p 301 - 303
p 372-378

# PUBLIC LAW IN ISRAEL

# PUBLIC LAW IN ISRAEL

ITZHAK ZAMIR

and

ALLEN ZYSBLAT

CLARENDON PRESS · OXFORD

1996

*Oxford University Press, Great Clarendon Street, Oxford* OX2 6DP
*Oxford New York*
*Athens Auckland Bangkok Bogota Bombay*
*Buenos Aires Calcutta Cape Town Dar es Salaam*
*Delhi Florence Hong Kong Istanbul Karachi*
*Kuala Lumpur Madras Madrid Melbourne*
*Mexico City Nairobi Paris Singapore*
*Taipei Tokyo Toronto*
*and associated companies in*
*Berlin Ibadan*

*Oxford is a trade mark of Oxford University Press*

*Published in the United States*
*by Oxford University Press Inc., New York*



*British Library Cataloguing in Publication Data*
*Data available*

*Library of Congress Cataloging in Publication Data*
*Public law in Israel / [edited by] I. Zamir and A. Zysblat*
*p. cm.*
*Includes index.*
*1. Judicial review—Israel. 2. Judicial review of administrative acts—Israel.*
*3. State actions (Civil rights)—Israel. 4. Human rights—Israel.*
*I. Zamir, Itzhak. II. Zysblat, A. (Allen)*
*KMK2461.P83 1996 347.5694'012—dc20 [345.6940712] 96–34948*
*ISBN 0–19–825853–4*

1 3 5 7 9 10 8 6 4 2

*Typeset by Hope Services (Abingdon) Ltd.*
*Printed in Great Britain*
*on acid-free paper by*
*Biddles Ltd.,*
*Guildford and King's Lynn*

# Preface

The inspiration for this book can be traced to a lecture on Israeli public law presented to a group of English lawyers in 1991. While the audience doubtless anticipated yet another story of English common law principles taking root in a far-flung part of the common law world, what it actually heard was quite unexpected. For the story of Israeli public law is essentially the story of the remarkable willingness of the Supreme Court of Israel to intervene in all kinds of government actions on behalf of basic civil rights and the preservation of the rule of law.

Working essentially with the basic English common law tools of constitutional and administrative law, and without the aid of a written bill of rights, the Supreme Court recognized that Israel's special political and social realities warranted an extraordinary judicial vigilance. Its rich bounty of jurisprudence reveals a judiciary prepared to deviate from the established common law rules concerning non-justiciability, administrative discretion, and judicial restraint, as well as the ordinary rules of *locus standi*, whenever faced with a denial of justice or a deprivation of basic civil rights.

The editors were urged to make the sources of Israel's public law available to a much wider audience, by making the leading decisions of Israel's High Court available in English translation. Thanks to the assistance of many individuals in England and Israel, and with the support of Oxford University Press, that wish is now a reality.

This book has three main parts. The first part is entitled 'Human Rights', and contains chapters on non-statutory (i.e. judicially-created) and statutory human rights. The second part, 'Administrative Action', contains chapters on three important administrative laws (on administrative tribunals, administrative offences, and the duty to give reasons for decisions) and a chapter each on conflict of interests and administrative contracts and promises. The third part, 'Judicial Review', includes chapters on judicial review of statutes and proceedings of the Knesset, Israel's parliament; judicial review on the ground of unreasonableness; and judicial review of military orders in the occupied territories. Each chapter begins with an introductory note by a scholar presenting an overview and analysis of the subject. It is followed by selected primary sources—either laws enacted by the Knesset or decisions of the Supreme Court.

The judgments contained in this book do more than simply present Israeli law. In many ways, they are chapters in the history and development of the country. They deal, for example, with the conflict between freedom of speech and public order (*Kol Ha'am* in Chapter 2); the exemption of orthodox youth from military service (*Ressler* in Chapter 9); the expropriation of Arab land in the occupied territories for Jewish settlements (*Elon Moreh* in Chapter 12); and the imposition of judicial review on parliamentary proceedings (*Sarid* in Chapter 10). These are not dry legal issues. They touch the heart of Israeli society.

In reproducing judgments of the High Court, we have attempted, as far as possible, to retain the judgments in their original form. We hope this will enable the reader to become familiar with the styles of decision making of our Court. But we must stress that we have presented these judgments in translation, and we are only too aware of the fact that, however we might have tried, we could not fully reproduce the spirit and vigour of the original Hebrew.

* * *

The project of translating and editing the material contained in this book would not have been possible without the dedicated assistance of many people.

Three young lawyers deserve special mention. Sandra Azancot of the Ministry of Justice co-ordinated the editorial and technical efforts throughout the entire project with admirable skill and patience. Jeffrey Lubell and Adam Dodek, two recent Harvard Law School graduates, combined their work at the Supreme Court of Israel with long hours of work on this project. Each contributed his considerable editorial skills and professional insight to this project.

We are happy to acknowledge as well the assistance of a fine young group of volunteers: Jonathon Gillis, Lori Weizman, Karen Golden, Avi Bell, Felicia Zeidman, Michelle Karby, Elana Brown, Andrea Shahin, and Elisheva Paton.

Finally, we would like to acknowledge the financial assistance of the Israel Ministry of Justice and the Faculty of Law of the Hebrew University of Jerusalem, as well as that of a group of English lawyers who considered the project of sufficient interest and value for lawyers in the United Kingdom and other common law jurisdictions.

Without the dedicated support of all these people, this book could not have been published.

# *Foreword*

JUSTICE AHARON BARAK

*President of the Supreme Court of Israel*

The system of public law in Israel is based on the foundations of English law, incorporated into the law of this country during the thirty years of the British mandate. However, since the establishment of the State of Israel in 1948, the legal system has felt itself to a great extent free to deviate from English law. It has striven to mould the law of the land to suit the special circumstances and needs of Israel. To this end we have used the principles of English common law to arrive at rules somewhat different from those prevailing in England.

Since its inception, Israel has been fortunate to absorb many lawyers trained in various legal systems. Some of them served in positions of leadership in the legislature, the government, and the judiciary. We have benefited from their knowledge and experience to learn about other systems of law, not only common law systems but also other European systems. Not only have we had resort to foreign systems of law, as a source of inspiration, but we have also had recourse to our rich heritage of Jewish law. We have thus developed some legal institutions and rules which are unique to Israel.

Israel is unique in other ways as well. Its people have gathered from the four corners of the world, many of them from countries which knew no democracy, to find themselves in a poor country, overburdened with severe economic and social problems, and threatened by surrounding neighbours. In spite of the constant pressure, Israel has always aspired to create an enlightened democracy. The task of promoting the principles of human dignity, freedom, and equality, and of establishing rules of fair government, fell largely to the Supreme Court. The Court has responded to the challenge.

The Supreme Court has been willing, especially in recent years, to hear and determine a vast range of social and political issues and to closely scrutinize almost all acts of virtually every public institution. It has substantially narrowed the scope of non-justiciable matters, demonstrating its willingness to examine agreements between political parties and to review parliamentary proceedings; it allows every person, without any personal interest, to bring to the Court matters of public concern pertaining to the rule of law; and it requires all public authorities to act fairly, avoiding a conflict of interest, personal or institutional, reasonably, and proportionally. For better or for worse, the Supreme Court has introduced, over the years, what has been described as a judge-made bill of rights and a system of high standards in public life.

In addition, our legislature, the Knesset, has enacted laws, some of which are original creations, regulating various aspects of administrative activity. Such are the laws imposing a general duty to state reasons for decisions, regulating the appointment and the work of administrative tribunals, and establishing a system of administrative offences in regulatory matters.

In 1992, the Knesset, in its capacity as a Constituent Assembly, enacted the Basic Law: Human Dignity and Liberty and the Basic Law: Freedom of Occupation. These Basic Laws entrench some (though not all) fundamental rights, including the right to human dignity. Recently, the Supreme Court has held that it is empowered to review the legality of any new law, and invalidate a law which is inconsistent with these Basic Laws.

Our enacted law as well as our case law are written in Hebrew, our ancient language which has been revived to serve all needs of a modern State. Thus, unfortunately, our law is practically inaccessible to lawyers outside Israel.

It has quite often been suggested to us that we find a way to open our system of law to lawyers in other countries through a translation of at least a selection of our legal sources. Happily, the editors of this volume have been able to respond with an admirable collection of leading cases and introductory notes.

This book does not pretend to present public law in Israel in a systematic and thorough manner. It presents only a selection of some important topics of public law, in which the law of Israel has taken a specific turn. It is a fair and representative sample. It offers an insight into a system of law which, like a distant cousin in a remote land, bears similarity to other common law jurisdictions, and yet, having been detached from the family for so long a time, has developed in its own way.

Jerusalem, February 1996 A.Barak

# Contents

# *Contributors*

**Eyal Benvenisti** is a Senior Lecturer at the Faculty of Law, Hebrew University of Jerusalem.

**Yoav Dotan** is a Lecturer at the Faculty of Law, Hebrew University of Jerusalem.

**Judith Karp** is Deputy Attorney General of Israel and a Member of the United Nations Committee on the Rights of the Child.

**David Kretzmer** is Professor of Law at the Hebrew University and a Member of the United Nations Committee on Human Rights.

**Moshe Landau** is a former President of the Supreme Court of Israel.

**Shimon Shetreet** is a Professor of Law at the Hebrew University of Jerusalem and a former Minister of Religious Affairs.

**Tana Spanic** is Deputy Attorney General of Israel.

**Itzhak Zamir** is a Justice of the Supreme Court of Israel and a former Professor of Law at the Hebrew University of Jerusalem.

**Allen Zysblat** is Senior Director of Legislation and Legal Counsel at the Israel Ministry of Justice and former Professor of Law at the University of British Columbia.

# *Abbreviations*

| | |
|---|---|
| AC | Appeal Cases (UK) |
| ADA | Administrative Detention Appeal |
| ALA | Application for Leave to Appeal |
| All ER | All England Law Reports |
| *Am. J Comp. L* | *American Journal of Comparative Law* |
| *Am. J Int. L* | *American Journal of International Law* |
| *Aust. LJ* | *Australian Law Journal* |
| CA | Civil Appeal |
| *CJQ* | *Civil Justice Quarterly* |
| *CLJ* | *Cambridge Law Journal* |
| Cr. A | Criminal Appeal |
| *Crim. LR* | *Criminal Law Review* |
| DH | Divrei HaKnesset (Records of Knesset proceedings) |
| DLR | Dominion Law Reports (Canada) |
| DP | Deputy President |
| EA | Election Appeal |
| F. 2d. | Federal Reporter, second series (U.S.) |
| FH | Further Hearing |
| F. Supp. | Federal Supplement (U.S.) |
| *Harv. LRev* | *Harvard Law Review* |
| *Hast. Cont. LQ* | *Hastings Constitutional Law Quarterly* |
| HC | High Court of Justice |
| HH | Hatza'ot Hok (Legislative bills of the Knesset) |
| IDF | Israel Defence Forces |
| *Is. LR* | *Israel Law Review* |
| *Is. YB on HR* | *Israel Yearbook on Human Rights* |
| *JPL* | *Journal of Public Law* |
| KB | Kings Bench (UK) |
| KH | Kovetz HaTakkanot (Official publication of subsidiary legislation) |
| LEd. | Lawyer's Edition, Supreme Court Reports (U.S.) |
| LSI | Laws of the State of Israel (authorized English translation of Laws of the Knesset) |

| | |
|---|---|
| *LQR* | *Law Quarterly Review* |
| MA | Miscellaneous Applications |
| MK | Member of Knesset |
| N.E. | Northeastern Reporter (U.S.) |
| P | President |
| PPA | Prisoner's Petition Appeal |
| PD | *Piskei Din* (judgments, an official publication of judgments of the Supreme Court of Israel) |
| PE | *Pesakim Elyon* (an unofficial publication of judgments of the Supreme Court of Israel) |
| *PL* | *Public Law* |
| PLO | Palestinian Liberation Organization |
| QB | Queen's Bench (UK) |
| S.Ct | Supreme Court Reporter (Unofficial Reporter of the US Supreme Court) |
| SH | Sefer HaHukim (official publication of laws of the Knesset) |
| SJ | Selected Judgments of the Supreme Court of Israel (English translation) |
| US | United States Reports (Official Reporter of the US Supreme Court) |
| *Yale LJ* | *Yale Law Journal* |

# SECTION 1: INTRODUCTION

# 1

# *The System of Government*

ALLEN ZYSBLAT



## 1. Historical Background

### *A. Before the Establishment of Israel*

To understand the central features and sources of public law in Israel, it is necessary to go back some seventy-five years in Israel's history, to the time when General Allenby led his troops through Jerusalem's Jaffa Gate—thus beginning some thirty years of British rule over Palestine.

The British civil administration, which was installed in 1920[1] found itself

[1] The Mandate did not actually come into force until 1923. See generally, D. Friedmann, 'The Infusion of Common Law into the State of Israel' (1975) 10 *Is.L.R.* 324. Indeed, the author owes a special debt of gratitude to this study of Prof. Friedmann's, together with the other parts of his larger study: *The Effect of Foreign Law on the Law of Israel* (Israel Law Review Association, Jerusalem, 1975).

inheriting the laws and legal institutions that had been put in place by the Ottoman (Turkish) Empire during its 400-year rule over Palestine prior to the First World War.[2]

The Ottoman legal system was a curious mix of Moslem traditional law and an amalgam of continental European codifications: on the one hand, the Ottoman civil code—the *Megelle*—which was promulgated in 1869, was in effect a restatement of the civil rules of the *Sharia*, the Moslem religious law, as expounded by the *Hanafi* School of Moslem Jurists.

On the other hand, Ottoman Palestine also inherited some of the products of the Young Turk revolution and of its immediate predecessors who undertook the modernization of Turkey and its legal system. The method employed here was simply to translate *en bloc* huge sections from French, and later Swiss and other continental, laws. The translation into Turkish left a great deal to be desired and made interpretations and applications notoriously difficult.

The British administration's conviction that the Ottoman law was confusing and generally unsuitable for the solution of modern legal problems led to a steady anglicization of the legal system over the life of the mandate period.

This process of anglicization took a number of forms, first, by means of statutes based on English legislation or original codifications of the common law. Thus, in the field of commercial law, new Palestinian legislation appeared based on statutes enacted in Westminster (e.g. the Bills of Exchange Act, the Companies Law) whereas in other cases notably in the Civil Wrongs Ordinance of 1944, and partly in the Criminal Code Ordinance of 1936,[3] the legislation attempted to give a statutory form to what in the United Kingdom, was only common law.

Secondly, and most importantly, by means of Article 46 in an overriding 'constitutional' Order-in-Council[4] passed in 1922, the mandate laws provided for the adoption of 'the substance of the common law and the doctrines of equity in force in England insofar as there were lacunae in the local law, and as the circumstances of Palestine permit'.

The impact in Palestine of the introduction of the substance of the common law and principles of equity was immense. In the ordinary course of events, and because many of the leading judges in Palestine were British (the Chief Justice of the Supreme Court was always a British jurist), the courts were only too happy to give a liberal and broad interpretation to the specific language of Article 46. Such interpretation included a rather

[2] See e.g. D. Friedmann, 'The Effect of Foreign Law on the Law of Israel: Remnants of the Ottoman Period' (1975) 10 *Is.L.Rev.* 192; 'The Israel Legal System', 16 *Am. J Comp. L* 405 (1968–9).

[3] The main substance of these ordinances is still the law in Israel.

[4] See Friedmann, n. 1 above, at 325.

clear disdain for the Ottoman law. In many instances, an application of the relevant Ottoman legislation was narrowed by construction, and at times it was ignored altogether. In other cases, Ottoman legislation was construed in such a way that it found itself imbued with English law content.

In other words, through the widened gateway of Article 46 of the Order-in-Council, Palestine was suddenly given direct access to the traditions and was able to share in the heritage and experience of close to 1,000 years of English law.[5]

Finally, mention should be made of the less formal causes of the anglicization of the law and legal institutions of Palestine: Palestinian judges were usually trained in Israel, and young Palestinian lawyers were educated in law schools built and administered on the English model;[6] the English language became part of the law of Palestine, and therefore there was a natural introduction of the techniques of the common law, as well as its underlying ideology, conceptions, and the stability implicit in its doctrine of *stare decisis*. English law was often applied even where no *lacuna* existed in the Ottoman law and beyond the limits set by the Order-in-Council, simply because of the orientation of the Bench and Bar.

In conclusion, by the time the English authorities left for home in 1948, Palestinian law had very much become a part of the English common law world, and this was at least as true in the field of public law as in any other.

## *B. The Establishment of the State of Israel*

With the creation of the new State of Israel on 15 May 1948, it was assumed that the legal source of the rule of law in the new State, and its dedication to basic rights and freedoms, would take the form of a written constitution.

Indeed, the 1947 United Nations Resolution calling for the establishment of a Jewish State and an Arab State in former Palestine mandated that each would enact a democratic constitution, including entrenched guarantees for the civil rights of all citizens. Israel's own Declaration of Independence specified that the provisional bodies of state would govern until an election would be held 'pursuant to the provision of a constitution to be prepared . . . no later than 1 October, 1948'.

For a whole host of reasons, Israel's tumultuous first year of existence did not include the preparation of a constitution. The political debates soon revealed deep divisions on central issues,[7] and the decision was

[5] *Ibid.*

[6] The English-style legal education in Palestine is described in G. Frumkin, *The Life of a Jerusalem Judge* (Davir, Tel Aviv, 1955) (Hebrew).

[7] See R. Gavison, 'The Controversy over Israel's Bill of Rights' (1985) 15 *Is. YB on HR* 113 and I. Zamir, 'Rule of Law and Civil Liberties in Israel' [1987] *CJQ* 64, at 65.

taken—in the famous Harrari Resolution of 1950[8]—to postpone the adoption of a constitution as one document and instead to prepare it piecemeal—chapter by chapter—in a series of basic laws which would eventually be brought together to form the constitution.

One argument advanced at the time to justify postponing the entrenching of basic civil liberties in a written constitution was that British experience had proven that a formal constitution was not essential for democracy.[9] Many countries have totalitarian regimes with admirable constitutions, while Britain, the model for parliamentary government, does not have a written constitution at all. Since Israel's Provisional Council of State had already issued a Proclamation declaring that the mandatory law that was in effect in Palestine at the time of the establishment of the State, including 'the substance of the common law', would continue in force,[10] the new courts of Israel could be counted on to defend the rule of law and basic individual liberties in the best British democratic tradition.

Indeed, it was pointed out at the time, and is worth noting today, that the new Jewish State inherited more that just the British tradition of democracy. Democracy, as a way of conducting public affairs, has been a typical feature of Jewish communities in many countries, especially in Europe, for generations. Many of these communities, striving to maintain a Jewish way of life, established networks of institutions, not only religious, but of a cultural and social nature as well. As they had no formal authority or coercive power over their members, they had to rely on popular consent and voluntary co-operation. Consequently, their social institutions and political movements were organized on democratic principles. The Zionist movement was one such movement, and the Zionist Congress was a democratic assembly as much as any house of representatives in a democracy. This form of democracy, with its various institutions, including the system of elections, was transferred by the Zionist pioneers to Palestine about 100 years ago. Even before the establishment of the State of Israel, the Jewish population in Palestine was well organized as a democratic society under a non-democratic government. The State of Israel was established on this foundation. It inherited from the Zionist movement not only the tradition of democracy but also some of its institutions, including the proportional system of national elections. This tradition was undoubtedly the most effective guarantee of democracy in Israel.[11]

As will be seen in some detail in the following chapters, the Supreme Court of Israel proved itself admirably worthy of the trust vested in it by

[8] I. Zamir, 'Rule of Law and Civil Liberties in Israel' [1987] *CJQ* 64, at 65.

[9] Zamir, n. 7 above.

[10] See A. Maoz, 'The System of Government in Israel' (1988) 8 *Tel Aviv Studies in Law* 9, at 10. Indeed, much of this survey is based on the excellent and comprehensive work of Dr Maoz, to whom the author owes a great debt of thanks.

[11] Zamir, n. 7 above, at 65.

the founders of the new State of Israel to protect basic civil rights. Nor can there be any doubt that it was guided by more that just the British traditions of democracy. As one prominent member of the Supreme Court has written:

> it makes no difference whether we will have a written bill of rights or we continue living without it . . . . Even without a statute defining and laying down the various human rights, all those rights which could possibly or foreseeably be so defined and laid down are in actual practice legally recognized, protected and enforced. We derive these fundamental rights and freedoms not only from the constitutional conventions which form part of the common law of England, and are thus, *mutatis mutandis*, the residuary law applied here as long as no other law has been enacted on the subject-matter; but it has been held time and again that the State of Israel, as a modern parliamentary democracy, will uphold and protect all those individual liberties that are of the essence of the rule of law and which may now be regarded as forming a part of universally recognized principles of international law.[12]

## 2. The Principal Institutions of the State

### *A. The Legislature*

The State of Israel is a parliamentary republic.[13] Israel's parliament, the Knesset, is the elected 'house of representatives of the State'. It is the Knesset that elects the President of the State, and the Government is dependent on the Knesset's confidence.

In the tradition of democratic regimes, the Knesset is the legislative branch of the State.[14] Its uniqueness stems from the fact that the Knesset is, at one and the same time, the constituent assembly. In this aspect, the Knesset differs from its British peer, the veteran Parliament of Westminster, which serves as a valuable source of inspiration. Unlike the British Parliament, the Knesset can bind later legislatures by virtue of its constituent authority.

In the absence of a constitution, there are no restrictions on the Knesset's legislative activities other than a handful of technical limitations set out in a few clauses of the Basic Laws. These clauses require a special majority of the Knesset in order to change certain sections of the Basic Laws. The Supreme Court, sitting as the High Court of Justice, validated these provisions, declaring that the Knesset can, if it so wishes, deviate

[12] Justice Haim Cohn, 'The Spirit of Israel Law' (1974) 9 *Is.LR* 456, at 459.
[13] See the text accompanying n. 10 above.
[14] See Law and Administrative Ordinance, 1948 and Transition Law, 1949.

from the entrenched clauses by mobilizing the required majority at the various legislative stages.[15]

Until recently, there were only limited examples of such 'entrenched' provisions, amendable only by special procedures of future parliaments. A major change in this regard took place in 1992, when two entrenched Basic Laws on human rights were enacted: the Basic Law: Human Dignity and Liberty, and the Basic Law: Freedom of Occupation, the significance of which is discussed in Chapter 3 by Professor Kretzmer.

As the Israeli parliament and embodiment of its sovereignty, the Knesset is supreme over the other branches of the State. On the legislative level, this supremacy means that the will of the Knesset, under the cloak of law, obligates all other authorities of the State. It also indicates that the source of power of the other branches stems, directly or indirectly, from the Knesset.

The supremacy of the Knesset is expressed primarily in its relations with the Government, which serves by virtue of the confidence of the Knesset, and which resigns upon the election of a new Knesset or upon the Knesset's expression of no-confidence. A substantial portion of the Knesset's activities is devoted to supervision of the operation of the Government. The Knesset has several instruments to achieve this purpose, in addition to its power to express no-confidence. One important instrument is the supervision of the Government's income and expenses, which the Government must submit for legislative approval by the Knesset.

It should be emphasized that the Government as a body, and each of its Ministries, is responsible to the Knesset for actions within the scope of its responsibilities, as will be elaborated upon when we deal with the Government.

Despite the various methods of reviewing governmental activities, the Knesset's influence on the Government is diminished by its structure. As with the British model, in Israel the Government is drawn from the Knesset itself, and virtually all the Ministers serve at one and the same time as members of the Knesset. This model, which emphasizes the parliament as the supreme political organ of the State, is appropriate for Great Britain which has a two-party system. There is, however, some doubt, whether it is as compatible with a multi-party system such as Israel's.[16]

There are 120 members in the Knesset. At its head sits the Speaker, officially called the Chairman of the Knesset, and Vice-Chairmen, chosen by party-group affiliation, comprising the presidium of the Knesset. The Speaker and the Vice-Chairmen are elected by an open vote of the Knesset. Once elected, the Speaker is an impartial figure, and thus does not serve on any of the Knesset committees except the Interpretation Committee. He

[15] See *Bergman* v. *Minister of Finance* (1969) 27(2) PD 785 (excerpted in ch. 10).
[16] See Maoz, n. 10 above, at 16.

does not participate in Knesset discussions and usually does not vote. He is not required to sever all ties to his party, and in fact often belongs to its leadership, but may not hold an executive position within it.

The Speaker has pre-eminent status. He officiates as Interim President of the State if the President temporarily ceases to carry out his functions or the position of the Presidency has become vacant and the new President has not yet started to hold office.

The Knesset serves for four years unless it is dissolved earlier by law. Most of the Knesset's activities are conducted in full plenary session. The Knesset acts by majority decision but there is no requirement for a quorum, which occasionally results in poor participation in decisive debates and important legislation. Generally, votes are open, and, according to Section 27 of Basic Law: The Knesset, sessions are public 'unless it has been decided that it shall sit *in camera* under such conditions and in such manner as has been prescribed by the Rules'. The Knesset's procedures are primarily determined through rules approved by that body.

Elections to the Knesset are national and proportional. For electoral purposes, the entire country is considered a single electoral constituency. Electors vote directly for the competing lists. Mandates for each list are determined according to its proportional attainment in elections. Due to the existing electoral system, and the minimal qualifying threshold of 1.5 per cent, many party-groups are represented in the Knesset.

Every Israeli citizen is eligible to vote at the age of 18, but cannot exercise this right if he is outside the State on Election Day, unless he is on an Israeli vessel.

Any Israeli citizen at least 21 years old has the right to be elected to the Knesset, unless he has been sentenced to a prison term of five years or more for crimes against national security and is less than five years away from completion of service of the sentence.

## B. The Government

The Government is the head of the executive branch in Israel.[17] It is a cabinet government composed of the Prime Minister and other Ministers. Under the Basic Law: The Government, the Prime Minister must be a member of the Knesset while any other minister need not be a member of the Knesset. Nevertheless, in accordance with the British tradition, Ministers are generally also members of the Knesset.

In theory, the status of the Prime Minister is only that of *primus inter pares*, 'a mere chairman'.[18] He does not have substantial powers according to law. However, his resignation or removal from office is treated as the

[17] Basic Law: The Government, S. 1.

[18] P. Elman, 'Basic Law: The Government' (1969) 4 *Is.LR* 242, at 251.

resignation of the Government, and he has the power to remove a Minister from office. These powers, coupled with his power as leader of the majority party, make him in fact very powerful.

Usually, ministers are in charge of ministries, although there may also be ministers without portfolio. The present law does not dictate the number of ministries or their nature, as that is left to the Government itself, although it remains subject to confirmation of the Knesset.

Much of the present law relating to the formation of the Government and the distribution of powers is in the process of change. In 1992, pursuant to growing pressure to enhance the constitutional status of the Prime Minister, a new Basic Law: The Government[19] was passed, to be implemented for the first time together with the Knesset elections of 1996).

The most dramatic change included in the new legislation is the introduction of direct, national elections of the Prime Minister,[20] who will also have enhanced powers concerning the composition and functioning of the Cabinet. The new law requires that a candidate for election to the position of Prime Minister during regular elections, i.e. contemporaneous with Knesset elections, be the head of a Knesset election list, and at least 30 years of age. A candidate in extraordinary elections will have to be a member of the sitting Knesset.

Among other new provisions are those that mandate a Cabinet of no more than eighteen and no fewer than eight members[21] in which at least half of the ministers must be Knesset members.[22] Moreover, much of the authority over the workings of the Cabinet that is presently vested in the Government as a whole will be transferred to the Prime Minister.[23]

Under the Israeli legal system, the Government—like every other political institution—is subject to the principle of legality which is an extension of the rule of law. This principle prescribes that the Government must base its actions on a law authorizing it to act, or its activities will not have the force of law. In one of the first opinions issued by the Supreme Court, the rule was formulated as follows:

> The Executive Branch is not free to impose restrictions as it sees fit, but only when the law grants it the authority to impose necessary limitations. If this power is not found in a certain law, the Executive Branch must convince and motivate the Legislator to grant it this power, but until that occurs, the Executive Branch is not entitled to take it upon itself, lest the doctrine of the rule of law, one of the guarantees of a democratic regime, become an empty phrase and all the laws useless.[24]

[19] Basic Law: The Government (of 14 Apr. 1992) replacing the original Basic Law: The Government of 1968.

[20] *Ibid.*, S. 3. [21] *Ibid.*, S. 33. [22] *Ibid.* [23] *Ibid.*, S. 39.

[24] *Sheib* v. *Minister of Defence* (1951) 5 PD 399, at 411 (*per* Ulshan J).

Since the government is—or at least has been—a cumbersome body, it has difficulty executing its many powers. Therefore, Section 31(a) of Basic Law: The Government authorizes the Government to delegate its powers to one of the ministers. Indeed, following the inheritance of the extensive former powers of the High Commissioner, by virtue of section 14 of the Law and Administration Ordinance, 1948, the Government delegated these powers to various ministers. Such designations were authorized by section 2(d) of the Ordinance, the predecessor of section 31(a).

Section 32 of Basic Law: The Government provides an additional source of authority for the ministers in charge of a certain law. They 'may, in so far as no contrary intention appears from the Law, assume any power, other than a power of a judicial character, vested in a State employee under that Law'. This was an important power, mainly because of the policy of the Mandatory legislator to grant powers directly to various officials, as the need arose. The Israeli legislator also from time to time grants powers directly to bureaucrats although with more reserve. As a rule, however, the Knesset grants authority directly to the relevant minister, especially authority of a legislative nature.

A substantial portion of the ministers' activities' involves subsidiary legislation. Thus, Israel joins a long line of democracies abandoning the doctrine of separation of powers in its strictest sense.

## *C. The President of the State*

The Supreme Court described the position of the President as follows: 'the President is supreme over the various branches of the Government in that he symbolizes the whole of the State and its institutions'.[25] This statement accurately describes the formal status of the President of the State. According to Section 1 of Basic Law: The President of the State, he 'shall stand at the head of the State' and 'in his personality, represents the State itself'.[26] However, the President's position is no more than that of a figurehead. The President lacks actual governing authority; and in this respect his status is similar to that of the President of France during the Third and Fourth Republics. It is inferior to the status of Presidents not only in presidential regimes but also in most parliamentary ones.

The President is elected by the plenary of the Knesset, and his service is limited to two consecutive terms of five years each. The President's powers, detailed in Section 11 of Basic Law: The President of the State, are primarily ministerial and ceremonial, requiring no exercise of discretion. These powers include signing laws, accrediting diplomatic representatives of Israel, receiving the credentials of foreign diplomatic representatives,

[25] *Attorney General* v. *Matona* (1962) 16 PD 430, at 471 (*per* Berinson J).

and signing treaties ratified by the Knesset. The President also receives from the Government a report on its meetings.

In addition to these powers set out in the Basic Law, the President has other ceremonial functions by virtue of various legislative provisions. For example, he appoints judges, religious judges, and other high officials after their appointment has been approved by another institution, with no presidential discretion in the matter. This is so even when the law attributes the appointment to an act of the President while the decision of the electing body, *prima facie*, is at the stage of recommendation or suggestion only. The formal appointment by the President is designed, mainly, to emphasize the official's transcendent position, and perhaps also his independence. As an additional example of the President's ceremonial power, he opens the first sitting of the Knesset by virtue of Section 13 of Basic Law: The Knesset.

Before the new law for direct election of the Prime Minister, the President had the important duty of assigning to a Knesset member the task of forming a Government. In effect, the President had the duty to appoint a Prime Minister. With the people electing the Prime Minister, the President no longer has a role to play in government formation. However, the new law for direct election of the Prime Minister gives the President a new power. Under the new law, the Prime Minister can dissolve the Knesset, triggering special elections for both the Knesset and the premiership, if a majority of the Knesset opposes the Government and the effective functioning of the Government is prevented as a result. However, the Prime Minister may dissolve the Knesset only with the President's assent.

The other important power of the President is 'to pardon offenders and to lighten penalties'. This power has always been liberally interpreted.[27] In a comprehensive decision rendered by the Supreme Court in 1986 in the *Barzilai* case,[28] Shamgar P. writing for the majority, stated:

> In our law it has been held that the President is vested with the widest form of the power of pardon (as regards offences), and clemency (as regards punishment), and is empowered to obliterate even the stain of the offence and not only its consequences.[29]

The Court emphasized that the power of pardon has been entrusted to the discretion of the President and that the Court will not intervene unless 'convinced that no reasonable authority in a similar situation could have arrived at that same conclusion'. Moreover, 'in exercising its jurisdiction

[26] *Attorney General* v. *Matona* (1962) 16 PD 430, at 465 (*per* H. Cohn J).
[27] See e.g. *Matona*, n. 25 above.
[28] *Barzilai* v. *Government of Israel* (1987) 40(3) PD 505 (1986) 6 SJ 1.
[29] *Ibid.*, 6 SJ at 37.

the Court will also have regard to the identity of the constitutional authority whose conduct is under review . . . the status of the authority and the nature of its power'.[30]

## *D. The Judiciary*

### i. The Court Systems

The judiciary acts as Israel's watchdog over the rule of law and individual rights. As such, it is not an exception to similar institutions in other democratic countries. However, in the absence of a complete written constitution including a bill of rights, and with regressive laws remaining from the Mandatory period, and the wide-ranging powers of the Israeli Legislature, the judiciary's tasks are enhanced to a much more important and delicate position. As will be seen in more detail in later chapters, the judiciary in Israel, with the Supreme Court at its head, has achieved its mission with impressive success.

The judicial system in Israel is divided into two main types: one, the general law courts, known as the civil or regular courts, and the other, tribunals and other authorities with judicial powers, other than general law courts. The difference between the two types of institutions is, *inter alia*, in the extent of their jurisdiction: while jurisdiction of the law courts is general, the jurisdiction of the other tribunals known as lower courts or lower tribunals is limited in terms of persons or matters or in both aspects.

### ii. Tribunals with Limited Jurisdiction

The Israeli legal system recognizes various types of tribunals, the most important of which are the military courts, the labour courts, and the religious courts. These tribunals are singled out from most other tribunals in terms of both their personal and material jurisdiction. Each tribunal is comprised of a judicial system with independent administration and an appellate system of its own, which includes legally-trained judges.

### iii. Military Tribunals

The military courts were established by the Military Justice Law 1955. They are competent to try a soldier for 'an act constituting a military offence' and for 'any offence whatsoever which is not a military offence: provided that . . . the Attorney General may . . . order that such a person be tried by another court'. Since the law defines the term 'soldier' to include those in the regular forces of the army—either in compulsory service or permanent or voluntary service—or those who serve in the reserve

[30] *Ibid.*, at 42.

forces, while in active service, the relative range of people subject to the jurisdiction of the military tribunals in Israel is wide. Civil employees in army service are also subject to this jurisdiction, with certain limitations. The same rule applies to persons 'to whom arms have been delivered on behalf of the Army' as well as to prisoners of war. The system of military tribunals includes lower courts and a Military Court of Appeal.

Military tribunals also exist by virtue of other laws. The best known are the military courts established under the Emergency Defence Regulations 1945. These courts have sole jurisdiction to try offences committed under part 3 of the Regulations, while the regular law courts have concurrent jurisdiction in the remainder of criminal matters.

### iv. Labour Courts

The Labour Courts were established by the Labour Courts Law 1969, in the recognition that the branch of labour law requires its own judicial system, to consolidate the accumulated experience, customs, and rulings, and to interpret existing and future labour laws.[31]

The Labour Courts consist of Regional Courts and the National Court. Regional Labour Courts are trial courts, while the National Labour Court hears appeals, but also sits as a trial court in actions between workers' unions and employers' organizations that 'arise out of matters pertaining to labour relations' and in disputes between parties to a collective agreement concerning its existence, application, interpretation, implementation, or infringement of, or any other matter arising out of, the agreement.

### v. Religious Courts

While military and labour courts are not exclusive to the Israeli legal system, the religious courts are. The Israeli legal system is unique among modern legal systems in the utilization of various personal status laws in the area of family law, applied by religious courts.[32] This phenomenon has historical and political roots: the British found this system when they conquered Palestine from the Turks, and determined to maintain it.

The basic source for the application of the personal status law and the jurisdiction of the various religious courts is found in the Palestine Order in Council 1922. This order provides in Article 51 that 'jurisdiction in matters of personal status shall be exercised . . . by the Courts of the religious communities'.

Article 64 of the Order grants jurisdiction to the District Courts in matters of personal status of foreigners who are non-Moslems, stating that they 'shall apply the personal law of the parties concerned'. In relation to foreigners, this was defined as 'the law of his nationality'. The case law

[31] See Maoz, n. 10 above, at 45, n. 218.
[32] See I. Shiloh, 'Marriage and Divorce in Israel' (1975) 5 *Is.LR* 479.

determined that, in relation to non-foreigners, 'the court . . . have . . . to apply the religious or communal law of the parties'.

The Palestine Order in Council recognized eleven religious communities: Moslem, Jewish, and nine Christian denominations. The Israeli government added the Presbyterian Evangelical Church and the Bah'ai faith to this list. The Knesset also enacted a law vesting jurisdiction in the Druze religious courts.

### vi. Administrative Tribunals

In Israel, as is the case in many other Western legal systems, there is a growing trend to put specific legal issues in the hands of special administrative tribunals, designed to fulfil important quasi-judicial functions.

The older and more common kind of administrative tribunal in this regard is that designed to be appeal tribunals from administrative agencies determining social benefits, tax liability, or compensation for injury. Among the many examples in this category is the tribunal hearing appeals on compensation for injuries resulting from military service, and the tribunal hearing appeals concerning liability for property tax.

More recently, the Knesset has established tribunals having a much broader set of quasi-judicial functions. Thus, the Standard Contracts Tribunal considers actions brought with regard to unfair terms in standard-form contracts, and the Restrictive Trade Practices Tribunal plays an important role in ruling on the whole range of uncompetitive practices.

### vii. Supervision of the Regular Law Courts over Special Tribunals

A characteristic of the judicial system outside the regular system of law courts is that, in one way or another, it is subject to the regular law courts; namely, these special institutions are not completely separate from the regular judicial system since they are under its supervision. This subjection is either by way of appeal or through the supervision of the High Court of Justice. Section 15(d)(3) of Basic Law: The Judiciary grants the Supreme Court, sitting as the High Court of Justice, jurisdiction 'to order Law Courts, Tribunals and bodies and persons having judicial or quasi judicial powers under law . . . to hear, refrain from hearing, or continue hearing a particular matter or to void a proceeding improperly taken or a decision improperly given'. Subsection (4) of the same Section gives the High Court of Justice more limited authority in relation to religious courts.

### viii. The Regular Law Courts

The system of law courts that is discussed in the Basic Law: The Judiciary has three levels: the Supreme Court, District Courts, and Magistrates' Courts. The two latter levels are trial courts, and they are distinguished according to the gravity of the matter. Thus, in the criminal sphere, the jurisdiction of the Magistrates' Courts is limited to matters of relatively limited maximum sentences. In civil law, the jurisdiction of the Magistrates' Courts is limited according to the amount of the claim, to claims regarding possession or use of immovable property, and counter-claims regardless of their value. The jurisdiction of the District Courts is residual and includes 'any civil or criminal matter that is not within the exclusive jurisdiction of another tribunal'. In addition, the District Court rules on 'appeals from judgments and other decisions of the Magistrates' Courts'.

The Supreme Court is primarily an appellate court, considering appeals from trial court judgments in its appellate jurisdiction. The Supreme Court also sits as the High Court of Justice. In such instances, it sits as a trial court from which there is no appeal. In this capacity, the jurisdiction of the High Court of Justice parallels that of the English High Court of Justice, and as with it, is authorized to issue prerogative writs against branches of the state and other authorities operating by virtue of law. This very important power has earned the Supreme Court the title of 'Guardian of Civil Liberties',[33] the justification for which will hopefully become apparent in the following chapters.

### ix. The Independence of the Judiciary

The impressive achievements of the judicial system in Israel, with the Supreme Court at its head, in the enforcement of the rule of law and defence of human civil rights is, to a great extent, a result of the independence given to judges in the Israeli legal system. The judges enjoy both substantive and personal independence. Substantive independence is set out in Section 2 of Basic Law: The Judiciary: '[a] person in whom judicial power is vested shall, in judicial matters, be subject to no authority but that of the law.'

It should be emphasized that the general language of this section applies to any person vested with judicial power, and not only to judges within the regular law courts.

In addition to substantive independence, the judges have wide personal independence that begins with the procedure for their selection and continues during their term of office.

Judges are selected by the Judges' Election Committee, constituted to ensure that a majority of the Committee are members of the legal community. The Committee includes the President of the Supreme Court and two other Supreme Court judges, the Minister of Justice and one other minister, two members of the Knesset, and two representatives of the Chamber of Advocates. There is also a tradition that the members of the

[33] S. Shetreet, 'Reflections on the Protection of the Rights of the Individual' (1977) 12 *Is.LR* 32, at 34.

Knesset and the Government's representatives are jurists by training. Furthermore, a convention exists that a candidate for the Supreme Court will not be selected if the choice is not acceptable to representatives of that Court.

The judge's independence continues throughout the entire period of his term of office. The appointment of a judge is permanent, and continues until retirement at age 70, a higher age than that allowed in other public offices. A judge cannot be removed from office except by a decision of the Court of Discipline, consisting of judges appointed by the President of the Supreme Court, or upon a decision of the Judges' Election Committee at the proposal of the Minister of Justice or the President of the Supreme Court. The decision must be supported by seven of the nine members of the committee.

## *E. The State Comptroller*

One of the more recent in the expanding series of Basic Laws[34] deals with a very important part of public life and law in Israel—the State Comptroller.[35] Although the office of State Comptroller is obviously not unique to Israel, the breadth of the Israeli office-holder's functions, and the central role that this office has in fact played in Israeli public life and administration, are undoubtedly unusual.

The State Comptroller, who is elected for periods of five years in special sessions of the Knesset, is mandated to review the activities of the Government, its ministries, and all other public enterprises, corporations, and institutions assigned by law. Such review includes an assessment of the legality, propriety, good administration, and efficiency of public bodies and their activities. In carrying out his duties the comptroller is independent of the Government and answerable only to the Knesset.[36]

The State Comptroller is also assigned the task of public ombudsman—mandated to receive and consider complaints from the public about the operation and activities of public bodies.[37]

## *F. The Attorney General*

The last, but by no means least, public figure in the preservation of the rule of law in Israel is the Attorney General,[38] a figure who has not been the subject of a Basic Law or any other formal legislative sanction.

The office of the Attorney General in Israel, while based on British

[34] Basic Law: The State Comptroller (1988).
[35] In fact, the institution of the State Comptroller far predates the Basic Law.
[36] N. 34 above, S. 6. [37] *Ibid.*, S. 4.
[38] The description in this section is taken from Zamir, n. 7 above.

roots, has undergone a transformation. The Attorney General of Israel, similar to his counterpart in Britain, is the chief legal adviser to the Government and the head of the prosecution. However, even in these two capacities some marked differences exist between the Israeli and English models.

In his capacity as the legal adviser to the Government, the Attorney General of Israel is the head of the Government legal service which includes, informally, all legal advisers in all government ministries. This network of legal advisers, including the Attorney General, possesses the exclusive power to advise the Government in legal matters. The Government as a body, or any government minister or official, may not seek the advice of a private attorney without the consent of the Attorney General. Moreover, the opinions of the Attorney General in legal matters, as far as the Government is concerned, present an authoritative exposition of the law. Accordingly, the Government is bound to abstain from any course of action which in the opinion of the Attorney General is unlawful.

In his second capacity, the Attorney General is the head of the national litigation branch, which includes, in addition to a criminal department, other departments in various fields of the law. Here, too, the Attorney-General possesses the exclusive power to represent the State through attorneys in the litigation branch, in all courts, tribunals, and in all matters, criminal (with the exception that in minor offences the police have the power to prosecute, subject to control by the Attorney General), civil (including tax and labour matters), and administrative (i.e. judicial review of administrative action). This power also means that it is for the Attorney General to decide whether or not to initiate legal proceedings in any matter on behalf of the State or to defend the State (or any organ of the State) when it is sued in court. Again, whether or not the Attorney-General is ready to represent the State in any particular case, the Government may not hire the services of a private attorney without the consent of the Attorney-General, and such consent is only exceptionally given.[39]

However, the main difference between the Attorney General in Israel and his counterpart in Britain is that the Attorney General of Israel is not a member of the Executive, nor a member of the Legislature, nor is he a politician of any kind. Rather, although he is appointed by the Cabinet, he is traditionally expected to have had no active political background or association. The apolitical nature of the office is meant mainly to serve the independence of the office. This independence, which is acknowledged by the Government, is widely considered to be of great importance for the proper discharge of the functions of the Attorney General as legal adviser to the Government and as head of the litigation branch. Even more so, it

[39] See Zamir, n. 7 above, at 73.

is widely considered essential for the proper discharge of his unofficial function as watchdog over the Government in legal matters. The Attorney General has come to be regarded as the guardian of the rule of law, and indirectly as the guardian of civil liberties. In this sense he is not only the Government's lawyer but also the people's lawyer. He regularly attends all Cabinet meetings, not only to advise on legal questions, but also to see to it that the Cabinet acts within its powers. Nor is this power merely theoretical: as has been mentioned, it is the rule that the Government may not pursue a course of action which in the opinion of the Attorney General is unlawful; and if the Government should nonetheless choose to act against his opinion, and the act is then challenged in court, he may refuse to defend it, thus leaving the Government with no legal defence whatsoever.

The powers and the prestige of the Attorney General in Israel have contributed to the development of a practice according to which Government ministers and officials often seek his advice and consent before making decisions whose legality is in doubt. He thus serves as an effective internal check on governmental action in legal matters which is, in many ways, even more useful than the external check exercised by the courts.

# 2

# *Administrative Law*

ITZHAK ZAMIR



## 1. Introduction

In Israel, administrative law is, in a sense, more than just administrative law. It accounts for many of the norms and values which make Israel a free society governed by the rule of law. In many countries this may be attributed to constitutional law. In Israel, however, in the absence of a written constitution,[1] basic principles such as the rule of law, individual freedoms, equality before the law, and fair government originated in administrative law, mainly through judicial review of administrative action.

* This article was also published, with slight variations, in I. Zamir and S. Colombo (eds.), *The Law of Israel: General Surveys* (Sacher Institute for Legislative Research and Comparative Law, Hebrew University of Jerusalem, Jerusalem, 1995).

[1] See Allen Zysblat's note 'Protecting Fundamental Rights in Israel without a Written Constitution', in Section 2 of this book.

This is of special significance in Israel. Israel is a new country, poor in natural resources, struggling with the mission of absorbing waves of immigrants from all over the world, establishing a sound economy and promoting the values of western civilization. These, and other circumstances, account for the development of a very centralized and powerful government in Israel. Furthermore, from its inception, Israel's existence has been threatened by enemies from without, and public peace has been disturbed by terrorists from within. This, together with recurrent wars, has led to the imposition of a constant state of emergency and to the emergence of a strong army. National security is at the top of national priorities, and the military establishment is very prestigious and influential.

Such a situation could serve as fertile ground for a totalitarian regime. Israel has, nevertheless, escaped this danger and averted totalitarian manifestations. The Supreme Court, sitting as a High Court of Justice, constitutes the main administrative court of the State and is commonly acknowledged to have played a central role in promoting democratic values and safeguarding human rights. The High Court has become a popular synonym for fairness and justice in the relationship between the government and the governed.

## 2. Administrative Power

### *A. Administrative Legality*

The main principle governing the exercise of administrative power is that of administrative legality. This principle, well anchored in the case law, prescribes that an administrative authority possesses only such power as has been vested in it by law. Law in this connection means enacted law, as distinct from judge-made law. Enacted law may encompass, not only ordinary legislation made by the Knesset, but also subordinate legislation, that is, regulations and bye-laws made by various public bodies, notably ministers and local authorities. But the principle of administrative legality requires that the ultimate source of power, where the immediate source is a general regulation or even an individual order, be anchored in ordinary legislation.

Furthermore, according to this principle of administrative legality, the power exercised must fall within the limits prescribed for that power by legislation, primary or subordinate; otherwise, the exercise of power is unlawful and may be invalidated.

The principle of administrative legality serves not only to check administrative power, but also to safeguard human rights. Israel, lacking a written constitution, does not even have a comprehensive law prescribing human rights.[2] Thus, to a large extent human rights are safeguarded primarily by a common law rule emanating from English case law. This rule provides, on the one hand, that every person has the right to do whatever is not prohibited by law and, on the other hand, that an administrative authority may not interfere in this right unless empowered to do so by law. Freedom of expression, for instance, exists to the extent that there is no law curtailing this freedom, such as the law of libel or the law concerning state secrets.

The Knesset, being sovereign, may enact laws granting extreme powers to the administration, thus severely curtailing human rights, but it is for the court to interpret and implement the law. The court can strictly interpret laws granting powers to the administration and thus, relying on the principle of administrative legality, protect human rights. In practice this has often been done, so that human rights are enjoyed in Israel much the same as in other democracies in which such rights are protected by a written constitution.[3]

## B. *Extent of Power*

The Legislature has vested the Executive with vast powers in virtually all fields of life. This reflects the concept of the welfare State or the interventionist State. The State, according to this concept, bears responsibility for protecting the weak, providing basic services, such as social security, education, health, and supervising private enterprise so as to serve the public interest. The extent of powers vested in the myriad of administrative

[2] Several attempts were made over the years to enact a basic law prescribing human rights in a comprehensive manner. They all failed on grounds relating mainly to religious interests and national security considerations. Recently, however, two basic laws were enacted prescribing certain human rights. The first—the Basic Law: Freedom of Occupation, 1992—safeguards freedom of occupation only. The second—the Basic Law: Human Dignity and Liberty, 1992—provides for personal freedom, human dignity, the right to travel abroad, privacy, and freedom of property. These rights are now partially protected from infringement by other laws. Other human rights, including freedom of expression, are still not anchored in legislation. On these basic laws, see Section 3 of this book.

[3] See sect. 2E below on the interpretation of powers. See also generally on human rights in Israel, B. Bracha, The Protection of Human Rights in Israel' (1982) 12 *Is. YB on HR* 110; R. Gabison, 'The Controversy over Israel's Bill of Rights' (1985) 15 *Is. YB on HR* 113; A. Maoz, 'Defending Civil Liberties without a Constitition—The Israeli Experience' (1988) 16 *Melbourne University LR* 815; A. Rubinstein, *Constitutional Law of the State of Israel* (4th edn., Schocken, Tel-Aviv, 1991), 701 ff. (in Hebrew); I. Zamir, 'Rule of Law and Civil Liberties in Israel' (1988) 7 *CJQ* 64. In a paradoxical manner, it may be that the success of the Court in safeguarding human rights without a constitution helped defeat the attempts to enact a human rights law. However, the situation may have changed with the enactment of the new Basic Law: Freedom of Occupation and the Basic Law: Human Dignity and Liberty. On these basic laws see n. 2 above. Recently the Sup. Ct. has held that it is empowered to review and invalidate any new law inconsistent with these basic laws. See *United Mizrahi Bank Ltd.* v. *Migdal Cooperative Village* (1995) (not yet reported). On judicial review of legislation infringing human rights specified in these basic laws, see David Kretzmer's note in Section 3 of this book.

authorities allows Israel, like many other modern States, to be described as an Administrative state.

In most cases the Legislature bestows defined powers on specific authorities. In a typical case it provides that a certain authority is empowered, subject to certain conditions, to give a certain licence or benefit. However, in some matters the Legislature avoids regulating a certain field, and instead grants an administrative authority sweeping powers to regulate it, without providing any legislative standards or guidance. In the matter of State lands, for example, the law establishes the Israel Lands Administration 'to administer Israel Lands', but does not prescribe any rules or standards for that administration.[4]

The most important instance of sweeping powers is that of the Government. Section 29 of the Basic Law: The Government provides as follows: '[t]he Government is competent to do in the name of the State, subject to any law, any act the doing of which is not enjoined by law upon another authority.'[5] This provision is the source of intensive activity, not regulated by specific laws, in various fields, such as: foreign relations, housing, absorption of immigrants, and subsidies. But the power granted by this provision, broad and undefined as it is, is subject to two restrictions. First, the government is not empowered to act in a matter vested by law in any other authority. It cannot, for example, permit telephone-tapping, because a specific law provides that a permit to tap telephones must be received from a judge. Secondly, the power of the Government must be exercised subject to law, including the common law rule concerning human rights.[6] Accordingly, the Government may not rely on this provision to restrict, for example, free speech.

## *C. Nature of Power*

The pure doctrine of separation of powers, according to which each of the three main branches of government exercises a distinct kind of power, is honoured in its breach, especially by the executive branch. The Executive is vested by the Legislature with vast powers of a legislative (or quasi-legislative) nature, as well as with vast powers of a judicial (or quasi-judicial) nature.

No general power to make subordinate legislation is vested in the government, a minister, or any other authority. To make subordinate legislation in any matter, power must be granted by the Legislature specifically for that matter. However, virtually every law expressly provides that a specified minister, according to subject-matter, is charged with the

[4] Israel Lands Administration Law, 1960, S. 2 (14 LSI 50).

[5] Basic Law: The Government of 1968, S. 29 (22 LSI 257).

[6] On this rule see sect. 2A above.

implementation of that law and, to that end, may also make regulations necessary to implement the law. Such regulations (called *secundum legem*) can only lay down rules of a secondary nature needed to implement rules of a primary nature in the enabling law. In addition, laws often empower various authorities to make regulations in specific matters in which the enabling law does not prescribe any rule of a primary nature. In such instances the regulations (known as *praeter legem*) can regulate a specified field, without any guideline or standard having been laid down by the legislature. For example, the whole field of civil procedure is regulated by rules made by the Minister of Justice, pursuant to a provision in the Courts Law, empowering the Minister to make regulations in the matter of court procedure.[7] Also, the Legislature may empower a minister to make regulations (called *contra legem*) which may, as an exceptional measure, contradict the provisions of ordinary legislation. The most telling instance is that of emergency regulations. In a state of emergency, which has formally existed in Israel since the War of Independence, ministers are empowered to make emergency regulations. Such regulations—in force for only three months, unless extended by law—prevail over ordinary laws.[8]

The vast power to make subordinate legislation is subject to strict scrutiny in several ways. First, not infrequently the enabling law provides that regulations may only be made with the approval of a Knesset committee. Secondly, all regulations, whether or not approved by a Knesset committee, are subject to judicial review and may be invalidated by the court on any of the recognized grounds of review, including unreasonableness.[9] Finally, regulations may not impinge upon human rights, unless this is expressly authorized by the enabling law.[10]

Administrative authorities also possess vast powers of a judicial nature. Such powers may be vested in authorities which simultaneously exercise

[7] Courts Law [Consolidated Version], 1984, s. 108 (38 LSI 271).

[8] Law and Administration Ordinance, 1948, s. 9. (1. LSI 7). On emergency regulations generally, see A. Rubinstein, *Constitutional Law of the State of Israel* n. 3 above, 616–31 (in Hebrew). The present situation with regard to the state of emergency is due to change according to the new Basic Law: The Government, 1992 . The law (as provided in s. 63) entered into force and replaced the present Basic Law: The Government, 1968, after elections were held for the new (the 14th) Knesset, in May 1966. Among the changes introduced by the new Law (in secs. 49 and 50), it is noteworthy that the Knesset will be able to declare a state of emergency only for a period not exceeding one year, but it may extend the period, each time for a period not exceeding one year. Also, the power of the Government to make emergency regulations in such a period is subject to limitations. Among the limitations, the government may make such regulations, and such regulations may be relied upon by administrative authorities, only to the extent required by the state of emergency.

[9] This applies also to emergency regulations. See I. Zamir, 'Courts and Politics in Israel' [1991] *Public Law* 523, 528.

[10] See sect. 2E below on the interpretation of powers. On subordinate legislation generally see A. Barak, 'Subordinate Legislation', 16 *Scripta Hierosolymitana* (Jerusalem, 1966) 219; B. Bracha, *Administrative Law* (Schocken, Tel Aviv, 1986), 76–96 (in Hebrew); I. Zamir, 'Secondary Legislation: Procedure and Directives' (1986) 11 *Tel Aviv Uni. LR* 339 (in Hebrew).

non-judicial powers. In many cases, however, judicial powers are vested in administrative tribunals especially and exclusively established by law to hear and determine appeals from administrative decisions. Such tribunals exist in many areas such as taxation, social security, planning and agriculture. The tribunal is usually composed of three members appointed by a Minister. The law often requires that the chairman be a judge, a retired judge, or a lawyer. The other two members are usually lay persons, either representatives of the public or experts in the relevant field. The tribunal is meant to offer informal, speedy, and inexpensive adjudication. It is, therefore, not bound by the rules of procedure or evidence applicable in a court of law, although it is bound by the rules of natural justice (concerning bias and the right to a hearing) and subject to review by the court.

Each administrative tribunal is governed by the special provisions of the law under which it is established. However, a recently enacted law—the Administrative Tribunals Law of 1992—is meant to apply to administrative tribunals in general. At present it applies to fifteen kinds of tribunal enumerated in the Schedule to the Law, but more tribunals are meant to be gradually added to the Schedule, which is eventually to include most tribunals. The Law regulates the appointment and terms of office of members of the tribunal; conflict of interests; procedure and evidence, including powers to summon witnesses and to appoint an expert witness on behalf of the tribunal; appeal from the decision of the tribunal; and other matters. The Law is, however, of a residuary nature, i.e. it applies to a tribunal enumerated in the Schedule only in matters in which there is no specific provision relating to that tribunal in another law.

The Law also establishes a Council on Tribunals to be appointed by the Minister of Justice. The main functions of the Council are to advise the Minister of Justice or any other Minister on all matters relating to administrative tribunals, request reports on specific tribunals, and issue publications in all matters pertaining to tribunals. Its functions relate to all administrative tribunals and not merely to those enumerated in the Schedule to the Law.[11]

## *D. Auxiliary Powers*

Powers given to an administrative authority, be they of an executive, legislative, or judicial nature, are supplemented by auxiliary powers. Auxiliary powers are expressly granted by law to all authorities.[12] They can also be

[11] On administrative tribunals generally, see B. Bracha, n. 10 above, 97–128 (in Hebrew). On the Administrative Tribunals Law of 1992, see Ch. 5 of this book.

[12] Sec. 17(b) of the Interpretation Law of 1981 (35 LSI 370) provides: 'Any empowerment to do or enforce the doing of something implies the conferment of auxiliary powers reasonably required therefor.'

implied from the enabling law. However, they are restricted to such powers as are reasonably necessary to enable the authority to exercise its main power. Thus, the use of auxiliary powers in order to infringe upon human rights would generally be held by the court to be unreasonable. This would be in line with the general rule concerning the interpretation of powers.

### *E. Interpretation of Powers*

Faced with the vast powers granted by law to administrative authorities, the courts have developed rules of interpretation meant to mitigate the impact of such powers on the individual. Such rules derive guidance from the basic values of a democratic society as expressed, *inter alia*, in the Declaration of Independence of 1948. The Declaration, said by the courts to express the faith and vision of the people, states that Israel shall be founded on the principles of freedom, justice, and peace and shall secure equality of rights for all its citizens. Freedom and equality have thus been held by the courts to be guiding principles for the legislature and the executive alike. Accordingly, the courts have established a presumption that by granting power to an administrative authority, the legislature does not intend to allow that authority to curtail individual freedoms or to discriminate against individuals or groups. To act contrary to this presumption, an administrative authority must be expressly empowered by the legislature to do so. Thus, if a law empowers a Minister to make regulations in a certain matter, this in itself does not allow him to make regulations which would limit any individual freedom, such as freedom of speech. Furthermore, ambiguous terms will usually be interpreted so as to be consistent with the presumption of freedom and equality. This presumption has thus enabled the courts in many cases to protect human rights against administrative power as if they were founded in a written constitution.[13]

## 3. Administrative Authorities

### *A. The Government*

The Legislature grants power to the Executive by specifying the competent authority. The competent authority is often a public official within a government ministry, such as the Inspector of Traffic in the Ministry of Transportation, the Commissioner of Water in the Ministry of Agriculture, or the Director of Customs in the Ministry of Finance. Such authority

[13] See e.g. *Miterani* v. *Minister of Transportation* (1983) 37(3) PD 337 (included in Ch. 2 of this book). See also I. Zamir, n. 3 above, 68.

enjoys in law (though hardly in practice) a position of semi-independence. It is presumed that the law vesting power in the competent authority intends that the power will be exercised by that authority and not by others. The competent authority is, therefore, required to exercise its own discretion, and is forbidden to act upon superior orders, even if issued by the responsible minister.

The competent authority is, however, allowed to take into account superior policy or advice and adopt it as its own policy or decision. This in itself may usually suffice to induce the competent official, being dependent for his career on the goodwill of his superiors, not to disregard their will. Also, the law generally allows the minister charged with the implementation of a law to take upon himself powers granted by that law to other public officials.[14] The combined effect is that the rule forbidding the competent authority to act upon superior orders is, in practice, largely a fiction.

The presumed intention that power vested by law in the competent authority should be exercised by that authority also explains the rule against delegation of power. According to this rule the competent authority may not delegate its power, unless this is expressly provided or can be clearly inferred from the enabling law.

These rules offend a basic principle of sound administration, namely, the principle of administrative hierarchy. This principle is generally considered essential to ensure responsibility and efficiency within the administration. However, these rules have largely been neutralized by a recent legislative trend to vest powers in ministers, rather than in subordinate officials. The position of ministers as central figures in the operation of the administration has thus been strengthened. This does not necessarily mean that the administration will in practice become more centralized. The ministers are expressly authorized by law to delegate their powers (with the exception of the power to make regulations) to other public officials.[15] This they regularly do. Under the case law the minister is still able to maintain control over the delegated powers: he remains a competent authority, and can therefore exercise the power alongside the delegatee, issue guidelines, or withdraw the power from the delegatee and, depending on the circumstances of the case, cancel a decision made by the delegatee.

## *B. Statutory Corporations*

Powers are also vested by law in various public bodies outside the central government bureaucracy, notably in local authorities and in statutory corporations. A statutory corporation is established by law to carry out specific functions of a public nature. Important examples of such corporations

[14] Basic Law: The Government, s. 32 (22 LSI 257). [15] *Ibid.*, s. 31.

are the Broadcasting Authority, the Postal Authority, and the Airports Authority. The statutory corporation is endowed by law with a legal entity separate from that of the Government. The relationship between the corporation and the responsible minister is prescribed by law. Usually the corporation is subject to the strong influence of the minister. However, in its daily operation it enjoys a measure of independence and flexibility not enjoyed by a government department, which is intended to improve performance.

The relative success of various statutory corporations may partly explain the recent trend to remove from government ministries certain functions, which involve semi-economic activity, and vest them in newly established corporations.[16]

## *C. Government Companies*

Another channel of government activity is that of the government company. This form of organization is used when the Government, sometimes jointly with private capital, engages in economic activity that does not require statutory powers. There are scores of such companies, including some of the major economic bodies in Israel, such as the Electricity Company and the Telecommunications Company. Such companies are usually established, pursuant to a decision by the Government, under the general law of companies.[17] They are governed simultaneously by this general law and by the Government Companies Law of 1975. The latter Law requires, on the one hand, that the government company shall generally conduct its affairs according to ordinary business considerations that guide any other company (section 4). On the other hand, it provides for government control, to ensure that the company serves government policy and the public interest. For example, some members of the board of directors are appointed by the ministers responsible for the company; decisions of the company in certain matters, specified in the Law, require government approval; the Government may decide, in certain circumstances, to dissolve or merge government companies; and it may also decide, with the approval of the Finance Committee of the Knesset, that a government company should deviate from ordinary business considerations.[18]

The government company does not generally possess statutory powers. Consequently, it is not to be considered an administrative authority, nor is

[16] See generally, U. Yadin, 'The Public Corporation in Israel', in W. G. Friedman and J. F. Garner (eds.), *Government Enterprise* (Stevens, London 1970), 248.

[17] The Companies Ordinance (New Version) of 1983. This is a new version of the Companies Ordinance of 1929 which was based on the English Companies Act of 1929. A new Companies Bill has recently been drafted by the Ministry of Justice.

[18] Government Companies Law, 1975 (29 LSI 162).

it, generally, subject to the rules of administrative law.[19] However, certain government companies, notably public utilities companies, may be held bound by certain basic principles of administrative law, namely, fairness, good faith, equality, and reasonableness.[20]

## 4. Administrative Procedure

Israel does not have a comprehensive law of administrative procedure. Administrative authorities are nonetheless bound to follow various procedural rules. Procedural rules may be specific, that is, laid down by the law enabling a specific authority to exercise a specific power. Thus, for instance, a law empowering a specific authority to expropriate private land may impose upon that authority the duty to conduct an inquiry, to consult particular persons or bodies, to publish a certain notice and to give a hearing to an aggrieved person. Procedural rules may also be general, that is, applicable to administrative authorities in general. Such rules are partly laid down by enacted law, notably the Interpretation Law of 1981 and the Administrative Procedure Amendment (Decisions and Statement of Reasons) Law of 1958 and 1969, and partly by case law.

### *A. Duty to Act*

The Interpretation Law of 1981, section 11, requires all authorities to act in due time.[21] This means that the authority must take action within reasonable time, according to the circumstances of the case. It also means that action taken by the authority should be completed without undue delay.

In case of unreasonable delay, the court can order the authority to act within reasonable time or within a specified time. In case of extreme delay, the court may decide the case on the merits, for example, by holding that the applicant is entitled to the licence requested. In such a case the court may also annul administrative proceedings which, having started, were not completed in due time.[22]

[19] Exceptionally the law may vest powers in a government company. For instance, the Electricity Company and the Telecommunications Company are vested by law with certain powers, such as a power to enter upon private premises in order to build a communications installation. In exercising such a power the company is subject to judicial review on the general grounds of review as any administrative authority. See e.g. *Micro-Daf* v. *Israel Electricity Co., Ltd.* (1987) 41(2) PD 449.

[20] *Ibid.* It is also possible that other kinds of private bodies fulfilling functions of a public nature, such as burial societies, will be subjected to certain principles of administrative law. See *Chevra Kadisha* v. *Kestenbaum* (1992) 46(2) PD 464.

[21] 35 LSI 370.

[22] e.g. in *Amitai* v. *Local Committees for Planning and Building* (1988) 42(4) PD 89, a local

The court has also ruled that an administrative authority may not act upon unreliable presumptions or rumours. Instead, it must act on a sound evidentiary basis, that is, on reliable information. To this end, it must collect relevant information and assess its significance. The information to be relied upon must meet the so-called administrative evidence test, which is similar to the American substantial evidence rule. Under this test, the decision must be supported by such evidence as a reasonable person could have relied upon to reach that decision.

## *B. Rules of Natural Justice*

The administrative authority is bound to observe two rules of natural justice that have been developed by case law: the rule against bias and the rule concerning the right to a hearing. Originally, these rules applied only to judicial (or quasi-judicial) acts. The High Court has, however, extended their application, and they now also apply to purely administrative acts.

The first rule provides that an administrative authority may be disqualified for bias or for conflict of interests. Bias exists where the authority has a personal interest, pecuniary or otherwise, in the matter to be decided, or some other connection with that matter, which gives rise to a real likelihood (or, according to another version, to a reasonable suspicion) of bias. Conflict of interests is an extension of bias. It relates mainly to a potential conflict between two positions held by the authority. In such a case, if there is a real likelihood (or a reasonable suspicion) that the authority, acting in one capacity, may be unduly influenced by interests pertaining to the other capacity, it may be required to give up one of the conflicting capacities. In other cases, depending on the circumstances, the authority may only be restricted in the exercise of its power, so that it will have to avoid making decisions in matters in which such conflict exists.[23]

The second rule of natural justice prescribes a right to a hearing. The High Court has held that a person is entitled to a fair hearing by an administrative authority where a decision of the authority may adversely affect his person, property, profession, status, etc., by decision of that authority.[24] In such cases, the authority must notify the person in due time of the pending decision, provide him with information necessary to enable him to prepare his case, and, apparently, also allow him to inspect relevant material in the file of the authority. He should then be given an opportunity to

authority announced its decision to expropriate a certain plot of land in order to build on it a nursery school. But it did not complete the process of expropriation for 26 years as it did not have the resources necessary to compensate the owner. The Court annulled the decision to expropriate the land on the ground of undue delay.

[23] The leading case on conflict of interests is *The Likud Party in the Municipality of Petach Tikvah* v. *The Petach Tikvah City Council* (1980) 34(2) PD 566 (included in Section 4 of this book).

[24] *Berman* v. *Minister of the Interior* (1958) 12 PD 1493.

present his case, personally or by a lawyer, in writing or (depending on the circumstances of the case) orally, and (again, depending on the circumstances of the case) also to examine witnesses. Furthermore, he may be entitled to a second hearing, where this is required to enable him to rebut adverse evidence received by the authority after the first hearing. The terms of the hearing may change from one case to another. A fairness test is used to determine the nature and extent of the hearing.

## *C. Decisions, Reasons, and Publications*

The Administrative Procedure Amendment (Decisions and Statement of Reasons) Law, 1958,[25] commonly referred to as the Decisions and Reasons Law, provides that an administrative authority, requested in writing to exercise statutory power, is obliged to make a decision and answer the request in writing as soon as possible, and not later than than forty-five days. This obligation is subject to certain exceptions specified in the Law. For example, a decision may be made after the prescribed time if another law specifically requires an inquiry into the matter or prescribes a different period for decision, or if it has been found, upon examination by the authority, that the matter requires further examination. In such a case, the authority must notify the person concerned and their superior, in writing and as soon as possible, of the reason for the delay and give details of the expected time of decision.

The Decisions and Reasons Law also provides that an authority which refuses a written application to exercise statutory power must notify the applicant in writing of the reasons for the refusal. Here, again, the Law lays down certain exceptions. Thus, the authority does not have to state its reasons if this may jeopardize national security or foreign relations, unlawfully prejudice the rights of another person, or reveal trade secrets or information made secret by any law, or if another law exempts the authority from stating the reasons for specific decisions. The very refusal to state reasons must be reasoned in writing, and may be appealed to the Minister in charge.

There is no duty to publish all administrative decisions. However, regulations and other administrative acts having legislative effect must be published in the official gazette, and in the absence of such publication they may be held invalid.[26] Furthermore, some statutes require publication of specific decisions, such as certain governmental appointments, in the official gazette or elsewhere.

[25] 13 LSI 7 and 23 LSI 160.

[26] Interpretation Ordinance [New Version], s. 17 (1 LSI [New Version] 5). See e.g. *Attorney General* v. *Alexandrowitz* (1957) 11 PD 695.

## 5. Enforcement and Sanctions

Specific provisions for the implementation or enforcement of administrative decisions are sometimes included in the enabling law. For example, the law may expressly empower a specified authority to carry out a demolition order, to enter private premises for inspection, or to seize property or documents. The Taxes (Collection) Ordinance of 1929, for example, lays down rules for the collection of taxes, governmental as well as municipal. In certain matters the law states that the authority cannot implement its decision, e.g. to tap telephones or enter upon expropriated land, except with the consent of the court or some other authority.

Failure to obey an administrative decision is an offence. In addition to provisions in various laws, which make disobedience to specific decisions an offence, the Penal Law generally provides that disobedience to a lawful order made by a person acting in an official capacity is an offence punishable by imprisonment of up to two years.[27]

The Administrative Offences Law of 1985 has introduced a reform in this sphere. It provides that criminal offences under certain regulatory laws, enumerated in the Schedule to the Law, shall be administrative offences. At present some forty laws are enumerated in the Schedule, regulating matters of taxation, employment, safety, consumer protection, public health, and so on. Administrative offences are usually punished by administrative fines fixed by regulations at specified amount for each specific offence. The fines are imposed by specially appointed inspectors. The offender may pay the fine, in which case his offence is expiated and he is not regarded as having been convicted of an offence, or he may request to be tried for the offence in criminal proceedings before an ordinary court of law.[28]

## 6. Misuse of Power

Misuse of power may invalidate the administrative decision. The court has categorized forms of misuse that constitute grounds of illegality.

[27] Penal Law, 1977, s. 287 (LSI, Special Vol., 4).

[28] On this Law, see I. Zamir, 'The Administrative Offences Law: An Introductory Note' (1986) 21 *Is. LR* 201 (reproduced in this book in Section 7). For an English translation of the Law, see Section 7 of this book.

### A. Excess of Power

The original ground of illegality, and in a sense the basis of other grounds, is excess of power. The principle of administrative legality requires every administrative authority to act within the limits of its power, as prescribed by law, expressly or impliedly. If the authority exceeds these limits, for whatever reason, its act is unlawful. Such unlawfulness is usually considered a grave defect which may render the decision null and void.

Although excess of power is generally regarded as a distinct ground of illegality, it is actually only the result of another ground of illegality, often an error of law or an error of fact. Such an error may cause the authority to overstep the four corners of its power and perform an act of a kind it has not been authorized to do. The act will then be defective as being *ultra vires* and, at the same time, erroneous in law or in fact, as the case may be. But this is not necessarily so. The authority may err in law or in fact without exceeding the limits of its power. This is evident in case of an administrative tribunal which, like a court of law, can make a decision which is wrong in law or in fact, and yet within its jurisdiction. This may also happen with other administrative authorities. In such a case the error, in law or in fact, is clearly a distinct and possibly the only ground of illegality.

### B. Default

At the other end of the spectrum of the misuse of power is default, that is, neglect or refusal to exercise power. An authority, vested with power, is not only authorized to act, but may also be bound to act if the circumstances so require. It is, in any case, obliged to consider whether it should, under the circumstances, exercise its power. This it must do within a reasonable time. Neglect or refusal to do so, if unjustified in the circumstances of the case—for example, if based on irrelevant considerations—will be unlawful. Such a defect may be rectified by an order of the court.[29]

Default, like excess of power, is usually the result of some other ground of illegality. It may sometimes be attributed to a defect in the exercise of discretion or to an error of law or an error of fact.

### C. Defects in Law, Fact, and Procedure

Where the law provides for an appeal from the administrative decision to a court of law, there is no doubt that the court, in its appellate jurisdiction, can review all errors of law. Where the law does not provide for such an appeal, judicial review may be exercised by the Supreme Court in its

[29] See sect. 4A above. On judicial review of administrative default see e.g. *Berger* v. *Minister of the Interior* (1983) 37(3) PD 29.

supervisory jurisdiction, sitting as a High Court of Justice. In such cases, the rule used to be, following English law, that the Court could only intervene if an error of law was apparent on the face of the record. But this rule, said by the Court to be unjust, has been replaced by another rule according to which the Court, in its supervisory jurisdiction, can review all errors of law, whether or not apparent on the face of the record.[30] The new rule has greatly narrowed the difference between appellate review and supervisory review of administrative action.

With regard to errors of law there is a difference of opinion among judges on the question whether the Court should substitute its own conclusion for that of the administrative authority.[31] No such difference of opinion exists with regard to errors of fact. Here it is agreed that the authority is bound to collect the relevant information, assess it, and determine the facts in accordance with the administrative evidence rule.[32] However, the Court, on review, will avoid an independent examination of the evidence to determine the facts. It will not intervene in findings of fact, especially in matters which call for some expertise, if there is substantial evidence to support them. The test is that of the reasonable person, that is, the Court will usually refrain from intervention if the evidence before the authority reasonably supports the findings of fact.[33]

The intervention of the Court on the ground of a defect in administrative procedure is less predictable. It is clear that in principle the authority should observe all procedural rules, whether it is a statutory provision requiring prior consultation or publication, or the common law rule concerning the right of hearing, or any other procedural requirement.[34] It is also clear that a serious breach of a procedural rule may invalidate the decision. However, some procedural requirements are of a technical nature or of minor importance. The Court does not tend to invalidate a decision for breach of such a requirement. It may hold that such a requirement is only directory, and not mandatory. However, this seems to be a doubtful classification, since it is not to be presumed that the legislature, when prescribing a procedural requirement, is indifferent as to whether or not it is observed. Indeed, the Court has tended to avoid the distinction between mandatory and directory requirements as a test for validity. When it is not inclined to invalidate a decision for a procedural defect, it will usually hold that the defect is slight, or that it does not go to the root of the matter, or

[30] See *Trudler* v. *Election Officers to the Agricultural Committees* (1963) 17 PD 2503.

[31] Cf *Khatib* v. *National Labour Tribunal* (1986) 40(1) PD 673 and *Milferder* v. *National Labour Tribunal* (1987) 41(2) PD 210. The controversy relates to cases in which the law is not clear and reasonably allows more than one conclusion. In such a case, should the Court intervene if the administrative authority reached one such conclusion and the Court would have preferred another conclusion?

[32] See sect. 4A above.

[33] See e.g. *Berger* v. *Minister of the Interior*, n. 29 above, 37.

[34] On administrative procedure see sect. 4 above.

that it has not caused injustice. If one is to derive a test from the cases it may be this: can it reasonably be presumed that, had the authority observed the required procedure, its decision might have been substantially different? The test examines the presumed consequences of compliance with the procedural requirement. If the answer is that, presumably, compliance would not have changed the decision, the Court will not tend to intervene. According to this test, the Court will usually tend to intervene where the authority denied a right of hearing, but this is not always the case. If it is clear, in the circumstances of the case, that a hearing would have been a mere formality, since there was nothing to be argued that could possibly have changed the decision, the Court may uphold the decision despite the absence of a hearing.

## *D. Abuse of Discretion*

Review of administrative discretion is of special importance since most administrative powers are discretionary. In practice, the prospect that an administrative authority will wrongly exercise its discretion is greater than the prospect that it will exceed its power, err in law or in fact, or contravene a procedural rule. Not surprisingly, judicial review of administrative decisions on the ground that the authority abused its discretion is more frequently sought than review on any other ground.

The starting point in the review of administrative discretion is the presumption that the legislature intended the competent authority to exercise its own discretion; hence, the rule that the court should not intervene to substitute its own discretion for that of the authority. However, this rule applies only to discretion lawfully exercised, that is, in accordance with certain rules laid down by the court. The court presumes that the legislature intended the authority to exercise its discretion for the purpose for which the power was given, free from irrelevant considerations, and reasonably. If the authority acts to the contrary, it acts unlawfully, which constitutes a ground for the intervention of the court.

The basic rule concerning the exercise of administrative discretion is that the authority must aim at achieving the purpose (usually more than one purpose) for which the legislature (expressly or impliedly) granted the power. The exercise of power for another purpose, i.e. an improper purpose, is unlawful. If the improper purpose is just one of several purposes, it may invalidate the decision if it had a substantial effect on the authority or if it was the dominant purpose.[35]

The legislative purpose also determines, to a great extent, the relevant

[35] *Emma Berger* v. *District Committee for Planning and Building* (1973) 27(2) PD 764, 773; *Dweikat* v. *Government of Israel* (*The Elon Moreh Case*) (1980) 34(1) PD 1, 20 (included in this book in Section 12).

considerations. Other relevant considerations may depend on the circumstances of the case. The rule, derived from the rule concerning improper purpose, requires the authority to take into account the relevant considerations and to disregard irrelevant considerations.

The Court has gone further to regulate the decision making process of the administrative authority. The authority, the Court has held, should take into account two main kinds of relevant considerations. First, there are specific considerations which are relevant to the case at hand. For example, in case of a request for a building permit, the particular considerations are those emanating from the Planning and Building Law of 1965 and other considerations pertaining to building. Secondly, there are general considerations which apply to administrative powers generally. The general considerations are common to all administrative powers since they derive from the basic values and principles of the legal system. These values and principles reflect the democratic nature of society. Prominent among them are individual freedom and equality before the law. Freedom and equality were declared as guiding principles in the Declaration of Independence of 1948. Accordingly, they should guide all administrative authorities. This means that they are relevant considerations to be generally taken into account in the exercise of administrative powers. If an authority fails to do so, in a case in which individual freedom is involved or equality before the law may be affected, the Court may hold that the discretion has not been lawfully exercised.[36]

Further, it is not sufficient for the lawful exercise of discretion that it is exercised for the proper purpose and on relevant considerations. It must also be exercised reasonably. An unreasonable decision, for the purpose of judicial review, is a decision so unreasonable that no reasonable authority could have arrived at it. But this formula is clearly a tautology and, as such, not very helpful. What, then does unreasonableness mean?

A decision may be unreasonable because it is tainted by an improper purpose or irrelevant considerations. In such a case, unreasonableness is not really a distinct ground of review, but rather the result or the symptom of another ground. In practice, however, it serves as a useful ground of review, because it allows review of decisions even in cases in which the purpose and the considerations of the authority are not revealed and cannot be proved and thus remain unknown. The unreasonableness of the decision in such cases may serve as an indication of a defect in the exercise of discretion. This may be sufficient to shift the burden of proof from the aggrieved person to the deciding authority.

Unreasonableness, however, is not only a symptom of another defect. It

[36] See e.g. *Poraz* v. *Municipality of Tel Aviv* (1988) 42(2) PD 309. Here the Court overruled a decision of the Municipality of Tel Aviv that discriminated against women, because it had disregarded equality of women as a guiding principle.

may also be a distinct ground of review in a case in which the authority acts for a proper purpose and on relevant considerations. In such a case the defect in the exercise of discretion may lie in the weight given by the authority to the relevant considerations. While the weight to be given to relevant considerations is, indeed, a matter for the authority, there is a limited range of weights which may reasonably be given to any consideration. This is called the range of reasonableness. If the authority remains within the limits of this range, the court, even if it might have preferred some different weight, will not intervene. But if the authority substantially oversteps these limits, by giving excessive or insufficient weight to any consideration, it may be said to be acting unreasonably.[37]

It is not only the weight given by the authority to a specific consideration that may be undue; the relative weights given to competing considerations may also be wrong. For example, a military censor may have given, in a particular case, insufficient weight to the value of free speech as compared to that given to the interest of national security. In such a case the Court may hold that the authority acted on a wrong balance of interests. Balance of interests is thus an extension of the rule concerning reasonableness and has recently become a common technique for the review of administrative discretion. The Court often examines whether the balance of interests made by the authority reflects the proper balance of interests, that is, the balance of interests which appears proper to the Court. Such examination allows the Court closer scrutiny of administrative discretion especially in cases in which individual freedoms are involved.

The Court, examining the balance of interests, can go further than declaring that the balance reached by the authority in the particular case is wrong. It can offer a criterion for the balance to be aimed at in that kind of case. The criterion may lay down the proper relationship between the competing considerations (rather, the main considerations) in cases of that kind. Thus, in cases of censorship the court has repeatedly held, in spite of a very broad legislative power of censorship, that free speech may only be restricted if there is a 'near certainty' that a publication will cause 'substantial damage' or 'substantial danger' to public order or to national security.[38] The substance of the criterion may depend upon the nature of the competing interests and vary according to their relative importance, as evaluated by the Court. For example, for cases in which free speech conflicts with the judicial process, such as the case of *sub judice* publications,

[37] See e.g. *Dapei Zahav* v. *Broadcasting Authority* (1981) 35(1) PD 421; *Ganor* v. *Attorney General* (1990) 44(2) PD 485 (included in this book in Section 11).

[38] See e.g. *Kol Ha'am* v. *Minister of the Interior* (1953) 7 PD 871. In *Laor* v. *Board of Censorship of Films and Plays* (1987) 41(1) PD 421, the Court applied the same criterion to plays. Consequently, the mandatory ordinance providing for censorship of plays was abolished by the Knesset. In *Schnitzer* v. *Chief Military Censor* (1988) 42(4) PD 617 (reproduced in this book in Section 2) the Court applied this criterion to military censorship based on security considerations.

the Court laid down a different criterion, namely 'reasonable possibility' of substantial damage to the judicial process.[39]

There is a marked difference between a case in which the Court simply declares that the authority acted on a wrong balance of interests and a case in which the Court lays down a criterion for the proper balance of interests. By laying down a criterion, the Court not only reviews the exercise of power retrospectively, but also provides a guideline, which is to serve the authority prospectively, in repeated exercise of that power.

Recently a new ground of review has emerged, which has been in latent existence for a long period of time. The Court has held on several occasions that even where an authority may exercise its power, as where the balance of interests allows restriction of free speech, the power should be exercised proportionally, that is, in proportion to the need or danger. Excessive use of power may invalidate the decision. It may be said, as it was said with regard to reasonableness, that it is the presumed intention of the legislature that the authority would exercise its power proportionally. To this end, the authority should take into account the legislative purpose and the particular circumstances of each case. For example, in the case of a pornographic film, subject to censorship, it may be disproportionate, and therefore wrong in law, to ban the film if the legislative purpose may be adequately served by less drastic measures, such as cutting out certain scenes or excluding minors from the cinema.[40]

## *E. Special Instances*

The Court has traditionally considered itself restricted in the review of administrative discretion in certain special instances. This has been attributed to the language of the enabling law, the position or qualifications of the competent authority, or the nature of the power reviewed. Recently, however, the Court has largely removed such self-imposed restrictions.

First, the Court used to distinguish between ordinary discretion and subjective discretion. Discretion was considered subjective where the enabling law used special language supposedly indicating broader discretion than in ordinary cases. These were cases in which the law stated that the authority could act if it were satisfied that a certain situation existed, or if in its opinion it was necessary to take a certain course of action, or if in its discretion (or even its absolute discretion) it saw fit to do a certain thing, and the like. The Court used to accept such language as restricting judicial review. Recently, however, the Court has changed its position on this matter, and has gradually cast aside the differences in review of the two kinds

[39] *Azulai* v. *State of Israel* (1983) 37(2) PD 565.

[40] See e.g. *Euronet Gold Lines (1992) Ltd.* v. *Minister of Communications* (1995) (not yet reported); *Ben Atiya* v. *Minister of Education* (1995) (not yet reported).

of discretion. Today the Court maintains that so-called subjective discretion is subject to review much as ordinary discretion.[41]

Another instance of self-imposed restraint in the review of administrative discretion relates to the Attorney General. Traditionally, the Court held that the decisions of the Attorney General whether or not to institute or to stay criminal proceedings were subject to review only on the ground of bad faith. In practice this meant that the Court would not intervene in such decisions. This rule probably reflected the high position and special qualifications of the office of the Attorney General. But this, too, has been lifted. The Court recently stated that the decisions of the Attorney General are subject to review on the same grounds as those of other administrative authorities. Indeed, in two recent instances the Court held that decisions of the Attorney General not to prosecute were invalid on the ground of unreasonableness.[42]

The nature of administrative power can also account for self-restraint in judicial review. This is the case in matters concerning national security. It seems to be a universal phenomenon that courts are very cautious in such matters, possibly more than in any other matter. Such matters, usually clouded in secrecy, appear to be intrinsically connected with issues of high policy vital to national interests. The Court, therefore, tends to leave the responsibility in such matters to the competent authorities, political or professional, civil or military. Such an attitude may be especially understandable, and possibly justifiable in Israel, given the State's constant exposure to security risks. Yet, the Court seems to have somewhat modified its attitude to security matters in recent years. It is now more willing to examine such matters on the merits, and intervene in the exercise of discretion by military authorities, applying the ordinary grounds of review. Indeed, in a number of cases the court overruled decisions of military authorities on grounds of improper purpose, insufficient evidentiary basis, unreasonableness, inequality, and the like.[43]

[41] See e.g. *Kardosh* v. *Companies Registrar* (1961) 15 PD 1151; *Companies Registrar* v. *Kardosh* (1962) 16 PD 1210; *Schnitzer* v. *Chief Military Censor* (1988) 42(4) PD 617 (included in Section 2 of this book).

[42] *Sheftel* v. *Attorney General* (1989) 43(4) PD 356; *Ganor* v. *Attorney General* (1990) 44(2) PD 485 (included in this book in Section 11). Also, in *Tzofan* v. *Military Advocate General* (1989) 43(4) PD 718, the Court held that a decision of the Military A.G. not to prosecute a high-ranking officer in a military court was unreasonable and, therefore, that prosecution should be instituted.

[43] For recent cases see *Schnitzer* v. *Chief Military Censor*, n. 41 above; *Association for Civil Rights in Israel* v. *Commander of the Central Region* (1989) 43(2) PD 529; *Morcus* v. *Minister of Defence* (1991) 45(1) PD 467; *Nimmer* v. *Commander of the West Bank Region* (1991) 45(3) PD 625; *Raffel* v. *Minister of Defence* (1992) 46(1) PD 397. And see S. Shetreet, 'The Scope of Judicial Review of National Security Considerations in Free Speech and Other Areas: The Israeli Perspective' (1988) 18 *Is. YB on HR* 35; I. Zamir, 'Media Coverage of Military Operations', *ibid.* 61; Y. Dinstein, 'The Israeli Supreme Court and the Law of Belligerent Occupation: Reunification of Families', *ibid.* 173; I. Zamir, 'Rule of Law and Control of Terrorism' (1988) 8 *Tel Aviv University Studies in Law* 81; I. Zamir, 'Human Rights and National Security' (1989) 23 *Is.LR.* 375.

What is the reason for this change? While no reason has been formally given, there is probably more than one simple reason. It can possibly be assumed that the change may be paradoxically attributed in part to the precarious situation of Israel. What in other countries is a passing emergency, which may therefore be viewed as an exceptional situation, is in Israel a way of life. For many years now the Court has been regularly presented with many applications (about one fifth of all applications for judicial review) challenging decisions of military commanders and other security authorities, usually from inhabitants of the West Bank and the Gaza Strip. The sheer volume of such applications makes it increasingly difficult for the Court to view such matters as exceptional. Virtual immunity from judicial review, when it relates to a bulk of cases, may eventually reflect upon the position of the Court. In any case, the Court has made it clear that security matters, including discretion exercised in military matters, are not immune from review on the merits.

However, it should not be inferred from such recent developments that the Court does not continue to differentiate between different kinds of power and authority. In practice, even if not in theory, the Court is still especially cautious in reviewing certain matters, notably security matters. The reasons which for many years have induced it to act in self-restraint in such matters have not entirely disappeared, and may still be discerned in the manner and scope of judicial review. Only exceptionally will the Court overrule decisions in matters of national security on grounds of abuse of discretion.

## 7. Judicial Review

### *A. Appellate Review and Supervisory Review*

No administrative decision is immune from judicial review. Some laws, granting power to administrative authorities, provide for an appeal from the administrative decision to a court of law. Other laws (more than 100 in number) provide for an appeal from the administrative decision to an administrative tribunal.[44] Review on appeal is broad. This is especially so with regard to review by an administrative tribunal, possibly because of its special composition and qualifications. At least some tribunals are empowered to substitute their own discretion for that of the administrative authority.[45] All administrative tribunals are subject to review by a court of

[44] On administrative tribunals, see sect. 2C above.

[45] S. 18 of the Interpretation Law, 1981 (35 LSI 370) provides: 'Any empowerment to hear and determine an objection to or any other contestation of a decision of an authority implies empowerment to confirm the decision, with or without variations, to set it aside and give another decision instead, or to return the matter, with instructions, to the authority which gave the decision.' A

law and eventually by the Supreme Court, either by way of appeal, where this is prescribed by law, or else by resort to the supervisory jurisdiction of the Supreme Court.

A right of appeal depends upon an express provision in the law to this effect. If the law does not provide for an appeal from the decision, whether of an administrative tribunal or of any other administrative authority, review of the decision may take place by resort to the supervisory jurisdiction of the Supreme Court. The Supreme Court, which usually sits as a court of appeal in civil and criminal matters, sits as a High Court of Justice when reviewing administrative decisions. In this capacity it fulfills a function similar to that of the High Court of Justice in England when hearing applications for judicial review.[46]

It is clearly an anomaly that the Supreme Court sits in administrative matters as a court of first instance and final appeal. This anomaly can only be understood against the historical background. In 1922, the British mandatory government introduced, for the first time in this country, the concept of judicial review, to be exercised by means of the prerogative orders e.g. *certiorari* and *mandamus*. It did not trust the lower courts, with their majority of native judges, with the delicate task of supervising governmental decisions. It therefore entrusted this task to the Supreme Court which, throughout the mandatory period, had a majority of English judges.

Naturally, the High Court of Justice exercised its supervisory jurisdiction during the mandatory period much as an English court. Since independence the jurisdiction of the High Court of Justice has remained unchanged. But it did not take long for judges of the Supreme Court to break away from the English tradition and to introduce important innovations in the theory and practice of judicial review. The English origins are still evident: the substantive rules and the remedies are similar. Yet the differences between the two jurisdictions are marked in detail and in approach.

similiar provision, using almost indentical language, is included in s. 37 of the Administrative Tribunals Law, 1992. The meaning of these provisions has not yet been authoritatively determined. But in some cases concerning specific tribunals it was held that the tribunal could make the decision that in its opinion the administrative authority should have made.

[46] In addition, judicial review may be exercised in a proper case in any other court by way of collateral attack, that is, when the question of the legality of an administrative decision is incidentally raised in civil or criminal proceedings, e.g. as a defence. Collateral attack is available even in the very few instances in which direct attack is excluded by an express provision in the law, e.g. a decision by the President to pardon an offender. See e.g. *Barzilai* v. *Government of Israel* (1987) 40 (3) PD 505; published in English translation in (1986) 6 *Selected Judgments of the Sup. Ct. of Israel* 1. Supervisory jurisdiction over administrative authorities is vested not only in the Sup. Ct. sitting as a High Ct. of Justice, but also in ordinary courts, such as District Cts. However, the extent of this jurisdiction is still undefined. In practice it is rather narrow. See e.g. *Pasternak* v. *Minister of Housing* (1991) 45(5) PD 50. It is clear that ordinary courts, when reviewing administrative decisions, whether directly or collaterally, by way of appeal or otherwise, apply the same rules of administrative law applicable in the Sup. Ct. sitting as a High Ct. of Justice. See *ibid.*

## *B. Scope of Review*

The function of the High Court of Justice, as the Court itself perceives it, is twofold. It is, first and foremost, to settle disputes between the executive branch and an aggrieved person. But in addition it is the guardian of the rule of law, in a broad sense of the concept, which includes basic values and administrative fairness.

This approach is reflected in the scope of review. The Court has expanded the scope of review to cover loopholes in the application of the rule of law. The expansion has taken place in two main directions: in private law and in public law.

First, judicial review has been carefully applied to certain activities of the executive branch in the field of private law. The Executive, as the Court repeatedly declared, is a trustee of the general public. It cannot escape the basic duties of a trustee when it acts in the field of private law. Accordingly, discrimination is forbidden by any administrative authority in its private law dealings, such as buying, selling, or letting property.[47] Also, the bids issued by administrative authorities, such as a bid for the performance of public works or a bid for the supply of equipment to the authority, are subject to special rules, established by the Court, to ensure equality among the bidders.[48] Finally, government companies are not entirely free from the rules of public law, nor from judicial review. At least some governmental companies which provide public utilities are bound to observe some basic principles of administrative law, such as equality, good faith, and fairness.[49]

The expansion of judicial review in the field of public law has taken place by greatly loosening the threshold requirements of standing and justiciability.[50] Traditionally, the rule concerning standing required an applicant to have a personal interest in the matter brought before the Court. There are, however, cases in which administrative authorities are alleged to have acted contrary to law, and there is nobody with a personal interest, or those who have a personal interest are not willing to come forth and challenge the act in court. The victim in such a case may be the rule of law. The Court, as guardian of the rule of law, has therefore decided to modify the rule concerning standing. At present the rule provides that no personal interest is required if the matter brought before the Court is alleged to reveal corruption or if it may affect constitutional principles or the rule of law itself. In such cases, which cover a wide spectrum, the court may

[47] See e.g. *Peretz* v. *Kfar Shemaryahu* (1962) 16 PD 2101.

[48] See e.g. *Beit Ariza Rehovot Ltd.* v. *Minister of Agriculture* (1962) 16 PD 20.

[49] *Micro-Daf* v. *Electricity Company of Israel Ltd* (1987) 41(2) PD 449, 463.

[50] For a more detailed examination of this development, see the note by Shimon Shetreet in Section 9 of this book.

open its gates to applicants who have no other interest but the interest, common to everybody, that the rule of law be upheld.[51]

Also, the rule concerning justiciability has been dramatically reformed. The rule was previously used to exclude from the Court matters relating to high policy pertaining to other branches of government, notably the Legislature and the President, and other matters having a strong political flavour. Some such matters have recently been brought within the domain of the court. For example, the question of whether students of religious institutions should be drafted for military service, which had several times been held to be nonjusticiable, was later heard and determined on the merits.[52] Most striking is the intervention of the Court in parliamentary proceedings. The Court has held that such proceedings are justiciable. The Knesset, although sovereign to do or undo any law, must respect the rule of law. Accordingly, if it is alleged to have violated the law, including the Knesset rules which regulate its proceedings, the Court may intervene. However, out of respect for the Knesset the Court has stated that it will only intervene in matters that affect the fabric of parliamentary life and substantive values of the constitutional regime. Under this test the Court has in fact intervened and held several decisions of the Knesset or its organs to be unlawful and invalid.[53]

## C. *Procedure, Evidence and Remedies*

The procedure in applications for judicial review in the High Court of Justice, now regulated in broad lines by rules of procedure made in 1984, is simple.

The Court inherited archaic rules, overburdened with technicalities, with regard to the prerogative orders. These rules were, however, quickly discarded. The Court did not even wait for a formal reform. It simply ignored the old rules, and they faded out, some forty years ago, to be replaced by a uniform procedure for the different kinds of order: *mandamus*, *certiorari*, injunction, declaration, and the like. In this respect, the application to the High Court of Justice is similar to the modern English application for judicial review which was introduced in England by rules of court in 1987. The

[51] See e.g. *Ressler* v. *Minister of Defence* (1988) 42(2) PD 441 (included in this book in Ch. 9); *Ganor* v. *Attorney General* (1990) 44(2) PD 485 (included in Ch. 11 of this book). See further I. Zamir, n. 3 above, 69.

[52] *Ressler* v. *Minister of Defence* (1988) 42(2) PD 441 (included in Ch. 9 of this book).

[53] See *Sarid* v. *Knesset Speaker* (1982) 36(2) PD 197. And see e.g., *Kach Faction* v. *Knesset Speaker* (1985) 39(3) PD 141 (denying a one-member faction the right to move for a vote of no-confidence); *Kahane* v. *Knesset Speaker* (1985) 39(4) PD 85 (refusing to lay before the Knesset a Private Member's Bill on the ground that it was racist); *Miari* v. *Knesset Speaker* (1987) 41(4) PD 169 (removing the immunity of a Knesset member). See further D. Kretzmer, 'Judicial Review of Knesset Decisions' (1988) 8 *Tel Aviv Uni. Studies in Law* 95; I. Zamir, 'Courts and Politics in Israel' [1991] *Public Law* 523.

applicant does not even have to specify what kind of order he seeks from the court.

A practical problem exists, however, with regard to evidence in the High Court of Justice. The evidence is to be submitted by affidavit, and only exceptionally will the Court allow cross-examination on the affidavit. This may occasionally cause difficulties for the applicant, who must overcome the presumption of legality, behind which the authority may seek shelter. The presumption may be especially difficult to overcome in a case in which abuse of discretion is alleged. How can the applicant penetrate the mental process of the authority and, without cross-examination, prove an improper purpose or irrelevant considerations? The difficulty may sometimes be overcome by resort to such grounds as reasonableness, proportionality, or discrimination. This, however, may be inapplicable in the circumstances of a specific case. The Court, being aware of this difficulty, has recently stated that it may be willing to rely upon data, statistical or otherwise, presumptions, and other facts from which abuse of discretion may be reasonably inferred. Such evidence may be sufficient to shift the burden of proof as to the purpose and considerations supporting the decision from the applicant to the authority. In one case, for example, the applicant, who failed in an examination held by the Council of Land Assessors, claimed that his failure was attributable to an undisclosed policy of the Council to restrict the number of land assessors, in order to reduce competition in this field. This claim could not be proved by direct evidence. The Court, however, held that the unreasonably high proportion of candidates who annually failed these examinations might serve as *prima facie* evidence supporting the argument of the applicant as to the motive of the Council.[54] The Court may thus occasionally alleviate the difficulty encountered by applicants, but this cannot entirely solve the problem. It appears that in this matter some reform in the practice of judicial review is needed.

A reform appears to be needed also in connection with the remedies available on judicial review. Generally speaking, the High Court of Justice offers an impressive choice of remedies and usually succeeds in granting a remedy which suits the case.[55] There is, however, one serious deficiency in the range of remedies available in the High Court of Justice, and it involves

[54] *Moskowitz* v. *Council of Land Assessors* (1990) 44(2) PD 236.

[55] In other courts, such as District Courts, a problem exists with regard to the remedies available against the State or organs of the State. By law, the courts (with the exception of the High Court of Justice) may not issue coercive orders such as an injunction or specific performance against the State or organs of the State. But they can instead give declaratory judgments. About 15 years ago the Supreme Court also sanctioned the innovation of an interim declaration, which can be used against the State or organs of the State instead of an interlocutory injunction. See *Yotvin* v. *State of Israel* (1980) 34(2) PD 344. Recently a Bill has been presented to the Knesset to allow all courts to issue coercive orders against the State.

the award of damages. In principle there is nothing to prevent the Court from granting damages to an aggrieved person, even if there exists no cause of action in contract or in torts.[56] But in practice (with a few exceptions) the Court has chosen not to do so. The applicant who seeks damages is referred to another court, where he must bring a new action for damages, and establish a recognized cause of action. This does not make much sense from the point of view of the aggrieved person. On the other hand, it may be understandable from the point of view of the Court. The Supreme Court is clearly not a suitable forum to hear evidence on damage caused to the applicant and to assess the damages. This may be one more reason for a reform of the anomalous situation in which the Supreme Court sits as a court of first instance. Transferring judicial review to a lower court could solve some problems in the field of judicial review. It could, for example, make it possible to cross-examine witnesses and to receive damages alongside public law remedies.

A related issue is that of the consequence of the defect in the administrative decision. A traditional theory holds that defects are divided into two classes: first, defects which go to jurisdiction and make the decision void *ab initio*; secondly, defects which remain within the jurisdiction and make the decision only voidable. The Court, however, is gradually casting off this theory and replacing it by a new theory called relative nullity. This is a very flexible theory which has not as yet been clarified or crystallized. It is clear, however, that, according to the new theory, the consequence of a defect (and the ensuing remedy) does not depend (or, at least, does not wholly depend) upon the defect's classification as being inside or outside the jurisdiction of the authority. It rather depends on the severity of the defect, on the circumstances in which the decision is challenged (as, for example, on whether the applicant is the person directly aggrieved by the decision or whether it is a direct or a collateral challenge) and, generally, on the balance of relevant considerations.[57] Such flexibility seems welcome.

## 8. Conclusion

The High Court of Justice is seemingly the most respected institution in the country. It is also a most influential institution. By means of judicial review it has established rules which have had a strong impact on the working of public authorities and on the relationship between the authorities and the

[56] See e.g. *Binui Upituach Banegev Ltd.* v. *Minister of Defence* (1974) 28(2) PD 449.

[57] See e.g. *Shapira & Co.* v. *State of Israel* (1982) 36(1) PD 337 and 36(3) PD 645; *Petrochemical Industries Ltd* v. *State of Israel* (1990) 44(3) PD 812.

individual. The principles of English administrative law were a good starting point. They are still the backbone of our administrative law. However, the Court has felt free to deviate from these principles and to shape them so as to suit evolving concepts.[58]

The main achievement of the High Court of Justice has been the instilling of concepts of modern democracy, the rule of law, and fair administration into the fabric of a new government in a young country with no democratic tradition. Without the support of a written constitution, it has succeeded in establishing a judge-made constitution based on the principles of individual freedom and equality before the law.[59]

These achievements were possible partly due to the fact that judicial review has been exercised by the Supreme Court sitting as a court of first instance and final appeal. The personal stature and great prestige of the justices of the Supreme Court have made them an undisputed authority on matters of governmental norms and ethics. The direct and easy access to the High Court of Justice, with the publicity attending its deliberations and decisions, have had a strong deterrent effect on administrative authorities.

On the other hand, some disadvantages are inherent in the situation in which judicial review is exercised by the Supreme Court sitting as a court of first instance. The price of this anomaly is paid, first, by applicants for judicial review. They are at a disadvantage, *inter alia*, by not being allowed to cross-examine the administrative authority or to obtain damages. The price is also paid by the Supreme Court itself, by being overburdened with a huge load of cases, many of which are of little importance and significance, that in other countries would not have reached the Supreme Court.

Consequently, there is now a trend to transfer administrative matters from the Supreme Court to a lower court, mainly the District Court, with a right of appeal to the Supreme Court. This is a process gradually carried out by means of legislation and judicial decisions. A public committee, referred to as the Landau Committee, in 1980, recommended that an administrative division be established in the District Court, with specialized judges to hear and determine such matters. If such a division is established, it may be expected that a reform will ensue in certain practical aspects of judicial review, mainly in matters of procedure, evidence, and remedies.[60]

[58] For a survey of developments in the case law of the High Court of Justice, see D. Kretzmer, 'Forty Years of Public Law' (1990) 24 *Is. LR* 341; I. Zamir, 'Administrative Law: Revolution or Evolution?' (1990) 24 *Is. LR* 356.

[59] See e.g., A. Barak, 'Constitutional Law Without a Constitution: The Role of the Judiciary', in Sh. Shetreet (ed.), *The Role of Courts in Society* (Martinus Nijhoff, Dordrecht, 1988), 448.

[60] Recently, the Ministry of Justice drafted a Bill designed to regulate the transfer of administrative matters from the jurisdiction of the Supreme Court to the jurisdiction of the District Court sitting as an administrative court (with specialized judges).

# PART I
# *Human Rights*

# SECTION 2: NON-STATUTORY HUMAN RIGHTS

# 3

# *Protecting Fundamental Rights in Israel without a Written Constitution*

ALLEN ZYSBLAT



## 1. Introduction

For the first forty-five years of its existence, Israel lived without a written constitution or any other written statement of the basic rights and freedoms of its citizens. The decision of Israel's Knesset to postpone the attempt to forge a legislative balance between public authority and individual freedoms[1] meant that the task of safeguarding the basic liberties in Israel—as in England—was left to the courts.[2]

This judicial task was an especially daunting one in Israel. From the very beginning, Israel has been a 'democracy under siege'.[3] The constant security crisis, the endemic social and ethnic tensions, as well as the

[1] In the *Harari* Resolution of 1950. On this development see generally, R. Gavison, 'The Controversy over Israel's Bill of Rights' (1985) 15 *Is.YB on HR* 113.

[2] For more detailed analysis of this phenomenon, see B. Bracha, 'The Protection of Human Rights in Israel' (1982) 12 *Is.YB on HR* 110; A. Shapira, 'The Status of Fundamental Individual Rights in the Absence of a Written Constitution' (1974) 9 *Is.LR* 497; G. Hausner, 'The Right of the Individual in Court' (1974) 9 *Is.LR* 477; J. Albert, 'Constitutional Adjudication Without a Constitution: The Case of Israel' (1969) 82 *Harvard LRev.* 1245; S. Shetreet, 'The Reflections on the Protection of the Rights of the Individual: Form and Substance' (1977) 12 *Is.LR* 32; I. Zamir, 'Rule of Law and Civil Liberties in Israel' (1988) 7 *CJQ* 64; A. Maoz, 'Defending Civil Liberties Without a Constitution—The Israeli Experience' (1988) 16 *Melbourne University LR* 815.

[3] Bracha, n. 2 above, at 110.

discouragingly common excesses of a Government only too ready to regulate every aspect of life in the new State, challenged Israel's Supreme Court far more severely than was the case in other common law jurisdictions.

The general consensus is that Israel's judiciary has met this challenge admirably. In a rich and well-crafted case law—enlarged by the unique direct access that every Israeli resident has to the Supreme Court sitting as a High Court of Justice[4]—the Court forged a remarkable statement of basic rights and freedoms. The continuing call for a written bill of rights[5] for Israel was in no sense an indictment of the Supreme Court in this area. Rather, it was the expression of a desire further to anchor basic civil rights that the Supreme Court had so often expressed.[6] Justice Shamgar was surely correct when he said:

> The new draft Basic Law: Human Rights is designed to consolidate certain principles and mark their boundaries. Its central function is to enshrine these in an enacted law in order to protect them from the dangers that come with the various crises that arise from time to time. Its purpose is to serve as an expression of those values by which the citizen may be guided and to block in advance those who would trespass on their rights. But even now . . . basic freedoms are enshrined in the foundation of our legal system and form an intrinsic part of the law in Israel.[7]

## 2. The Basic Principle

What were the sources of this 'common law' protection of civil liberties and the rule of law? The principal concept is doubtless to be found in the common law rule that every person is permitted to do everything that is not forbidden by law.[8] The fundamental rights of the individual can be negated or curtailed by authority of the Legislature alone, in an enacted law.[9] This authority is vested exclusively in the Legislature whose pronouncements in the matter must be expressed in clear and unambiguous terms. The Knesset may, of course, delegate its power to other bodies, and does so, mainly to administrative organs, but it must voice such an intention in unequivocal language.

As Justice Haim Cohn said:

[4] For the background to this rule see the n. in Ch. 1 of this volume, 'The System of Government in Israel'.

[5] An excellent review of the history and substance of the debate about a written bill of right for Israel is found in Gavison, n. 2 above. See also Maoz, n. 2 above, at 830.

[6] See M. Shamgar, 'On the Written Constitution' (1974) 9 *Is.LR* 467; B. Akzin, 'The Place of the Constitution in the Modern State' (1967) 2 *Is.LR* 1; Shapira, n. 1 above, at 508.

[7] *Ha'aretz* v. *Electricity Company* (1977) 31(2) PD 281, 294–5.

[8] See e.g. Shapira, n. 2 above, at 499; Zamir, n. 2 above, at 64.

[9] Shapira, n. 2 above.

It must be imputed to the Legislature that it will not seek to deny the right . . . except by way of an express law . . . . In a State where the rule of law prevails, no person—no matter how dangerous a criminal and contemptible a traitor he may be—shall be deprived of his right, except according to law alone. . . . The Knesset is the legislative authority and none but itself may authorize others, should it so wish, to do a person according to his deeds and his misdeeds. In the absence of such authorisation from the Legislature, neither logic nor necessity, patriotism and any other consideration whatever—can justify the making of one's own law in denial of another's right.[10]

The force of the rule permitting any activity unless clearly prohibited by law is particularly powerful when examining *secondary* legislation. Here the courts can demand not only clear general legislative intent, but also assume that the administrative authority adopted such modes of operations and patterns of conducts that are commensurate with the fundamental rights of the individual. In a long line of cases, the Supreme Court has made it clear that in the absence of an unequivocal statutory authorization directing or permitting an administrative authority to act otherwise, the latter must be guided by the principle of individual freedom and chart its action in a manner that does not derogate from basic human rights.[11]

A relatively recent example of this is to be found in the *Miterani* decision,[12] where the issue was the validity of secondary legislation affecting the basic freedom of occupation of the petitioners. Justice Shamgar explained the approach of the Supreme Court in the following terms:

Examination of secondary legislation according to the limits marked out for it in the primary legislation is, understandably, especially exacting when the limitation of a basic right is involved . . . . As to the special constitutional status of a basic right, a meticulous investigation should be made to see if it can really be inferred from the authority set out in the primary legislation, if such exists and whether at its root lay the genuine intention to grant an authority to the secondary legislator to alter the bounds and scope of the basic right. It follows from what we have said that if the grant of authority is general and non-specific, it will be interpreted in such a way as would block the grant of an authority to limit a basic right.[13]

## 3. Statutory Interpretation

It should not be assumed, however, that the Supreme Court was often prevented from protecting basic rights by an alleged limitation contained in

[10] *Yeredor* v. *Chairman of the Central Elections Committee* (1965) 19(3) PD 365, 377, 379.
[11] Shapira, n. 2 above, at 300.
[12] *Miterani* v. *Minister of Transport* (1983) 37(3) PD 337 (included in this Section).
[13] *Ibid.* 358.

*primary* legislation. Here, of course, the main tool employed by the Court was that of 'creative' statutory interpretation.[14]

The basic starting point in this regard is the presumption that the Knesset was cognizant of basic individual rights when it shaped the legislative measure at issue. Hence, when a law is amenable, *prima facie*, to two different interpretations—one consistent with the right under discussion and the other repugnant to it—the Court will prefer the interpretation that upholds such right. And the greater the encroachment of the enactment in the domain of fundamental rights, the more pronounced will be the court's inclination to construe it as restrictively as possible.[15]

But the real test of a court's commitment to the protection of fundamental rights is whether it is prepared to engage in 'creative interpretation' in this regard, i.e. by showing a willingness—in Justice Haim Cohn's terms—to interpret statutes curtailing civil liberties contrary to the legislature's assumed intention whenever the language used by it enables the court to do so.[16]

The clear evidence is that Israel's Supreme Court was quite willing to engage in the boldest forms of 'creative' interpretation of statutes, and to achieve what Professor Albert has called a 'constitutional status'.[17] Indeed, as early as 1953, in a case that is probably Israel's most famous and most influential civil rights case—the *Kol Ha'am* decision[18]—the Supreme Court gave clear notice not only that it was prepared to 'interpret away' repressive legislation limiting fundamental human rights, but also that it was opening the Court to the widest possible range of sources and ideas upon which to base fundamental rights protection.

In what is probably the most quoted judgment in Israeli constitutional law, Justice Agranat declared:

The system of laws under which the political institutions . . . have been established and function are witness to the fact that this is indeed a State founded on democracy. Moreover, the matters set forth in the Declaration of Independence—especially as regards basing the State 'on the foundations of freedom' and securing freedom of conscience—mean that Israel is a freedom loving State. It is true that the Declaration 'does not include any constitutional law laying down any rule regarding the maintaining or repeal of any ordinances or laws' . . . but in so far as it 'expresses the vision of the people and its faith' . . . we are bound to pay attention to the matters set forth therein when we come to interpret and give meaning to the laws of the State, including the provisions of a law made at the time of the Mandate and adopted by the State after its establishment, through the channel of Section 11 of the Law and Administration Ordinance, 1948; for it is a well-known

[14] See e.g. the discussion in Shetreet, n. 2 above, at 35 ff.

[15] Shapira, n. 2 above, at 503.

[16] Yeredor, n. 10 above, at 369.

[17] Albert, n. 2 above, at 1249.

[18] *Kol Ha'am* v. *Minister of Interior* (1953) 7 PD 87 (included in this Ch.).

axiom that the law of a people must be studied in the light of its national way of life.[19]

Thus, in protecting the principle of freedom of speech and expression, the Court declared that a standard close to the American standard of 'clear and present danger' should be met by the Minister of Interior before he may exercise his draconian authority to close a newspaper. In so doing, the Court thereby replaced the subjective test of the legislation with a rather objective criterion.[20] As Professor Bracha has pointed out:

> By using the declaration of Independence as a canon of interpretation, the High Court of Justice managed in this case to read into a British-colonial ordinance—which was enacted in order to restrict the freedom of the press—some constitutional principles taken from democracies having written constitutions, including a Bill of Rights chapter. Justice Agranat adopted the American constitutional doctrine of 'clear and present danger', hardly mentioning that it was developed in the United States on the basis of the First Amendment of the Constitution, which guarantees the freedom of speech.[21]

## 4. The Normative Sources

As has already been noted, the *Kol Ha'am* decision was an inspiration not only for the judicial creativity and activism that were so often to animate the Supreme Court in this area, but also for the construction of Israel human rights case law on the broadest possible base of normative sources. Thus, Israeli constitutional scholars have discovered dozens of general normative sources[23] such as 'a universal principle in every democratic country', basic principles of equality, liberty, and justice which are the heritage of all orderly and enlightened States and 'the liberal tradition and principles of natural justice'. Moreover, various benches of the Supreme Court have been prepared to seek guidance from such diverse sources as American constitutional case law,[23] the principles of Jewish law and tradition,[24] and the Universal Declaration of Human Rights.

Whatever the normative sources cited in particular cases, the Court's dedication to individual freedom and its willingness to employ judicial techniques to guard against unwarranted legislative and administrative threats against such freedoms have preserved fundamental civil rights in

[19] *Ibid.* [20] Maoz, n. 2 above, at 820. [21] Bracha, n. 2 above, at 117–18.

[22] See especially Shapira, n. 2 above, at 505.

[23] Indeed, it was observed as early as 1966 that 'apart from the courts of the United States, the Israeli Supreme Court possibly makes more frequent use of American jurisprudence than any other court in the common law world': Apelbom, 'Common Law à l'Americana' (1966) 1 *Is.LR* 562.

[24] See Maoz, n. 2 above, at 826 ff.

Israel. In addition to the freedom of expression and freedom of occupation already discussed, the Supreme Court of Israel has defended freedom of the person, the right of incorporation, freedom of assembly, the right not to be deprived of property without due process of law, freedom of religion and conscience, freedom from discrimination, and more.[25]

The recognition that Israel's political and social realities warrant special judicial vigilance has also led to another result of the Supreme Court's 'judicial activism': established common law rules of non-justiciability, administrative discretion, and judicial restraint, as well as rules of *locus standi*, are largely disregarded by the Court when faced with a denial of justice, deprivation of civil rights, and infringement of the rule of law.[26]

The Supreme Court of Israel has held that in cases which raise problems of the constitutional nature of matters concerning the rule of law it may, in its discretion, make an exception to the general rule requiring sufficient interest. In such cases the Court would tend to open its gates to every person, as if the application for judicial review was an *actio popularis*. The reasons for this exception are:

(1) that in matters of constitutional importance it is desirable to have an authoritative statement of the law;
(2) that the rule of law, requiring the prevention of unlawful governmental action, should not be compromised on procedural grounds; and
(3) that in some cases dismissal of an application for lack of standing is practically tantamount to a grant of immunity from judicial review.

Two recent cases demonstrate the position of the Supreme Court on this matter. In one case, concerning the so-called Shin Bet (Israel's General Security Service), the head of the Shin Bet was suspected of having committed various offences. Before the police began their investigation, he was pardoned by the President of the State. Thereupon the legality of the pardon was challenged in the Supreme Court on the ground that the President had no power to pardon before conviction. The applicants—lawyers, professors of law, and others—clearly had no personal interest in the matter. Their motivation for bringing the case was simply to ensure that the charges against the Shin Bet head be investigated and the President not exceed his powers. Nevertheless, the Court held that they had standing, and decided the case on its merits.[27] In the second case, the Minister of Justice refused to order the extradition of a person accused of murder in France after the courts in Israel had declared him extradictable. Here, too, a group of citizens with no interest in the case except to vindicate the rule

[25] See especially Bracha, n. 2 above, at 123–4.
[26] Maoz, n. 2 above, at 822; Zamir, n. 2 above, at 68.
[27] See *Barzilai* v. *Government of Israel* (1987) 40(3) PD 505.

of law challenged the decision of the Minister in the Supreme Court on the ground that under the relevant statute he should have decided to the contrary. Again the Court acknowledged their standing and gave its decision on the merits.[28] It is noteworthy that in both these cases the people who had a personal interest in the decisions under attack, namely the person pardoned by the President and the person whom the Minister decided not to extradite, were happy with those decisions. The only possibility of reviewing the legality of those decisions was to give standing to people with no personal interest. In these cases, the interest of the rule of law was considered to be sufficient interest.

## 5. Scope of Judicial Review

The general rule is that acts of all public bodies and officials are subject to judicial review. This rule, however, is subject to an exception, in Israel as elsewhere, according to which certain public acts are unjusticiable. Public acts may be considered unjusticiable, and as such not amenable to the judicial process, either because they are not governed by legal rules or because they are too closely involved with the political process. In one such case, the Knesset Speaker decided that a party which was represented in the Knesset by only one member could not move for a vote of no-confidence. The Court held that this decision was contrary to the Knesset rules and was thus invalid.[29] In another case, the Speaker and his deputies refused to lay before the Knesset a private member's bill on the ground that it was racist. The Court held that there was no power under the Knesset rules to disqualify such a bill by reason of its contents, repulsive as they might be, as distinct from its form.[30]

This far-reaching intrusion by the Supreme Court into the domain of the Knesset demonstrates the strong commitment of the Court to the concept of the rule of law. But it also raises the question, especially when this is compared with the position of courts in other countries, whether it is right and wise.[31] Public opinion in Israel seems to support the interventionist stance of the Court, believing that it has clearly strengthened the rule of law.

Indeed, the determination of the Supreme Court to intervene whenever it seemed necessary has continued to take it into previously unchartered

[28] *Aloni* v. *Minister of Justice* (1987) 41(2) PD 1. The Court ordered the Minister of Justice to reconsider his decision. In fact, the Minister eventually ordered the extradition.

[29] *Kach Party Faction* v. *Knesset Speaker* (1985) 39(3) PD 141.

[30] *Kahane* v. *Knesset Speaker* (1985) 39(4) PD 85.

[31] Indeed, the debate has taken place among justices of the Supreme Court itself, see *Miari* v. *Knesset Speaker* (1987) 41(4) PD 169.

territories. Thus, the Court has not only shown itself again willing to review the Attorney General's decision not to prosecute certain criminal activity,[32] but also—in what is surely one of the most remarkable examples of judicial activism—held that political parties are obliged to make their coalition agreements public.[33]

In this regard it is worth noting the dicta of Justice Barak in the Le'or case,[34] which may serve as an appropriate legal bridge between the era of common law human rights protection and the recent appearance of entrenched basic laws on fundamental civil rights. In Le'or, Justice Barak suggested that the Supreme Court possesses jurisdiction to review laws of the Knesset even in the absence of an entrenched basic law, where such law conflicts with the fundamental principles of the Israeli democratic regime, but refrained from doing so in light of the prevailing social-legal consensus on the proper role of the Court.[35]

[32] See *Ganor* v. *Attorney General* (1990) 44(2) PD 485 (included in Section 11).
[33] See *Shalit* v. *Peres* (1990) 44(3) PD 353.
[34] *Le'or Movement* v. *Knesset Speaker* (1990) 44(3) PD 529 (1990). [35] *Ibid.* 554.

# 4

# "Kol Ha'am" Company Limited
# v.
# Minister of the Interior

[H.C. 73/53, 87/53]
[(1953) 7 P.D. 871]

*Agranat J, Sussman J, and Landau J*

Israeli cases referred to:

[1] Cr.A 95, 99/51—*Podamski and Others* v. *Attorney-General*; 6 PD 341, 355.
[2] Cr.A 24/50—*Gorali* v. *Attorney-General*; 5 PD 1145, 1160.
[3] HC 10/48—*Zeev* v. *Gubernik, District Commissioner, Urban District of Tel Aviv and Another*; 1 PD 85.

English cases referred to:

[4] *R.* v. *Cuthell* (1799) 27 How.St.Tr. 642.
[5] *Wilkes* v. *Wood (*1763) 19 How.St.Tr. 1167.

American cases referred to:

[6] *Abrams et al.* v. *United States*, 40 S.Ct. 17 (1919).
[7] *United States* v. *Associated Press*, 52 F.Supp. 362 (SDNY 1943).
[8] *Whitney* v. *People of the State of California*, 47 S.Ct. 641, 649 (1926).
[9] *Schenck* v. *United States*, 39 S.Ct. 247, 249 (1918).
[10] *Dennis et al* v. *United States*, 71 S.Ct. 857, 891 (1951).
[11] *Cantwell et al.* v. *State of Connecticut*, 60 S.Ct. 900 (1939).

## JUDGMENT

**Agranat J:**

Section 19(2)(a) of the Press Ordinance, as amended, provides as follows:

(2) The High Commissioner, either with or without having caused the proprietor or editor of a newspaper to be warned under subsection (1) hereof, may:

(a) if any matter appearing in a newspaper is, in the opinion of the High Commissioner in Council, likely to endanger the public peace,

. . .
by order in council suspend the publication of the newspaper for such period as he may think fit and shall state in the said order the period of such suspension.

The Minister of the Interior now takes the place of the High Commissioner.

Relying on the provision I have cited, the respondent, on 22 May 1953, ordered the suspension of the publication of the newspaper *Kol Ha'am* (which belongs to the petitioner in file No. HC 73/53) for a period of ten days, and, on 14 April 1953, ordered the suspension of the publication of the newspaper *Al-Ittihad* (the petitioner in file No. HC 87/53) for a period of fifteen days. The immediate reason that led the Minister of Interior to make the orders suspending the publication of the aforementioned newspapers was the printing in each of them of a leading article, namely in *Kol Ha'am* on 18 March 1953 under the title 'Let Abba Eban Go and Fight Alone . . .' and in *Al-Ittihad* on 10 March under the title 'The People will not Permit Speculation in the Blood of its Sons'. The ground for the criticism that was voiced in both of the articles was a news item published in the newspaper *Ha-aretz* on 9 March 1953, in these words:

Mr Henry Morgenthau stated that Georgei Malenkov was obviously worse than Stalin, and when the fatal hour came, Israel would place 200,000 soldiers at the side of the United States.

Israel's Ambassador, Mr Abba Eban, expressed his agreement with Mr Henry Morgenthau's statement that Israel could place 200,000 soldiers at the side of the United States in the event of war, and added that Mr. Morgenthau did not sufficiently appreciate Israel's recruiting capacity.

The authors of the two articles regarded this news item as a typical sign of the 'anti-Soviet policy' of the Government of Israel, as at present constituted, that is to say, of the policy of readiness 'to fight at the side of the United States in the event of war against the Soviet Union'; and each of them warned against this policy in the manner described below. Copies of the full contents of the said articles are appended as a supplement to this judgment, and we shall therefore confine ourselves at this point to quoting certain passages in order to determine, on the one hand, in what form the authors voiced their protest against the matters contained in the news item published in *Ha-aretz* and in order to ascertain, on the other hand, the attitude of the Minister of the Interior who was of the opinion that each of the two articles contained material likely to endanger the public peace.

The article in *Kol Ha'am* concludes with these three paragraphs:

Despite the anti-Soviet incitement, the masses in Israel know that the Soviet Union is faithful to the policy of the brotherhood of peoples and peace. The speeches of Comrades Malenkov, Beria and Molotov have once more confirmed that. If Abba Eban or anyone else wants to go and fight on the side of the

American warmongers, let him go, but go alone. The masses want peace and national independence, and are not prepared to give up the Negev in return for joining the 'Middle East Command'.

Let us increase our struggle against the anti-national policy of the Ben-Gurion Government, which is speculating in the blood of Israel youth.

Let us increase our struggle for the peace and independence of Israel.

In the course of the evidence he gave on behalf of the respondent, Mr. Moyal (the Director General of the Ministry of the Interior) declared, that it was mainly the second paragraph that constituted the basis for the Minister of Interior's decision concerning the suspension of the publication of the newspaper *Kol Ha'am.* The article in the newspaper *Al-Ittihad* concluded (according to the translation from the Arabic original) with the following two paragraphs:

And so all forms of surrender by the Ben Gurion Government, and all her demonstrations of faithfulness, will not avail her with her American masters; moreover, her economic, political and state bankruptcy, internal and external, are beginning to be revealed to the masses, who have started to understand whither this Government is dragging them—not only to unemployment, poverty and hunger, but even to death in the service of imperialism, feeding them as fodder to their war machine, whilst those masses do not want that fate and will demonstrate their refusal.

If Ben Gurion and Abba Eban want to fight and die in the service of their masters, let them go and fight by themselves. The masses want bread, work, independence and peace, will increase their struggle for those objectives, and will prove to Ben-Gurion and his henchmen that they will not allow them to speculate in the blood of their sons in order to satisfy the will of their masters.

In the body of the order that was issued for the suspension of that newspaper, the ground given—and repeated by Mr Moyal in his evidence before us—was that, essentially, it was the matter contained in the first paragraph that moved the Minister of the Interior to order the temporary suspension of the newspaper in the Arabic language.

For the sake of completeness, it should be noted that, on 23 March 1953, the Prime Minister announced in the Knesset, in reply to a question that had been put to him, that the news item published in the newspaper *Ha'aretz* was a 'piece of journalistic imagination', and that all that the Israeli Ambassador had declared on the occasion in question was:

The Governments of the free world are well aware of the declared purpose of Israel to defend its borders and its form of government against revolution and attack. ('Divrei Haknesset', Second Session, Issue No. 19, p. 1096).

From time to time, a case reaches this Court which raises some fundamental problem, demanding the reconsideration of ancient and well-worn principles. The two cases in question here belong to that group, and we are called upon to define the relationship that exists between the right to freedom of the press on the one hand, and the other, the power held by the authorities, by virtue of the said section 19(2)(a), to place a limit on the use of that right. We regard the freedom of the press as one specific form of the freedom of expression, and we shall not hereafter, for the purpose of our judgment, distinguish between the two concepts.

A. The principle of freedom of expression is closely bound up with the democratic process. In an autocratic regime, the ruler is looked upon as a superman and as one who knows, therefore, what is good and what is bad for his subjects. Accordingly, it is forbidden openly to criticize the political acts of the ruler, and whoever desires to draw his attention to some mistake he has made has to do so by way of direct application to him, always showing an attitude of respect towards him. Meanwhile, whether the ruler has erred or not, no-one is permitted to voice any criticism of him in public, since that is liable to injure his right to demand obedience. The historian of the criminal law in England teaches us that, in the light of that approach, until the end of the eighteenth century, every act of criticism in writing of persons performing public functions in England, concerning their conduct in such capacity, or of the laws and institutions of that State, was regarded as falling within the scope of the offence of 'sedition' (Stephen, *Criminal Law*, Volume II, p. 348). On the other hand, in a state with a democratic regime—that is, government by the 'will of the people'—the 'rulers' are looked upon as agents and representatives of the people who elected them, and the latter are entitled, therefore, at any time, to scrutinize their political acts, whether with the object of correcting those acts and making new arrangements in the state, or with the object of bringing about the immediate dismissal of the 'rulers', or their replacement as a result of elections.

This simple understanding of the democratic regime inevitably leads, therefore, to the enforcement of the principle of freedom of expression in every State where such a form of government exists; that is to say, that it embraces a logical justification for the application of that principle. But anyone who confines himself to that notion alone and pursues it to its logical extreme must, whether he likes it or not, come to the conclusion, as Stephen notes (*ibid.*, p. 300), that in accordance therewith, there remains in fact no possibility of imposing any prohibition on any criticism of the government in power, except perhaps to prohibit incitement calculated to result in the immediate injury to the life, limb, or property of another. In other words, such a definition of the character of the democratic regime does not provide us with any serious contribution to the solution of the problem with which we are faced—a problem which is fundamentally one of placing proper limits—having regard to the general good and the interests of the State—on the wrongful exploitation by the individual citizen of the right of freedom of expression. In order to find such a solution, we must first of all consider the values involved in the exercise of that important right. It is important that we should previously acquaint ourselves with the interests that that right is designed to protect. But, for that purpose, we must necessarily arrive at a deeper understanding of the nature of the democratic regime than that which we have described above.

Democracy consists, first and foremost, of government by consent, the opposite of government maintained by the power of the mailed fist; and the democratic process, therefore, is one of selection of the common aims of the people and the means of achieving them through the public forum of negotiation and discussion, that is, by open debate and the free exchange of ideas on matters of public interest (see *Reflections on Government*, by E. Barker, p. 36). 'Public opinion' plays a vital part in that discussion, carried on through the political institutions of the State, such as parties, general elections, and debates in the legislature—and it plays that part not only when the citizen goes to the polls, but at all times and in all seasons. To the sensible statesman, it is evident—as that learned author, Lindsay, explains (see his book, *The Modern Democratic State*, Volume 1, p. 270)—that he must take public opinion into account from day to day, since it is the ordinary citizen who is affected when the statutes are incompatible with his needs; he is the one who knows whether 'the shoe pinches' too much, and where it pinches. 'The public, it is true, is not acquainted with details', notes Prof. Roth, in Chapter I, 'Government of the People by the People' (p. 19):

> He only knows, for example that war disturbs him or that the price of essential commodities is greater than his financial capacity. A very important part of the tasks of democracy is to make it possible for those feelings to come out into the open and be solved in a legal way fixed in advance, and the feelings are plain enough even to the ordinary man, even though he is not expert in the scientific analysis of the causes and their solution. 'A man's heart feels the bitterness of his own soul'; and if the ordinary man does not know how to put things right, he certainly knows what it is that needs putting right.

There exists, in fact, not only the perpetual process of clarification of public opinion, but also its *shaping*. There is considerable educational value for the ordinary citizen in that system of public discussion and general negotiation. By following, to a greater or lesser extent, in the press the speeches and debates conducted in the legislature, for example, he learns what he needs and is thus assisted in determining his attitude (Roth, *ibid.*, p. 39).

Basically, the whole of the aforementioned process is none other than a process of investigating the truth, in order that the State may learn how to reach the most satisfactory objective and know how to select the line of action most calculated to bring about the achievement of that objective in the most efficient manner. Now, the principle of freedom of expression serves as a means and an instrument for the purpose of investigating that truth, since only by considering *'all'* points of view and a free exchange of *'all'* opinions is that *'truth'* likely to be arrived at. In his famous judgment in the case of *Abrams* v. *US* [6] Justice Holmes said:

But when men have realized that time has upset many fighting faiths, they may come to believe . . . that the ultimate good desired is better reached by free trade in ideas—that the best test of truth is the power of the thought to get itself accepted in the competition of the market, and that truth is the only ground upon which their wishes can be safely carried out.

Another American judge expressed a similar idea when he noted that freedom of expression is founded on the assumption that 'right conclusions are more likely to be gathered out of a multitude of tongues, than through any kind of authoritative selection' (from the observations of Learned Hand J in the case of *US* v. *Associated Press* [7]).

* * *

B. * * *

C. Nevertheless, the right to freedom of expression does not mean that a person is entitled to proclaim, by word of mouth or in writing, in the ears and eyes of others, whatever he feels like saying. There is a difference between freedom and licence. In *Podamski* v. *Attorney-General* [1], we explained that side by side with the rights to freedom (and that, in effect, is their legal significance), there are restrictions imposed by the law, and we demonstrated this idea as follows: 'Everyone has the right to freedom of speech and freedom of expression, but the use of that right is subject to the restriction of the law' [1]; and in *Gorali* v. *Attorney-General* [2], we stated: 'The object of the local criminal law in making the uttering of slander and the publishing of libel offences is to restrict that fundamental right whenever a person abuses it' ([2] at 1160). That is to say, that just as the right to freedom of action in other fields does not extend to the use of a man's profession, business, or property in a manner injurious to others, so also the right to freedom of speech and the press does not entail the abuse of the power of the tongue or the pen. 'The liberty of the press is dear to England', Lord Kenyon once said, in *R.* v. *Cuthell* [4], 'The licentiousness of the press is odious to England.' That is to say, that certain interests also require protection and for the sake of these it is essential to place clear limits on the right to freedom of expression.

One interest of this kind was previously hinted at: the need for protecting the good name of the citizen (Criminal Code Ordinance, 1936, sections 201 and 202). Other kinds of interests requiring the raising of a barrier against the effect of statements by word of mouth and written publications are: the securing of a fair trial and the doing of justice to parties before the courts (*ibid.*, sections 126 and 127), the prevention of outrage to religious feelings (*ibid.*, section 149) and the prohibition of obscene publications which offend against moral values (*ibid.*, section 179). We do not intend to exhaust the list of those interests, and we shall mention only the most important of them, namely, the interest included under the heading, 'State security'. Here we are concerned indeed with a composite and broad concept, but generally speaking, it may be said that it refers to all that is involved in avoiding the danger of invasion by the enemy from without; in suppressing any attempt at forcible overthrow of the existing regime by hostile factors from within; in maintaining public order and securing the public peace. It is quite obvious that the object of reinforcing State security, too, requires some limit to the freedom of expression on certain terms, for were that not so, a situation might be created in which the State would be unable to achieve its aim or to conduct its affairs in a proper manner; everyone would be deprived of his freedom, including the freedom of speech and the press, and instead of freedom of liberty, anarchy and chaos would reign in the State.

D. * * *

E. So far, we have dealt with the problem in a general way, and have established that the solution must come by weighing the interests of State security on the one hand against freedom of expression on the other; that the great social value of the principle which protects the latter interest is worthy of particular attention; and that preferring the former interest is justifiable only when the situation definitely calls for it. It is clear that this approach by itself does not amount to a mathematical formula which can be accurately adapted to every single occasion. The legislator does, in point of fact, sometimes do the work of weighing and balancing by himself, that is, he himself determines in advance the kind of material that is not to be published, or the terms on which its publication is to be prohibited by considerations based on State security. This he did, for example, in the Official Secrets Ordinance. But sometimes the legislator leaves the discretion in this field to the hands of others, such as the Executive. In the last group of cases, the question must inevitably arise (particularly because that approach does embody a concise narrow formula), what is the rational principle that ought to guide the Executive when engaged in the aforementioned process, in order to settle the question in favour of one or other of the two interests. If we consider this last question in the light of section 19(2)(a) of the Press Ordinance, as we propose now to do, and if we bear in mind the interest of 'public peace' instead of 'State security', then it would be right to state the question in this form: what is the test which the Minister of the Interior should apply when he comes to decide whether the material that has been published is 'likely to endanger the public peace' to the degree which justifies the suspension for a certain time of the newspaper in which it has been published? In fact, the moment we are successful in finding a definition suitable to the expression, 'endangers the public peace', the question will become confined to the interpretation we ought to give to the term 'likely'.

So what do we mean by 'endangers the public peace'? Once more we are dealing with a broad and complex notion. In the case of *Cantwell* v. *Connecticut* [11]. Justice Roberts (of the Supreme Court of the United States), considered the offence of 'breach of the peace', as understood in the common law, and after noting that it embodies 'a concept of the most general and undefined nature', added: 'The offence known as breach of the peace embraces a great variety of conduct destroying or menacing public order and tranquility. It includes not only violent acts but words *likely* to produce violence in others.' It may well be that, in fact, the offence of 'breach of the peace', as so understood, was what was in the mind of the legislator when he limited the use of the power mentioned in section 19(2) in the way he did. We do not propose to lay down any hard and fast rules in this respect, nor shall we try to mark the outer limits of the concept, 'endangers the public peace', but for the purpose of the present discussion, it will be sufficient to hold that any publication leading to the use of violence by others, to the overthrow by force of the government in power or of the existing regime, to the breach of the law, to the causing of riots or fighting in public, or to the disturbance of order endangers the public peace.

But section 19(2)(a) says, '*likely* to endanger'. What is the purport of the term 'likely'? The answer to that question depends on the choice of one of two possible approaches. According to one approach it is sufficient, in order to satisfy the condition stated in the section in question that the publication reveals only a tendency—even a slight or remote tendency—in the direction of one of the consequences that we have included in the notion, 'endangers the public peace'. While according to the other approach, the Minister of the Interior must be convinced beforehand that there has been created, having regard to the circumstances in which it takes place, a link between the publication and the possibility of one of the said consequences occurring, which must lead to the inference that the occurrences of that consequence are probable. We think that the second approach represents the intention of the legislator in section 19(2)(a).

It is easy to discern that this approach of 'a bad tendency' means—as Stephen once commented in his analysis of the offence of incitement to rebellion in its original form—a refusal of the right of serious political discussion (*History of the Criminal Law in England*, Volume II, p. 359). 'And the most powerful weapon in their hands (i.e. of those who oppose freedom of the press)', Professor Chafee once stressed, 'is this doctrine of indirect causation under which words can be punished for a supposed bad tendency long before there is any probability that they will break out into unlawful acts' *(Free Speech in the United States* (1948), 24).

* * *

To sum up: the approach of 'a bad tendency' is perhaps suitable to a political system employed in a State based on an autocratic or totalitarian regime, but it obstructs, or at least renders inefficient, the use of that process which constitutes the very essence of any democratic regime, namely, the process of investigating the truth.

The system of laws under which the political institutions in Israel have been established and function is witness to the fact that this is indeed a State founded on democracy. Moreover, the matters set forth in the Declaration of Independence, especially as regards the basing of the State 'on the foundations of freedom' and the securing of freedom of conscience, mean that Israel is a freedom-loving State. It is true that the Declaration 'does not consist of any constitutional law laying down in fact any rule regarding the maintaining or repeal of any ordinances or laws' (*Zeev* v. *Gubernik* [3]), but in so far as it 'expresses the vision of the people and its faith' [3], we are bound to pay attention to the matters set forth in it when we come to interpret and give meaning to the laws of the State, including the provisions of a law made in the time of the Mandate and adopted by the State after its establishment, through the channel of section 11 of the Law and Administration Ordinance, 1948; for it is a well-known axiom that the law of a people must be studied in the light of its national way of life. Thus, there we have a first sign indicating that we must interpret the term 'likely', when we read it together with the other matters stated in section 19(2)(a), in the sense of 'near certainty' rather than in the spirit of the view which favours the doctrine of the 'bad tendency' and 'indirect causation'.

As for the second sign, which goes hand-in-hand with the first: the procedural means available for suppressing or restricting the freedom of the press are of two kinds. One measure is to punish the objectionable publication after it has taken place. The other measure is preventive, that is, by way of taking steps directed to obstructing the publication of the improper material in advance or to prevent the continued appearance of the newspaper in which that material has been published. In the last instance, too, which is the present case, we are concerned with a preventive measure, which bears no criminal character in the regularly understood sense, seeing that its primary and immediate purpose is to secure the non-publication of the newspaper, because it is likely to contain similar improper material in the future.

Indeed, it has long been recognized that the same 'preventive' measure—which is, after all is said and done, nothing more than censorship, pure and simple—is the more powerful of the two measures that have been mentioned. 'The censor', says Chafee, 'is the most dangerous of all the enemies of the liberty of the press, and ought not to exist in this country unless *made necessary by extraordinary perils*' (Chafee, *Free Speech in the United States* (1948), 29). The history of many peoples, and of the people of Israel first and foremost, is full of innumerable examples of men who have dared and ventured, without being deterred by the fear of punishment, to publish what their conscience dictated, notwithstanding its prohibition on the part of the ruling authorities. However, it is clear that such display of courage has never been, nor is it today, any sufficient guarantee against the effective stay, by preventive measures, of disseminating views or thoughts that are entirely novel. What endows the use of a measure of the preventive kind with its powerful and drastic character is the general acknowledgment 'that no official yet born on this earth is wise enough or generous enough to separate good ideas from bad ideas, good beliefs from bad beliefs' (*ibid.*, p. 61). Accordingly, even during the period in which the rule of incitement to rebellion in its original form was still in force in England, the common law recognized the principle that the Executive ought to be slow in making use of measures preventing the publication of the forbidden material in advance, and that its sole alternative was the bringing of the offender to trial after the act for having disseminated the inflammatory remarks in public.

* * *

F. (1) * * *

F. (2) It must indeed be admitted that even the test of 'near certainty' does not constitute a precise formula that can be easily or certainly adapted to every single case. We mean by that that, when making his decision regarding the exercise of the power given him by section 19(2)(a), the Minister of the Interior is not expected to forecast with absolute certainty that one of the consequences contained in the definition of 'endangering the public peace' is bound to occur by reason of the act of publication in question, if he does nothing to prevent it. The most that is demanded of him is only an estimation that that is how things are likely to turn out, that is to say, an estimation that a proximate (and not necessarily a certain) result will follow if he does make prompt use of his said powers. This estimation means, as we have already suggested more than once in the course of our remarks, an estimation made *according to the circumstances surrounding the act of publication. . . .*

* * *

F. (3) It is important to stress that the circumstances which the Minister of the Interior is entitled to take into account are liable to be varied and of different nuances. For instance, he must consider not only the *immediate* external facts, that is, that a direct connection has been created between the circumstances and the publication, but also the general background, such as the state of emergency existing in the country at the time of publication or the tension prevailing in international relations at the moment. It is indeed obvious that, since life is continually in a state of development, there is no point in our trying to exhaust or classify the circumstances referred to or in our making hard-and-fast rules concerning the possible effect of one or other of these circumstances. As stated, that effect is liable to alter from case to case, and what is always of importance is the estimation of the combined effect of the circumstances in each individual instance. Nevertheless, it is worthwhile adding—for the sake of guidance only, and without setting up any strict rules—the following observations:

First, generally speaking there will be no need to consider the bad intention of those responsible for the publication in question. The choice is the following: either the contents of the matters published are true, in which case, it makes no difference what the author or publisher had in mind; or they are untrue, in which case only the possible effect of the published matters themselves on the public peace is of importance and not the disclosed intention of those who have caused their dissemination. True, this will not apply in every case, since in certain conditions the intention formed in the mind of the author or publisher may be of great assistance in estimating the danger that will probably result from the publication. For example, where the matters published may be understood in different ways, the discovery of that intention is likely to throw light on the real meaning to be given them, on their dangerous character, and on the objectionable purport lying behind them.

Moreover, in certain circumstances it would not be out of place to take into consideration the strong tone, the offensive language, and the emotional tinge in which the contents of the article or the piece of information published have been clothed. But we should not exaggerate this, since without being able to connect the form of the writing with other facts which might endanger the public peace, it would not be right to regard the form of language as a factor likely to affect the public peace; holding otherwise would disregard the principle which safeguards the freedom of expression and which recognizes that the meaningful discussion of an event in the sphere of politics cannot always be restricted to polite criticism. As Chafee stated: 'The greater the grievance, the more likely men are to get excited about it, and the more urgent the need of hearing what they have to say' (*loc. cit.*, p. 43).

Finally, it will not, *generally speaking*, be right for the Minister of the Interior to take into account, among his considerations, the personality or character of those responsible for the improper publications. The observations of Lord Chatham when supporting the struggle of *John Wilkes* [5] a person of the most dubious past, for the freedom of the press in England, are most enlightening on this point: 'In his person though the worst of men, I contend for the safety and security of the best' (Chafee, p. 242 ff.).

F. (4) We must, in this connection, make one more point clear. The test of 'near certainty' which we favour does not mean that the Minister of the Interior must be satisfied in every case that the danger to the public peace is likely to occur shortly after the matters are published in the newspaper in question. A finding of 'near certainty' does not necessarily mean a finding of the danger in the sense of proximity in time. Indeed, the consideration that, as a consequence of the publication, an imminent danger has been created to the public peace strengthens the estimation that that danger is probable, just as the consideration that the publication is likely to show signs of its effect on the public peace only after a certain lapse of time reduces the likelihood of there being any danger at all. But if the Minister of the Interior becomes aware, in the light of circumstances, that the publication makes it possible, amounting almost to a certainty, that serious harm will be caused to the public peace, then there is nothing to prevent him from exercising the power given to him by section 19(2)(a), even where he estimates that it is not a case where harm will be caused forthwith.

It should be noted that in the United States, when Justices Holmes and Brandeis were defining the guarantee of freedom of speech and the press found in the American Constitution, they held as an essential condition to the restriction of that freedom that the publication in question must be liable to cause serious and immediate harm to the interests that the legislator was seeking to safeguard. 'The question must be liable to cause serious and immediate harm to the interests that the legislator was seeking to safeguard. The question in every case is whether the words are used in such circumstances and are of such a nature as to create a clear and present danger that they will bring about the substantive evils that Congress has a right to prevent. It is a question of proximity and degree' (see *Schenck* v. *US* [9] at 249; *Abrams* v. *US* [6] at 22; *Whitney* v. *California* [8] at 649; see also the judgments collected on this point in the addendum to the judgment of Justice Frankfurter, in the case of *Dennis* v. *US* [10] at 891; cf. the new approach of the majority opinion in the last-mentioned case). Now it is very evident, in view of the approach we have indicated above, that we cannot go to the extreme of demanding that the Minister of the Interior be satisfied, before ordering the paper to be suspended, that the danger to the public peace created in consequence of the publication is also proximate in time. The dictionary definition, at the very least, of the term 'likely' in section 19(2)(a), the meaning of which is, as stated, the presence of a near certainty that the effect on the public peace must take place at some time in the future, and not necessarily the immediate future, prevents us from so doing. However, we take the view that, in weighing the interests involved in securing the public peace on the one hand, and safeguarding the freedom of the press on the other, the Minister of the Interior would do well to pay attention to the general directions that the aforementioned judges employed in shaping the rule of law and of some of which we have already made mention in an earlier part of our judgment. Those directions—which we quote here not as hard-and-fast rules, but as guiding principles only—are:

(a) As a general rule, there is a good chance that truth, in the end, will prevail; so that if there is enough time to spare, it is better to act through discussion, education, and counter-explanation, in order to cancel out the effect of the false information published in the newspaper in question or in the article for which space was found. 'If there be time to expose through discussion the falsehood and fallacies, to avert the evil by the processes of education, the remedy to be applied is more speech, not enforced silence' (*per* Justice Brandeis, in the case of *Whitney* [8] at 649). Accordingly, it would be advisable to reflect, for example, whether instead of suspending the newspaper for publishing the incorrect information, it would not be preferable to oblige the editor, in accordance with section 17 of the Press Ordinance, to publish a denial.

(b) It often happens that the very act of oppression—the actual suspension of the newspaper in which the matters objected to have been published—endows them with an exaggerated value in the eyes of the public. Where 'the enemies of liberty are met with a denial of liberty, many men of goodwill will come to suspect that there is something in the proscribed doctrine after all. Erroneous doctrines thrive on being expunged. They die if exposed' (from the observations of Haley, quoted in the case of *Dennis* v. *US* [10] at 889; see also the observations of Justice Holmes in *Abrams* v. *US* [6] at 22).

(c) Finally, in cases in which there is no danger of causing *immediate*, or even *probable*, harm to the public peace, it would be best to weigh very carefully the gravity of the danger which the Minister of the Interior sees in the offing as a result of the publication in question. The current view is that any act of suppression of the appearance of a newspaper of itself occasions harm to the public interest, that is, to the important interest connected with the freedom of expression. The point is that every such act of suppression of necessity fills the owner of the newspaper that has been suspended and its editor, and others as well, with fear and apprehension; that fear and apprehension in turn contribute to the imposition of a self-censorship on the part of the latter; and in that way, those very arguments that ought in particular to see the light of day for the purpose of investigating the truth and advancing the democratic process, are silenced (see Chafee, p. 561). On the other hand, since we are concerned only with the estimation of a potential danger, that is to say, one which is probable, but as regards which there is no assurance that it will necessarily occur—and in any event, there is no fear of its occurring in the near future—it is possible (even assuming that the possibility is a distant one) that the public peace will not suffer on account of the objectionable publication. In which case, it is important to consider whether the gravity of the danger that the Minister of the Interior foresees as the result of the publication of the matters objected to, is indeed so great as to be comparable to the public harm to the other public interest, that is, the harm to the interest of freedom of expression, which the suspension of the newspaper is in any event likely to cause.

G. The rule to be applied in the present case may be, therefore, summed up as follows:

The use of the power stated in the said section 19(2)(a) calls, on the part of the Minister of the Interior, for the weighing of the interests involved in the public peace on the one hand, and in the freedom of the press on the other, and preferring the former interest only after full weight has been given to the public need for freedom of expression. The guiding principle ought always to be: is there a near certainty that as a consequence of the publication, a danger to the public peace has been disclosed; the bare tendency in that direction in the matter published will not suffice to fulfil that requirement. Moreover, the Minister of the Interior is bound to estimate the effect of the matter published on the public peace only according to the standard of what is reasonable in the light of the surrounding circumstances; and in that estimation, the length of time likely to pass between the publication and the consequent event which constitutes the harm to the public peace is liable to be an important factor, though not necessarily a decisive one. Finally, even if the Minister is satisfied that the danger caused by the publication is 'nearly certain', he ought to consider carefully whether it is so grave as to justify the use of the drastic power of suspending the newspaper or whether effective action is not available for the purpose of canceling out the undesirable effect consequent upon the publication, by less stringent means, such as discussion, denial and counter-explanation.

* * *

[*Applying the above rules to the article in* Kol Ha'am, *Justice Agranat concludes as follows*:]

Can the publicly declared description of that policy as self-humiliation before a foreign State and surrender of the interests of Israel to the latter's will (however much that description may be mistaken) be regarded as creating at least a *near certainty* of 'danger to the public peace', within the meaning I have given to that phrase? Would the article have such an effect even if we consider the state of emergency in which our country finds itself at the moment when no permanent peace treaty has been signed with our neighbours, the Arab States? Would it be right to interpret the matters published as incitement to the use of violent means in order to bring about a change in the supposed policy of the Government? Does there exist any sufficient foundation for inferring that they are advocating non-enlistment for service in the Israel Defence Forces within the framework of the Defence Service Law? It is quite obvious that we must give negative answers to each on of those questions.

* * *

To sum up: if we do not wish to put obstacles in the way of discussion and free investigation in the political sphere and in that way divest ourselves of all interest involved in the freedom of the press, and if we do not also desire utterly to depart from the test which requires that the negative effect of published matter on the public peace be regarded in the circumstances as at least probable, then we shall have no alternative but to decide that, in making the order for the suspension of the newspaper *Kol Ha'am*, for a period of ten days, for having published the article referred to, the respondent gravely exceeded his jurisdiction.

* * *

[*Turning next to the article in* Al-Ittihad, *Justice Agranat analyses the arguments for and against suspension of the newspaper and concludes*:]

In these circumstances—when, on the one hand, the very essence of the view advocated in the two passages cited is dependent on that news item of 9 March 1953 being an accurate reflection of the official policy of the present Government of Israel and, on the other hand, it became clear, only a few days after the publication of the article, that the news item was incorrect and without any foundation in fact, so that the condition abovementioned does not exist at all—in these circumstances, can it logically be estimated that that appeal would have the effect of endangering the public peace? Could anyone really imagine that, after reading what was written in the article in question, 'the masses' might at some time arise and employ violent means or refuse to carry out their lawful duty of enlisting for military service, just in order to bring about the reversal of the policy which, as it appears, was not in any wise declared by those qualified to do so to be the official policy of the Government of Israel at this time? We can give a negative answer—and a negative one alone—to those questions. And if it be said that the day may come when Israel's policy will turn into the policy against which the author of the stated article was agitating, that the readers will then recall the matters written therein, and that, as a result thereof, they will act in the manner in which they were called upon to act by the author, so that the public peace will be seriously endangered, we would reply that that approach is none other than the approach of the 'bad tendency' and 'indirect causation' that we disapproved of as a standard proper to be employed by the Minister of the Interior when deciding whether to exercise the power stated in the said section 19(2)(a).

It follows that in making the order for the suspension of the newspaper *Al-Ittihad*, too, for a period of fifteen days, the respondent exceeded his jurisdiction.

For these reasons, we have decided to make absolute the orders nisi given in each of these two cases.

Orders *nisi* made absolute

Judgment given on 16 October 1953.

## APPENDIX A—The Article in *Kol Ha'am*

'Topic of the Day: Let Abba Eban Go and Fight Alone . . .

The Ben-Gurion–Bernstein Government has not reacted in any way to Abba Eban's announcement concerning his readiness to provide 200,000 Israeli troops in the war against the Soviet Union. The official silence can only be interpreted as complete agreement with the remarks of A. Eban. More than that. The Ambassador of the Ben-Gurion–Bernstein Government cannot be assumed to have made his pronouncement in his own name and not in the name of the Government as a whole.

A. Eban's pronouncement is exceptional, even in the Atlantic camp, since every government within the aggressor Atlantic bloc is endeavouring, with all its might, to place as few troops as possible at the disposal of the American generals. The confirmation of the war pacts of Bonn and Paris has so far met with great difficulties. Many countries in Asia and Europe, Britain and India among them, are seriously criticizing the policy of Eisenhower-Dulles.

It seems, therefore, that the Ben-Gurion Government is pushing its way into the front ranks of the warmongers' camp; it is quicker than any other government, even within the aggressor Atlantic bloc.

The finance bosses of America do not feel obliged to take into account the 'war effort' of Ben Gurion, Sharett, and Abba Eban. The Lebanese newspaper, *Az-Zaman*, has quoted American officials as stating that John Foster Dulles, the American Foreign Minister, and Anthony Eden have reached agreement on a common policy which calls for the consent of Israel 'to the annexation of the Negev to Jordan, in order that the British army stationed in the Suez Canal Zone can transfer to the Negev' and their consent to other concessions, such as the transfer of Haifa port to the Atlantic command, etc.

The White House is trying very hard indeed to increase the arms race in the Middle East, and the dispatch of American weapons to the value of 11 million dollars leaves no doubt as to that. And that is not all. The State Department has delivered an ultimatum to the Ben-Gurion Government regarding the evacuation of the grounds of the Arab College in Jerusalem. The Ben Gurion Government has obeyed the ultimatum without a murmur.

The anti-Soviet policy of the Ben-Gurion–Bernstein Government resembles the policy of the Polish reactionaries, Beck and Ridz-Smigly, who out of blindness and anti-Communist hatred brought national disaster on their country.

Despite the anti-Soviet provocation, the masses in Israel know that the Soviet Union is faithful to the policy of the brotherhood of peoples and peace. The speeches of Comrades Malenkov, Beria, and Molotov have once more confirmed that. If Abba Eban or anyone else wants to go and fight on the side of the American warmongers, let him go, but go alone. The masses want peace and national independence, and are not prepared to give up the Negev in return for joining the Middle East Command.

Let us increase our struggle against the anti-national policy of the Ben-Gurion Government, which is speculating in the blood of Israel Youth.

Let us increase our struggle for the peace and independence of Israel.'

## Appendix B—The Article in *Al-Ittihad*

'The People will not Permit Speculation in the Blood of its Sons.

At the opening of the 'Independence' Bonds Conference last week in New York, Abba Eban, Ben-Gurion's Ambassador in the United States, declared that the Government of Israel was prepared to supply 200,000 Israel troops to fight on the side of the United States in the event of war against the Soviet Union.

To this day, no reply has appeared on behalf of the Ben-Gurion–Bernstein Government to this grave pronouncement by its Ambassador and representative in New York. If that silence means anything at all, it means that the Government expresses full agreement that the pronouncement was not made save at its behest, that no official representative of any Government can express in his speeches and declarations anything other than the opinions and policy of his government.

This self-humiliation before the gates of American imperialists is not new on the part of the Ben-Gurion Government, its diplomats, and representatives. This Government has become accustomed to running as fast as it can before the chariot of American imperialism, in its endeavours to overtake all of its satellites and to express its faithfulness to its masters and warmongering supporters, and to prove to them by every form of compliance that it is the faithful servant whose services cannot be dispensed with, that it hopes to win a glance of satisfaction from it. At a time when American imperialism is meeting with many difficulties in carrying out its programmes in each of these satellite States, and at a time when those governments are trying to squirm and manœuvre and even dare at a time when a government like that of Naguib in Egypt and Shishakli in Syria are still afraid of binding themselves to any kind of guarantee to join the Mediterranean bloc, we see that the Ben-Gurion Government is crawling on all fours and asking and begging to be received into that bloc, and promising to hand over bases, ports, airfields, and cannon-fodder to the American war machine. But it seems that the lords of Wall Street and their representatives in the White House do not yet appreciate this Ben-Gurionic service given with such 'generosity' and do not see any need for giving a friendly glance at their Israeli lackeys for being in their 'pocket', after breaking off relations with the Soviet Union, and after becoming completely dependent, from the political and economic point of view, on the 'kindness' of American imperialism. Thus we see that rulers of America are trying to make up to Naguib, Shishakli, and Ibn-Saud, and are no longer interested in Ben-Gurion and his offers. This week, the Lebanese newspaper, *Az-Zaman*, wrote that Foster Dulles, at present on a visit to thc Middle East, is carrying in his pocket a programme for peace between Israel and the Arab countries, which includes stripping Israel of the Negev and annexing it to Transjordan, in order that the British troops evacuating the Suez Canal can be transferred there.

And so all forms of surrender by the Ben-Gurion Government, and all her demonstrations of faithfulness, will not avail her with her American masters; moreover, her economic, political, and State bankruptcy, internal and external, are beginning to be revealed to the masses, who have started to understand whither this Government is dragging them—not only to unemployment, poverty, and hunger, but even to death in the service of imperialism, feeding them as fodder to their war machine, whilst those masses do not want that fate and will demonstrate their refusal.

If Ben-Gurion and Abba Eban want to fight and die in the service of their master, let them go and fight by themselves. The masses want bread, work, independence, and peace, will increase their struggle for those objectives, and will prove to Ben-Gurion and his henchmen that they will not allow them to speculate in the blood of their sons in order to satisfy the will of their masters.'

# 5

# *Member of Knesset Rabbi Meir Kahane and the 'Kach' Movement*
# v.
# *The Executive Board of the Broadcasting Authority and others*

[H.C. 399/85]
[41(3) PD 255 (1987)]

*Barak J, Bach J, and Netanyahu J*

Israeli cases referred to:

[1] EA 2/84—*Neiman* v. *Chairman of the Central Election Committee to the Eleventh Knesset*; 39(2) PD 225.
[2] HC 73/85—*Kach* v. *Speaker of the Knesset*; 39(3) PD 141.
[3] HC 742/84—*Kahane* v. *Speaker of the Knesset*; 39(4) PD 85.
[4] HC 669/85—*Kahane* v. *Speaker of the Knesset*; 40(4) PD 393.
[5] HC 58/68—*Shalit* v. *Minister of the Interior*; 23(2) PD 477, 513.
[6] CA 165/82—*Kibbutz Hazor* v. *Rehovot Tax Clerk*; 39(2) PD 70.
[7] Cr.A 255/68—*State of Israel* v. *Ben Moshe*; 22(2) PD 427.
[8] HC 153/83—*Levi* v. *Commander of the Southern Police District*; 38(2) PD 393.
[9] HC 73, 87/53—*Kol Ha'am Co.* v. *Minister of the Interior*; 7 PD 871.
[10] CA 723/74—*'Ha'aretz' Newspaper Publishing Ltd* v. *The Israel Electric Co. Ltd*; 31(2) PD 281.
[11] FH 9/77—*The Israel Electric Co. Ltd* v. *'Ha'aretz' Newspaper Publishing Ltd*; 32(3) PD 337.
[12] Cr.A 95/51—*Podamski* v. *The Attorney General*; 6 PD 341.
[13] HC 112/77—*Fogel* v. *The Broadcasting Authority*; 31(3) PD 657.
[14] CA 7/79—*'Hahayim' Publishing Co.* v. *The Broadcasting Authority*; 35(2) PD 365.
[15] HC 372/84—*Klohfer-Nave* v. *The Minister of Education and Culture*; 38(3) PD 233.
[16] HC 1/81—*Shiran* v. *The Broadcasting Authority*; 35(3) PD 365.
[17] CSA 5/86—*Spiro* v. *Civil Service Commission*; 40(4) PD 227.

[18] HC 243/62—*Israel Film Studios* v. *Gary*; 16 PD 2407.
[19] HC 749/75—*Noah Film Co. Ltd* v. *The Film Censorship Board*; 30(1) PD 757.
[20] HC 14/86—*Leor and others* v. *The Film Censorship Board*; 41(1) PD 421.
[21] H.C 10/48—*Zeev* v. *Guberin*; 1 PD 85.
[22] CA 461/62—*Zim* v. *Maziar*; 17 PD 1319.
[23] HC 448/85—*Daher* v. *Minister of the Interior*; 40(2) PD 701.
[24] HC 355/79—*Katlan* v. *Prison Authority*; 37(3) PD 294.
[25] HC 243/82—*Zichroni* v. *Broadcasting Authority*; 37(1) PD 757.
[26] HC 876/78—*En Gal* v. *Film and Theater Censorship Board*; 33(1) PD 274.
[27] HC 206/61—*Israel Communist Party* v. *The Mayor of Jerusalem*; 15 PD 1732.
[28] HC 259/84—*'Milan'* v. *The Broadcasting Authority*; 38(2) PD 673.
[29] HC 351/72—*Kenan* v. *The Film and Censorship Board*; 26(2) PD 811
[30] HC 381/66—*The Attorney General* v. *The Film and Play Censorship Board*; 20(4) PD 757.
[31] HC 246/81—*Derekh Eretz Association* v. *The Broadcasting Authority*; 35(4) PD 1.

American cases referred to:

[32] *Columbia Broadcasting Services ('CBS')* v. *The Democratic National Committee*, 412 US 84 (1973).
[33] *Red Lion Broadcasting Co.* v. *Federal Communications Commission*, 395 US 357 (1963).
[34] *Abrams* v. *United States*, 250 US 616 (1919).
[35] *Garrison* v. *Louisiana*, 379 US 64 (1964).
[36] *Dennis* v. *United States*, 341 US 494, 71 S.Ct. 857, 905 (1951).
[37] *Whitney* v. *California*, 274 US 357 (1927).
[38] *New York Times Co.* v. *The United States*, 403 US 713, 91 S.Ct. 2140 (1971).
[39] *Southeastern Promotions Ltd* v. *Conrad*, 420 US 546 (1971).
[40] *Near* v. *Minnesota*, 283 US 967 (1931).

## JUDGMENT

**Barak J:**

What is the authority and extent of the discretion of the Broadcasting Authority in refusing to broadcast views and opinions that conflict with the democratic nature of the state because they spread hatred and anger based on racial or national origin? This is the question for us to decide.

## *The Facts*

1. The first petitioner, Rabbi Meir Kahane, was elected to the eleventh Knesset. He heads the 'Kach' party. The second petitioner, the 'Kach' movement, is a political movement represented in the Knesset by the First Petitioner. The question of Kach's participation in the elections to the eleventh Knesset was dealt with in *Neiman* v. *Chairman of the Central Elections Committee to the Eleventh Knesset* [1]. In that Election Appeal it was decided to overrule the Central Elections Committee and to approve Kach's participation in the elections. When the elections were held, the party won 25,907 valid votes ((1984) IP 3081, p. 3006) which resulted in the first petitioner's election to the Knesset. Upon his election, the first petitioner began political activity both inside the Knesset and outside it. The first petitioner's activity in the Knesset has been the subject of several appeals to this Court (*see Kach* v. *Speaker of the Knesset* [2]; *Kahane* v. *Speaker of the Knesset* [3]; *Kahane* v. *Chairman of the Knesset* [4]).

2. Soon after the elections to the eleventh Knesset, on 29 July 1984, a 'news forum' of the Broadcasting Authority was assembled. The second respondent, the General Manager of the Broadcasting Authority, chaired the meeting. The 'Managers of the Media' and other senior television and radio employees participated. The topic of the discussion was, *inter alia*, 'Kahane'. Various views were exchanged and the following 'conclusion' was adopted:

> In general, we do not ban or ignore. We cannot do so as journalists. Today it is Kahane, tomorrow someone else. The criterion must be: is it *news* or an attempt to make us into a tool? When a suspicion of 'playing to the cameras' arises, we shall not co-operate. The screen and microphone should not become an arena for conflicting extremes. The new political landscape lays a heavy burden of responsibility upon us. Everything must be shot and recorded; not everything should be broadcast. The criterion should be whatever deserves factual reporting on the front page of a newspaper.
>
> The Criteria Are:
>
> To shoot and record everything, [but] not to broadcast everything, including the Knesset;
>
> Everything that is clearly newsworthy, according to the editor's discretion, may be broadcast;
>
> Where a topic is considered sensitive, and in cases of doubt, a duty of consultation arises;
>
> We must now more than ever see to it that we do not become the tool of extremist elements engaging in attention-getting manœuvers.

3. On 1 August 1984, the above conclusion was presented to the Executive Board of the Broadcasting Authority (the first respondent). After a discussion the following resolution was adopted:

In order to ensure that the national broadcasting media do not serve as a stage for incitement against citizens and for declarations that damage the State of Israel and are contrary to the principles of the Declaration of Independence, the Executive Board approves the General Manager's announcement regarding the instruction given to the Managers of Radio and Television to check, in accordance with those principles, interviews with Meir Kahane and quotes from his activities, and to approve for broadcasting only those stories which are clearly newsworthy and do not contradict these principles and the letter and spirit of the Broadcasting Authority Act.

The meaning of this decision was that the reporters and technicians would shoot and record everything, but broadcast only what was 'clearly newsworthy'. The decision was also thus understood by the respondents. Instructions to this effect were given to the employees of the Broadcasting Authority.

4. Since then, the Broadcasting Authority has followed these guidelines. When the events relating to the petitioners are in the respondents' view 'clearly newsworthy', they are broadcast. Thus excerpts from the first petitioner's speech in the Knesset when voting no confidence in the Government, and a report of the petitioners' convention, were broadcast. But anything related to the views, opinions, and political positions of the petitioners was not broadcast. Moreover, the petitioners were not allowed to respond to the views, positions, and opinions of other political entities which attack the petitioners' positions. But if positions that the petitioners do not support had been ascribed to them, they would have been given a chance to deny them.

## *The Arguments*

5. The petitioners . . . argue primarily that the respondents have placed a 'ban' on them, thus injuring the petitioners' and the public's freedom of speech; that there has thus been a violation of the Broadcasting Authority Act, and discrimination against the petitioners. [The petitioners argue that] once the first petitioner has been elected to the Knesset, he must be allowed to express his political opinions equally to other Knesset members. Denying the petitioners' freedom of speech is a severe injury to democracy and the rule of law, and can negate the 'fairness doctrine' which the respondents follow. According to the petitioners, the respondents' actions constitute 'private censorship' and an injury to the principles of fairness and the preservation of equal opportunity for all.

In his oral argument [on behalf of the petitioners,] Mr Papu stressed the importance of the news media in general, and their obligation to broadcast the political platform of a party that had been elected to the Knesset. Only an explicit mandate to the contrary in the Act can absolve the Broadcasting

Authority from this duty, and there is no such explicit mandate in the Act. According to Mr Papu, the political views and opinions of a party in the Knesset must be broadcast even if an imminent certainty of injury to the public peace exists, because, in the realm of political opinions, unlike other realms, the near certainty test is inappropriate. In any case, the respondents did not consider this question, nor do they claim that such certainty exists. Finally, Mr Papu stressed that the first petitioner was not given a hearing nor given a chance to respond before the decisions concerning him were taken. In so acting the respondents violated the principles of natural justice, and this is another ground for invalidating their decision.

6. The respondents argue that no 'ban' was placed on the petitioners, since the respondents broadcast news relating to the petitioners that is clearly newsworthy. According to the respondents, they are authorized to refuse to broadcast the petitioners' views and opinions by section 3 of the Broadcasting Authority Act, 1965, referring to section 2 of the Public Education Act, 1953. Under those statutes, the Broadcasting Authority must further the drive for a society based on liberty, equality, tolerance, mutual aid, and love of your neighbour. This aim prevents broadcasting the petitioners' position, which entails violent racial incitement, preaching hatred among sections of the public, and injury to basic democratic principles. The Broadcasting Authority must not become a tool for the spreading of the petitioners' racist views. [According to the respondents,] it does not matter whether a near certainty of injury to the public order exists. The question of near certainty has not been checked by the respondents, and they do not claim that a near certainty of injury to the public order exists if the petitioner's views and opinions are broadcast. [Moreover, argue the respondents,] it cannot be said that the respondents discriminate against the petitioners, for they differ so distinctly from other groups. Therefore, the respondents do not contradict the 'fairness doctrine', for that doctrine does not require the respondents to enable the petitioners to 'balance' what had been said against them by spreading hatred, anger and violence between parts of the public, and by broadcasting their racist opinions.

7. . . . The question posed before us is whether the Broadcasting Authority is authorized to prevent the broadcasting of reports concerning the petitioners' views and opinions that are not clearly newsworthy. As we have seen, the petitioners' position is that a positive answer to this question is possible only if an explicit mandate to that effect is included in the Broadcasting Authority Act, and they claim that such a mandate is not found there. Are the petitioners correct?

8. The Broadcasting Authority Act, 1965 (henceforth the 'BA Act') states that the Broadcasting Authority, an independent statutory entity, will provide television and radio broadcasts to the public as a State service

(section 2). Section 3 of the BA Act defines the roles of the Broadcasting Authority as follows:

> The Authority will provide broadcasts to fulfill the following roles:
> (1) To broadcast educational, entertainment and informative programs in the fields of politics, society, economy, culture, science and art, in order:
> (a) to reflect the life of the state, its struggle, creativity and achievements;
> (b) to foster good citizenship;
> (c) to strengthen ties to Jewish heritage and the values thereof and deepen the understanding thereof;
> (d) to reflect the life and culture of all segments of the people stemming from various countries;
> (e) to broaden and spread knowledge;
> (f) to reflect the life of Jews in the diaspora; [and]
> (g) to further the aims of public education as described in the Public Education Act, 1953.

The aims of public education, to which section 3(1)(g) refers, are defined in section 2 of the Public Education Act, 1953 (henceforth the 'Public Education Act'), as follows:

> The aim of public education is to base education in the state on the values of Jewish culture and the achievements of science, on love of the Jewish people and patriotism, on training in agriculture and industry, on pioneering, and on a desire for a society based on liberty, equality, tolerance, mutual aid and love of neighbors.

Section 4 of the BA Act adds that, 'The Authority will ensure that the broadcasts properly reflect the various views and opinions prevailing in the public and broadcast trustworthy information.'

Mr Yarak, arguing for the respondents, stressed before us the mandate of section 3 of the BA Act. According to him, this mandate forbids broadcasting the petitioners' views and opinions, because these views flagrantly contradict the principles of liberty, equality, tolerance, and love of neighbours. [By contrast,] Mr Papu stressed, in arguing for the petitioners, section 4 of the BA Act, which provides that the Broadcasting Authority should properly reflect the various views and opinions prevailing in the public, including the petitioners' views and opinions.

9. Sections 3 and 4 of the BA Act set the framework in which the Authority operates. Naturally, this framework was stated in broad terms, assigning to the Broadcasting Authority a broad range of tasks. At first glance, those tasks may support both views argued before us. The duty to 'reflect the life of the State' can include the duty to reflect extreme political positions, whatever their political program. 'Fostering good citizenship' may lead both to supporting the petitioners' views and to refuting them, depending on the proper view of 'good citizenship'. Does fostering good citizenship require reflecting every opinion, including an opinion that spreads hatred between people and races? The aims of the Public

Education Act also create an ambiguity. What is the 'liberty' about which the youth should be educated? Does it not include freedom of speech, including the petitioners' freedom of speech? Does 'equality' not mean broadcasting all views and opinions? Should a society based on tolerance not be tolerant of views that foster intolerance? Does the duty 'properly' to reflect various views and opinions prevalent in the public include the duty to reflect views that contradict vital interests of the State? The text of sections 3 and 4 of the BA Act and section 2 of the Public Education Act are not the end of the interpretative process but its beginning. These sections are based on general values and principles, which themselves need interpretation, confrontation and balancing according to their weight.

The petition before us poses the question of the scope of freedom of enraging and dissonant speech; speech that spreads hatred and anger based on racial or national/ethnic origin. Let us call such speech for the purpose of this appeal 'deviant' speech. I am willing to assume for the purposes of this appeal, without it being proven before us, as counsel for the petitioners had to assume, that the petitioners' views are 'deviant' in the above sense. The question is whether, despite this, the petitioners are entitled to have their deviant views broadcast by the respondents.

Does the task of reflecting the life of the State, fostering good citizenship, basing society on liberty, equality, tolerance, mutual aid, and love of neighbours permit or forbid the expression of such 'deviant' speech? The answer must derive from the basic principles of our legal regime. The BA Act does not have its own principle, and the answer to this question, within the scope of the BA Act must depend, as the Act shows, on the status of 'deviant' speech in our national life. The BA Act does not stand alone. The law is, as President Sussman once stated, 'a creature existing in its environment' (*Shalit* v. *Minister of the Interior* [5]) and the law's environment includes, *inter alia*, 'broader circles of accepted principles, basic aims and fundamental criteria, deriving, as President Landau has put it, from the "springs of social consciousness of the people to whom the Judges belong"' (*Kibbutz Hazor* v. *Rehovot Tax Clerk* [6] (Barak J.) ).

The tasks of the Broadcasting Authority, including its authority to broadcast or forbid broadcasting views and opinions, should be interpreted against the background of our legal system, and on the basis of our law's conception of freedom of speech on the one hand, and its limits on the other.

## *The Broadcasting Authority's Authority: Freedom of Speech and its Limits*

10. We have seen that the authority of the Broadcasting Authority to broadcast or not to broadcast the petitioners' views is to be determined

according to the position accorded the principle of freedom of speech in our law. What is the essence and scope of freedom of speech in Israel, and does it extend to 'deviant' political speech? . . . The point of departure is the principle that the entire body of laws and principles of Israel indicate that it is a democratic State. Freedom of speech, which is the living breath of democracy and 'dearest to it' (Agranat J, in *State of Israel* v. *Ben Moshe* [7] at 435) and which occupies 'a place of honour in the temple of man's basic rights' (*Levi* v. *Commander of the Southern Police District* [8] at 398 (Barak J)), derives from the democratic character of the State. This right is considered a 'superior right' (Agranat J, in *Kol Ha'am Co.* v. *Minister of Interior* [9] at 878, and Shamgar J, in *'Ha'aretz' Newspaper Publishing Ltd* v. *The Israel Electric Co. Ltd* [10] at 295).

11. Freedom of speech is '[the citizen's] freedom to say what he wants and to listen to what others have to say' (Landau P, in *The Israel Electric Co. Ltd* v. *'Ha'aretz' Newspaper Publishing Ltd*, [11]). In its essence, freedom of speech is a liberty in its Hohfeldian meaning (*see* G. Williams, 'The Concept of Legal Liberty', 56 *Colum. L. Rev.* 1129 (1956) ). To guarantee that liberty the law gives its possessor other rights derived from it (*see Podamski* v. *The Attorney-General* [12] at 355; *Fogel* v. *The Broadcasting Authority* [13] at 662). Among these we may mention the right to receive information and to respond to it. Thus, 'freedom of speech' in its broader meaning is a bundle of rights, in whose centre lies the speaker's and listener's liberty, and beside this liberty [lie] other rights designed to fulfil and defend the said freedom. On this complexity of freedom of speech Professor Emerson has said:

> A system of freedom of expression, operating in a modern society, is a complex mechanism. At its core is a group of rights assured to individual members of the society. This set of rights, which makes up our present-day concept of free expression, includes the right to form and hold beliefs and opinions on any subject, and to communicate ideas, opinions, and information through any medium—in speech, writing, music, art or in other ways. To some extent it involves the right to remain silent. From the adverse side it includes the right to hear the views of others and to listen to their version of the facts. It encompasses the right to inquire and, to a degree, the right of access to information.

(Emerson, *The System of Freedom of Expression* (1970), 3). The freedom of speech and the rights derived from it . . . fit into the general constitutional framework, and are a cornerstone of the State's democratic essence.

12. The liberties and rights composing 'freedom of speech' apply to television and radio broadcasts. Professor Klinghoffer has noted the 'importance of assuring that broadcasts be made under the conditions of freedom of speech . . .' (Klinghoffer, *On the Freedom of Speech* (1984), 15). The application of freedom of speech [to broadcasting] is twofold: *first*, the Broadcasting Authority enjoys the same freedom of speech as any person

who wishes to express an opinion (*see* Fiss, 'Free Speech and Social Structure', 71 *Iowa L. Rev.* 1405 (1985–6) ). *Secondly*, the Broadcasting Authority must ensure the freedom of speech of others. That is freedom of speech *through* the Broadcasting Authority. The first aspect regards the Broadcasting Authority as a speaker. The second regards it as a stage, like an electronic street-corner, on which the freedom of speech of speakers and listeners is carried out. The general problem of the Broadcasting Authority is to find a balance between its right as a speaker and its duty as a stage.

The second aspect [of freedom of speech *through* the Broadcasting Authority] is particularly meaningful. 'The broadcast emitted from the television tube is heard from one end of the world to the other, and no place is free from it' (Elon J, in '*Hahayim' Publishing Co.* v. *The Broadcasting Authority* [14] at 369). In the modern age, it is possible to exchange opinions and persuade and be persuaded only if the mass media (radio and television), 'whose speech and sight attract a mass audience, and who know their influence on the audience's opinions and taste' (Cohn DP, in [14] at 368), serve as a stage for fulfilling the freedom of speech. President Shamgar noted this in *Klohfer-Nave* v. *The Minister of Education and Culture* ([15] at 238), stating:

> The democratic process is conditional upon the possibility of openly discussing the problems facing the state and freely exchanging opinions concerning them. . . . In the said discussion and debate the mass media fill an immensely important role. They enable meaningful mass publication of information on all spheres of life, which makes such information public, and they are a prime tool for explaining doctrines and opinions and for open public debate concerning them.

Indeed, in the modern age, it is difficult to maintain meaningful freedom of speech without using radio and television. As Professor Barron has observed:

> In the era of mass communication, the words of the solitary speaker or the lonely writer, however brave or imaginative, have little impact unless they are broadcast through the great engines of public opinion—radio, television, and the press.

(Barron, *Freedom of the Press—For Whom*) XIII (1973) ).

Therefore, the public and its members have a right *vis-à-vis* the Broadcasting Authority and the Broadcasting Authority is obliged to maintain freedom of speech on the airwaves. 'The public's right is that freedom of speech be maintained in the media—radio and television—and that these media be run in a way which fulfills such freedom in practice. The right that is preserved is mainly the right of the general public, namely the listeners and viewers, and not just that of those who wish to broadcast the program . . . because the airwaves belong to the public and not to this or that individual.' (Shamgar P, in *Shiran* v. *The Broadcasting Authority* [16] at 378). [United States Supreme Court] Brennan J made a similar observation in *Columbia Broadcasting System Inc.* v. *Democratic National Committee* (*'CBS'*) [32] at 94, stating:

In light of the unique nature of the electronic media, the public has strong First Amendment interests in the reception of a full spectrum of views—presented in a vigorous and uninhibited manner—on controversial issues of public importance.

The duty of the Broadcasting Authority in a democratic society is thus not only to broadcast the news fully and objectively, but also to express the views and opinions of all segments of the public (*see* Barron, 'An Emerging First Amendment Right of Access to the Media?', 37 *Geo. Washington L. Rev.* 487 (1969) ). Brennan J made this point in *CBS* [32] at 190:

Nor are these cases concerned solely with the adequacy of coverage of those views and issues which generally are recognized as 'newsworthy'. For also at stake is the right of the public to receive suitable access to new and generally unperceived ideas and opinions.

White J summed up this issue comprehensively in *Red Lion Broadcasting Co.* v. *Federal Communications Commission* [33]:

the people as a whole retain their interest in free speech by radio and their collective right to have the medium function consistently with the ends and purposes of the First Amendment. . . . It is the purpose of the First Amendment to preserve an uninhibited market-place of ideas in which truth will ultimately prevail rather than to countenance monopolization of that market.

Section 4 of the BA Act gave expression to this view by obliging the Broadcasting Authority to ensure that its broadcasts properly reflect the various views and opinions prevalent in the public. It is another question how this mandate can be exercised, for broadcasting time is limited. We shall deal with this question below. At this stage we are only discussing the basic principle that the Broadcasting Authority is not only a 'speaker' but also a 'stage' and must give proper expression to views and opinions, even if they are not clearly newsworthy.

13. I have discussed freedom of speech and its application to radio and television broadcasts. [A question arises as to] the scope of that freedom, and the degree to which it obliges the Broadcasting Authority to broadcast ['deviant'] speech. . . . To answer this question, we should examine the basic arguments supporting that freedom. The question [of scope and degree] has occupied philosophers for centuries. It was comprehensively discussed in Milton's *Areopagitica*: *A Speech for the Liberty*, *Unlicensed Printing*, and in Mill's essay *On Liberty*. Various thinkers have expressed differing opinions concerning the reasons for freedom of speech and various explanations have been given (for a summary, see Emerson, *The System of Freedom of Expression* (1970); Nimmer, *Freedom of Speech* (1984); Barendt, *Freedom of Speech* (1985)).

Indeed, freedom of speech does not have one single explanation, but many and varied ones. I consider this phenomenon very welcome (*see* Shauer, *Free Speech*: *A Philosophical Inquiry* 82 (1982); Schlag, 'An Attack on Categorical Approaches to Freedom of Speech', 30 *UCLA LRev*. 1671 (1983) ). Freedom of speech is a broad system of rights and liberties linked to one another, and it is only natural that such a complex system cannot be justified by a single explanation, but requires many varied arguments expressing various aspects of freedom of speech. Only thus may the scope of freedom of speech be reflected (*see* Tribe, *American Constitutional Law* 579 (1978) ).

* * *

. . . The justifications for freedom of speech are complex and interconnected. It is the freedom of the individual to fulfill himself and form a view of life by setting free his creative and receptive, impressing and impressed, spirit; it is the freedom of the individual and the community to bring truth to light by the free and constant conflict between truth and falsehood; it is the freedom of members of society to exchange tolerantly, without fear and with respect to each individual's autonomy, views, and opinions, and to persuade one another, in order to stabilize, anchor, and develop the democratic regime. Some of those justifications are utilitarian, others are not; some focus on the individual and his happiness, others on the public and on defending its values (*see* Shamgar P, in *Spiro* v. *Civil Service Commission* [17]). Let us examine briefly the main arguments.

14. The *first* argument is based on the desire to bring out the truth. Freedom of speech should be assured to enable various and differing views and ideas to compete. Truth will emerge from such competition, and not from the governmental imposition of a single 'truth', because truth is destined to prevail in the conflict of ideas. As Agranat J noted in *Kol Ha'am* ([9] at 877):

> Fundamentally, the said development is nothing but a gradual discovery of the truth, so that the state can aim for the wisest goal and choose the route that leads to that goal in the most efficient manner. To find out that truth, the principle of freedom of speech serves as a tool, for only by examining '*all*' views and freely exchanging *all* opinions may that 'truth' be discovered.

In the course of [his opinion,] Agranat J quotes Holmes J in *Abrams* v. *United States* [34] at 630:

> But when men have realized that time has upset many fighting faiths, they may come to believe even more than they believe the very foundations of their own conduct that the ultimate good desired is better reached by free trade in ideas—that

> the best test of truth is the power of the thought to get itself accepted in the competition of the market, and that truth is the only ground upon which their wishes can be carried out.

The test of truth is not the government power supporting it but its inner power to persuade. The way to deal with falsehood is not to silence it but to rectify the misconception through education and explanation. Falsehood fails through exposure, not through suppression. The solution is not to limit speech but to strengthen it. For that purpose, it is essential to assure freedom of speech, for without speech there is no conflict, and without conflict truth may not emerge.

15. The *second* argument is based on the need of man to seek fulfillment. Only by assuring freedom of speech can such self-fulfillment be ensured. Without the freedom to speak or be heard, write or read, talk or be silent, man's personality is damaged. His spiritual and intellectual development is based upon his ability freely to shape his world view (*see* Scanlan, 'A Theory of Freedom of Expression', in Dworkin (ed.), *The Philosophy of Law* 153 (1977) ). Freedom of speech is an essential element in such fulfillment. As Agranat J notes in *Kol Ha'am* ([9] at 818):

> The importance of the principle is based also upon the protection it bestows upon a distinctly *private* interest, namely every man's wish, being a man, fully to express his own attributes and personal characteristics; to develop and foster to the greatest possible extent his personality; to express his opinion on every subject he considers crucial; in short to say what he believes in, so that life may seem worthwhile to him.

That need is not just the need of the speaker. It is also the need of the listener, and therefore of the general public. As White J stated in *Red Lion Broadcasting Co.* ([33] at 390):

> It is the right of the viewers and listeners, not the right of the broadcasters, which is paramount. It is the right of the public to receive suitable access to social, political, aesthetic, moral, and other ideas and experiences which is crucial here.

Shamgar P recently expressed the same idea in *Spiro* ([17] at 240):

> Not just the speaker exercises his rights and enjoys his privileges as a member of a free society. The audience of potential listeners or readers has a right to hear or read what others say, and limiting such listening and reading is not just an injury to the rights of the speaker or writer but to the same extent an injury to the rights of the people being addressed.

This argument ties freedom of speech to the dignity of man, and to other liberties such as freedom of religion and conscience, but also identifies it as an end in its own right. Man's nature is to seek fulfillment by self-expression.

16. The *third* argument bases freedom of speech on democracy (*see* Kretzmer, 'Demonstrations and the Law', 19 *Isr. LR* 47 (1984) ). 'The principle of freedom of speech is tied fast to the democratic process' (Agranat J, in *Kol Ha'am* [9] at 876). Freedom of speech is an essential condition for the existence and development of a democracy. As the US Supreme Court said in *Garrison* v. *Louisiana* [35] at 74–5: 'Speech concerning public affairs is more than self expression; it is the essence of self-government.' Freedom of speech ensures a public exchange of views, and thus enables citizens to form opinions on public matters. Thus the government may be formed, observed, and changed. 'Only thus may he form an independent opinion, so far as possible, on the question facing society and the state, the resolution of which ultimately lies in his hands since he has the right to elect the authorities of the State' (Landau J, in *Israel Film Studios* v. *Gary* [18] at 2415).

If the 'truth' argument seeks to discover the truth, the 'democratic' argument seeks to share that truth with all members of the public, so that they can shape the future of society (*see* Meiklejohn, *Political Freedom*: *The Constitutional Powers of the People* 75 (1965) ). The free exchange of information, views, and opinions which are not dictated from above, in an attempt at mutual persuasion, is an essential condition for the existence of a democracy based on the rule of the people, by the people, for the people. Only thus may every individual in society be assured of getting the maximum information needed to make decisions regarding politics and government. Such a free flow of opinions enables an orderly change in the structure of powers supporting the regime. Without freedom of speech democracy loses its soul.

This Court has often noted the insoluble tie between freedom of speech and democracy. It was the basis for the Court's opinion in *Kol Ha'am* [9]. Agranat J re-emphasized this connection in *State of Israel* v. *Ben Moshe* [7] at 435, noting the 'intimate tie between the principle of freedom of speech and debate and the proper functioning of the democratic process'. This was stressed in *Spiro* [17]. It was also noted by Shamgar J in *Shiran* [16] at 378:

> The democratic regime is dependent upon and nourished by the free flow of information from and to the public, concerning the main topics influencing society and the individual. Therefore, the free flow of information is a key to the operation of the entire democratic system.

* * *

17. Another aspect of the democratic argument is the important contribution of freedom of speech to social stability, and hence to democracy (*see* Gromewalt, 'Speech and Crime' [1980] *ABF Res. J* 647, 672). By virtue

of freedom of speech and social pressures, discontent is expressed in the placid sphere of expression and not in the violent sphere of action. Society, which is sometimes stagnant and oblivious to hidden dangers, can prepare itself by being aware of the dangers which freedom of speech reveals. As Douglas J observed in *Dennis* v. *United States* [36] at 905):

> Free speech has occupied an exalted position because of the high service it has given our society. Its protection is essential to the very existence of a democracy. The airing of ideas releases pressures which otherwise might become destructive. When ideas compete in the market for acceptance, full and free discussion exposes the false and they gain few adherents. Full and free discussion even of ideas we hate encourages the testing of our own prejudices and preconceptions. Full and free discussion keeps a society from becoming stagnant and unprepared for the stresses and strains that work to tear all civilizations apart.

Moreover, democracy is based on tolerance (*see* Bollinger, *The Tolerant Society* (1986); Richards, *Toleration and the Constitution* (1986) ). It is based on tolerance even for the other's opinions and deeds. It is based on tolerance even for the intolerant. In a pluralistic society like ours, tolerance is the force that unites us, and enables us to live together (*see Noah Film Co. Ltd* v. *The Film Censorship Board* [19] at 764—Witkon J). Freedom of speech enhances tolerance and strengthens democracy. On this triple link between tolerance, freedom of speech, and democracy, Elon J said in *Neiman* [1] at 296:

> That is the theory of leadership and rule in Jewish heritage—to be tolerant of each individual and each group, in accordance with their world views and opinions. That is the great secret of tolerance and listening to what others have to say, and the great strength of the right to voice an opinion for each individual and each community, that they are not just necessary, for an ordered and enlightened regime but also essential for its creative force, since in the real world 'two opposing elements join and make each other fruitful, *a fortiori* in the spiritual world' (Rabbi A. I. H. Kook).

The European Human Rights Court noted the same connection in *Glimmerveen and Hagenbeek* v. *Netherlands* (1980) 23 Yearbook of European Commission of Human Rights 366, 380:

> Freedom of expression constitutes one of the essential foundations of a democratic society, one of the basic conditions for its progress and for the development of every man. . . . Subject to paragraph 2 of Article 10, it is applicable not only to 'information' or 'ideas' that are favorably received or regarded as inoffensive or as a matter of indifference, but also to those that offend, shock or disturb the state or any sector of the population. Such are the demands of that pluralism, tolerance and broadmindedness without which there is no 'democratic society'.

18. This connection between freedom of speech and democracy places freedom of speech in a unique position. Freedom of speech ensures the

democratic regime, which in its turn ensures other rights. Hence the importance of freedom of speech, on which other rights depend.

* * *

. . . Against this background, the question arises whether freedom of speech includes freedom for 'deviant' speech—namely annoying and irritating speech, which spreads anger and hatred, based on racial or ethnic origin.

19. Freedom of speech is not just the freedom to express or hear widely accepted views. Freedom of speech is also the freedom to express dangerous, annoying, and deviant views, which the public abhors and hates. *See State of Israel* v. *Ben Moshe* [7] at 434 (Agranat P); *Leor* v. *The Film Censorship Board* [20]; *Neiman* [1] at 322; (Barak J) and at 325 (Beiski J). As I noted in *Levi* ([8] at 411):

> The freedoms of speech and assembly are not just the freedom to express nice things. Freedom to march is not just the freedom of children carrying flowers to march through the street, but also the freedom to march of people whose views are not accepted, and whose marching annoys and irritates.

Similarly, Shamgar P stated in *Neiman* ([1] at 277):

> The true test for the existence of a right arises not in times when the current events express composure, tolerance and understanding, but at moments of pain and vexation, when there is little sympathy for the person claiming a certain right or for his views.

* * *

20. We have seen that according to our established view freedom of speech includes 'intrinsically' the freedom to express dangerous, annoying, and deviant opinions. Does this freedom extend to racist views? Does not the racist substance of the speech exclude it from the scope of freedom of speech? The reasons for freedom of speech, it may be argued, do not extend to racist speech. Thus, for instance, if freedom of speech is explained through a desire to uncover the truth, racism is fundamentally false, and cannot contribute to finding the truth. Nor should we support the self-fulfillment of a false prophet. The democratic argument too can support a view that excludes racist speech from the scope of freedom of speech, for racist speech injures democracy.

In my opinion, such arguments are not determinative, and are based on an incomplete comprehension of the reasons for freedom of speech. Racism is false, but this truth can emerge only through that free competition of ideas and views. Through a free debate with racism on the stage of opinions and views, racism will be exposed in all its ugliness and man's equality and dignity strengthened. The falsehood of racism supports giving it expression, for the free competition of ideas and views will expose that fallacy. . . . The argument about self-fulfillment [also] supports my view, because to fulfill ourselves we must listen to and be aware of racist views as well. Only thus can we know how to fight them (*See* Meiklejohn, *Political Freedom* 55 (1948) ).

This result is required also by the democratic argument. Through exchanging views and opinions, the public can form its own view as to a racist opinion, and destroy it or weaken it in the political struggle, based on tolerance, in a democratic society. From such an open struggle against racism, democracy will emerge strengthened and more robust. Therefore, I believe that freedom of speech includes 'intrinsically' the freedom of racist speech as well (*see* Shauer, *supra*, at 163; Nimmer, *supra*, at 2–30, 3–16; Barendt, *supra*, at 167). I am aware that an opposite view is possible, that racist speech is outside the scope of freedom of speech. I do not favour this view. I consider it dangerous to freedom of speech and to democracy. Nor do I believe that racist speech can be clearly isolated from other speech; the result of such a view would ultimately be to allow the government to encroach broadly and openly upon freedom of speech.

21. My approach, which extends freedom of speech even to racist 'deviant' speech, applies particularly to the freedom of speech of a political party in parliamentary life. The petitioners were allowed to participate in the parliamentary election. Over 20,000 voters supported them. How can a democratic society allow a party to participate in the election, but prevent it from expressing its views afterwards? It may be argued that, by allowing the racist speech of a political party, the party itself is approved of. I do not accept this view. In extending freedom to racist speech, democratic society (in general) and the court (in particular) do not legitimize racist speech. As Professor Gabizon has stated:

> In our tradition, there is no direct passage from saying that a certain speech is not illegal, or that some step to silence it is not legal, to substantive support of that speech. It is easy to understand that a man may refrain from legally prohibiting speech which he opposes, and we have grown accustomed to such decisions in our court. But rightly we regard these decisions as a jurisprudential achievement.

(Gabizon, 'Twenty Years after Yeredor—the Right to be Elected and the Lessons of History', *Shimon Agranat Jubilee*, Volume 145, 170 (1986) ).

Moreover, if we agree to silence a racist political opinion, are we not in danger of crossing the line at some stage? 'Is there no danger that the line will not be observed, and that a stigma of racism and incitement be stamped on the views of a political opponent just because they are unusual?' (*Neiman* [1] at 322—Barak J). True, the recent past indicates that anti-democratic forces have often used the freedom of speech given by democracy to bring about democracy's downfall. But while that historical experience must be kept before us, it should not be decisive. As Shamgar P noted in *The Israel Electric Co.* ([11] at 361):

> One must beware of reaching conclusions as to limiting freedoms just because some totalitarian movements managed to use them for their notorious ends. Such an attitude by itself can lead to dangerous and far-reaching conclusions. We had better abandon analogies whose connection and similarity to our modern social reality and legal system are weak and uncertain.

While we should learn from the experience of others, our approach to freedom of speech should rest on our own experience, our political strength, moral health, and national culture.

22. * * *

23. In Israel, no constitutional provision determining the permissible limits on freedom of speech has yet been enacted. Therefore, every law limiting freedom of speech is constitutionally valid. But as in the United States, Germany, Canada, England, and other countries, it is the courts—and within the court system, the Supreme Court—that should interpret the limiting law and determine its scope (*see* Boyle, 'Freedom of Expression as a Public Interest in English Law' [1982] *Public Law* 574). This interpretation is made in light of the basic principle of freedom of speech. However, freedom of speech is not the only principle to be considered, for in a democratic society other basic principles must be taken into account, such as the dignity of man, the right to property, the integrity of the judicial process, and the public peace.

Where these basic principles clash, they should be balanced. The balance is determined first by the legislature itself. The court should, of course, interpret the legislative language, and that is its contribution to the balancing task. Sometimes the legislature does not indicate a position in the balancing issue, and it is wholly performed by the court. When a judge sets the balance, he frequently faces a choice between principles. 'Frequently the judge faces basic principles that contradict one another. Often every principle has its opposite, every thesis its antithesis . . . indeed, basic principles of the system often march two by two, each in its own direction' (*Neiman* [1] at 308, *per* Barak J).

The task of the judge-interpreter is to locate the clashing values, to contrast them, assign them weight, and find that balance which most adequately reflects the nation's 'beliefs' (Zmoira P, in *Zeev* v. *Guberin* [21]); its 'national way of life' (Agranat J, in *Kol Ha'am* [9] at 884); 'society's basic political views' (Shamgar P, in *Klohfer-Nave* [15] at 241); and what has been called 'views accepted by the enlightened public' (Landau J, in *Zim* v. *Maziar* [22] at 1335); *Shalit* v. *Minister of the Interior* [5] at 520).

24. 'These expressions—balance, weight—are but metaphors. Behind them lies the conception that not all principles are considered of equal importance by society and that without legislative direction, the court should estimate the relative social importance of the various principles. Just as no man lacks a shadow, there is no principle without weight. Setting the balance on the basis of weight means giving a social evaluation of the relative importance of the various principles' (*Leor* [20] at 434, *per* Barak J).

The task of balancing belongs first and foremost to the legislature. Where the legislature has refrained from setting the balance, the court must do it by putting the principle of freedom of speech 'on the scales' (*Kol Ha'am* [9] at 878) and comparing it to the other principles that arise from the case. It is natural that the balance changes from case to case according to which values are striving for supremacy. Therefore one should not adopt a single criterion, but rather varying ones, according to the weight of the conflicting values (*Levi* [8] at 401; *Daher* v. *Minister of Interior* [23]). The balancing points vary according to their character and essence. For instance, some balancing points concern the causal relationship between cause and effect, and some concern the scope of various liberties. But despite the differences among the criteria, they all share the same principled character. We are looking for a 'rational principle' (Agranat J, in *Kol Ha'am* [9] at 881) and not an *ad hoc* decision. The balance between principles cannot be fortuitous and changing from opinion to opinion. We must seek a principle applicable to a class of cases. We must seek a 'criterion giving value-laden guidance' (Shamgar J, in *Israel Electric Co.* [11] at 361), avoiding a 'fortuitous paternalistic criterion, whose aim and character nobody can foresee' (*ibid.*). 'The balance should be based on a criterion giving value-laden and rational guidance' (*Spiro* [17]).

25. * * *

26. The deviant speech in our case may hurt the dignity and human feelings of a group of people in our state. It may undermine the social order, social tolerance, and the public peace. It contradicts the essence and fundamental characteristics of a democratic State, and the principle of equality between people that exists in it. It negates our national character and beliefs. We may adopt Elon J's words concerning the petitioners' platform (in *Neiman* [1] at 302):

> The content of 'Kach's' platform and the aim of its founders and leaders, as they appear in the record, are in striking contradiction to the world of Judaism, its ways and thoughts; to the past of the Hebrew nation; and to its future aspiration. They totally negate basic principles of human and nationally morality, Israel's Declaration of Independence, and the basis of today's enlightened democracies, and copy into the Jewish state ideas and deeds adhered to by the worst nations of the world.

These injuries may be subsumed under the title 'social order'. The deviant speech may indeed injure the social order, for it may injure democracy, the public's peace and security, and its members' dignity and religious, moral, ethnic, and other feelings.

27. We have seen that deviant speech may injure the social order, which is but a set of values (democracy, the public's peace and security, human dignity, and public feelings). Are these values protected in Israeli law? The positive answer to this question is self-evident. Israeli law does not protect only freedom of speech. It protects another set of values it holds dear, which reflect its beliefs; thus, Israeli law protects the State's democratic character (*see Katlan* v. *Prison Authority* [24] at 298); and the public's feelings (*see Leor* [20]). We learn this from our very essence as a democratic State and from the development of our 'national way of life' (Agranat J, in *Kol Ha'am* at 584). This conclusion is strengthened by various mandates in our legislation. So, for instance, publication of incitement to racism is a criminal offence (1446(a) of the Criminal Code). Injury to religious feelings (173 of the Criminal Code) and publication of obscene materials (214 of the Criminal Code) are also criminal offences. Indeed, Israeli law protects besides freedom of speech other values included in the 'public order' as well (*see Leor* [20], *supra*).

28. In this clash between the principle of freedom of speech and the values upholding public order which prevails? That is not a new question before us. It has arisen in the past. It was decided that public order prevails. Thus we have held that speech in demonstration that leads to bloodshed or violence is subject to the need to preserve the public peace (*see Levi* [8]). A long line of opinion concerning the authority of the Film and Theater Censorship Board holds that speech which hurts the public's religious and moral feelings is set aside by the need to preserve such feelings. Freedom of speech also yields to the need to protect public service (*see Spiro* [17]) and the public peace (*see Zichroni* v. *Broadcasting Authority* [25]).

The reasons for this preference [for public order] reflect the common view in enlightened states that 'liberty is not licence', and that various values exist that should be protected even when they clash with freedom of speech. Thus, it has been said in various international agreements that racism is a phenomenon that should be combated (*see e.g.* the International Agreement on Eliminating Racial Discrimination, to which Israel is a party; *see* Dinstein, *Public International Law*, 126 (1979)). Indeed, while freedom of speech protects and exposes truth, an enlightened democratic society is not always willing to have the truth revealed at any price. For instance, we do not tolerate the beating of an accused by his interrogators, even if as a result truth emerges. We punish libel even if it contains an element of truth. Moreover, an enlightened democratic society is usually willing to set limits to man's self-fulfillment. Publishing obscenity is a crime even if it is a result of its creator's self-fulfillment.

While freedom of speech protects democracy, it must be concluded, sometimes, that it can also injure it. Such an injury can occur when the speech is racist and leads to injury to public feelings; an expression of hatred which causes a disturbance of the public peace; and other injuries that may arise from publication of racist speech. An enlightened democracy may protect itself from a cancer wishing to destroy it. Democracy is willing to protect freedom of speech, as long as freedom of speech protects democracy. When freedom of speech becomes a weapon to injure democracy, there is no reason why democracy should bare its throat. 'The freedom of speech assured everyone in Israel does not mean freedom for incitement and injury from abroad and destroyers from inside' (Landau J in *En Gal* v. *Film and Theater Censorship Board* [26] at 278); 'a constitution is not a recipe for suicide and civil rights is not a stage for national destruction . . . democracy does not have to kill itself to prove its vitality' (*Neiman* [1] at 310, 315, *per* Barak J).

29. We have said that in the clash between freedom of speech and 'public order', the latter prevails. Two questions arise in this context: *first*, does every injury, even a slight one, to public order justify limiting freedom of speech? *Secondly*, what probability of injury justifies limiting freedom of speech? As to the first question, the accepted view in Israel is 'that freedom of speech yields only where the injury to public order is harsh, serious and severe' (*Leor* [20]). The special value we bestow upon freedom of speech justifies this approach. As Agranat J noted in *Kol Ha'am* ([9] at 892):

> It is important to consider whether the seriousness of the danger that the Minister of the Interior foresees upon publication of the depraved material is great enough to compensate the public injury, namely the injury to freedom of speech, which stopping the publication of the newspaper in which they appear must occasion.

I noted the same consideration in *Neiman* ([1] at 311): 'The question is always if the magnitude of the damage, discounted by the chance that it will not happen, justifies the injury to civil rights to prevent it.' The same approach is common in American jurisprudence. Thus Brandeis J said in *Whitney* v. *California* ([37] at 376):

> To justify suppression of free speech there must be reasonable ground to fear that serious evil will result if free speech is practiced. . . . There must be reasonable ground to believe that the evil to be prevented is a serious one.

Prohibition of free speech and assembly is a measure so stringent that it would be inappropriate as the means for averting a relatively trivial harm to society.

Because of the central importance of the principle of freedom of speech, only a serious and real injury to the public order can justify limiting freedom of speech.

30. What is the causal connection between publication and a real injury to public order, which would justify limiting freedom of speech? That, too, is not a new question before us. It was thoroughly discussed in *Kol Ha'am*. Since that landmark case, we follow the doctrine set in it, which says that freedom of speech may be limited in our State [only] where a near certainty exists that the speech will be followed by deeds which will palpably injure public order, public peace, or the foundations of democracy. This approach regarding the limits of protecting freedom of speech when a near certainty exists of a real injury to public order is followed throughout this Court's opinions. The beginning, as we said, is in Agranat J's opinion in *Kol Ha'am*: 'Only when the publication goes beyond explaining an idea and becomes preaching that creates in the circumstances at least a *near* possibility of action endangering public peace, may governmental authorities intervene to suppress the publication or prevent its recurrence' ([9] at 888). Landau J repeated this approach in *Zichroni* ([25] at 2426), regarding the authority of the Board according to the Films Act:

> We should adopt the main arguments of this Court in *Kol Ha'am* v. *Minister of the Interior* also in the case before us. It was held there that as to prevention of a danger to the public peace, the test should be if a 'near certainty' exists that the publication will jeopardize the public peace.

Since then, this Court has followed that principled criterion in all situations where freedom of speech clashes with the principles of public peace, public order, or the foundations of democracy.

* * *

31. * * *

32. . . . In his argument before us [on behalf of the petitioners,] Mr Papu claimed that even if the near certainty test applies to freedom of speech in general, it should not be applied to political speech of a political or parliamentary party. I cannot accept this view. The values of the existence of democracy, the public's peace and security, and the public's feelings are protected in a democratic society *vis-à-vis* every speech, and I can see no way of judicially creating an exception for the political speech of a party. Whoever wants to make a political speech an 'absolute' value, which may not be limited, must point to a statutory mandate from which such a conclusion can be drawn. This is what Black J and Professor Meiklejohn did in interpreting the First Amendment (*see* Meiklejohn, 'The First Amendment is an Absolute', 1961 *Sup. Ct. Rev.* 245). We have no 'First Amendment', and our laws contain nothing from which we can deduce that political speech is absolutely protected.

Certainly, the democratic argument behind freedom of speech (*see* section 16, *supra*) is particularly strong as regards the freedom of political speech (*see* Sussman J, in *Israel Communist Party* v. *Mayor of Jerusalem* [27] at 1728; Agranat J, in *State of Israel* v. *Ben Moshe* [7] at 435; Shamgar P, in *Klohfer-Nave* [15] at 239). But we have never held that political speech is absolute and may not be limited where a near certainty of real danger to the public order exists. On the contrary, the cases on freedom of speech which adopted the said test dealt mainly with political speech, including the political speech of a party (*see* e.g. *Neiman* [1]).

In my opinion, the near certainty test of a real danger to public order extends also to the political speech of a party. Indeed, just as I do not think that racist political speech should be excluded from freedom of speech, so I do not believe it should be excluded from its limits. In my opinion, the proper balance between freedom of speech and its limits stemming from public order is found in the near certainty test, and this balance applies to racist political speech as well.

33. * * *

34. Since the respondents' decision was taken and their arguments were heard by this Court, the Penal Act (20th Amendment), 1986, was enacted. That Act adds to the 1977 Penal Act sections 134(a)–144(e). Section 144(a) defines racism as follows:

> Racism—persecution, degradation, humiliation, a manifestation of enmity, hostility or violence, or incitement to hatred toward the public or parts of the population, only because of their color or their racial or national/ethnic origin.

Section 144(b) establishes a criminal offence of publishing an incitement to racism as follows:

> (a) Whoever publishes anything, intending to incite to racism, shall serve five years in prison.
> (b) For the purposes of this section, it does not matter if the publication led to racism or not or whether it was true or not.

Section 144(c) defines a permitted publication and states *inter alia* 'that the publication of a truthful and fair report of an act defined in Section 144(b) will not constitute a violation of that section, as long as it was not intended to lead to racism.' . . .

35. In my opinion, the respondents are entitled to and must prevent publication of a racist speech if by publishing it they will be committing a criminal offence. The question whether in publishing racist speech the respondents violate section 144(b) of the Penal Act has not been examined by me and I will not express any opinion concerning it (*see* in this regard section 144(c) of the Act, which gives the Broadcasting Authority a defence in certain cases). I will continue to analyse my approach based on the

assumption that the Broadcasting Authority itself is not committing any crime in broadcasting a racist report, and focus upon the question whether the Broadcasting Authority must not broadcast it because of its criminal/racist nature, and whether it may refrain from broadcasting it.

We cannot say that the criminal nature of the publication *requires* the Broadcasting Authority to prevent it prospectively. The Broadcasting Authority can determine that the penal sanction for the publication shall be applied to the criminal after the fact, and that it is too unjustified under the circumstances to prevent publication beforehand (*see* Ben-Porat J, in '*Milan*' [28] at 680).

36. But may the Broadcasting Authority—even if it does not have to—prevent publication of a racist speech just because of its criminality, because it does not wish to assist the commission of a crime by the publisher? It may certainly do so if it believes that publication creates a near certainty of a real injury to the public order (whether this is a factual element of the crime or not). Thus, the Film and Play Censorship Board may prevent performance of a play that can injure the religious feelings of part of the public, a violation of section 173 of the Penal Act (*Kenan* v. *The Film and Play Censorship Board* [29]). [In that case,] Landau J noted that performing the play would constitute 'blasphemy against the Christian religion, plus profanity', and this fulfills in my opinion the near certainty of a real injury to public peace test, since public peace includes the public's religious feelings. Similarly, in *Attorney General* v. *Film and Play Censorship Board*, a play was banned which violated section 41 of the Courts Act, 1957, concerning a publication which may influence the Court (today, section 71 of the Courts Act (New Version), 1984). Silberg J stressed on the one hand that a possible influence on the court is enough to establish the violation, and on the other that 'the danger I have just mentioned is not just remote, but immediate and very near given the particular actuality of the plot'. What is the rule if there is no near certainty of an injury to the public peace by publication, even though it is a criminal offence; may the Broadcasting Authority exercise prior restraint of the broadcast for this reason only?

37. In my opinion, the answer is no. The centrality of freedom of speech means that only a near certainty of a real danger to the public peace justifies limiting freedom of speech prospectively. In so far as the criminal norm applies to the speech itself ('bad tendency') without that near certainty being present, the speech may not be banned, but the publisher can be prosecuted. Criminal responsibility is neither a necessary nor a sufficient condition for prior restraint. It is not a necessary condition, because a prior restraint is possible of a publication that will almost certainly injure public order, even if it is not a crime. And it is not a sufficient condition, because the principle of freedom of speech justifies prior restraint on such

freedom only when near certainty of danger exists. When no such near certainty exists, and the criminal prohibition applies to the speech without regard to its result, prior restraint is unjustifiable. That is in my view the necessary result flowing from Agranat J's view in *Kol Ha'am*, which distinguished criminal responsibility from prior restraint and limited the latter as an 'extremely severe and serious' act, to be used only when a near certainty of substantial injury to public peace exists.

38. * * *

## *The Authority of the Broadcasting Authority: Summary*

39. * * *

## *The Exercise of the Broadcasting Authority's Discretion*

40. The authority of the Broadcasting Authority is to give expression to views and opinions that do not entail a near certainty of a real injury to public order. That authority should be exercised according to the accepted criteria for exercise of a statutorily-bestowed discretion by a public authority. Thus, the Broadcasting Authority should act fairly, *bona fide*, reasonably, without discrimination or arbitrariness, and taking into account all relevant considerations and them alone (*see Zichroni* [25] at 768). Naturally, broadcasting time is limited, and it is impossible to broadcast all views and all opinions at each time. As Ben-Porat DP noted in *Klohfer-Nave* [15] at 243:

> Nobody will claim that freedom of speech, without legislative intervention, allows *everyone* who wants to express *his opinion*, even in a matter of public importance, to *require* the Broadcasting Authority (despite its legally authorized role) to broadcast his views on T.V.

The Broadcasting Authority must determine, within its time frame, an order of priorities which satisfies the appropriate standard. In establishing this order of priorities the Broadcasting Authority must act fairly and equitably. Of course, it does not have to give the same time to all views and opinions. But it must not discriminate between them (compare *Derekh Eretz Association* v. *The Broadcasting Authority*, [31]). As we have seen, section 4 of the Broadcasting Authority Act requires it to give proper expression in the broadcasts to views and opinions prevalent in the public. There can be no doubt that in this framework the views and opinions of a political party represented in the Knesset should be expressed. The scope of speech should be determined by the Broadcasting Authority, as long as it is 'proper'. Moreover, if a political view has been criticized, fairness requires a chance to reply. As Ben-Porat DP stated in *Spiro* ([17] at 370):

Naturally, criticism invites response, and I have no doubt, that if the Appellant wants to explain on T.V. or otherwise why the criticism against it is baseless or exaggerated, it must be allowed to do so as a matter of course.

* * *

41. We have seen that the Broadcasting Authority is authorized to refrain from broadcasting views or opinions which nearly certainly will cause a real injury to public order. By this authority the Broadcasting Authority should examine each view and opinion and decide whether the said test has been fulfilled. The decision in this matter cannot be sweeping and general, but must be anchored in the circumstances of each case. Indeed, beside the authority to limit freedom of speech in certain cases, there is the lack of freedom to limit it in all cases (*see* Shamgar P, in *Neiman* [1] at 266). My colleague Bach J noted this in *Zichroni* ([25] at 781), where he criticized 'a sweeping decision to ban radio and T.V. interviews with a certain class of people absolutely, whatever the topic'. My esteemed colleague quoted approvingly Brennan J's words in *Columbia Broadcasting System, Inc.* v. *Democratic National Committee* [32] at 196: '[I]n the light of the current dominance of the electronic media as the most effective means of reaching the public, any policy that *absolutely* denies citizens access to the airways necessarily renders even the concept of "full and free discussion" practically meaningless' And on page 202, 'the issue in these cases is not whether there is an *absolute* right to access but, rather, whether there may be an *absolute* denial of such access. The difference is, of course, crucial' (emphasis added by Bach J in *Zichroni* [25]).

Of course, in the matter before us, the Broadcasting Authority does not absolutely bar its doors before the petitioners, because it does broadcast matters pertaining to them that are clearly newsworthy. But as regards the petitioners' views and opinions, in so far as they are not clearly newsworthy, its doors are totally barred before the petitioners. Such a total bar does not fit the near certainty test, which requires a case by case examination of every speech. The decision to broadcast or refrain from broadcasting the petitioners' views and opinions, just like those of others, must be made *ad hoc*, through examining the question whether a near certainty exists of real damage to the public order if a given opinion is broadcast at a given time. This may require the Broadcasting Authority to tape the speech beforehand, and decide after it has been recorded. We have been told that this technique is common at the Broadcasting Authority and does not pose special difficulties. As noted, the 'news forum' decided, *inter alia*, to 'film and tape everything' (*see* Section 2 above).

## *Judicial Review*

42. * * *
43. * * *
44. * * *
45. * * *

## *From the General to the Particular*

46. The legality of the respondents' decision in the case before us should be examined in light of the general principles I have noted above. The necessary conclusion is that the respondents erred in interpreting the law and formed a mistaken test; therefore, their decision is illegal and must be overruled. The Broadcasting Authority believed that the content of the petitioners' views is enough to prevent broadcasting them in any context except news. This view is erroneous. The Broadcasting Authority must broadcast the petitioners' political views and opinions not only as news, but also in programmes devoted to views and opinions prevalent in the public, just as they do the views and opinions of other political parties. The argument between the parties whether the Broadcasting Authority 'boycotted' the petitioners is just semantic, because the Broadcasting Authority must broadcast not only newsworthy items concerning the petitioners, who are a political and parliamentary party, but also matters pertaining to their views and opinions which are not newsworthy.

In meeting this [obligation], the Broadcasting Authority must be fair, reasonable, and equitable. It must determine criteria that enable it to broadcast views and opinions of the various political sections of Israeli society within the time allotted to it. But the Broadcasting Authority may refrain from broadcasting the petitioners' opinions and views if in its opinion broadcasting them creates a near certainty of a real injury to public order. As we have said, this consideration of the impact of the petitioners' words on public order was never taken into account by the Broadcasting Authority. We repeatedly asked the Broadcasting Authority's attorney if its position is based on the view that broadcasting the petitioners' opinions creates such a near certainty. The answer was that this was not taken into account. The Broadcasting Authority erred in acting thus. It must consider this question. As we have seen, such consideration must be *ad hoc* on the basis of the special circumstances of each case. Not the 'bad tendency' of the petitioners' views and opinions, but the near certainty of real injury caused by them, can justify not broadcasting them over the public airwaves.

47. Before I conclude, I want to stress again that my legal approach, according to which the petitioners' views and opinions must be broadcast,

as long as there is no near certainty of a real injury to the public order, is not based upon agreement with those views and opinions. I am not interested in the substance of the petitioners' views, but in their right to express them even if I find them unacceptable. Regarding a playwright's right to have his play performed, I noted that my approach is entirely based on the playwright's freedom of speech, and not on the play's artistic merit (HC 14/84, *supra*). The same applies in this case. The views and opinions of the petitioners make me shudder, but I insist upon their right to express them. In this approach there is no approval of their views. I consider them unacceptable, but my approach validates their right to express such unacceptable views as long as there is no injury to public order. Democracy is tested according to a speaker's freedom of speech, not by the value of his words. Moreover, my approach is not based on a view that the petitioners' views and opinions do not entail a near certainty of real danger to public order. As I have noted, this question was not considered by the Broadcasting Authority, and so I have not addressed it.

The result is that we make the temporary order absolute, so that the Broadcasting Authority's decision as to broadcasting the petitioners' views and opinions should be to broadcast, just as those of other political parties on a basis of equality, unless the Broadcasting Authority believes in each concrete instance that the broadcast creates a near certainty of real injury to public order; that is, to the democratic structure, the security and existence of the public, and the feelings of the public or parts of it.

The respondents will pay the petitioners' expenses in the total sum of 3,000 NIS, bearing interest and index-linked to the date it is paid.

**Bach J:**

1. I agree with my esteemed colleague Barak J that the decision of the Executive Committee of the Broadcasting Authority regarding the petitioners cannot stand, and that the temporary order should therefore be made absolute. Nevertheless, I must dissent from part of the reasoning of my esteemed colleague relating to important points of principle, which may have real operative impact on the meaning of the order we are giving.

2. It seems to me, that to clarify my position I should first list the points in which I agree with my esteemed colleague:

(a) I agree that freedom of speech and expression are a supreme value in a democracy and an utmost effort should be made to preserve them.
(b) The principle of freedom of expression is tested not when conventional and widely accepted views are expressed, but rather when we are dealing with deviant views, which many people, or even the majority, consider aggravating, disturbing, disgusting, and antagonizing. A really strong democracy must ensure that the confrontation with such opinion is not through banning their spread from above, but through

open and free debate through which each individual in the society can form his own view.

(c) Notwithstanding the importance of this superior principle, sometimes another public interest prevails over it, and then freedom of expression is curtailed, usually by statutory fiat. That is the situation regarding obscenity, libel, revealing state secrets, and publications that may affect ongoing trials.

(d) Among the grounds on which freedom of expression may be limited is the danger of disturbing the public order by publication, and I agree with my esteemed colleague Barak J that in this case publication should be prevented only when a 'nearly certain danger' exists for such a danger to materialize. I also agree with my colleague that 'injury to the public order' includes real injury to the feelings of the public or part of it.

(e) The mass media, radio, and TV are of particular importance for a man or organization that intends to bring its political and social views before the public and try to convince them of their justice. Therefore any order that prevents or limits in sweeping fashion the access of a person or class of persons to those media is a severe injury, and without special justification it is illegitimate discrimination. I have explained my view on this topic in my opinion in *Zichroni* [25], parts of which were quoted by my colleague Barak J in his opinion.

(f) Therefore, I agree that the respondent's order, according to which only 'clearly newsworthy' words of the petitioners are to be broadcast, is invalid and should not be maintained. Public figures, including politicians, often say things that are merely 'newsworthy' and not 'clearly newsworthy', yet their words are broadcast. Representatives of various views in social and political matters, especially those who hold extreme and deviant views, are invited to participate in debates and symposia in the media. Excluding the petitioners *a priori* from such debates without even considering the topic is undue discrimination, especially regarding the representative of a political party which this Court allowed to participate in the elections to the Knesset, and whose candidate was elected to it.

3. But we differ on the topic to which my colleague devoted a substantial part of his opinion, regarding publication and speech that constitute incitement to hatred among different sections of the public based on their race, ethnic or national origin. Because of the views expressed consistently and regularly by the petitioners, and in view of the respondent's argument in which he tried to justify the decision of the Executive Committee (respondent No 1), it is clear that this topic is not merely theoretical, but relates to the main cause and reason for the respondents to adopt this directive which is the subject of this appeal.

Therefore, my colleague did well explicitly to clarify his view on this topic as well. It can be summarized in the following sentence from his opinion: 'Deviant speech—that is annoying and irritating speech, spreading hatred and anger, based on racial or ethnic/national origin—is included in the scope of the principle of freedom of speech.' In my colleague's view, even when the words of respondent No 1 include clear racist incitement, and even if the respondents believe in good faith that publication constitutes a criminal offence, the public media, TV and radio *must* broadcast them. Those responsible can refrain from broadcasting only when a 'near certainty of a real injury to the public order' exists because of the publication. My esteemed colleague further adds that in 'marginal cases freedom of speech must not be limited'. I shall try to explain below why I cannot join my esteemed colleague's position on this point.

4. I do not believe that in the State of Israel, in light of our people's tragic and traumatic experience, I have to explain the destructive nature of incitement to racist hatred. There is no verbal behaviour more potent than such incitement, whose negative side effects include a call for violence, an appeal to the basest and most despicable instincts of mankind, and the degradation of those parts of the populace against whom the incitement is levelled.

Therefore, if there are topics on which freedom of expression should be limited through regard for a superior public interest, is it not necessary to include the interest in preventing the inflammation of hatred and anger on racial and ethnic grounds? Is this interest any less valuable than the prevention of libel? Would we force the Broadcasting Authority to broadcast a libelous report which it does not wish to air for that very reason? I accept David Kretzmer's words in his article 'Freedom of Speech and Racism', 8 *Cardozo Law Review* 445, 447 (1987): 'Among the values of a democratic regime is "recognition of the inherent dignity and of the equal and inalienable rights of all members of the human family"' (the quotation is from the preamble to the United Nations Universal Declaration of Human Rights, GA Res. 217, UN Doc. A/810, 71 (1949)—GB). Racist speech is not merely speech which advocates abrogation of this recognition: it is speech which in itself is an affront to the inherent dignity of man. It is not clear why speech must be allowed in a democracy when it clashes with this basic value.

5. Moreover, my esteemed colleague rightly notes that an 'injury to the public order' can be an injury to the feelings of the public or of part of it. His opinion states, *inter alia*:

> As we have said, the near certainty of a real injury is to the public order. That term is not limited to security or the prevention of violence. It includes also, *inter alia*, preserving human dignity and the public's feelings, either of the majority or of a minority. . . . If a broadcast over radio or T.V. entails a near certainty of a real

injury to the feelings of the whole public or of part of it, such a broadcast may be prevented.

It should be asked: can racist incitement somehow *not injure* the feelings of the public, or at least that part of the public, it is levelled at? And that not just with *'near certainty'*, which would be enough to ban it, but with *absolute certainty*? Therefore, it seems to me that including publication of racist incitement in the list of topics protected by the principle of freedom of expression is unjustified and artificial.

6. But my esteemed colleague Barak J goes further and holds that his view does not change despite his awareness that such a broadcast may constitute a criminal offence. Publishing words that may engender hatred and anger among different parts of the populace is, and *was* when the decision on which this appeal is based was taken, a criminal offence of 'incitement to rebellion' according to sections 134(a) and 136(b) of the Penal Act, 1977, henceforward the 'Penal Act'. Moreover such action is a crime of 'libel on a group of people or part of the public' according to section 4 of the Libel Act, 1965. According to section 1 of the same Act, libel is, *inter alia*, what may 'humiliate a person or render him an object of hatred, division or spite', or 'shame a person because of his origin or religion'. In the meantime the legislature found it necessary to strengthen the public's awareness of this problem and added to the Penal Act, in Penal Act Amendment No 20 1986, [including] sections 144(a) and 144(b) (quoted in Barak J's opinion), which makes publishing something with an intention to incite to racism a crime punishable by five years' imprisonment. And the term 'racism' is defined broadly, to include 'persecution, humiliation, derogation, manifestation of hatred, enmity or violence, or arousing anger towards the public or parts of it, based on color or racist or ethnic/national origin'.

My esteemed colleague believes that not only does the criminality of publication not *require* the Broadcasting Authority to prevent it, but it *must* publish despite the criminality, unless a nearly certain danger exists of a real injury to public order. My colleague writes, 'when no such near certainty exists and the ban is laid on the speech itself without considering its results, no such prior restraint is justifiable'. Therefore, in such a case the Broadcasting Authority must broadcast, and afterward criminal prosecution can be directed at the person who delivers the racist message.

7. With all due respect, I dissent from my colleague's reasoning on this point, on several grounds:

(a) My esteemed colleague agrees that the Broadcasting Authority is not obliged to broadcast when in doing so it commits a crime itself, but he is willing to assume that the Broadcasting Authority is not liable if it broadcasts a report knowing that it contains criminally racist material. My colleague mentions section 11(c)(a) of the Penal Act, which states 'The publication of a fair and true report of an act mentioned in section 144(b) shall not violate that section, as long as there was no intention to lead to racism.' I do not believe that this subsection protects the Broadcasting Authority effectively. It may prevent prosecution only when it objectively and fairly reports events such as a speech in the Knesset or a demonstration. But when a report prepared by the radio or TV is broadcast, not live so that the editors have no control, then section 144(c)(a) cannot protect the Broadcasting Authority when it knows that the report includes 'racist' speech intended to lead to racism. In making such a broadcast possible, the Broadcasting Authority makes itself an accomplice. This Court should not force the Broadcasting Authority to put itself in this position.

(b) My esteemed colleague relies on opinions, both here and in the United States, according to which the court will prevent broadcasts, or an authorized body limit freedom of speech, only in extreme cases when a real danger to public order will ensue from publication. But in my opinion, one should distinguish cases in which a man was forbidden by a government body or a court to publish what he wants, and this case, in which the court is asked to *force* the Broadcasting Authority to publish what it does *not* desire to broadcast. This does not apply to public advertisement, or election propaganda, where the Broadcasting Authority is only a *technical tool*, through which they are published. But when an interview with the petitioner is broadcast on the news, or a symposium in which the petitioner participates and voices his views is aired, the broadcast is not just an advertisement of the petitioner, but *a publication of the Broadcasting Authority itself.* Therefore the Court should be careful before it *orders* the Broadcasting Authority to broadcast against its will, when such a refusal stems from a feeling that publication is a criminal offence, even if the *Court* would not have *forbidden* publication had the Broadcasting Authority desired it.

(c) Israeli case law on which my colleague relies, does not in my view support his far-reaching thesis on the point. When it was said in *Kol Ha'am* that 'only when the publication under the circumstances creates at least *near* certainty of actions endangering the public peace is there a place for government intervention to suppress the publication or prevent its recurrence' ([9] at 888), the reference was to words whose publication was not explicitly banned in a specific section of Criminal Law. The words of Shamgar P in *Shiran* [16] and *Neiman* [1], quoted by my esteemed colleague, seem to me to indicate clearly that a sharp distinction should be made between ordinary deeds that are in themselves not illegal, but that can be banned because of the danger they pose to the public order, and deeds that violated the criminal law. Let us quote these words again. In *Shiran* [16] it was said:

For this court to *forbid* someone who is responsible for broadcasts to publish a given program, there must exist extreme circumstances from which a tangible and nearly certain danger arises to the peace of the public at large (*Kol Ha'am* [9]) *or another kind of clear and patent illegality*.

Ben-Porat DP likewise affirmed this point in *Milan* [28] at 680. In *Neiman* [1], [Shamgar P] held: 'One does not deny a liberty prospectively except in the context of a near and inevitable certainty *of the commission of a crime or an injury to security or the public peace*' (emphasis mine, GB). My colleague indeed states that one should understand these words in context, but in my view these holdings are self-explanatory, and indicate that one may ban broadcasts that violate the criminal law even if no near certainty of an injury to public order exists.

(d) Nor does it seem to me that the American precedents mentioned in my esteemed colleague's opinion can lead us in the direction he suggests. In *New York Times Co.* v. *United States* [38], the Supreme Court struck down a government decision to ban publication of a classified historical study regarding American policy in Vietnam. The Solicitor General could find no legal basis of such a ban and it was therefore declared illegal. In *Southeastern Promotions* v. *Conrad* [39], the Court decided that there was no legal basis to ban a musical because it alleged immorality, without legal authority. In the well-known case of *Near* v. *Minnesota* [40], the Supreme Court struck down a decision based on Minnesota law banning publication of a newspaper because it 'is a malicious, scandalous or defamatory newspaper, as defined by law'. Under the circumstances the Court believed that to ban future publication is unjustified prior restraint. That case fits in particular the words of the Court in *Southeastern Ltd* v. *Conrad* [39], quoted by my colleague Barak J, that 'it is always difficult to know in advance what an individual will say'. Needless to say, all American precedents should be understood against the background of the First Amendment, which states 'Congress shall make no law . . . abridging the freedom of speech or of the press.'

In my opinion, one should not apply these decisions to the case at bar, which deals with the right of public authorities to prevent broadcasts of specific programs banned by an explicit law. My colleague Barak J rightly noted that such broadcasts do not have to be live ones, and are usually prerecorded and can be checked before broadcasting. If the Broadcasting Authority decides not to air a specific programme because it contains criminally 'racist' words, this is different from closing down a newspaper or limiting freedom of speech prospectively without legal grounds and against a constitutional mandate.

(e) My esteemed colleague says: 'in allowing racist speech, freedom, democratic society and the court do not legitimize it', and finds support in Professor Gabizan's article, which says *inter alia*: 'in our tradition there is no direct passage from saying that certain speech is not illegal, or a certain act to ban it is illegal, and substantive support for such speech'. I agree with Professor Gabizon, that there is no *support* or *affirmation* of such ideas in such freedom of speech or in forcing the public media to air them, but I am afraid that this does give them *legitimacy*, and weakens the criminal statute forbidding such publications.

(f) My colleague writes further: 'a tort or breach of contract are also forbidden. Why should the Broadcasting Authority not be allowed to ban such publication either?' I would not suggest forcing the Broadcasting Authority to air a programme that will cause a tort action against it or breach a valid contract. The Broadcasting Authority has often been sued at tort for libel, included in a programme it had broadcast, and I see no harm in the Broadcasting Authority deciding not to publish tortious words; *a fortiori* criminal ones.

(g) My colleague Barak J stresses that as long as no court had held that a given broadcast includes racist speech, we cannot be sure that the speech is criminal. He raises the question whether 'the Broadcasting Authority should be authorized to prevent a speech prospectively on the basis of a suspicion of a crime', and adds, 'the central position of the principle of freedom of speech in our legal system must lead to a negative response to this question'. I find it difficult to agree.

It is true that only courts, and not the Broadcasting Authority or another authority, can establish with certainty that a given publication constitutes a criminal offence. But as we have noted above, and as Barak J says, we are not concerned with live broadcasts but with prerecorded programmes that might be checked afterwards. If the petitioner believes that banning a given programme was mistaken or in bad faith, the doors of this Court are open to him. And if after examination, it is decided that the programme does not include racist speech as defined by law, and that the Broadcasting Authority's decision was clearly erroneous or in bad faith, with the claim of criminal racism only an excuse for the desire to limit the petitioners' freedom of speech, we shall not hesitate to overrule it. But the possibility that the Broadcasting Authority be mistaken in a given case is not enough to deny it the right to refuse to air a programme whose publication is a criminal offence.

(h) When the Broadcasting Authority people say 'we refuse to broadcast in the public media a given programme, first because it includes racist incitement, which we find objectionable (and needless to mention, there is no difference between anti-semitic programmes and other racist programmes), and second because we believe publication would be a crime and we are unwilling to be accomplices to it', it seems to me unacceptable for us as the High Court of Justice to come and order them to broadcast the programme, [especially] if we do not disagree with their belief that the publication is racist as defined in the Penal Act.

9. To sum up my position:

(a) Racist or national/ethnic incitement injures the feelings of most of the public, and necessarily injures deeply the feelings of those against whom it is levelled, and publishing them injures the public order; in any case there is undoubtedly a near certainty that publication will lead to such a result. Because of this alone, the respondents may refrain from publishing programs with such content or meaning.

(b) Additionally and alternatively, if we theoretically assume that there may be cases in which racist incitement does not create a near certain danger of injury to public order, the Broadcasting Authority may refrain from broadcasting them when it reasonably and in good faith believes that publication constitutes a criminal offence and not an objective news report protected by section 144(c) of the Penal Act.

(c) Nevertheless, the sweeping decision of the Broadcasting Authority is an unjustified limitation of the petitioners' right to voice their views on the public media and discriminate against them by comparison with other political bodies. There are many topics of public interest, regarding which there is no fear of speech constituting a criminal offence, or a near certainty of injury to public order, and the petitioners may not be denied the right to participate in such broadcasts. Even regarding 'sensitive' topics one should not ban the words of the petitioner and its representatives beforehand, and in those rare cases in which a live interview must be held, one cannot ban it prospectively because of the fear that racist words *may* be uttered. But one must in my opinion allow the Broadcasting Authority to check each recorded programme and prevent its broadcast under the circumstances noted in sections (a) and (b) above.

Therefore, and subject to what has been said above, I agree to make the temporary order absolute.

**NETANYAHU J:**

I agree that the temporary order should be made absolute.

I do not express an opinion on the question if in publishing racist speech of the petitioner, the respondents violated section 144(b) of the Penal Act. My agreement to make the order absolute does not of course intend to force the respondents to commit a crime.

Decided according to the judgment of Barak J.

Judgment given 27 July 1987.

# 6

# *Meir Schnitzer and Others*
# v.
# *The Chief Military Censor and Others*

[H.C. 680/88]
[42(4) P.D. 617 (1988)]

*Barak J, Maltz J, and Wallenstein J*

Israeli cases referred to:

[1] HC 5/48—*Leon* v. *The Acting Supervisor of the Tel Aviv Municipal Area*; 1 PD 58.
[2] HC 222/68—*Nationalist Groups, A Registered Association* v. *The Minister of the Police*; 24(2) PD 141.
[3] HC 107/52—*Assad* v. *The Chief of Staff of the Armed Forces*; 6 PD 339.
[4] FH 29/84—*Kossoi* v. *Feuchtwanger Bank*; 38(4) PD 505.
[5] Cr.A 667/83—*Borochov* v. *Yeffet*; 39(3) PD 205.
[6] HC 953/87—*Poraz* v. *The Mayor of Tel Aviv-Jaffa*; 42(2) PD 309.
[7] HC 58/68—*Shalit* v. *The Minister of the Interior*; 23(2) PD 477.
[8] CA 165/82—*Kibbutz Hazor* v. *Rehovot Revenue Agent*; 39(2) PD 70.
[9] EA 2/84—*Neiman* v. *The Chairman of the Elections Committee for the Eleventh Knesset*; 39(2) PD 225.
[10] CA 65/57—*Haetzni* v. *Ben Gurion*; 11 PD 403.
[11] CA 81/55—*Kochavi* v. *Baker*; 11 PD 225.
[12] Cr.A 108/66—*'Dan' Cooperative for Public Transportation Ltd* v. *The Attorney General*; 20(4) PD 253.
[13] HC 262/62—*Peretz* v. *The Kfar Shmaryahu Local Council*; 16 PD 2101.
[14] HC 301/63—*Shetreet* v. *The Chief Rabbi of Israel*; 18 PD 598.
[15] HC 243/62—*Israel Movie Studios Ltd* v. *Grey*; 16 PD 2407.
[16] HC 39/64—*El-Ard Company Ltd* v. *The Supervisor of the Northern Region, Nazareth*; 18 PD 340.
[17] Cr.A 126/62—*Dissenchik* v. *The Attorney General*; 17 PD 169.
[18] Cr.A 696/80—*Azulai* v. *The State of Israel*; 37(2) PD 565.
[19] HC 448/85—*Daher* v. *The Minister of the Interior*; 40(2) PD 701.

[20] HC 399/85—*Kahane* v. *Broadcasting Authority*; 41(3) PD 255.
[21] Cr.A 255/68—*The State of Israel* v. *Ben Moshe*; 22(2) PD 427.
[22] HC 372/84—*Klopper-Naveh* v. *The Minister of Education and Culture*; 38(3) PD 233.
[23] HC 73/53—*Kol Ha'am Company Ltd* v. *The Minister of the Interior*; 7 PD 871.
[24] CA 723/74—*'Ha'aretz' Newspaper Publication Ltd* v. *The Israel Electric Company Ltd*; 31(2) PD 281.
[25] HC 14/86—*Leor* v. *The Council for Review of Movies and Plays*; 41(1) PD 421.
[26] HC 562/86—*Al-Hatib* v. *The Ministry of the Interior*; 40(3) PD 657.
[27] HC 343/82—*Zichroni* v. *The Broadcasting Authority*; 37(1) PD 757.
[28] Cr.A 495/69—*Omer* v. *The State of Israel*; 24(1) PD 408.

American cases referred to:
[29] *New York Times Co.* v. *United States*, 403 US 713 (1971).
[30] *Near* v. *Minnesota*, 283 US 697 (1931).

[*This case addresses the power of the Military Censor to prohibit publication of information concerning Israel's foreign security service, known as the 'Mossad'. The General Security Service (the GSS or the 'Shabak') is Israel's internal security service, comparable to the American FBI while the Mossad is comparable to the American CIA.*]

## JUDGMENT

**BARAK J:**

What is the power of the 'Military Censor', operating in accordance with the Defence (Emergency) Regulations 1945, to prohibit publication of a newspaper article which is critical of the role of the Chief of the Institute for Intelligence and Special Operations ('Mossad'), and which contains information related to forthcoming changes in the leadership of the Mossad? This is the question that stands at the centre of the petition before us.

### *The Petition*

1. Mr Schnitzer (the first petitioner) is the editor of *The City* (the third petitioner), a weekly newspaper in Tel-Aviv. Aluf Ben (the second petitioner) is a journalist employed by this newspaper. Mr Ben prepared an article dealing with anticipated changes in the leadership of the Mossad. The article was submitted to the Chief Military Censor (the first respondent) and

was prohibited by him on 3 August, 1988. The reason given for the prohibition was that publication of the article would be prejudicial to the security of the State. A few days later, on 11 August, 1988, the Editor submitted to the Censor an alternative version of the article. This new version was also prohibited, and again the reason given concerned the security of the State. The Censor approached the newspaper requesting a revised article and this was submitted to him on 14 August 1988. This version was not authorized for publication (15 August 1988), on the ground that individuals were identified by name. A few days later, on 23 August 1988, the article was submitted to the Censor in its final form. He allowed the article for publication, with the exception of thirty-two items, which were prohibited. It is against this decision that the appeal before us is directed.

2. The items banned from publication deal with three subjects; first, a profile of the Chief of the Mossad. In the opinion of the Censor, these items are not to be published because they are liable to lead to his identification and thus endanger his personal safety. Secondly, criticism of the activity of the Chief of the Mossad, casting aspersions on his efficiency. In the opinion of the Censor, criticism of the Chief of the Mossad is prejudicial to the operational capability of the Mossad, at all its levels. In particular, it was noted that the matter would be prejudicial to State security, in regard to relationships both with parallel organizations in other States and with operators in the field. Thirdly, the timing of the replacement of the Chief of the Mossad. The position of the Censor is that the reporting of information regarding the anticipated departure of the present Chief of the Mossad is forbidden, because certain interested parties are liable to focus an intolerable degree of attention on the man, his movements, and his activities, and make full use of this knowledge to expose the identity of the Chief of the Mossad, especially outside Israel. In the opinion of the Censor, this constitutes a real danger to the safety of the Chief of the Mossad.

3. Mr. Liblik, the petitioners' representative, agreed that all items in the article dealing with a profile of the Chief of the Mossad should be excised, and this issue is no longer in contention before us. On the other hand, he considers that the other two subjects—criticism of the Chief of the Mossad and the date of his replacement—are suitable for publication and prohibition of them is unlawful. Mr Liblik stresses the importance of freedom of expression and the public's right to know in a democratic society. In his opinion, the Censor is entitled to prohibit publication of an article only when there exists a near certainty of prejudice to State security, and even then he must act reasonably. In the view of Mr. Liblik, publication of criticism of the Chief of the Mossad and of the date of his replacement does not constitute a near certainty of prejudice to State security, and prohibition is therefore unreasonable.

In his presentation to us, Mr Liblik stressed the public importance of the function of the Chief of the Mossad—especially since the Yom Kippur War—and the vital need that the most suitable person be chosen for this post. Hence, it is the duty of the petitioners to warn and to remind those responsible that the appointment of the new Chief of the Mossad should be considered in a responsible manner, and that the choice should not be influenced by politics, by inter-party rivalry, or by an attempt to find a compromise which will lead to the appointment of a mediocre candidate. Mr Liblik stressed the point that the petitioners mention no names in the article, and make no recommendation of candidates. They seek only to underline the obligation to appoint the most suitable people, in such a way that the derelictions of the past are not repeated.

Mr Liblik agrees that the activity of the intelligence services needs to be secret and protected from publicity, but there is no justification, in his view, for preventing publication of criticism of the Chief of the Mossad. Public criticism is in fact likely to lead to greater caution on the part of the Chief of the Mossad. Finally, Mr Liblik noted that the report of the anticipated appointment of a new Chief of the General Security Service was approved for publication and there is no basis for distinguishing between the Chief of the Service and the Chief of the Mossad. He also drew attention to an article published in September 1987 and approved for publication by the respondent, which spoke of increasing unrest in the Mossad with regard to the appointment of the next Chief of the Mossad. Mr Liblik also notes that the Military Censor has not prohibited published criticism of the Chief of the General Security Service, of the Chief of Army Intelligence, and of the Chief of the General Staff. In his opinion, there should be one law regarding public criticism applicable to the chiefs of all the security organizations.

4. In her reply, Ms Arad, on behalf of the respondents, stressed that the Military Censor accepts the need to respect the right of expression and freedom of expression, which are among the fundamental principles of our system. This is the guiding premise in his deliberations. Furthermore, the Military Censor accepts that he is authorized to prohibit a report only when there exists a near certainty that publication of the report will be prejudicial to State security. [However, Ms Arad submits that] publication of criticism of the Chief of the Mossad and publication of the date of his replacement constitute near certainty of prejudice to security, and it is therefore reasonable to prevent publication of this information.

The reasons given by the Military Censor for prohibiting criticism of the Chief of the Mossad and the ban on revealing the fact of his replacement have already been noted. Ms Arad [added] that the Military Censor did not prohibit the sections which criticize the Mossad and its activities in general. The prohibition applies [solely] to criticism of the outgoing Chief of the Mossad. The reason is, as mentioned above, that as long as the Chief of the Mossad continues in office, close attention to his role is liable to prejudice State security. In her submission, criticism of the Chief of the Mossad is not the same as criticism of the chiefs of the other security organizations, because of the special nature of the operations of the Mossad. Thus, for example, according to existing practice, information is released on behalf of the Government regarding the appointment of a new Chief of the Mossad. Once the new appointment had been made it is permitted, for the first time, to publish the identity of the previous Chief. This practice does not exist with regard to the chiefs of the other security organizations. Ms Arad added and stressed that the appointment of the Chief of the Mossad is already subject to public scrutiny. The Chief of the Mossad is appointed by the Prime Minister. Scrutiny of the Chief of the Mossad is in the hands of the Prime Minister, the Government, the Foreign Affairs and Security Committee of the Knesset, the Knesset, and the State Comptroller.

5. As this case has progressed, the area of contention between the parties has narrowed. Of the thirty-two items prohibited by the Military Censor, the ban on eight of them has been lifted. The petitioners themselves have agreed, on their own initiative, to waive six of the items prohibited by the Censor. It thus emerges that the area of disagreement relates to eighteen items, which are all concerned with criticism of the alleged misconduct of the outgoing Chief of the Mossad and with his imminent replacement. The question with which we are faced is, therefore, whether the position of the Military Censor in these matters is lawful.

## *The Normative Framework*

6. 'Military censorship' exists under the provisions of the Defence (Emergency) Regulations 1945 (hereinafter, 'Defence Regulations'). Section 8 of the Defence Regulations concerns censorship. Regulation 87(1) states:

> The censor may by order prohibit generally or in particular the publishing of matters the publishing of which, in his opinion, would be, or be likely to be or become, prejudicial to the defence of Palestine or to the public safety or to public order.

The censor is entitled to demand presentation of material for censorship before publication (Regulation 97). The publication of prohibited material constitutes an offence against the Defence Regulations. The censor was [originally] appointed by the High Commissioner. This authority now belongs to the Minister of Defence. The censor is a military officer, and the exercise of censorship in accordance with Section 8 of the Defence Regulations is performed in a military framework—hence his title 'Military Censor'.

It should be noted that, in practice, the authority of the Military Censor is not applied to those newspapers which are parties to the agreement between the Editors' Committee and the Minister of Defence (for the agreement and its application, see Chafets, 'Press and Government in Israel', 14 *Isr. YB on HR* 134 (1984); Lahav, *Press Law in Modern Democracies* (1985) 265, 275). The petitioner newspaper is not a member of the Editors' Committee and is not a party to the agreement with the Minister of Defence, and therefore the legality of the conduct of the Military Censor is to be tested directly according to the Defence Regulations, without any reference to the agreement with the Editors' Committee.

7. The provisions of the Defence Regulations regarding censorship raise, in connection with the petition before us, four questions: first, in what circumstances of prejudice to the defence of the State, public safety, or public order is the Military Censor entitled to forbid publication? Secondly, what are the restrictions imposed on the deliberation of the Military Censor? Thirdly, what is the scope of judicial review over decisions of the Military Censor? Fourthly, does the decision of the Censor in the matter before us pass the appropriate tests, and is there a case for our intervention in his decision? These questions will be addressed in turn.

## *The First Question: The Circumstances Justifying Prohibition of Publication*

8. The Defence Regulations were instituted by the High Commissioner by virtue of the authority vested in him by Article 6 of the Orders in Council for Palestine (Defence) 1937. These Regulations are therefore an article of Mandatory legislation. . . . Under Article 11 of the Law and Administration Ordinance of 1948, they became a part of Israeli law. This transference from Mandatory to Israeli legislation is not merely technical, but also entails a change of content. Thus, Article 11 of the Ordinance states that the law which existed in the country on 14 May 1948 will remain in force 'subject to the changes emanating from the establishment of the State and its rights'. Initially this Court took the view that these changes were solely of a technical nature (*Leon* v. *The Acting Supervisor of the Tel Aviv Municipal Area* [1], at 69). However, it was later determined that the 'changes' are not solely of a technical nature, but of a substantive nature (*Nationalist Groups* v. *The Minister of the Police* [2]). Zilberg J insisted on this point in *Nationalist Groups* at 157–8, commenting as follows on the technical approach adopted in *Leon*:

> With the greatest of respect to the learned judges, I am not entirely convinced of the validity of the formal interpretation given to these words on that occasion. I consider that there would be *capitis diminutio* (devaluation) of the prodigious

historical event of the creation of the Jewish State in the Land of Israel if we were to say that the judicial change we are faced with, after two thousand years of exile, with the establishment of our independent State, is of the order, for example, of the change of frontiers made in the year 1948, when it became necessary to drop the Allenby Bridge from the list of 'legal' points of entry to the country, published in 1943. . . . I admit without shame that I am incapable of grasping this concept. My heart is with those 'maximalist' dreamers of national independence: deliverance, the Third Temple, the renewal of national life. And if this is the reality of independence, is it not possible, in principle, to examine the cogency of every Mandatory law and to see if it accords with the vibrant spirit of the laws of our free and independent State?

Indeed, in place of colonial administration there came national independence. In place of autocratic rule came a democratic system, which is government of the people, based on representative government, operating according to the view of the majority, and guaranteeing human rights. This change, by its very nature, has brought with it a new perception of the law and the legal system. The effects of this change vary with the circumstances. Sometimes the change is solely technical (see *Assad* v. *Chief of Staff* [3]). However, the change is sometimes of a more substantive nature, and thus an article of Mandatory legislation may not become a part of Israeli law (see *Nationalist Groups* [2]). This would happen only on rare occasions, and has been ever rarer with the passage of time (see *Nationalist Groups* [2] at 209).

9. One of the 'changes emanating from the establishment of the State and its powers' consists in the approach to interpreting articles of Mandatory legislation.

The conclusion to Article 11 emphasizes the essential fact that national independence also brings in its wake changes in the domain of law and its interpretation. The more urgent the matter, the more legitimate is the basis for independent interpretation of the law and independent realisation of the theoretical change' (Shamgar J in *Kossoi* v. *Feuchtwanger Bank* [4], at 511).

This change in the interpretation of Mandatory legislation is twofold: first, articles of Mandatory legislation will not be interpreted according to the rules of interpretation practised in the period of the Mandate. Rather, they will be interpreted according to the rules of interpretation practised in the State of Israel; secondly, an article of legislation is to be interpreted on the basis of the fundamental principles of our legal system. (See *Borochov* v. *Yeffet* [5]; *Poraz* v. *Mayor of Tel Aviv* [6].) Thus, articles of Mandatory legislation will not be interpreted on the basis of the fundamental principles of the legal system as practised in the period of the Mandate. Instead, Articles of Mandatory legislation will be interpreted on the basis of the fundamental principles of the legal system practised in Israel.

* * *

A legal norm—whether enacted or theoretical—is not a creature existing independently. A legal norm is 'a creature living in its environment' (Sussman J in *Shalit* v. *Minister of the Interior* [7], at 513). It is involved in its environment, influencing it and being influenced by it. The 'judicial environment' which influences every legal norm

> includes not only close legal connections but also broader circles of accepted principles, fundamental aims and criteria which emerge, in the words of Justice Landau, from 'the social consciousness of the people among whom the judges live'. . . . These principles do not need to be reiterated in regard to every single law, but they constitute a kind of 'normative umbrella' covering all articles of legislation. (*Kibbutz Hazor* v. *Rehovot Revenue Agent* [8] at 75.)

Furthermore:

> An act of legislation. . . is not a unique act divorced from general experience. The law takes on skin and sinew in the context of a given political and judicial system. It constitutes one brick of the overall structure, which is founded on the basis of the precepts of government and law which constitute the fundamental axioms of that society. (*Neiman* v. *Chairman of the Knesset Election Committee* [9], at 37.)

Thus, a normative legal principle which constituted a part of Mandatory law is accepted into our law if it does not 'deviate from the fundamental principles of the legal structure of our State' (Landau J in *Haetzni* v. *Ben Gurion* [10], at 409), and it continues to be operative in Israeli law, on the basis of the fundamental principles of Israeli law. [But] its form is determined by its new environment. (Compare *Kochavi* v. *Baker* [11], at 236). This rule applies to any enacted norm which constituted a part of the Mandatory judicial system. This norm is accepted into our law, and if it accords with the basic principles of our legal structure, it continues to be operative in Israeli law, on the basis on the fundamental principles of Israeli law. Hence the aspiration towards 'legislative harmony' (in the words of Sussman J in *'Dan' Cooperative for Public Transportation Ltd* v. *The Attorney General* [12], at 261). The various articles of legislation—those whose historical origin is Mandatory and those that are the product of our independent legislature—need to be combined to work in a comprehensive system. (*Poraz* [6], at 328.)

The nature of the fundamental principles can be learned from various sources. One of the most important of these is the Declaration of Independence, 'which constitutes a legal norm expressing the revealed values of the nation' (*Poraz* [6], at 330). This point was reinforced by Sussman J, who said of the Declaration of Independence:

> The way of life of the citizens of the State is determined by it, and its principles should be taken by every power in the State as its guiding light. (*Peretz* v. *The Kfar Shmaryahu Local Council*, [13] at 2116.)

The Declaration of Independence is not the only source from which one may learn of the fundamental values of the State. Thus, for example, the Supreme Court sometimes has recourse to 'basic principles of equality, freedom and justice, which are the property of all developed and enlightened nations' (H. Cohn J in *Shetreet* v. *The Chief Rabbi of Israel* [14], at 612) and to 'basic rights which are unwritten but emanate directly from the nature of our state as a democratic and freedom-loving state' (Landau, J in *Israel Movie Studios Ltd* v. *Grey* [15], at 2414).

10. The Defence Regulations were established by a colonial legislator. They are not the product of legislation in a democratic society. With the foundation of the State it was claimed that their continuance in force in the State of Israel is inconsistent with the changes emanating from the establishment of a democratic state. This claim was rejected by the Supreme Court (*Leon* [1]; *El-Ard Company Ltd* v. *The Supervisor of the Northern Region, Nazareth* [16]). A number of parliamentary attempts were made to repeal them in their entirety, but these attempts proved fruitless (see Rubinstein, *The Constitutional Law of the State of Israel* (3rd. edn. 1980), at 219). On the other hand, the Israeli legislature has seen fit to repeal parts of the Defence Regulations and to put in their place Israeli Provisions (see, for example, the Law of Emergency Powers (Detention) 1979). No such legislative change has been applied to the authority of the Military Censor. Section 8 of the Defence Regulations, which relates to military censorship, remains in force in the State of Israel.

However, the interpretation to be given to the Defence Regulations in the State of Israel is not identical to the interpretation which was appropriate in the period of the Mandate. The Defence Regulations today are among the laws of a democratic state. They must be interpreted on the basis of the fundamental principles of Israeli law.

* * *

11. What are the basic values which mould the interpretation of the Defence Regulations? First and foremost stand considerations of security which extend over the full range of the Defence Regulations. State security, public safety, and public order are the essential purpose for which the Defence Regulations were enacted, and the [Regulations] must be interpreted in light of this purpose (cf. Article 6 of the Orders in Council for Palestine (Defence) 1937).

Alongside considerations of security there exist other values, in the light of which every article of legislation in a democratic society must be interpreted, and on which the Defence Regulations have a bearing. Thus, for example, the Defence Regulations deal with military courts. It is only natural that in this connection the value associated with integrity of judgment should be taken into account. (See *Dissenchik* v. *The Attorney General* [17]; *Azulai* v. *The State of Israel* [18].) . . . Another part of the Defence regulations deals with orders restricting freedom of movement. Freedom of movement is, likewise, a value which must be taken into consideration. (*Daher* v. *The Minister of the Interior* [19].) [Similarly,] that part of the Defence Regulations which imposes military censorship is prejudicial, first and foremost, to freedom of expression.

* * *

12. * * *

13. In the appeal before us the value of State security opposes the values of freedom of expression, publication, and the public right to know. [Each of] these clashing values is an integral part of our judicial system. Without security there can be no State, and there cannot be the public consent on which it is based, and there can be none of the personal freedoms which the State is required to uphold. Hence the centrality of the values of security in the scheme of values of the judicial system.

[Likewise,] without freedom of expression, it is impossible to expose the truth, impossible for the individual to realize his potential, and impossible for a democratic system, which depends on the exchange of ideas, to exist. Free exchange of information, opinions, and views is a vital condition for the existence of a democratic system, based on government of the people by the people for the people. Without freedom of expression democracy loses its soul. (*Kahane* v. *Broadcasting Authority* [20], at 274.) Indeed, on more than one occasion this Court has commented on the 'close association that exists between the principle of freedom of expression and debate and the correct operation of the democratic process' (Agranat J, in *State of Israel* v. *Ben Moshe* [21], at 435). Similarly it has been noted that 'freedom of expression is a pre-condition for the existence and correct operation of democracy' (Shamgar J, in *Klopper-Naveh* v. *Minister of Education and Culture* [22], at 238). Hence the special status of the social value in regard to freedom of expression. Freedom of expression guarantees the democratic system, which in turn guarantees other fundamental rights. (See *Kol Ha'am* v. *Minister of the Interior* [23], at 878; *Ha'aretz* v. *Israel Electricity Company* [24], at 295.)

14. How is one to resolve the conflict between the values of security and the freedom of expression? It seems to me that if the conflict between the values is 'head-on', so that one cannot exist at the same time as the other, then the value in respect to security will gain the upper hand. The reason for this is twofold: First, because the value in respect of state security is the material purpose essential to the Defence Regulations, and the interpreting judge must, first and foremost, uphold this purpose; secondly, because

democracy needs to exist in order to uphold itself. 'The democratic system is prepared to protect freedom of expression so long as freedom of expression protects democracy. But when freedom of expression becomes an axe with which to strike at democracy, there is no requirement for democracy to lay its head on the block.' (*Kahane* v. *Broadcasting Authority* [20], at 287.)

* * *

15. The 'balancing formula' in the conflict between State security and freedom of expression assumes, in any case, the upholding of the value of State security. At the same time, because of the centrality of the fundamental value of freedom of expression, it seeks to limit the damage to this fundamental value as far as possible, and only if the damage to freedom of expression is vital to the preservation of State security will this damage be allowed. In this matter, the judgment of this Court rests on two fundamental questions: first, what is the degree of damage to security which justifies infringing freedom of expression? Secondly, what is the degree of probability that the damage to State security will come about if freedom of expression is not restricted? The guiding approach of our judgment is that 'the question is always whether the scale of the damage, when adjusted to reflect the prospect that it will not occur, justifies the denial of the rights of the citizen in order to prevent the danger' (*Neiman* [9], at 311).

It has been determined that in a conflict between State security on the one hand and freedom of expression on the other, 'freedom of expression yields only where the damage to public order is serious and severe' (*Leor* v. *The Council for Review of Movies and Plays* [25], at 435). Hence, only severe and substantial damage to public order is sufficient to justify the limitation of freedom of expression. Similarly, it has been determined that the probability [of damage] which justifies limitation of freedom of expression is that of 'near certainty'.

* * *

16. [I]n various statutory contexts (such as the Police Ordinance, Newspapers Ordinance, Law of Broadcasting Authority, Public Performances Ordinance) this Court has taken the judicial-compromise approach, whereby it is possible to limit freedom of expression in the interests of defending the security of the State and public order only when there exists a near certainty of substantial damage to the security of the State and to public order in the absence of the limit on freedom of expression. . . .

There is nothing exceptional about the Defence Regulations which justifies deviating from the general concept accepted in Israel in similar cases.

There is no material difference between 'military' and 'civilian' censorship, and in both cases there is a need to give the same consideration to State security on the one hand and to freedom of expression on the other. . . . True, the security dangers which the Defence Regulations are intended to prevent are likely to be—although are not always—more severe than the dangers to public safety with which the other regulations are intended to deal. This expression of relativity is reflected in the fact that sometimes it is easy to demonstrate that the danger of damage to security is substantial and severe, and that the likelihood of the danger of damage to security is indeed close to certain. (See e.g. *Al-Hatib* v. *The Minister of the Interior* [26].)

However, there is no reason why this difference in the seriousness of the danger existing in some cases should reveal itself in different tests of principle. Indeed, when considering the question of information that should not be divulged in broadcasts in matters relating to interviews with a representative of the PLO, this Court relied on the test of near certainty. [In that case,] D. Levin J observed that 'the important right to freedom of expression is negated by the public interest when there exists a near-certainty that exploitation of this right is liable in a given case to endanger public safety or the security of the State' (*Zichroni* v. *Broadcasting Authority* [27], at 766). The same approach was adopted by Shamgar P when he observed that 'no right is abrogated *ex ante* except in relation to the existence of a near and unavoidable certainty of the commission of a crime or of damage to security or to public safety' (*Neiman* [9], at 266).

At the heart of the matter, it seems to me that the test of near certainty of real damage to the security of the State is the proper test. It reflects correctly the social importance of the conflicting principles, and does so according to the criterion of the 'enlightened public', the standard which we have adopted in cases of this kind (*Shalit* [7], at 520).

> The dividing line between the permitted and the forbidden is for the Court to decide in every case according to its judgment, in accordance with the enlightened views current in contemporary society, remembering that any restriction on the freedom of expression is redolent of censorship, and in borderline cases the tendency should be to permit and not to forbid (Landau J, in *Omer* v. *State of Israel* [28], at 411).

On the one hand, this test protects State security and public order, as it prevents publication in which there is near certainty of real damage to these values. On the other hand, this test protects freedom of expression in broad and comprehensive areas, and thus permits the achievement of the objectives of freedom of expression. Any attempt to impose a more severe test on freedom of expression is likely to have serious consequences for freedom of expression and for democracy. It must not be forgotten that we are discussing censorship, which prevents publication in advance, and thereby not only 'chills' freedom of expression but 'freezes' it (see A. M. Bickel, *The Morality of Consent* (1975), 61). Moreover, this freezing takes place without judicial process and without judicial decision. In these circumstances, it is particularly important to insist that denial of information to the public will not take place except in extraordinary and exceptional cases. The test of near certainty expresses this approach.

It is not irrelevant to note that in the United States the test for 'prior restraint' is much more severe. The principle is that prior restraint is forbidden, unless there is an inevitable, direct, and immediate influence on the security of the State, such as an influence on the physical safety of participants in a military operation (*New York Times Co.* v. *United States* [29]; *Near* v. *Minnesota* [30]). In Israel we have not adopted this test. On the other hand, we note that the distinction on which it is based—between prior restraint of publication and punishment of the publisher after publication—is sufficient to justify the fact that in Israel we adopt the test of near certainty in relation to prior restraint of publication and not a lighter test.

* * *

Indeed, Israeli society today, which sees the need to defend security and public safety on the one hand and freedom of expression on the other, can find no more suitable balance between them than the test of near certainty. Shamgar P reinforced this point when he observed:

> If there is a near certainty that use of a particular right will be prejudicial to public safety and public order in a specific case, the statutory power vested with this authority may restrain the practical application of this right in the circumstances stated (*Neiman* [9], at 265).

In the absence of near certainty of real danger, it is important that the free exchange of opinions and ideas be maintained. This matter is no less important in matters of security than in other matters. Precisely because of the 'life and death' implications of security issues, it is important that the public be made aware of the various problems, so that it may reach informed decisions regarding the fundamental problems that concern it. . . .

* * *

And precisely because of the bearing that decisions of a security nature have on the life of the people, it is appropriate to open the door to the frank exchange of opinions on security issues. In this context, it is particularly important that the press should be free to provide a forum for the exchange of opinions and criticism in matters vital both to society and to the individual. It thus seems to me that the test of near certainty is an appropriate test for gauging the powers of the Military Censor according to the Defence Regulations.

17. In conclusion: the Mandatory Defence Regulations are interpreted on the basis of the values of the State of Israel. In their interpretation there must be a balance between State security and public order on the one hand and freedom of expression on the other. This balance means that it is legitimate to restrain freedom of expression, as a last resort, only when there exists a near certainty of substantial damage to State security and public order.

## *The Second Question: Limitations Imposed on the Deliberation of the Censor*

18–21. * * *

22. Article 87 of the Defence Regulations states that the censor is empowered to prohibit publication if, in his opinion, publication is likely to be prejudicial—i.e. there exists a near certainty of substantial prejudice to the security of the State. . . . The censor—he and none other—is empowered to act in this matter, and if there exist a number of legal possibilities in the matter, the choice is made by him and by nobody else. This ruling does not mean that the censor is entitled to reach his decision in any manner that seems to him appropriate. Indeed, the decision of the censor must be reasonable, in the sense that a reasonable censor would act accordingly in the circumstances of the case. . . . In establishing the reasonableness of the Military Censor's decision, account is to be taken of an assessment of the facts on the one hand, and of near certainty of substantial prejudice on the other. The question in each case is whether a reasonable censor is entitled to reach the conclusion that, on the basis of assessment of the given facts, publication is likely to cause (i.e. there exists a near certainty that publication will cause) severe or substantial damage to the security of the State.

23. * * *

## *The Third Question: The Scope of Judicial Review*

24–27. * * *

## *The Fourth Question: Evaluating the Censor's Decision*

* * *

## *Criticism of the Chief of the Mossad*

29. It is the Censor's position that the casting of aspersions directed towards the Chief of the Mossad, and the casting of aspersions on his efficiency and the results of his role, and the legitimization [of this criticism] that would be implied were publication to be permitted in Israel alone (leaving aside the question of publication abroad) would be prejudicial to the operational capabilities of the Mossad at all its levels, including its relations with parallel organizations in other countries and with operators in the field.

The Military Censor adds that 'on the other hand, it is appropriate to stress that there has been no excision of those passages where the writer of the article has expressed an opinion critical of the Mossad and its activity in general'. The censor concludes his argument in this matter with the observation that:

> the essence of the business is not the prohibition of publication on the ground of personal injury to the individual who is the subject of the report, but on the ground that for as long as he continues to serve in his post, such detailed and factual attention to him, regarding his activity and its results in the field, . . . in the assessment of the censor, constitutes injury to the security of the State. And this is based on the most practical of considerations.

30. Perusal of the Military Censor's statement indicates that he is not complaining that the article involves publication of the activities of the Mossad or of the Chief of the Mossad, and that such publicity is prejudicial to State security. [Rather,] the Censor's statement is directed towards prejudice to the efficiency of the role of the Chief of the Mossad if the criticism of him is published. In this respect, the Military Censor distinguishes between criticism of the Chief of the Mossad which is prejudicial, in his opinion, to State security and is therefore not to be published, and criticism of the Mossad itself, publication of which is not prohibited.

In my opinion, this argument does not pass the test of review. In publication of criticism of the role of the Chief of the Mossad there is created no near certainty of substantial prejudice to State security. What we have before us is a remote possibility—a 'bad tendency' to quote Agranat J in *Kol Ha'am* [23]—which is not to be taken into account in our judicial system. On the contrary, it is proper to allow, in a democratic State, the expression of criticism of persons holding public office. Of course, criticism is not pleasant, and is sometimes injurious. This applies to criticism of the Chief of the Mossad or the Prime Minister or any other public functionary. But the lack of pleasantness is not enough to silence criticism in a democratic society based on the exchange of ideas and public debate.

It may be assumed, for example, that criticism of the Prime Minister creates a possibility of prejudice to his role, to the public's trust in him, and to his conduct of negotiations with the leaders of other States. [But] this possibility does not establish a sufficient basis for prohibition of publication. Freedom of expression is also freedom of criticism, and the freedom to ask questions which may be uncomfortable to those in power. Sometimes the criticism is not justified. Sometimes it is malicious; sometimes it is harmful. None of these are sufficient to justify the prohibition of publication. [In this respect,] it is appropriate to repeat and underline the decisive statement of Landau J, in *Israel Movie Studios Ltd* [15], at 2416:

> A government which takes on itself the power to decide what is good for the citizen to know will eventually decide what is good for the citizen to think. There is no greater deviation than this from genuine democracy.

* * *

In deciding to forbid publication of criticism of the Chief of the Mossad, the Military Censor has not given adequate weight to the principle of freedom of expression. Admittedly, the Censor has repeatedly declared before us that he has 'no quarrel whatsoever with the obligation to respect the right of expression and the freedom of expression—in the press, in the present case—which are vital to our system. This factor has guided his deliberation.' But rhetoric is not enough. A principled approach is needed when establishing a practical decision. It is not enough to say that freedom of expression is a fundamental principle of our system. The statement must be given operative meaning. . . .

31\. * * *

This is the ruling in our case. Any prior restraint of freedom of expression bears a heavy presumption of unlawful prejudice to freedom of expression. A heavy burden rests on the one seeking to demonstrate that prior restraint of freedom of expression is lawful. The Military Censor has not discharged this burden.

## *Timing of Replacement of the Chief of the Mossad*

32\. The Military Censor has forbidden the petitioners to publish details of the timing of the replacement of the Chief of the Mossad. The reason for this is that:

> certain interested parties are liable to focus an intolerable degree of attention on the man, his movements and his activities, and make real use of this knowledge to expose the identity of the Chief of the Mossad, especially outside Israel. This constitutes real danger to the safety of the Chief of the Mossad.

In my opinion, this conclusion also fails to pass the test of review. The possibility that publication of the timing of the forthcoming replacement of the Chief of the Mossad increases the danger to the safety of the outgoing Chief of the Mossad seems to me merely speculative. No information has been placed before us—besides the above-mentioned assessment—which is capable of supporting this claim. And what is the claim—that hostile elements will be able to identify the Chief of the Mossad by noting an increase in the number of flights from Israeli airports? In my view this claim has no validity. . . .

33. * * *

## *Conclusion*

34. * * *

We declare the order nisi absolute, meaning that there is to be no prohibition of publication of those parts of the article wherein there is criticism of the Chief of the Mossad or reference to the date of the forthcoming replacement of the Chief of the Mossad. We repeat and affirm that publication of any item likely to identify the Chief of the Mossad is forbidden. It is also assumed that those items waived by the petitioners in the course of the hearing will not be published, and those items conceded by the respondents in the course of the hearing will be published.

The respondents are to bear the costs of the petitioners, in a sum to be determined hereafter.

**Maltz J**: I concur.

**Wallenstein J**: I concur.

Judgment given on 10 January 1989.

# 7

# *Shlomo Miterani and others*
# v.
# *Minister of Transport and another*

[H.C. 337/81]
[37(3) P.D. 337 (1983)]

*Shamgar DP, Barak J, and Bach J*

Israeli cases referred to:

[1] HC 1/49—*Bejerano et al.* v. *Minister of Police et al.*; 2 PD 80.
[2] CA 723/74—*Haaretz* v. *Electricity Company*; 31(2) PD 281.
[3] HC 73/53, 87/53—*Kol Ha'am* v. *Minister of Interior*; 7 PD 87.
[4] HC 200/57—*Bernstein* v. *Bet Shemesh District Council*; 12 PD 264.
[5] HC 144/50—*Sheib* v. *Minister of Defence*; 5 PD 399.
[6] HC 252/77—*Bebajni* v. *Tel Aviv-Jaffa Municipality*; 32(1) PD 404.

## JUDGMENT

**Shamgar DP:**

1. The subject of this petition is the continuing work of the petitioners in the business of submitting requests for vehicle checks and registration on behalf of vehicle owners.

The immediate cause for their approaching this Court was the publication in the Ministry of Transport of internal regulations prohibiting registration offices and licensed garages from accepting documents for vehicle checks and registration from anyone not listed among the following: the vehicle owner himself, a member of his family, someone in his permanent employ, an employee of a licensed garage, and a vehicle dealer. This internal regulation will, according to the petitioners, deprive them of their livelihood, since for years they have made their living dealing with requests for vehicle checks and vehicle registration on the basis of a service for all.

2. The respondents do not deny their intention of bringing to an end the

practice of the petitioners and of others performing the same task. It would be appropriate at this juncture to quote the explicit statement made by Mr Eliezer Cohen, head of the registration office for the Tel Aviv–Jaffa and central areas in the Ministry of Transport, in the affidavit presented to this Court:

In the temporary injunction the respondents are being asked to give reason why they should not allow the petitioners to continue their business, submitting people's requests for vehicle checks and registration, and why the regulations should not be changed accordingly. The petitioners present themselves as being 'permanently in the business of submitting applications for vehicle checks and registration' and that this has been their sole occupation for many years. In doing so they thus form part of a group of people, numbering to the best of my knowledge, around 13 to 15, commonly known as 'fixers'—a word not used in its positive sense here.

In other words this petition raises a question commonly referred to as the problem of the fixers in the Ministry of Transport—i.e. people with the right contacts who are somehow able to produce results in vehicle registration checks which the vehicle owners themselves would be hard put to achieve.

3(a) With these opening words the nub of the respondent's position in this petition is presented here: to put an end to a practice that is both anti-social and generally undesirable and which has been subjected to increasing and justifiable criticism; to uproot such a practice entirely after numerous attempts at restricting it and regulating it in other ways have failed.

(b) Consideration of the public good—the very same consideration which the petitioners themselves invoked at the end of their petition—is what ultimately prompted the respondent to act as it did, acting moreover in accordance with its powers under the law.

4(a) The problem is not in fact new. In one way or another it has reared itself since the founding of the State (see *Bejerano* v. *Minister of Police* [1]). If, however, this Court raised a question *then* over the possible harm to the public stemming from the occupation of the petitioners and others, today there should be no doubt about it. Nor can the opinion of the court then, that the police had reached their conclusions over the petitioners without a thorough investigation of the matter, remain true today. The problem has been a priority issue for the respondents for some time now. Over that time various solutions have been tried, various modes of operation put into effect—all to no avail, until finally the Minister of Transport realized that the only way to deal with the problem would be through transport regulations, i.e. the very same method now being attacked in the present petition.

(b) It would seem that in this way an important distinction has now been made between the present instance and that decided in the 1949 judgment. There the Court made it quite clear that 'it [would] not [have found] anything wrong with the respondent's decision had the legislation required the appearance in person of vehicle owners' (by 'legislation' here both statute and regulation are implied, as the context makes quite clear). In our case therefore, the matter has now been dealt with by a legal instrument, determining who is entitled to present their vehicle for its annual test.

3. The various legal provisions governing the practice of handling requests for vehicle licensing that might have some bearing on the matter before us here, are the following:

**(a) Regulations 271(a) and 273(a) of the Transport Regulations 1961:**

*Requests for vehicle registration, licensing and license renewal*

271(a). Anyone wanting to register a motor vehicle or trailer, likewise anyone desiring a vehicle licence renewal or registration, should submit their application to the vehicle licensing office of his home or work district.

*Bringing a vehicle for inspection*

273(a). Anyone applying for a vehicle licence or its renewal shall bring their vehicle to the vehicle licensing office where he submitted his application, or to another place as the licensing office shall direct.

The wording of the above would indicate that the application had to be submitted by the person wanting registration or licence as appropriate. However, from a legal standpoint the wording was not universally taken to preclude giving an agent the licence to perform the above on behalf of those who, by law, were bound to apply for the registration or licence themselves. The regulation did not contain any prohibition from giving such authority to someone else, nor did it require the vehicle owner to act in person. In fact, substantively, there were no grounds for concluding that an application for registration or licence had to be brought to the authorities by the vehicle owner in person.

(b) * * *

(c) * * *

(d) Following the public outcry that resulted from the appreciable reduction in the number of those entitled to handle applications for licences as the term was used in Regulation 271 after its amendment in 1980, the rules were relaxed slightly in 1981 and a new system was brought into being. It is this that the petitioners are now complaining about. The following is the wording of the definition of the term 'owner' in Regulation 271(e) of the Transport Regulations after its amendment in 1981; it is this that has been brought here for our adjudication:

(E) In this regulation 'the owner' includes one of the following:
(1) If the owner of the vehicle is a company—one of the managers or employees of the company who has been authorized in writing by the company.
(2) A member of the vehicle owner's family or someone permanently employed by him if he has been given power of attorney by the vehicle owner.
(3) The owners of a licensed garage or a permanent employee of the garage if requested by the vehicle owner; all of which provided both of the following are adhered to:

—the garage presents a certificate to the licensing authority on a form to be determined by the latter, attesting that the vehicle was inspected by the garage or that work on it or a part of it was carried out in that garage immediately prior to the application and that all safety gadgets in the vehicle were found to be in satisfactory order.

—it is the garage owner or an employee satisfying the conditions of regulation 15B and authorized in writing by the licensing authority and under the conditions determined by the licensing authority in its authorisation; and provided that their number does not exceed three.

(4) Someone proving to the satisfaction of the licensing authority that he is a motor vehicle dealer or one of his employees, authorized by him and authorized also by the licensing authority—provided the vehicle was bought at that dealer's near the time when the application was made.

We may see therefore, that the application may now also be dealt with by the following: someone in the permanent employ of the vehicle owner bearing power of attorney, 'a permanent employee of a garage' authorized by the licensing authority, and also an employee of a motor vehicle dealer authorized by him and by the licensing authority—provided the vehicle was purchased from that dealer around the time when the application was submitted.

Following the amendment to Regulation 271, internal directives 10/81 were published by the licensing authority in the Ministry of Transport. These included the following guidelines:

A. In regulations vol. 4214 of 15.3.81 an amendment to regulation 271(e) was published setting out a new definition for 'owner' for the purposes of bringing a vehicle for licensing inspection. This definition included the registered owner, a member of the owner's family or someone in his permanent employ, employees of a garage authorized by the licensing authority and a motor vehicle dealer.

B. With regard to licensed garages, in line with the regulations we have checked the details of their employees to see whether they are indeed employed in the licensed garage and also whether they have criminal records, something which in our view would disqualify them from receiving the relevant authorization. Whoever has been deemed to satisfy the requirements of the regulations has been given a 'certification of employee in licensed garage' by the licensing authority; the certificate bears the owner's photograph.

Where the registered owner does not appear himself, the license may be renewed only when the application is submitted by:

(1) A company employee bearing the appropriate power of attorney, where the vehicle is registered in the name of the company and the company details and stamp appear in the application form. The power of attorney may be made out on form RS/35.

(2) A vehicle dealer with the appropriate valid written authorization from the licensing office and bearing the sale contract signed by the owner registered on the vehicle licence, showing that the vehicle was purchased from that owner within 30 days of putting in the application.

(3) A member of the family of the vehicle owner or someone in his permanent

employ bearing both power of attorney and the identity document of the vehicle owner. Here also the power of attorney may be made out on form RS/35.

(4) An employee of a licensed garage bearing a certificate from the licensing office with his photograph, authorizing him to bring the vehicle for its annual inspection. In addition to a power of attorney on form RS/35 and the vehicle owner's identity document, he shall also present a certificate of the vehicle's roadworthiness.

4–7. * * *

8. At this stage of our examination of the petitioners' pleas, we must address ourselves to the question whether freedom to pursue one's occupation may be limited by secondary legislation. No answer to this may be found in statute law nor has a Basic Law yet been introduced which would deal with this problem. In the published draft Basic Law: Civil Rights, the following forms part of section 7:

Every individual has the right to engage in any work, trade or profession. This right may only be limited by law.

The draft law distinguishes in its various sections, *inter alia*, between the expression—'on the basis of the law', and, on the other hand, 'by law'. The significance of these two versions has yet to be given an authoritative interpretation. I am of the opinion that one cannot regard the phrase 'on the basis of the law' as allowing for secondary legislation to limit a certain freedom, while at the same time the phrase 'by law' ensuring that any limitation on the freedom to pursue an occupation could only come from statute. It could well be that the linguistic distinctions are only the result of the drafter's particular use of language. In any case we are only talking about a proposed law which can have no direct influence on our examination of the problem before us. Be that as it may, in section 7 of the draft law dealing with the freedom to pursue an occupation, the phrase 'by law' is used and this usually has the connotation of a regular but direct enactment of the Legislature. It would therefore seem that if the draft law were to become a Basic Law, it would not be possible to make regulations limiting the freedom to pursue an occupation without there being express provision for this in an enactment of the Knesset or in another law, according to the meaning of the term in section 1 of the Interpretation Ordinance (new version). It follows that the intention of the proposed law should be interpreted with reference to the meaning of the terms as accepted at the time of the proposed law's submission to the Knesset. Since we are, however, only talking about a draft proposal, there is no point in making a detailed analysis of its possible consequences, were it even possible to apply the constitutional criteria embodied in it. However the above does provide an indicator of a definite underlying trend, i.e. that if we are to preserve the freedom to pursue an occupation, it may only be limited by the explicit word of the legislature. It goes without saying that the actual prohibition of an occupation represents the most extreme form of such a limitation. Thus the term 'limitation' in section 7 of the draft Basic Law, includes within it the term 'prohibition'.

9. In the seminal decision *Bejerano et al.* v. *Minister of Police et al.* [1], the High Court laid one of the cornerstones in the protection of the rights of the individual. In *Bejerano*, the Court for the first time looked at the status of the freedom to pursue an occupation. Justice Cheshin's words are worth quoting here:

> As a general rule, every individual has a natural and inherent right to carry on any work or occupation which he chooses, so long as such work or occupation is not forbidden by law. Where the law has set restrictions or limitations in the form of prior conditions for those adopting certain professions or trades, no one may follow those occupations without first fulfilling those prior conditions. Thus, for example, no one can practise as an attorney unless he is licensed to do so, as specified in the Attorneys Ordinance. Such a licence is only available to one who has acquired a proficiency in legal knowledge. So, too, no one may operate as an agent to release goods from the customs authority without the necessary licence under the Customs' Agents Ordinance. Anyone wishing to practise medicine, pharmacy or surveying must first acquire a special licence under the relevant Ordinance. Anyone who does not do so and yet continues to pursue the particular occupation is liable in law. There is, however, no limitation or restriction to be placed on people's desire to act as paid agents. We do not accept Mr Cohen's argument that where the law does not authorize the pursuit of a particular occupation, the right does not actually exist. On the contrary—so long as the law has not prohibited the chosen occupation and so long as the law has not imposed prior conditions for qualification to work in a particular profession, then the freedom to pursue an occupation exists as of right, the exercise of which cannot be prohibited except for reasons stated in the law.

From here it follows that, as a basic starting point, it is accepted in any free society that anyone can carry on any occupation or trade so long as no prohibitions or limitations have been laid down regarding the particular occupation. Such prohibitions or limitations cannot be imposed or sustained, except by an explicit and specific provision in the law.

The learned counsel for the respondents, Advocate R. Yarak, raised two arguments in this regard: first, he referred to the fact that, in dealing with an occupation of the same type as that of the petitioners here, the Court in *Bejerano* [1] considered the possibility of compelling the vehicle owner to appear in person. As the Court stated:

> We should not have found any flaw in the decision of the respondents if the law had required the personal appearance of the vehicle owners. In such case there would be no place for agents or messengers. But the fact is not so. The Road Haulage Regulations contain many provisions from which it appears that the vehi-

cle owner must appear in person for certain purposes. So, for example, regulation 83 provides that the Driving Licence Authority is entitled to require the applicant to undergo a medical examination and to submit to a test on his knowledge and suitability to act as a driver. It is obvious that for the purpose of this regulation it is essential for the applicant to appear in person. However, the purpose of regulations dealing with bringing vehicle for inspection, submission of certain forms of the payment of taxes and other such formalities which only require someone to stand in line and waste his time, it is not essential that the vehicle owner appear in person. In such cases a person's agent is as himself.

Secondly, he argued that it can be assumed that when Justice Cheshin used the term 'law' he had in mind the meaning of the term at that time i.e. before the new version of the Interpretation Ordinance had come into force. At that time the term 'law' was interpreted in part 2 of the Interpretation Ordinance (Amendment) of 1945 as follows:

> 'law' includes:
> (a) . . .
> (b) orders, regulations, rules, byelaws, . . .
> (c) . . .
> (d) . . .

The first argument provides no answer to our problem because it leaves the difficulty where it was. We are not just examining the question whether the licensing authority has the right to compel the vehicle owner or the driving licence applicant to be present personally at the office of the authority. If that were the only question here, it would only be necessary to decide whether such an obligation can be created on the strength of our administrative order or whether it requires secondary legislation which in turn draws its authority from a provision in statute law.

Such a question is purely theoretical now. On the basis of what is clearly stated in paragraph 21 of section 70 in the Transport Ordinance (new version), there is no doubt that the Transport Authority has been given the authority to make regulations on 'the procedure for submitting applications'. This version enables the authority to establish the rule which requires someone to appear in person. However, appearing in person is one thing, denial of the right of another party to carry on a trade or business is something else altogether. You might say, if we wish to respond not only to the question 'can someone be required to attend in person' (for identification, medical examination, and so forth) but also to the question 'can someone be prohibited from carrying on a trade in matters which even today do not require such personal attendance' (such as vehicle inspection), then the original question remains to be answered 'can such a restriction or prohibition stem from a regulation or does it require an explicit provision in statute law'.

The second argument of Mr Yarak does not constitute an answer to the problem before us. The judgment indeed used the term 'law' but the question of distinguishing between primary and secondary regulation did not arise before the court, and so was not addressed. The only matter examined was whether a restriction or a prohibition can be authorized simply by an administrative order. The various components of the term 'law' did not come up for discussion. It is superfluous to add that a court judgment is not an 'enactment', on the interpretation of which section 2 of the Interpretation Ordinance 1945 (then in force) would have taken effect. All that can be deduced from that judgment is that there must be a basis in law for any restriction on the freedom to pursue an occupation. A clarification of the finer distinctions as required in our case will have to be arrived at in other ways.

10. (a) From here we turn to the status of a 'basic right' and the significance and forms of changes in its scope.

The status accorded to any one of the basic rights of the individual within the political and social framework reflects the approach of that society and confirms its image. The constitutional and philosophical premise is that every basic right remains in force in its complete sense so long as it has not been limited by law (a term whose significance in this regard I will deal with later). Such a premise does not simply allude to the technical formal aspect of the various possible ways to limit the right nor does confirming such a premise merely serve to bolster the existence of the principle of constitutionalism. It is, first and foremost an expression of the legal supremacy of the basic right, in consideration of which any limitation on the right is conditional on putting into effect a prior legal process with a definite legislative aspect. The validity of the limitation is to be tested by looking at two aspects of the same problem—one intrinsic, the other, as it were, formal. The content, consequences, and implications of some legislative act determine its substance as legislation limiting the scope of a basic right. Bound up with this is the formal aspect of the manner in which the limitation is applied, since this provides a clear indication of the force of the type of legislation adopted to alter something already in existence. Establishing specific modes for altering a basic right is in large measure the chief means to ensure that the matter is properly tested for its inherent suitability. There should be no application of a limitation on a right without prior careful thought and discussion. This is because a possible corollary of reducing the scope of a right is a distortion in the character of the political or social order. As we have stated, the place of a basic right in the legal system is a factor by which the very existence of the rule of law can be measured. A change in the scope of the right has an inevitable consequence for the continuing existence of the rule of law. Hence the importance of specifying defined legislative modes by which means alone the scope and validity of a basic right may be altered.

There are a number of additional comments which are called for here on the subject of the place of basic rights in the legal system.

(b) An appropriate safeguard for the status of a particular freedom is not to be achieved solely by proclaiming its existence, even though one should not minimize the didactic value of a declaratory edict. Such an edict is a crucial starting point in the real process of a rights formulation wherein it acquires a perceptible reality. It is also the point from which the legal premise that underlies the edict penetrates areas beyond the law, such as the moral and social plane. It is worth adding here that it is doubtful if a particular basic right can have real life without a positive and mutual relationship persisting between the legal, moral and social spheres.

Recognizing the existence of a basic right means allocating a place to it as an actual constituent of our law. In other words we are not just talking about a declaratory principle representing beliefs and ideas, but about one of the basic constituents of the law which holds sway in Israel. On this matter the following was said in the case of *Haaretz* v. *Electricity Company* [2]:

> The absence in Israel of a single enactment with perceived legal status embodying constitutional principles does not mean that we lack legislative provisions with a constitutional element or that our legal system lacks constitutional principles which define the basic rights of the citizen.
>
> In our view the law which holds sway in Israel embodies the basic rules for the existence and protection of individual freedoms. This is so even before the draft Basic Law: Civil Rights becomes actual law.
>
> The new draft Basic Law is designed to consolidate certain principles and mark their boundaries. Its central function is to enshrine these in an enacted law in order to protect them from the dangers that come with the various crises that arise from time to time. Its purpose is to serve as an expression of those values by which the citizen may be guided and to block in advance those who would trespass on their rights. But even now, certain basic freedoms are enshrined in the foundation of our legal system and form an intrinsic part of the law in Israel. The integration of these rights into our law derives from the system of government we have chosen for ourselves (see also *Kol Ha'am* v. *Minister of Interior* [3]). But the duty to uphold them in practice does not just have a political, social or moral aspect, it also has legal status.

(c) Identifying a basic right as a constituent of substantive law, in other words determining its very existence, carries immediate implication for the force and validity of part of some legislative enactments, where a contradiction emerges with the basic right or where an attempt is being made to limit the basic right by means of these enactments.

I chose the term 'part' because this Court does not put the validity of Knesset legislation under critical scrutiny. (Unless it is the provision of a law whose acceptance by the Knesset was conditional on it receiving a special majority and it did not receive such a majority.)

However, where it is not the actual validity of the law that is in question, but its interpretation, or when we are investigating the most appropriate ways of setting limits to a particular basic right while preserving the essentials of the rule of law, then the basic right should always have a status in keeping with its intrinsic importance. This is so whether we are dealing with primary or secondary legislation.

With regard to the question of 'interpretation' I refer to what was said in *Haaretz* v. *Electricity Company* [2] regarding the basic right of freedom of expression and relevant to the subject now before us:

> Any limitation on the scope of a right which is inferred from the words of an enactment should be interpreted narrowly, with the objective of giving the said right maximum scope and not limiting it more than is clearly meant by the Act. Freedom of expression and the provisions in a Law which are designed to limit it do not have equal or identical status. So long as this can be reconciled with the actual text, one should give preference to the presence of the right over the provisions in an act which seem designed to limit the right. The standard by which we set the protection of freedom of expression is uppermost in our considerations when it clashes with another—such standard should inform both the legislator's formulation of legislative norms and also the actual interpretation of these laws and their implementation in circumstances where their practical application may be properly gauged.

Furthermore, the status of a basic right is not to be secured merely by following the paths of interpretation common to all legislation. In the case of secondary legislation, the supervision of the court is effected not only in its power to interpret the text but, first and foremost, in its examination of whether the secondary legislator has worked within the ambit of his authority, as spelled out in the primary legislation (A. Barak, *Supervision of the Courts over Secondary Legislation* 21 Hapraklit (1964–5) 463). Interpretation of the text of the enabling Act and of the secondary legislation in a case such as the one before us is the main instrument for effecting such judicial review.

11. From the point of view of the desired legislative policy in all that relates to the demarcation line between primary and secondary legislators, I agree with the view of Prof. H. Klinghoffer (*The Rule of Law and Secondary Legislation*). According to him:

> The Legislature must itself determine, where possible, the guidelines by which the administrative authority may be allowed to interfere with the freedom of the individual. If the Legislature leaves the setting of such guidelines to the administrative authority, it would thereby undermine the influence of the individual, by whom the legislative body has been chosen, on the formulation of such guidelines. In a State governed by the rule of law the authority to make primary regulations rests with the Legislature. Administrative organizations are permitted to make secondary regulations only, within the framework of the law.

Unfortunately, the line within which the secondary legislator must be restricted in setting out secondary regulations only, is not always incorporated into the law by the primary legislator. However, despite this being an unwelcome phenomenon in terms of preserving the substantive rule of law, there is nothing in it to invalidate secondary legislation. The validity of secondary legislation depends in every case on the wording of the primary legislation. It is this that provides the secondary legislator with the precise limits for his activity, devolving on him the authority to introduce secondary legislation on specified topics. Without such a grant of authority in primary legislation, the secondary legislator has no basis at all. The secondary legislator only derives power from the grant of authority in the parent law, setting out the bounds of action permitted him. In this respect it makes no difference whether the issue is the limitation of a basic right or any other matter. In every instance the secondary legislator only has the power granted him. A regulation cannot contradict a statute (section 16(4) Interpretation Ordinance (new version) ), and neither can it overstep the bounds marked out for it in the primary legislation. In other words not only will a substantive contradiction between primary and secondary legislation result in the cancellation of the latter, but also where the secondary legislation spreads to areas where it does not have specific authority, the result will be the same.

Examination of secondary legislation according to the limits marked out for it in the primary legislation is, understandably, especially exacting when the limitation of a basic right is involved. As already mentioned, the subsidiary legislator requires in all cases the clear authority of the primary legislation. Thus we return to the problem of interpreting the written word. As to the special constitutional status of a basic right, a meticulous investigation should be made to see if it can really be inferred from the authority set out in the primary legislation, if such exists, whether at its root lay the genuine intention to grant an authority to the secondary legislator to alter the bounds and scope of the basic right. It follows from what we have said that if the grant of authority is general and non–specific, it will be interpreted in such a way as would block the grant of an authority to limit a basic right.

A basic right can only be denied or limited by an unequivocal provision in the primary legislation and also by the secondary legislator specifically authorized by primary legislation, provided there is no Basic Law directing otherwise.

As we shall see in due course, in the case before us, the primary legislation does not include the grant of any authority to the secondary legislator to make regulations which could limit the freedom to pursue an occupation. Even if it were proposed to make inferences from the context in the primary legislation, and not merely from the actual text granting authority to make regulations, there would still be no indication that a grant of the necessary authority had been intended. That being so, we have no need to make a decision in this case on the question whether the granting of authority in primary legislation needs to be specific and unequivocal or whether it would suffice if such a grant of authority were merely implied.

My own view is that the granting of authority in this type of situation requires a specifically stated grant of authority. I would say that the grant is effective only where in the primary legislation it is stated clearly and specifically that it is granting authority to the secondary legislator to make regulations which set out prohibitions or restrictions on the pursuit of a particular occupation. This Court dealt with the subject before in the case of *Bernstein* v. *Bet Shemesh District Council* [4], where it was stated by Berinson J:

> This natural right, as it is called in that judgment [the reference is to the freedom to pursue an occupation], cannot be rescinded or diminished except by a clear and unequivocal provision in statute. In no way can I deduce from the provisions dealing with the power 'to enact' the authority either to prevent a person from carrying on a trade, or to make prior conditions, in addition to those already provided for in the law, which the applicant would be bound to observe before being allowed to pursue his occupation.

In a further judgment, *Sheib* v. *Minister of Defence et al.* [5], Olshan J stated:

> The executive authority is not at liberty to impose limitations, simply because it considers them to be desirable, unless the particular law grants it the power to impose such limitations where it deems necessary. If such an authority is not to be found in a particular law, the executive authority must then try to persuade the legislature to grant it. But so long as that authority has not been given, the executive is not entitled to assume it on its own. If it were to do so, then the whole principle of 'the rule of law', one of the guarantees of democratic order in the State, would become a mere empty slogan and all the laws that deal for example with the regulating of entering the various professions would be made redundant.

To sum up on this point: in the absence of a constitution establishing the legal status of fundamental civil rights, there is no limitation today on the provisions that may be included in normal primary legislation (apart from certain areas such as in section 4 of Basic Law: The Knesset). But secondary legislation derives its power only from what is authorized in primary legislation. When it comes to matters like the limitation of fundamental freedoms, the secondary legislator is only authorized to act in the said area if authority has been granted him clearly and unequivocally by the primary legislator.

This point can also be presented as follows: the best scenario would be if limitations on basic freedoms derived solely from the authority which the legislature reserved for itself alone, in other words where all such limitations and prohibitions emanated solely and directly from enactments of the Knesset. (Prof. Klinghoffer has noted, following Kelsen that the rule that 'the individual is free to do anything which is not prohibited' is accepted even by autocratic regimes.) What characterizes the difference between the autocratic system and a democracy are, *inter alia*, the riders and restraints embedded in the law which the primary legislator has actually imposed on itself. Beyond this, special importance attaches to the scope of powers granted to the executive or to what extent the secondary legislator has been empowered to limit fundamental individual freedoms. That is in fact what was proposed in the draft Basic Law, which was going to define basic rights (section 7 of draft Basic Law: Civil Rights). The Knesset, however, has yet to set limits on its normal prospective legislation, as far as concerns basic rights (with the exception of matters related to the electoral system or the permanence of existing Basic Laws in the face of emergency legislation). Thus, from a legal standpoint, we are unable to invalidate any enactment of the Knesset which gives the Executive the authority to make secondary enactments, including the authority to impose restrictions on a basic right.

However, because of the nature of the subject (the limitation of a basic right) and also because of the rules which normally apply to the validity of secondary legislation, we can stipulate that the secondary legislator does not, as a rule, have authority to limit the validity, effect, or scope of a basic right unless such authority has been granted clearly and unequivocally. I am not myself disposed to adopt the view that the authority to limit the freedom of the individual can be inferred from a general rule in the text of the law or from its known objective. However, as already explained, we do not need to make a ruling on this in the case before us.

12. Where the text of the authority granted by the primary legislator is ambiguous, for example where the content cannot simply be gleaned from the plain meaning of the words, the court will tend to interpret the grant of authority in a manner which would nullify any intention of the legislature to limit a basic right by such grant of authority. In *Bebajni* v. *Tel Aviv–Jaffa Municipality* [6] it was stated:

> We have always held that, when dealing with a limitation on the right to pursue an occupation any doubt will be interpreted in such a manner as will preserve the individual's freedom and not limit it.

This interpretive approach derives directly from the status which basic rights enjoy in our law. This is the interpretive rule which in my view applies to primary legislation and even more so to secondary legislation. It is an accepted approach which has been conspicuously present in the interpretation which this Court has adopted for various expressions used by the primary legislator when granting authority to the secondary legislator. Thus it has been adjudged that the power to make provisions in the field of licensing is equivalent to the power to 'regulate'. However, the expression 'to regulate' cannot be interpreted in a way which could include an authority to place a complete prohibition on pursuing a certain profession.

Of course the term 'to regulate' could acquire wider significance if the law in which the authority is given specifies as much (see for example section 5(b) of the Supervision of Goods and Services Law). But this will only be the case if the provision is, as we have said, specific. Furthermore, even if the executive has been given the power to regulate a certain area by way of prohibition, there still remains the question what exactly that area is. In this regard, the interpretive approach will once again come into operation. The power of the secondary legislator to make prohibitions in the field of freedoms of the individual will be subjected to the most searching examination in an attempt to discover whether he has, in fact, acted within the confines of the subject whose regulation has been entrusted to his authority.

13. (a) As already indicated, the regulations by which the Ministry of Transport seeks to prohibit the petitioners from continuing in their occupation derive from the provisions in sections 27 and 70 of the Transport Ordinance (new version). In line with what we have stipulated here, we must now look to see if there is anything in the provisions of the legislation, i.e. in sections 27 and 70, which would give the executive the power to prohibit the pursuit of the trade of submitting applications by proxy.

(b) Section 27 of the Transport Ordinance does not affect our case. It serves to all intents and purposes as a basis for other provisions which are included in the Transport Regulations (amendment no. 4).

(c) Section 70 contains numerous paragraphs giving details of those matters where the authority to make regulations has been granted, and as we stated earlier, the matters dealt with in subsections (21) and (22) are nearest to our purposes here.

(d) Subsection (21) deals with the manner of submitting applications and conducting checks and examinations for the purposes of granting or renewing driving licences, licences for driving instructors, for maintaining driving schools, and also vehicle licensing, and the arrangements for offices of the appropriate licensing authority.

The creator of the regulations, subject of this petition, apparently believed he was empowered to prohibit the petitioners from following their trade, as a result of being authorized to establish rules for the manner in which applications are to be submitted and for the organization of the licensing authority offices. Such a belief is erroneous. It is diametrically opposed to the guidelines for the validity of secondary legislation as set out above. Completely to prohibit the pursuit of a particular occupation (which is to make a direct assault on the freedom to pursue an occupation), it is not enough simply to rely for authority on a provision that relates in a general way to procedures for submitting licence applications or for the organization of offices. If the Legislature had intended to grant power to the Ministry of Transport to prohibit the trade of 'submitting applications by proxy', it should have spelled out its intention clearly and unambiguously—application of the rule, requiring such a provision to be clear and unambiguous, is conspicuously necessary in the case before us. No claim has been made before us here that when the Legislature enacted subsection (21) (in section 70) it was aware that the secondary legislator would rely on it to prohibit some occupation or other. All would agree that what we have here is a decision by the secondary legislator, after the legislature has already completed its work; in other words an interpretation of subsection (21) broad enough to allow for the prohibition of the trade of submitting applications by proxy. Such a widening of the powers of the Authority is unacceptable for the reasons stated above. It goes far beyond the power granted to the secondary legislator. So that there should be no doubt at all I would add here that the extent of any granting of authority will be tested in every instance in the light of the written text. The awareness of the Legislature of the problems relating to people submitting applications for pay and to the desire of the Executive to do something about it by making such prohibitions cannot help the Executive here when the text of the Law itself does not include the requisite explicit grant of authority.

Again to remove any doubt here, I should add that it is immaterial that the actual prohibition of the occupation is not mentioned specifically in the regulations but is only implied from the positive provisions specifying the classes of people who may submit applications. If the end (also the self-declared end) is the prohibition of a particular occupation, then for our part the result will be the same as if the composer of the regulations had actually used direct language and had sought to include provisions prohibiting the appellants and their like from pursuing their occupation.

There is, however, a further side effect from the fact of the regulations not making a direct prohibition on the appellants engaging in their trade, but instead setting out who can in fact submit applications. If the regulation had only included the prohibition, the Court would have considered it completely void since the secondary legislator had no authority to make such a prohibition. Where, however, the regulation contains other provisions on the manner of submitting applications and the kinds of people who can submit applications, then these regulations may stand, so long as they are not considered to imply that the appellants are forbidden to carry on their trade. The right of the appellants to carry on their trade remains firm; since there is no valid piece of legislation which could restrict it, they must therefore be permitted to continue to practise it. The provisions in the regulation also remain in force to the extent that they are of no effect in prohibiting the appellants' trade but are of effect in regulating other matters; they have no power to limit the freedom to pursue an occupation.

14. We also referred to subsection 22 of the Transport Ordinance (new version) as a possible basis for the setting out of regulations in the matter before us. However, close examination of the text of that subsection, which deals with traffic security, shows that there is nothing in it to support a grant of authority to prohibit the occupation of the appellants since that has nothing to do with traffic safety. Traffic safety, in so far as inspection of vehicles is concerned, can be safeguarded by the quality and scope of the inspection carried out on the vehicle and the standard of inspection and screening employed by the licensing authority and the licensed garages. The question of the employment of those engaged in submitting applications by proxy cannot be included under this heading.

15. For the reasons set out above I would accept the petition and make the injunction permanent. To remove any doubt here I would add that I have not dealt with additional claims which could have been examined in connection with the matter before us. For example, the matter of the assault on inherent rights, or the reasonableness of the regulations. These are matters which in my opinion, in light of the above, need not be addressed in the ruling which we are being asked to make here.

I would therefore overturn the absolute order.

**Barak J:** I concur.

**Bach J:** I concur.

Judgment given today, 10 July 1983.

# SECTION 3: STATUTORY HUMAN RIGHTS

# 8

# *The New Basic Laws on Human Rights: A Mini-revolution in Israeli Constitutional Law?*

DAVID KRETZMER*



## 1. Background

Until the Basic Law: Freedom of Occupation and the Basic Law: Human Dignity and Liberty were enacted in 1992 Israel had no bill of rights. Pursuant to the 1950 Harari Resolution, according to which Israel's formal constitution would be drawn up in a piecemeal fashion by a series of basic laws, basic laws were enacted covering virtually all aspects of Israel's constitutional system. However, these basic laws did not include a basic law on civil liberties or human rights.

The absence of a Bill of Rights was not for want of trying. Numerous attempts were made over the years by members of the Knesset, the Knesset Constitution and Law Committee, and Ministers of Justice to further passage of a Bill of Rights. In recent years the most adamant opposition to a

* This note is based on an earlier article of the same name published at (1992) 26 *Is.LR* 238.

general bill of rights came from the religious parties, who have a principled objection to judicial review. This objection rests on the not-unfounded conviction that a Bill of Rights will enable the Supreme Court to exercise judicial review over legislation that was passed because of the strategic position of the religious parties in Israel's coalition system, but that is inconsistent with fundamental freedoms and rights, such as freedom of religion and equality. The main examples of such legislation are the laws regarding religious marriage and Sabbath observance.

The two basic laws enacted in the last session of the outgoing Knesset before the 1992 elections grew out of the realization that, even were it impossible, for political reasons, to enact a general Bill of Rights, it might be possible to enact a bill that deals with those rights that are considered less controversial from the political point of view. Thus it was that the first basic law on civil rights passed in Israel deals with a right that is not specifically mentioned in many constitutions and human rights documents, namely what has been called 'freedom of occupation', i.e. the freedom to follow the vocation of one's choosing. The second law deals with a whole range of rights under the general rubric of 'human dignity and liberty'.

The assumption that the right to freedom of occupation raises issues that are not controversial, especially when it comes to the relationship between State and religion, did not stand the test of time. Some time after the original version of the Basic Law: Freedom of Occupation was enacted, the Supreme Court decided that import restrictions on meat on grounds of *kashrut* (i.e. that the meat does not comply with the dietary laws of the Jewish religion) were in violation of freedom of occupation.[1] The political echelons of government discovered that the Basic Law: Freedom of Occupation prevented them from 'remedying' this situation by ordinary legislation. As a result a political deal was reached under which that basic law was re-enacted. While the main object of the new version of thc basic law was to include an override clause, during the process of enactment some other changes were also introduced. Furthermore, the new basic law also amended the Basic Law: Human Dignity and Liberty.

## 2. The Status of Human Rights before Enactment of the Basic Laws

A Bill of Rights fulfills at least one of three normative functions in a legal system. Its first and most obvious function is to define those basic rights that are recognized and protected by the system. The second function is to

[1] See *Meatrael Ltd* v. *Minister of Commerce and Industry* (1993) 47(1) PD 521.

set standards for resolving clashes between the protected rights themselves and for balancing those rights and other values or policies recognized by the system. The final function is to establish the constitutional status of the recognized rights. This means determining whether the Bill of Rights binds the legislative body itself and whether legislation that is inconsistent with basic rights may be struck down by a court or by some other constitutional body.

Absence of a formal Bill of Rights did not mean that before the basic laws were enacted civil rights had no place in Israel's legal system. The Supreme Court filled part of the void left by lack of a Bill of Rights. In a long line of decisions, starting with Agranat J's landmark decision in the *Kol Ha'am* case,[2] the Court held that basic civil rights, as accepted in other democratic countries, are an integral part of the Israeli legal system. These basic rights enjoy the status of what I have elsewhere termed 'soft legal principles'.[3] They are *legal* principles because government authorities may not restrict them without express statutory authority, all authorities must be guided by them in interpretation of statutes and administrative authorities must give them appropriate weight when exercising administrative discretion. They are *soft* principles because they do not limit the legislative power of the Knesset. In the absence of a formal constitution or Bill of Rights, the Supreme Court was not prepared to subject primary legislation to judicial review in order to examine whether it places unacceptable restrictions on those basic rights that are recognized as legal principles.[4]

Given the central place basic rights play in judicial decision-making in Israel, a Bill of Rights was not needed to fulfill the first of the functions mentioned above: defining the protected rights. This is especially evident in the case of freedom of occupation, referred to frequently by the Supreme Court, which, in one of its earliest decisions, described this freedom as one of the natural rights of man.[5]

The Supreme Court also developed an extensive case law dealing with the tests for balancing basic rights, such as equality, freedom of speech, and freedom of movement with other rights and interests.[6]

The main contribution of a Bill of Rights to Israel's constitutional system would therefore be to enhance the status of basic rights by providing

[2] See *Kol Ha'am* v. *Minister of the Interior* (1953) 7 PD 871.

[3] See D. Kretzmer, 'Demonstrations and the Law' (1984) 19 *Is.LR* 47.

[4] See e.g. *Rogozinsky* v. *State of Israel* (1972) 26(1) PD 129; *Tnuat Laor* v. *Speaker of the Knesset* (1990) 44(3) PD 529.

[5] See *Bejarano* v. *Minister of Police* (1949) 2 PD 80, at 82.

[6] The decisions are too numerous to mention here. But see e.g. *Kol Ha'am* v. *Minister of the Interior*, n. 2 above; *Kahane* v. *Broadcasting Authority* (1987) 41(3) PD 255 (freedom of speech); *Dahaar* v. *Minister of the Interior* (1986) 40(2) PD 701 (right to travel abroad); *Poraz* v. *Mayor of Tel Aviv* (1988) 42(2) PD 309 (equality).

for judicial review over legislation that is inconsistent with those rights. The first task in discussing the two basic laws is therefore to examine whether they do indeed provide for such review.

## 3. The Entrenchment Provisions and Judicial Review

Although basic laws are supposed to be chapters in Israel's emerging constitution˙ the Supreme Court held in the past that in the absence of express provisions granting them preferred status, basic laws are not inherently superior to ordinary legislation.[7] Thus, in the case of a clash between a special provision in ordinary Knesset legislation and a general provision in a basic law, the former prevails.[8] Furthermore, the Court held that the Knesset may amend a provision in a basic law by ordinary legislation passed with a simple majority.[9] The only exception to this rule recognized before the new basic laws on civil rights were enacted related to those provisions in basic laws that are entrenched, such as section 4 of the Basic Law: The Knesset.[10] The Court exercised judicial review in order to ensure that legislation inconsistent with entrenched provisions was indeed enacted with the special majority expressly required by those provisions.[11]

Section 7 of the Basic Law: Freedom of Occupation states that this basic law may not be changed 'except by a Basic Law enacted by a majority of Knesset members'. The requirement that the change be effected not only by an absolute majority, but by a basic law, makes this entrenchment stronger than the entrenchment in section 4 of the Basic Law: The Knesset. According to the approach taken by the Supreme Court, the entrenched clause in that law may be changed by an ordinary law, provided it was passed with a special majority.[12]

As opposed to the Basic Law: Freedom of Occupation, the Basic Law: Human Dignity and Liberty does not contain an express entrenchment clause. Such a clause was included in the bill but was dropped at the second reading stage. This causes some interesting anomalies. Thus, section 1a,

[7] See *Kaniel* v. *Minister of Justice* (1973) 27(1) PD 794; *Ressler* v. *Chairman of the Central Elections Committee* (1977) 31(2) PD 556. For a full discussion of the status of the basic laws see D. Kretzmer, 'Judicial Review of Knesset Decisions' (1988) 8 *Tel Aviv Uni. Studies in Law* 95.

[8] See *Negev* v. *State of Israel* (1974) 28(1) PD 640.

[9] See A. Rubinstein, *The Constitutional Law of the State of Israel* (4th edn., Schocken, Tel Aviv, 1991) 459–60.

[10] 12 LSI 85 and (Amendment No. 3) 13 LSI 228.

[11] See *Bergman* v. *Minister of Finance* (1969) 23(1) PD 693; *Agudat Derech Eretz* v. *Broadcasting Authority* (1981) 35(4) PD 1; *Rubinstein* v. *Speaker of the Knesset* (1983) 37(3) PD 141; *Tnuat Laor* v. *Speaker of the Knesset*, n. 4 above.

[12] See *Kaniel* v. *Minister of Justice*, n. 7 above; *Ressler* v. *Chairman of the Central Elections Committee*, n. 7 above.

which was phrased on the basis of the assumption that the entrenchment clause included in the original bill would remain, states that the purpose of the basic law is to entrench human dignity and liberty in a basic law. A comparison between the two new basic laws would seem to imply that freedom of occupation is more important than such basic rights as the right to life, bodily integrity and dignity, and personal liberty of the individual.

Section 11 of the Basic Law: Human Dignity and Liberty states expressly that all governmental authorities are bound to respect the rights protected under that law. Furthermore, section 8 of that basic law states that no restrictions may be placed on protected rights except by a statute that meets defined substantive standards. These provisions would seem to leave little room for doubt that the basic law is meant to place restrictions on the legislative power of the Knesset. Nevertheless, given the existing case law of the Supreme Court regarding the status of basic laws, and the absence from that basic law of an express entrenchment clause, some doubts were raised whether legislation that did not meet the demands of the Basic Law: Human Dignity and Liberty would be regarded as invalid.

These doubts were dispelled in a decision handed down by an expanded bench of nine justices of the Supreme Court in November, 1995.[13] That decision related to legislation passed after the Basic Law: Human Dignity and Liberty was enacted which affected the rights of creditors to collect debts against agricultural settlements. Creditors argued that the legislation violated their property rights, protected under section 3 of the Basic Law, and that it did not meet the requirements of section 8. The Court was unanimous in holding that the property rights of creditors were indeed violated by the legislation but that the legislation fulfilled the requirements of section 8 and was therefore valid. It could therefore easily have avoided addressing questions relating to the binding force of the Basic Law and the power of judicial review over legislation claimed to be inconsistent with it. Nevertheless, some of the justices dealt with these questions at great length.

The majority of judges on the Court held that the Basic Law: Human Dignity and Liberty and the Basic Law: Freedom of Occupation have formal constitutional status and therefore enjoy a status superior to that of ordinary legislation.[14] Thus all legislation passed after these basic laws came into force must meet their demands. Furthermore, the courts have

[13] See *United Mizrachi Bank Ltd* v. *Migdal Co-operative Village* (C.A. 6821/93, not yet reported).

[14] There was some difference of opinion between the judges regarding the theoretical basis for the power of the Knesset to pass constitutional laws that have a superior status to ordinary legislation. Barak J relied on the theory, rejected in the past by the Court, according to which the Knesset possesses both legislative and constituent power. In passing basic laws the Knesset is exercising its constituent power and it may therefore place restrictions on the use of legislative power. This view appealed to at least three of the other justices on the bench. Shamgar J rejected the constituent power theory, but held that as a sovereign legislative body the Knesset could ascribe constitutional status to basic laws and could also place binding constraints on itself.

the power to review legislation in order to determine whether it does indeed meet those demands and to invalidate legislation that does not. The majority even went one step further and revised the previous position of the Court according to which a basic law may be amended by ordinary legislation. In future, changes in all basic laws must be made by expressly amending those basic laws or by enacting other basic laws. Only one of the judges on the Court, Cheshin J, refused to accept that the *Knesset* has the power to give legislation superior constitutional status, or to bind its legislative power in a way that exceeds the majority rule in a parliamentary democracy.[15]

## 4. Judicial Review and Existing Legislation

Introduction of judicial review over Knesset legislation immediately raises the question whether all existing legislation meets the standards set in the basic laws. This always provided a bone of contention in discussions of a Bill of Rights for Israel. The main concern was expressed not only by the religious parties, which feared that legislation enforcing religious norms would not stand up to review, but more particularly by the defence establishment, which realizes that much of the British Mandatory emergency legislation which is still in use does not meet those standards. Thus, for instance, the Supreme Court itself has described regulation 94 of the Emergency Regulations (Defence) 1945 that deals with licensing of the press as a provision 'that is inimical to basic conceptions of freedom of speech and expression in a democratic society'.[16]

The issue of existing legislation has been dealt with in different ways by the two basic laws. Freedom of occupation was not regarded as politically sensitive or threatening to existing security powers. The original version of the basic law passed in February 1992 therefore allowed a period of grace of two years for existing legislation, after which it would be subject to review under the exacting standards set by the basic law. This period of grace was extended for a further two year period under section 10 of the new version of the basic law passed in March 1994.

The rights ensured in the Basic Law: Human Dignity and Liberty are

[15] Cheshin J took the view that the *Knesset* may regulate the *type* of majority required for given decisions or legislation. Thus it may stipulate that in ordinary cases a simple majority is sufficient, while in special cases an absolute majority of its members is required. However, it does not have the power to entrench a statute by a requirement that exceeds an absolute majority. Cheshin J also expressed the view that the Knesset could overcome the demands of section 8 of the Basic Law: Human Dignity and Liberty by including an express provision in subsequent legislation that that legislation would be valid notwithstanding the provisions of the Basic Law.

[16] See *Al-Assad* v. *Minister of the Interior* (1980) 34(1) PD 505, 513.

regarded as far more problematic. Many of them are regulated by emergency legislation. Thus, for example, emergency laws in Israel provide for administrative detention and other restrictions on freedom of movement, including restrictions on the right of citizens to travel abroad, which violates the right ensured in section 6 (a) of the Basic Law. One would have hoped that the way to deal with these laws would have been similar to the approach adopted in the freedom of occupation law, i.e. a period of grace in order to allow legislative changes after which the Supreme Court could examine whether the legislation meets the standards of the Basic Law. This approach was rejected. Instead section 10 declares that nothing in the basic law 'affects the validity of law that existed prior to the coming into force of this Basic Law'.

There is little doubt that the immunity from review granted to existing legislation under section 10 of the Basic Law: Human Dignity and Liberty greatly weakens the import of that Law. Given the special provision dealing with emergency powers in section 12 of the Basic Law, it seems that the refusal to allow review of existing legislation under the standards of the Basic Law reveals a lack of confidence in the legitimacy of that legislation, even when examined in the light of the security situation in which Israel finds itself.

In spite of the fact that the courts may not invalidate existing legislation that is inconsistent with the terms of the Basic Law: Human Dignity and Liberty, some of the justices on the Supreme Court have taken the view that adoption of the new basic laws has changed the status of the protected rights.[17] As constitutionally protected rights they now have more weight than they had in the past. This means that judicial interpretations of legislation should be reviewed and that the courts should strive for interpretations that are consistent with the notion of rights that are constitutionally protected. According to this approach the new basic law will have an influence on existing legislation, even though it cannot be declared invalid if it is inconsistent with it.

## 5. The Override Clause

As opposed to the Basic Law: Human Dignity and Liberty, the Basic Law: Freedom of Occupation may not be changed 'except by a basic law passed by a majority of Knesset members' (section 7). However, under section 8 of the new version of the Basic Law, the Knesset retains the power to

[17] See the opinions of the majority in the case of *Ganimat* v. *State of Israel* (1995, not yet reported, decision in the appeal and further hearing) and the opinion of Dorner J in *Alice Miller* v. *Minister of Defence* (1995, not yet reported).

include an override clause in legislation. Such legislation will be valid, even if it restricts freedom of occupation in a manner inconsistent with the balancing provision, provided two conditions are met: 1. that the legislation was passed by an absolute majority of Knesset members, and 2. that it expressly states that it will take effect notwithstanding the provisions of the Basic Law. Such a law will automatically expire fours years after it came into force, unless the law itself provides for a shorter duration. Immediately after the new version of the Basic Law was published the Knesset used the override provision in order to enact the Import of Frozen Meat Law 1994 which prohibits import of meat that has not been certified as kosher.

The Canadian Charter of Rights and Freedoms was a model for the override clause in the Basic Law. However, there are some significant differences between the provision that appears in section 33 of the Canadian Charter and section 8 of the Basic Law: Freedom of Occupation. The Canadian provision states that the declaration that the statute will be valid notwithstanding that it restricts a basic right loses its effect after five years. Section 8, on the other hand, stipulates that the overriding statute itself expires after four years. Furthermore, the Canadian Charter expressly states that the legislature that enacted the overriding statute may re-enact the overriding declaration at the end of the five year period. There is no parallel provision in the Israeli statute. It remains to be seen whether the courts will take this as implying that the offending statute may not be re-enacted after it expires.

## 6. The Rights Protected

The Basic Law: Freedom of Occupation protects one right: the right of every citizen or resident of the State to engage in any occupation, profession, or trade. Under the general category of human dignity and liberty the second basic law includes a number of fundamental rights: the right to life, body, and dignity and to protection of these interests (sections 2 and 4); the right to property (section 3); the right to liberty of the individual (section 5); the right to leave and enter the country (section 6), and the right to privacy and personal confidentiality (section 7).

The absence of express mention of some of the most basic rights mentioned in international human rights declarations and treaties and in modern constitutions was not accidental. As mentioned above, the notion of piece-meal basic laws on human rights was meant to overcome the opposition in certain quarters to entrenchment of those rights that raise controversial questions on the political level, and especially those rights that are affected by religiously motivated legislation. It is clear that the most sensitive rights in this respect are freedom of religion and conscience and the right to equality. The former is clearly affected by the lack of civil marriage in Israel. The latter is affected by the jurisdiction granted to the religious courts in matters of marriage and divorce, as the law applied by both the Jewish Rabbinical and Moslem courts may be regarded as discriminatory towards women.

Many of the rights expressly mentioned in human rights covenants or charters are part and parcel of the rights listed in the Basic Law: Human Dignity and Liberty, even if not explicity mentioned. Thus, for example, the prohibitions against slavery and against torture and cruel, inhuman, and degrading treatment or punishment are covered by the right to human dignity. It also seems clear that the right to due process is bound to the right to liberty of the person and the legitimate restrictions on that liberty. The big question is whether the notion of human dignity should be extended to include those rights, such as equality, freedom of religion, and freedom of expression that were intentionally excluded from the rights mentioned in the basic law.

In a number of decisions some of the justices on the Supreme Court have taken the view that fundamental rights not expressly mentioned in the basic laws, such as equality and freedom of expression, are protected under the umbrella of human dignity.[18] Furthermore, in his extra-judicial writings Barak J, now president of the Court, has dismissed the idea that original intent should be the guiding principle in interpreting basic laws that are part of Israel's developing formal constitution.[19] Following Barak J's general theory of interpretation, the concept of human dignity must be interpreted in the light of its 'objective purpose', which can be gleaned from its meaning in international human rights documents and other democratic constitutions, and which in the end must include 'all those human rights that have a close substantive connection to human dignity and liberty according to prevailing concepts among the enlightened public in Israel'.[20] If one follows this approach it is almost self-evident that the concept of human dignity includes both equality and freedom of religion.

The wide view of the concept of human dignity was strengthened by the amendment to the Basic Law: Human Dignity and Liberty, introduced by

[18] See e.g. *Re'em Engineers Ltd* v. *Municipality of Nazareth Elite* (1992 ) 47 PD (5) 189, 201; *Dayan* v. *Commander of Jerusalem Police* (1993) 48 PD 456, 468; *Hupert* v. *Yad Vashem* (1995) 48 (3) PD 353, 360–3; *El Al Airlines* v. *Danilewitz* (1994, not yet reported); *Women's Network* v. *Minister of Transport* (1994, not yet reported).

[19] See A. Barak, *Interpretation in Law*, iii, Constitutional Interpretation ( New Jerusalem, 1994) 149 ff.; *ibid.*, 'Human Dignity as a Basic Right,' *Ha'aretz*, 3 June 1994, b5.

[20] See Barak, *Interpretation*, n. 19 above, 416 and *Vickselbaum* v. *Minister of Defence* (1993) 47(2) PD 812.

the new version of the Basic Law: Freedom of Occupation. Section 1 of both basic laws now states:

> Fundamental human rights in Israel are founded on recognition of the value of the human being, the sanctity of human life, and the principle that all persons are free; these rights shall be upheld in the spirit of the principles set forth in the Declaration of the Establishment of the State of Israel.

The principles set forth in the Declaration of the Establishment of the State of Israel include 'complete equality of political and social rights, irrespective of race, religion or sex' and freedom of religion and conscience. The argument that human dignity includes these rights may now be based not only on international and comparative materials but on interpretation of this concept in the spirit of these principles. Nevertheless, given the structure of the basic laws that expressly mention some, but not all, specific rights, and the clear political desire not to 'constitutionalize' all fundamental rights protected in other constitutions and international documents, it seems that the Court should develop a case law which allows for resort to the notion of 'human dignity' to address gross violations of rights not specifically mentioned, but does not turn the term into a catch-all phrase for all rights that were intentionally omitted from the basic laws.[21]

## 7. Balancing Tests

Most basic rights are not absolute. They may clash with other basic rights or with important social interests, such as State security or public order. There are three different systems of dealing with the need to resolve such clashes. The first, followed in the US constitution, is to ignore the issue in the constitution itself, which merely defines the protected rights. Forging balancing principles is left to the courts that must interpret the constitution and examine allegations that the government has exceeded its constitutional authority. The second system, prevalent in human rights treaties such as the European Convention on Human Rights and Freedoms, lays down specific balancing tests for different rights. The third system, adopted in the Canadian Charter of Rights and Freedoms, lays down one general

[21] The first signs of attempt to develop a case law along these lines is to be found in the opinion of Dorner J in *Alice Miller* v. *Minister of Defence* (1995, not yet reported). Dorner J suggested that a violation of human dignity occurs when a person is degraded. Not every type of discrimination involves degradation of the individual. However, all discrimination on the basis of race or gender degrades the individual and therefore constitutes a violation of his or her right to human dignity.

balancing test that must be employed in all cases in which restrictions have been placed on one of the protected rights.

The basic laws follow the Canadian model. The individual rights themselves are defined in absolute terms, but the laws provide a general balancing test that must be applied in all cases. This test, as it appears in section 8 of the Basic Law: Human Dignity and Liberty, states:

> The rights according to this Basic Law shall not be infringed except by a statute that befits the values of the State of Israel and is directed towards a worthy purpose, and then only to an extent that does not exceed what is necessary, or by regulation promulgated by virtue of express authorization in such a statute.

The questions of purpose and whether the extent of the incursion is necessary have arisen in other jurisductions and the courts will be able to look to them for guidance. The Supreme Court has already looked to Canadian case law and favours an interpretation of the 'necessary extent' requirement that is similar to the proportionality test developed by the Supreme Court of Canada.

More problematical is the reference to a statute that befits the 'values of the State of Israel'. This term must be read together with section 1a of the Law that refers to the 'values of the State of Israel as a Jewish and democratic state'. It merits separate attention.

## 8. A Jewish and Democratic State

Israel's constitutional system is based on two fundamental tenets: that the State is democratic and that it is also Jewish. The first tenet provided the original rationale for incorporation of basic civil rights, such as freedom of speech, as part of the legal system, even though they were not mentioned in any written law.[22] The second provided the original legal basis for excluding a list from participation in the Knesset elections, even though no statute made provision for its exclusion.[23] The constitutional challenge facing the State of Israel is to create a synthesis between these two principles.

The meaning of Israel as a Jewish State has been a subject of major debate. On the ideological level views have ranged from minimalists, who believe that the right of every Jew to immigrate to Israel is the only necessary element of its definition as a Jewish State, to those who would ascribe a messianic mission to the State itself. While the issue was left rather vague for a long time, a 1985 amendment to the Basic Law: The Knesset adopted

[22] See *Kol Ha'am* v. *Minister of the Interior*, n. 2 above.

[23] See the opinion of Agranat J in *Yardor* v. *Chairman of Knesset Elections Committee* (1965) 19(3) PD 365.

a highly controversial definition that served only to increase the tension between the two tenets. According to section 7A of the Basic Law: The Knesset, that was introduced by the said amendment, a list may not participate in the Knesset elections if, by its aims or actions, it expressly or by implication 'negates the State of Israel as the state of the Jewish people'.[24]

The definition in section 7A ignores the status of the non-Jewish citizens of the State, who comprise 18 per cent of the population. The section would seem to imply that, contrary to the democratic notion of the State being the State of all its citizens, the State of Israel is not the State of its non-Jewish citizens.[25] The implications of this particularistic approach were most clearly articulated in the opinion of Dov Levin J in his dissent in *Ben-Shalom* v. *Central Elections Committee for the Twelfth Knesset*.[26] Levin J took the view that a list that demands total equality between Jews and Arabs in Israel, on the group as well as the individual level, should be excluded under section 7A.

The definition adopted in section 1a of the Basic Law: Human Dignity and Liberty and section 2 of the Basic Law: Freedom of Occupation is a welcome change. Use of the term 'Jewish and democratic state' would seem to imply that there is no inherent contradiction between the two tenets and that some form of synthesis must be found between them. According to the basic laws a conception of the Jewish State that is inconsistent with democratic values must therefore be rejected.

The meaning of the term 'Jewish and democratic state' has already cropped up in decisions of the Supreme Court and has caused controversy among two leading justices. According to the view of Elon J, in cases in which various approaches to an issue are compatible with democratic values, the Court must look to the tradition of Jewish law and prefer the approach consistent with that tradition, thereby creating a synthesis between the notions of a democratic and Jewish State.[27] Barak J, on the other hand, has written that 'the values of the State of Israel as a Jewish state are those universal values that are common to members of democratic societies and which grew out of Jewish tradition and history'.[28]

The notion of restrictions on rights 'necessary in a democratic society' has been developed in the case law of the European Court of Human

[24] The s. also includes two further grounds for excluding lists from participation in Knesset elections: that the list negates the democratic nature of the State or that it incites to racism (Amendment No. 9, *SH* 1155, 196).

[25] I have recently discussed this issue elsewhere. See D. Kretzmer, *The Legal Status of the Arabs in Israel* (Westview, Boulder, Col., 1990) ch. 2.

[26] (1989) 43(4) PD 221.

[27] See *Chevra Kadisha Kehilat Yerushalayim* v. *Kastenbaum* (1992) 46 (2) PD 464; *Shefer* v. *State of Israel* (1994) 48 (1) PD 87; *State of Israel* v. *Azazmi* (1992) 46 (5) PD 72.

[28] See A. Barak, 'The Constitutional Revolution: Protected Human Rights' (1992) 1 *Mishpat Umimshal* 9, 31.

Rights, while the Supreme Court of Canada has given detailed attention to the question whether restrictions on basic rights may be 'demonstrably justified in a free and democratic society'. The question the courts in Israel will have to address is whether the notion of a 'Jewish and democratic state' leads to results that are different from those adopted in European and Canadian decisions.

# 9

# *Basic Law: Human Dignity and Liberty*

## Basic principles

1. Fundamental human rights in Israel are founded upon recognition of the value of the human being, the sanctity of human life, and the principle that all persons are free; these rights shall be upheld in the spirit of the principles set forth in the Declaration of the Establishment of the State of Israel.[1]

## Purpose

1A. The purpose of this Basic Law is to protect human dignity and liberty, in order to anchor in a Basic Law the values of the State of Israel as a Jewish and democratic state.

## Preservation of life, body and dignity

2. There shall be no violation of the life, body or dignity of any person as such.

## Protection of property

3. There shall be no violation of the property of a person.

[1] For the official English text of the Declaration see 1 LSI 1.

## Protection of life, body and dignity

4. All persons are entitled to protection of their life, body and dignity.

## Personal Liberty

5. There shall be no deprivation or restriction of the liberty of a person by imprisonment, arrest, extradition or by any other manner.

## Leaving and entering Israel

6.(a) All persons are free to leave Israel.
(b) Every Israel national has the right of entry into Israel from abroad.

## Privacy

7.(a) All persons have the right to privacy and to intimacy.
(b) There shall be no entry into the private premises of a person who has not consented thereto.
(c) No search shall be conducted on the private premises or body of a person, nor in the body or belongings of a person.
(d) There shall be no violation of the secrecy of the spoken utterances, writings or records of a person.

## Violation of rights

8. There shall be no violation of rights under this Basic Law except by a Law fitting the values of the State of Israel, designed for a proper purpose, and to an extent no greater than required, or by regulation enacted by virtue of express authorisation in such law.

## Reservation regarding security forces

9. There shall be no restriction of rights under this Basic Law held by persons serving in the Israel Defence Forces, the Israel Police, the Prisons Service and other security organizations of the State, nor shall such rights be subject to conditions, except by virtue of a Law and to an extent no greater than required by the nature and character of the service.

## Validity of laws

10. This Basic Law shall not affect the validity of any Law (*din)* in force prior to the commencement of the Basic Law.

## Application

11. All governmental authorities are bound to respect the rights under this Basic Law.

## Stability

12. This Basic Law cannot be varied, suspended or made subject to conditions by emergency regulations; notwithstanding, when a state of emergency exists, by virtue of a declaration under section 9 of the Law and Administration Ordinance, 5708–1948, emergency regulations may be enacted by virtue of said section to deny or restrict rights under this Basic Law, provided the denial or restriction shall be for a proper purpose and for a period and extent no greater than required.

Yitzhak Shamir
*Prime Minister*

Chaim Herzog
*President of the State*

Dov Shilansky
*Speaker of the Knesset*

# 10

# *Basic Law: Freedom of Occupation*

## Basic principles

1. Fundamental human rights in Israel are founded upon recognition of the value of the human being, the sanctity of human life, and the principle that all persons are free; these rights shall be upheld in the spirit of the principles set forth in the Declaration of the Establishment of the State of Israel.[1]

## Purpose

2. The purpose of this Basic Law is to protect freedom of occupation, in order to establish in a Basic Law the values of the State of Israel as a Jewish and democratic state.

## Freedom of occupation

3. Every Israel national or resident has the right to engage in any occupation, profession or trade.

## Violation of freedom of occupation

4. There shall be no violation of freedom of occupation except by a Law befitting the values of the State of Israel, enacted for a proper purpose, and to an extent no greater than is required, or by regulation enacted by virtue of express authorisation in such Law.

[1] For the official English text of the Declaration of the Establishment of the State of Israel, see 1 LSI 1.

## Application

5. All governmental authorities are bound to respect the freedom of occupation of all Israel nationals or residents.

## Stability

6. This Basic Law shall not be varied, suspended or made subject to conditions by emergency regulations.

## Entrenchment

7. This Basic Law shall not be varied except by a Basic Law passed by a majority of the members of the Knesset.

## Effect of nonconforming Law

8. A provision of a Law that violates freedom of occupation shall be of effect, even though not in accordance with section 4, if it has been included in a Law passed by a majority of the members of Knesset, which expressly states that it shall be of effect, notwithstanding the provisions of this Basic Law; such Law shall expire four years from its commencement unless a shorter duration has been stated therein.

## Repeal

9. Basic Law: Freedom of Occupation[2] is hereby repealed.

[2] This Basic Law: Freedom of Occupation repeals and replaces the former Basic Law on Freedom of Occupation, enacted in 1992 (SH 5752 114).

## Provisional measure

10. The provisions of any enactment which, immediately prior to this Basic Law would have been of effect but for this Basic Law or the Basic Law repealed in section 9, shall remain in effect two years from the commencement of this Basic Law, unless repealed earlier; however, such provisions shall be construed in the spirit of the provisions of this Basic Law.

Yitzhak Rabin
*Prime Minister*

Ezer Weizman
*President of the State*

Shevah Weiss
*Speaker of the Knesset*

# PART II

# *Administrative Action*

# SECTION 4: CONFLICT OF INTERESTS

# 11

# *Conflict of Interests in the Public Service*

TANA SPANIC



## 1. The Conflict of Interests Rule in the *Likud* Case

'It is a fundamental rule in our legal system that a public servant must not be found in a situation of conflict of interest.' Thus held Barak J in the landmark judgment in the *'Likud' Faction* case.[1] The rule had already been embodied in legislation and in judicial decisions regarding various public officials, but only in the *Likud* decision did the rule receive a thoroughgoing theoretical framework. In the *Likud* judgment one finds the rationale for the rule and its characteristic features:

The rationale for the rule regarding conflict of interests is twofold. . . . First, the pragmatic rationale. In exercising his authority, the public servant must take account of all considerations relevant to the exercise of that authority, and only those considerations. When a public servant is in a situation of conflict of interests there arises a concern that when he exercises his authority, he will take into account the conflicting interest. As a result an improper exercise of the authority may occur. The law aims to assuage this concern. Second, the justification from principle. The maintenance of an orderly and responsible public service with proper public stature requires public confidence that the decisions of public officials are pertinent, honest and fair. The fact that a public servant has a conflict of interests damages public confidence in the system of government. It raises in the

[1] HC 531/79. *'Likud' Faction, Petach Tikva Municipality* v. *Petach Tikva Municipal Council* (1980) 34(2) PD 566. 569 (1980) (hereinafter *Likud*). See excerpts from this judgment in this Ch.

public the gnawing fear that extraneous considerations guide public officials, and its confidence in government is impaired. The law aims to calm this fear.[2]

The first important feature of the rule is that it is a substantive rule, a basic principle for which no explicit legislative citation is necessary. Thus the existence of a legislative prohibition against conflict of interest does not in and of itself negate the application of the rule to areas without legislative reference.[3] What is involved is a principle upon which both legislative provisions are founded, as well as judicial pronouncements forming part of Israel's 'common law'.

Another characteristic is the broad range of the rule. It is not restricted to judicial or quasi-judicial bodies, but rather applies whenever a public servant exercises authority. Nor is the application of the rule limited to a conflict between governmental interest and a private interest; it also applies when a public servant is entrusted with two governmental interests.[4]

Yet another characteristic lies in the fact that the rule looks ahead to the future, and aims to prevent the evil before it occurs.[5] Thus the rule prohibits being in a situation in which there is liable to be a conflict of interests, and in this context the test is objective; existence of a conflict is not determined according to the subjective fears of one or another person.[6] However, as we shall see later, the *Likud* court made no finding on the question whether one must show a real possibility of conflict or whether a reasonable fear of such is sufficient.[7]

The judgment constitutes a turning point in that Barak J grounded the rule not only in principles of natural justice but also in the principle of trust placed in persons who are in a fiduciary position with respect to others.[8] Prior to this judgment, the judicial decisions addressed only the rule regarding bias, which is rooted in the notion that a person cannot properly deliberate when his own interests are involved.[9] The rule against bias

[2] HC 531/79. *'Likud' Faction, Petach Tikva Municipality* v. *Petach Tikva Municipal Council* (1980) 34(2) PD 571 (1980).

[3] *Ibid.* 573. [4] *Ibid.* 571–3. [5] *Ibid.* 572. [6] *Ibid.* 572.

[7] The question which is the appropriate test is still undecided as the judges are of different minds. Compare, e.g., the opinions of Maltz and Elon JJ in HC 244/86, *Rebibo* v. *Bentov, Head of Ofakim Local Council* (1988) 42(3) PD 183 (hereafter *Rebibo*). In HC 589/86 *Shimon* v. *Kiryat Malachi Municipal Council* (1987) 41(2) PD 617 Netanyahu J ruled according to the 'real likelihood' test (at 628–9). Despite this Bach J disqualified the conflict of interests (at 625). The reasonable apprehension test, which is the stricter of the two, was used by Y. Kahan J in HC 9/82, *Virshubsky* v. *Minister of Justice* (1982) 36(1) PD 645, 650.

[8] *Likud*, n. 1 above, at 570. It is worth noting that the fiduciary duty was already cited as a source of the rule against conflict of interests by Agranat J, in CA 254/64, *Hason* v. *Daliat al Carmel Local Council* (1965) 19(1) PD 17 (hereinafter *Hason*), but this was not developed in later Sup. Ct. judgments.

[9] See HC 279/60 *Ulamei Gil Ltd* v. *Ya'ari and Municipality of Tel Aviv* (1961) 15 PD 673; HC 353/66 *Levy* v. *Head of Be'er Ya'akov Local Council* (1967) 21(1) PD 449; HC 21/66 *Ka'atabi* v. *Levy, Mevasseret Zion Local Council* (1967) 21(2) PD 431, 434; HC 18/68, *Yisrael Footballpools Ltd* (*Ball Pool*) v. *Gambling and Sports Council* (1968) 22(1) PD 683, 689.

developed in the framework of the questions when and in what circumstances will a person be disqualified from serving as a member of a judicial or quasi-judicial committee.[10] On this issue the Court adopted two basic rules:

(1) Every monetary or material connection to the issue being adjudicated, however small or large, is an automatic disqualifier, as in such circumstances the law presumes bias;
(2) A person is not disqualified on the basis of 'ties' apart from a monetary or material connection with the matter being adjudicated, unless a real possibility of bias or corruption is shown.[11]

Since these rules were made with respect to a member of a quasi-judicial tribunal, it would appear that the rule is not applicable to a body that is not judicial or quasi-judicial, and this is the reason that the Supreme Court has found it difficult to apply the rule to an administrative body.[12]

Until the *Likud* judgment, then, the judicial decisions treated bias as a ground for personal disqualification of a member of a judicial or quasi-judicial body; only by anchoring the rule in another source, as was done in this judgment, could it be broadened into a rule forbidding conflict of interests generally.

After *Likud*, the rule regarding conflict of interests could be deemed independent from the bias rule. Judgments in the aftermath of *Likud* continued to consolidate and strengthen the rule. For example, in the *Yeshpe'er*[13] decision Netanyahu J enumerates the sources of the rule forbidding conflict of interests. To the fiduciary duty and the bias rule she adds other sources, such as the rules of orderly administration, the duty of fairness, and good faith. Basing the conflict of interests rule on these sources makes it clear that the rule is henceforth intended for administrative authority as well, and to the actions of public servants generally.

Another important aspect of the *Likud* decision is that it makes it clear that the rule applies to a conflict of governmental interests just as to a conflict between a governmental and a private interest,[14] although the decisions still distinguish between them with respect to the question whether the applicable standard is reasonable apprehension of conflict, or whether it is necessary to show a real possibility. For example, Elon J maintains in the *Rebibo* judgment that:

> In the case of a possible conflict between two governmental interests on the part of a public servant who holds two positions, as distinct from conflict between a

[10] See HC 174/54, *Shimel* v. *Authority for Seizure of Lands* (1955) 9 PD 459. [11] *Ibid.* 462.

[12] See HC 18/68, n. 9 above, 689. See also S. Shetreet, 'New Trends in Principles of Natural Justice' (1986) 37 *Hapraklit* 325, 327 (Hebrew) (hereinafter 'Shetreet').

[13] HC 35/82, *Yeshpe'er Ltd* v. *Minister of Defence* (1983) 37(2) PD 505 (hereinafter '*Yeshpe'er*').

[14] Prof. Shetreet advocates applying the rule to public bodies generally, but in his opinion this is presently only an emerging trend in the judicial decisions: see Shetreet, n. 12 above, 327–9.

governmental and private interest—the public servant must refrain from holding the two positions simultaneously only when there exists a real possibility of conflict of interests.[15]

## 2. Developments since the *Likud* Case

The subsequent development of the rule regarding conflict of interests was in its appearance in various laws, its adoption by numerous public bodies and, of course, in further judicial pronouncements.[16]

In including the rule in various laws, the Israeli legislator sometimes actually details the rule in the context of the particular law concerned. An example of this is contained in the Administrative Tribunals Law of 1992 as are provisions which make various bodies responsible for examining the existence of conflict of interests in the particular sector over which they have authority. Thus, the Civil Service Commission makes decisions with respect to civil servants, the Knesset (Parliament) Ethics Committee with respect to Knesset members, and an Advisory Committee undertakes a similar task with respect to elected municipal officials.

Two officials who have played a significant role in the development of norms in this area are the Attorney General and the State Comptroller, each in his own sphere of authority.

The courts, and particularly the Supreme Court of Israel, have issued a steady stream of judgments in the area of conflict of interests. The Supreme Court especially has made a series of restrictive decisions, especially from the perspective of efficient public administration. Not that the Court was unaware of this important aspect of its findings: in one case it specifically held that the need for administrative efficiency was heavily outweighed by the need for public confidence in the administration and its proper functioning.[17]

It would seem that the present form of the rule was expressed in *Shimon* v. *Danino*.[18] In that decision, the Supreme Court examined the subject of conflict of interests in the light of three questions: is there a conflict of interests between the official duties and other interests of the public official? Does this conflict reach the level of a conflict prohibited by law? What

[15] *Rebibo*, n. 7 above, 188.

[16] See the general survey in T. Spanic and V. Lusthaus, 'Conflict of Interest in the Public Service', in A. Barak and T. Spanic (eds.), *Essays in Honour of Uri Yadin* (Bursi, Jerusalem, 1990) (in Hebrew), ii, 315–55. This article emphasizes the practical application of the rule and suggests a working model.

[17] See HC 589/86, *Shulman* v. *Herzliyah Municipality* (1986) 40(4) PD 624.

[18] HC 595/89 (1990) 44(1) PD 409.

are the legal consequences that flow from the existence of such a conflict of interests?

In order to answer the first question, it is necessary to compare the two sets of duties which face the public servant in order to ascertain the existence of a potential conflict of interests. For these purposes it is important on the one hand to provide a detailed and exact description, as far as possible, of the public duty and its functioning, and on the other hand to collect all the relevant information on the second duty. This comparison of the two sets of duties permits the disclosure of potential points of contact which are liable to cause the public servant to consider more than one interest when taking his official decisions.

The answer to the second question is to be found in an intensive examination of the conflict of interests. This examination should not be subjective. However, even when we are talking about an objective test, the question remains: what kind of connection is relevant? The case law—as we have seen—has not finally determined whether the test is the existence of a *real* possibility of a conflict of interests, or whether it is sufficient to find a reasonable apprehension of conflict.

The importance of the *Shimon* v. *Danino* decision lies in the fact that it ties the general rule to an examination of different situations of conflict of interests and to the development of solutions for the prevention of such problematic situations.

The Court adopted the approach advocated by Spanic and Lusthaus,[19] namely that in not every case of a conflict of interests should a public servant be disqualified from exercising his public duty. Different situations of conflict require different solutions. Disqualification from office should not be the first option; indeed, since it is obviously the most drastic step, it should be the last option. In seeking the appropriate solution, it should not be forgotten that it is desirable for public servants to be active in their communities and to have other areas of interests. Senior public servants are, after all, chosen for their proximity to—and expertise in—the very subject that might lead to a conflict of interests.

In order to find the appropriate balance, one must—long before reaching the conclusion that the public servant be disqualified from a particular post—endeavour to 'neutralize' the conflict by means of one of the available solutions. The solution must be appropriate to the scope of the conflict, its intensity, and its centrality in the functions of the relevant public servant. Thus, if it is found that the conflict is extensive, central, and likely to arise with regularity, there may be no alternative to disqualifying the public servant from filling the relevant post. If, on the other hand, the conflict arises only in marginal matters, and is likely to be an

[19] N. 16 above.

infrequent occurrence, a much more 'moderate' solution can be considered.

In *Shimon* v. *Danino*, Barak J makes reference to a solution which would prevent the public servant from dealing with the particular matter which raises the potential conflict of interests, but there are of course other possible solutions, such as ensuring that certain public decisions are taken together with members of the public service, or requiring prior disclosure of the conflicting interest.

Moreover, the conflict of interests inherent in two different duties or activities may be avoided not only by solutions in the public sphere, but also by appropriate steps relating to the other duty or activities of the public servant. Thus, for example, it is possible to limit the public servant's activities outside his office, or to hold certain assets in a 'blind trust', all intended to permit the individual to continue with his public functions.

To complete the picture, it should be stressed that this paper has focused on the administrative consequence of situations of conflict of interests. That is, we have considered whether it is necessary to disqualify a decision of a particular public body, or disqualify an individual from serving in a particular office.

## 3. The Conflict of Interests Rule outside the Administrative Law Context

It is important to remember that conflict of interests has consequences in other spheres as well. Thus, it is possible that such a conflict could be considered to be a form of inappropriate conduct of a public servant for the purposes of disciplinary proceedings. Similarly, there could be consequences in the criminal field: the conflict could be considered a criminal violation of public trust, as has already been decided in Israeli case law, and one could theoretically find civil remedies for a conflict of interests, if one categorized the situation as one of breach of trust.

In sum, it is clear that a rule which may from some perspectives be seen as rather minor and inconsequential, can in fact have serious legal consequences.

# 12

# *The Likud Party in the Petach Tikvah Municipality* v. *The Petach Tikvah City Council and another*

[H.C. 531/79]
[34(2) PD 566 (1980)]

*H Cohn J, Bechor J, and Barak J*

Israeli cases referred to:

[1] HC 279/60—*Ulamei Gil Ltd* v. *Moshe Ya'ari and City of Tel Aviv-Yaffo*; 15 PD 676, 673.
[2] HC 18/60—*Fuzi Abd-Allah Al-Burie* v. *Head of the Local Council of Kfar-Yasif*; 14 PD 850, 853.
[3] HC 214/79—*Taran Rafik Abd Lachi* v. *Chairman of the Local Council of Tirah*; 34(1) PD 431.
[4] CA 793/76, Motion 506/78—*Michael Luckman* v. *Haim Schiff*; 33(2) PD 533, 557.
[5] HC 142/70—*Binyamin Shapira* v. *Jerusalem District Committee of the Chamber of Advocates*; 25(1) PD 325, 331.
[6] HC 262/62—*Yisrael Peretz, Meir Levin and Dina Friedan* v. *Chairman and Members of the Local Council and Residents of Kfar-Shmiryahu;* 16 PD 2101, 2115.
[7] HC 293/64—*Rejah Ali Hassin* v. *Aloni*; 19(1) PD 572, 576.
[8] MA 48/75—*Rachamim Yedid* v. *Government of Israel*; 29(2) PD 375.
[9] HC 332/61—*Perel H. Eisner* v. *Shoshana Finkelstein*; 16 PD 1841.
[10] CA 304/70—*Moshe Aviam* v. *State of Israel*; 25(1) PD 665.
[11] HC 174/65—*Avraham Diamantman* v. *Appeal Tribunal under the Claims by Victims of the Nazis Law* (*1957*); 19(4) PD 161.
[12] HC 290/165—*Zev Elteger* v. *Mayor and City of Ramat Gan*; 20(1) PD 29, 33.
[13] Cr.A 68/66—*Anonymous* v. *Attorney General*; 20(2) PD 322.
[14] HC 18/68—*Israel Footballpools* (*Ball Pool*) *Ltd* v. *Council for the*

*Regulation of Gambling in Sport*; 22(1) PD 683.
[15] ADA 9/55—*Anonymous* v. *Chairman and Members of the Legal Council*; 10 PD 1720, 1733.
[16] HC 289/79—*Israel Port Authority* v. *National Labour Court*; 34(2) PD 141.
[17] HC 405/74—*Shalom Bar Am* v. *Captain Amnon Madar*; 29(1) PD 54, 56.
[18] HC 598/77—*Eliahu Deri* v. *The Parole Board*; 32(3) PD 161.
[19] Cr.A 500/75—*Amos Barnes* v. *State of Israel*; 30(1) PD 208, 213.

## JUDGMENT

**Barak J:**

1. In the last local authority elections, Mr Tavori, a member of the Labour Alignment, was elected Mayor of Petach Tikva. The City Council, which is respondent no. 1, comprises twenty-three members. All political groups, with the exception of Likud, which represents the opposition, form the majority coalition, numbering seventeen members. The Council appointed various committees, among these the Management Committee and the Review Committee. On 15 July 1979 Mr Muhtar (respondent no. 1), a member of the 'Achvah' party, was chosen as chairman of the Review Committee. Mr Muhtar also serves as a member of the Management Committee, which has fourteen members. The demand of the Likud faction that one of its members be appointed as chairman of the review committee was rejected by the Council. In its petition before us, the Likud faction in the Council, represented here by its chairman, is requesting that we suspend the appointment of Mr Muhtar as chairman of the Review Committee and that we make an order for the appointment of a member of the Likud opposition as chairman of the Review Committee. The request is opposed by the Council and by Mr Muhtar.

There are two questions for us to answer here. The first is was the choice of a member of the Management Committee as chairman of the Review Committee a legitimate choice? The second is is the chairman of the Review Committee bound to be a member of the opposition group? These are two separate questions and we will deal with each one separately.

2. A fundamental rule in our legal system is that a public servant is prohibited from being in a position where there is a real possibility of a conflict of interests. There are a number of sources for this rule, the important ones being the principles of natural justice on the one hand and those of trust on the other. According to the principles of natural justice, a public servant is prohibited from being in a situation where there is a real possibility of partiality or bias. The main application of this rule is in the case

of a public servant who has a judicial or quasi-judicial duty to perform. But the rule is not limited to such cases alone. Every public body, no matter what its function, must do its job without preconceived or biased attitudes, without influence and without partiality. The significance of the terms 'partiality' and 'bias' has been interpreted by H. Cohn J:

> When we use the term 'partiality' in this case, we do not mean that the respondent will deliberately or knowingly show partiality to one of the parties; and when we use the term 'bias' or 'corrupted opinion' we do not mean that the respondent's attitude has been influenced by the receipt of an actual bribe. The idea is that partiality is something inherent to people, almost in the nature of things, even if unknowingly or unintentionally. A man is partial towards himself and at the same time does not see himself as in any way liable. The position he may have adopted in his former capacity and held with true conviction, and the interests which he represented and did so from being aware of their just and legitimate claims, these are the things which are going to be naturally close to his heart. He is going to identify with them, even if only subconsciously. The same will be true of an opinion which he may have formed about a particular issue which he dealt with in his former capacity, and which he must now deal with in his present capacity. The more certain and sincere his belief then, the harder it will be for him in his new capacity to detach himself from its influence (*Ulamei Gil Ltd* v. *Moshe Ya'ari and City of Tel Aviv-Yaffo* [1]).

If that is the scope of things in the case of the relationship between a public servant's previous and present function, how much more so is there a real possibility of partiality or bias when a public servant fulfils two functions at the same time, and when there is a real possibility of conflict of interest between them. Conflict of interest is what leads to partiality, and a real possibility of conflict of interest creates a real possibility of partiality. This Court has, on more than one occasion, discussed the connection between the rule on conflict of interests and the rules of partiality, in its handling of the provisions of section 46(a)(5) of the Municipalities Ordinance (now section 120 of the Municipalities Ordinance (new version)). According to this section, any paid employee of the municipality is disqualified from serving on the Council. In interpreting this provision and determining its parameters, the Court indicated that 'the intention of the Legislature here is that a salaried council official cannot also be a serving member of the council. A party to a dispute cannot be the judge.' [2] The same is true of section 101(4) of Local Councils Order (A) 1950 [3].

3. The rule which prohibits conflict of interests can also be justified in a different way. The law recognizes that in certain circumstances a person may owe loyalty to another. Such is the law in the relationship between an agent and his principal, a manager and a company, and between a trustee and the trust. The list is not closed and instances crop up in a large variety of legal relationships (Y. Kahan J in *Luckman* v. *Schiff* [4]). It seems

to me that what is common to all these situations is that the interests of one person are entrusted to another (see Sealy, 'Fiduciary Relationships' [1962] *CLJ* 69). There is always the fear that authority without supervision or restraint can lead to corruption. The purpose of the principles of trust is, *inter alia*, to create supervision and to impose restraint on the activity of the one who has been entrusted with authority. A public servant fulfilling a public function comes within the ambit of this test. Power and authority have been entrusted to the public servant. The purpose of the grant of such power and authority is to serve not one's own interests but the interests for which the power and authority were granted. As has been said by my colleague H. Cohn J in *Binyamin Shapira* v. *Jerusalem District Bar Association Committee* [5]:

> The private domain is not the same as the public domain. The former acts for itself and grants or refuses power at will, whereas the latter is only created for the purpose of serving the public and retains nothing for itself. Whatever it has is deposited as a trust; it has itself no rights or duties, beyond those which arise from the trust or which have been granted to it or imposed on it by force of law.

A public servant, therefore, must exercise his power and authority out of loyalty and fiduciary duty (see *Peretz* v. *Kfar Shmiryahu* [6]). He should always have in mind the interest entrusted to him and no other. From here we derive the principle that a public servant must not place himself in a position where there is a real possibility of a conflict of interest, i.e. between the interest entrusted to him and any other interest, whether the latter relates to himself personally, to his property, or to any other interest which has been entrusted to him. A real possibility of a conflict of interest is inconsistent with his fiduciary duty since this latter requires that he cut himself off from any conflicting interest.

4. It is the principles of natural justice on the one hand and those of trust on the other which together create the rule that a public servant must never be in a position where there is a real possibility of conflict between the exercise of his power and authority and any other interest with which he is connected. It is appropriate here that we dwell briefly on the reasons, the scope, and the implications of this rule.

(a) The *reasons* for the rule in the matter of conflict of interests are twofold (see *Taran Rafik Abd Lachi* v. *Chairman and Local Council of Tirah* [3]). First, a practical reason. A public servant who has been invested with authority is duty-bound to exercise his power while having in mind only those considerations which are relevant to the exercise of that authority. Where the public servant finds himself in a position of conflict of interests, the suspicion arises that he may take a conflicting interest into consideration, with a resulting inappropriate use of his authority. The law exists to prevent or allay this suspicion. Secondly, a value-based reason.

For the maintenance of an orderly and responsible public service it is essential that the public have confidence that its servants make decisions based on relevant considerations and that such decisions are made in good faith. The fact that a public servant is in a position of conflict of interests damages the public faith in the system. The public begins to suspect that outside interests are influencing the decisions and its faith in the system is impaired. The law is intended to remove this suspicion.

(b) The *scope* of the rule in the matter of conflict of interest extends, first and foremost, to a conflict between the interest of the governing authority and that of the individual, whether it is a personal interest or one related to a property. This is why a public servant cannot serve on a committee of tender offers which is handling a matter in which his relative has an interest. But the rule on conflict of interests is not limited to this type of conflict alone. A public servant must not be in a position where there is a conflict between two separate government interests, where he has been appointed over both. For example, it has been adjudged that a public servant cannot at one and the same time act as the body responsible under the Land Leasing Law (temporary provision) 1959, and at the same time as the deputy director of the Israel Lands Authority, within whose framework the abovementioned authority operates (*Rejah Ali Hassin* v. *Aloni* [7]). Berinson J has stated:

> A person is, however, partial to himself, his office, his department and their interests. He is liable very easily and unintentionally to identify with them without at all feeling that he is adopting a biased attitude towards the body of which he is the chairman and for whose interests he is chiefly concerned. As is well known in such instances, not only is it essential to avert the danger of justice not being done but also of justice not being seen to be done. If it is important that justice be seen to be done, it is even more important that justice indeed be done (*Aloni* [7]).

* * *

Furthermore, the prohibition does not only apply to the exercise of discretion in the performance of some action or duty. It extends to being in a position where there is likely to be a conflict of interests. The object of the rule is to eliminate the evil before it occurs. The rule looks to the future. It makes no difference if in practice the deliberations are fair and appropriate. The aim of the rule is to remove temptation from an honest and upright person, in the sense of not putting him to the test. So it is not in fact necessary to prove that there is an actual conflict of interests. It is enough that a real possibility of the conflict exists (*Rachamim Yedid* v. *Government of Israel* [8]). The 'real possibility' is measured objectively and not by the subjective suspicions of one side or another (*Eisner* v. *Finkelstein* [9]). One good question here is must there be a real possibility of a conflict of interests, or is it enough that there is a reasonable suspicion that a conflict of interests could arise? In the case law of this Court there is support for both viewpoints (see *Aviam* v. *State of Israel* [10]), and in the case before us there is no need to take a position on this (see Alexis, 'Reasonableness in the Establishing of Bias' [1979] *PL* 143).

(c) The *implications* of the prohibition of conflict of interest extend to all areas of the law. Thus for example, in the field of 'private law' actions in which there is a conflict of interest, there could be the basis for a right of restitution of money received whilst the recipient was in breach of the rule (see *Aviam* [10]). In criminal law the behaviour of a public servant could, through a conflict of interests, form the basis for an offence of bribery or breach of fiduciary duty. On occasion the behaviour could also amount to a disciplinary offence. There could also be consequences in administrative law from a breach of this rule, so that an action already performed could be annulled, or, if not already carried out, prevented. If a conflict of interests not only affected an isolated action but extended to a wide section of an official's function, the conflict of interests would constitute a flaw in the choice of the official and his appointment (*Ulamei Gil* [1]).

5. As we have seen, Israeli law recognizes the principle which forbids a public servant from being in a position where there is a real possibility of a conflict of interests between his public function and some other interest, be it his own private interest or be it another public interest for which he is responsible. The principle is reflected in a great many laws (see for example section 120(6) of the Municipalities Ordinance (new version); section 13 of the Bank of Israel Law 1954; section 7 of the State Comptroller Law (consolidated version) 1958; section 8 of the Salaries of Knesset Members Law 1949). All these provisions contain the said principle but the principle itself does not have its origin in them. The principle on the conflict of interests is part of the Israeli equivalent of the Common Law, originated and formulated in the case law of this Court. At times it takes the form of a rule of interpretation, according to which there is a presumption that the Legislature, in granting authority to a public servant, does so with the intention that the authority be not exercised from a position of conflict of interests (see *Ulamei Gil* [1]). The principle, however, does not exist solely as a rule of interpretation. It is a substantive principle forming part of our public law. From it are derived rights of the individual on the one hand and the powers of government on the other (see Shetreet, 'The Relationship Between the Rules of Natural Justice and Procedural Provisions in Legislation', 31 *Hapraklit* 42–66). This substantive principle is sometimes to be found reflected in a piece of legislation, while other legislation will not mention it at all (see *Elteger* v. *Ramat Gan* [12]). The silence on the part of the law, however, does not mean that the principle

is not actually there, since its existence does not depend on a provision in a law. Nor is the silence of a particular law to be taken as indicating a negative provision with regard to the rule; the absence of the rule in the law merely stems from recognition of the existence of the rule as a product of the case law of this Court.

* * *

However, in the absence of a fixed constitution, the rule dealing with conflict of interests should not enjoy special normative status. There is nothing to prevent the Legislature from abolishing the rule in a law and substituting for it a provision which actually allows for a conflict of interests. As faithful interpreters of the law we are bound to give legal force to such a law and not pretend that the meaning is otherwise (*Anonymous* v. *Attorney General* [13] and *Israel Footballpools* [14]). It should be emphasized, however, that only a clear and unambiguous provision in the law will suffice to abolish the application of the existing rule on conflict of interests. And where a provision may be interpreted in more than one way, we will give preference to the interpretation which preserves the rule on conflict of interests (*Anonymous* v. *Chairman and Members of the Legal Council* [15]).

* * *

Up to now I have dealt with two extreme situations: the first, where the law has defined and conferred the necessary authority but without stipulating any specific provision in respect of the principles of natural justice. In such a case the rule is that these principles continue to apply. The second, where the Legislature has defined and conferred the necessary authority and has abolished the application of the rules of natural justice in clear and specific terms. Clearly, in such a case, the laws of natural justice will not apply. But what of an intermediate situation, where the law has defined and conferred the necessary authority and has even made a number of provisions concerning right of audience, partiality, or conflict of interest, but where such provisions do not deal with all the scenarios covered by the rules of natural justice. Do we say that once a statutory provision has been made it has the capacity to limit the application of the rules of natural justice, or rather that, in so far as it has not been specifically stipulated otherwise, the laws of natural justice will continue to apply alongside the statutory provisions?

It seems to me that the answer is to be found in the interpretation of the law which created the authority and conferred the necessary power and which also instituted provisions in matters of natural justice. It may be that the interpretation of the law will lead to the inevitable conclusion that the law is a comprehensive provision and designed to replace the rules of natural justice emanating from this Court. But it could be that interpretation of the act will lead to the conclusion that its provisions are not there to undermine the laws of natural justice but rather to complete, emphasize and complement them, and sometimes to alter them in some limited area.

Sometimes the meaning of the law is clear and simple. But at other times, the task of interpretation is difficult, particularly when the intention of the legislature is not sufficiently clear. In such cases, the trend of any interpretation ought to be that the rules of natural justice, in so far as they have not been specifically changed, will continue to have legal force alongside statutory law. A statutory provision dealing with the rules of natural justice but without encompassing them all should be regarded as supplementing and underscoring those rules of natural justice, not as an all-embracing provision (see *Nicholson* v. *Secretary of State* [1978] JPL 38 (27) quoted by Garner, *Administrative Law* (5th edn., Butterworths, London, 1979) ). This is the only way to explain the following principle of interpretation (in Israeli case law): '[t]he assumption should be that the Legislature has no intention of abolishing any principle of accepted natural justice unless it says so clearly and unambiguously' [15].

Finally it should be noted that there could well be situations in which the substance of the case requires that there be a contraction or limitation in the application of the rules of natural justice even without a clear and unambiguous provision in the law. Thus, for example, we have ruled that in labour relations within collective labour agreements there are considerations which may restrict the right of the individual to bring a claim (*Israel Port Authority* v. *National Labour Court* [16]). Similarly, in military disciplinary courts, there may well be special considerations which would justify restricting the application of the natural justice rule on partiality (*Shalom Bar Am* v. *Captain Amnon Madar* [17]). The same could be true for the rule on conflict of interests whose application might be restricted or set aside depending on the special nature of the matter at hand. At times the actual matter at hand contains within it the seed of possible conflict of interests. In such a case the aim of the rule should be to prevent this seed from growing out of control. There are also principles of necessity, or 'the needs of the moment' which may set aside the application of the rules of natural justice and conflict of interest (See *Eliahu Deri* v. *The Parole Board* [18]). Thus, for example, even a judge who is affected by partiality may be bound at times to hear a case because otherwise 'the orderly workings of the wheels of justice would be frustrated', in the words of Agranat P in *Barnes* v. *State of Israel* [19]. The same is true in the case of the rules on conflicts of interest. In all these situations it is unavoidable that authority will be legally applied though the person wielding such authority acts out of a conflict of interest. Nevertheless, the application of the doctrine of 'necessity' should be restricted to what is vitally necessary only. It should not be made into a way of undermining the main rules on conflict of interest (see Schwartz, *Administrative Law* (1976) 316).

6. Against the background of the above principles, we now turn to an examination of the case before us. We are interested in deciding whether a real possibility of conflict of interest exists between the functions of Mr Muhtar (the second respondent) as a member of the Management Committee and as a member of the Review Committee. Our examination requires an understanding of the nature of Mr Muhtar's functions in both committees. When we have defined these functions we can decide whether the performance of the functions places Mr Muhtar in a position where there is a real possibility of a conflict of interests.

7. As to the Management Committee, we learn the following from the provisions of section 147 The Municipalities Ordinance (new version) which states:

> (A) The Council may choose from among its members a permanent Management Committee whose functions will be to advise the Mayor in all that relates to the execution of his duties. It will also constitute a committee to deal with any item not covered by the authority of any other permanent or temporary committee.
>
> (B) The members of the Management Committee will be—the Mayor, his deputies and other members of the Council whose number shall be determined by the Council. The latter shall also be elected by the Council.

The Management Committee is, therefore, a direct aid to the Mayor who is himself the executive authority of the municipality (section 126(a) of the Municipalities Ordinance). He is responsible for ensuring that all tasks, which are the function of the municipality, are properly executed (section 126(b) ). The Management Committee advises the Mayor on everything affecting the execution of his duty. It is worth noting that, in general, the Council committees, whether permanent or temporary, have as their function 'to advise the Council on specific cases or events' (section 150 of the Municipalities Ordinance). The Management Committee, on the other hand, advises the Mayor and not the Council. This provision appears to be left over from the days before the Mayor was elected by direct personal election (under the Local Authorities Law (Election of head of authority and of deputies and their terms of service) 1975). It constitutes a 'mixed breed'. It is an organic part of the Council, but it functions as an advisor to the Mayor. Needless to say, the Mayor is not bound to accept the committee's advice. He can accept or reject it at will.

8. The Review Committee is a statutory permanent committee which every council is bound to elect. This is provided for in the law amending the Municipalities Ordinance (Amendment no. 24) 1978, which added section 149 as follows:

(a) The Council will appoint a Review Committee from among its members. Its task will be to consider all reports of the State Comptroller reviewing the Municipality as well as all reports of the Municipality Comptroller. The committee will submit its conclusions and suggestions to the Council.

(b) The number of the committee's members will not exceed seven. The composition will represent, as far as possible the party composition in the Council. The Mayor and his deputies will not be members of the Review Committee.

(c) The chairman of the Review Committee will belong to a different party group from that of the Mayor, unless the Council comprises one party group only.

The Review Committee is a committee of the Council and submits its summaries and recommendations to the Council. Its task is to receive from the State Comptroller and the Municipality Comptroller the results of their reviews, to receive from the Mayor his comments on the reports of the Municipality Comptroller, to consider all these reports and comments, and to formulate summaries and suggestions which it will submit to the Council.

We learn from the legislative record that, in addition to improving the status of the Mayor as a result of altering election policy and making the appointment of the Mayor subject to direct personal election and also concentrating executive authority in his hands, the Legislature also sought to strengthen supervision of his actions. To this end the Municipalities Ordinance was changed to provide that the duty of the Municipality Comptroller was 'to examine all the activities of the municipality including the legality of actions carried out under the Planning and Construction Law 1965, whether such actions were performed by someone in authority, with due probity, adhering to proper standards of efficiency and economy' (section 170(a)(1) ). As we have seen, it is provided in the amendment that 'a municipality acts through the Mayor' and that 'the Mayor is responsible for ensuring that all the functions imposed on the municipality in this ordinance or in any other law are appropriately executed' (section 126 of the Municipalities Ordinance). It follows that the review by the Municipality Comptroller extends to the actions of the Mayor himself. In order to fulfil his duties it is stipulated that the Municipalities Comptroller is the one to decide on the subjects to be reviewed, the scope of the review, and the methods for carrying it out. The findings of the Municipality Comptroller are passed on to the Review Committee which also receives the report of the State Comptroller. It is true that the Review Committee does not perform any review function itself, just as the Council does not perform any review function. But the Review Committee does disclose the results of the review to the Council, which in turn suggests what actions are called for as a result.

9. Mr Muhtar is a member of the Management Committee. In this role he is required to advise the Mayor on all matters related to the perfor-

mance of his duties. He is also a member and chairman of the Review Committee. In the latter role he is required to adopt a position and draw conclusions from the review findings in relation to the actions of the Mayor and the advice given to the Mayor by the Management Committee. The result is that, in his capacity as member and chairman of the Review Committee, Mr Muhtar is required to take up a position in respect of his own actions as member of the Management Committee. This position becomes particularly stark when the Management Committee is considering the review reports and recommending to the Mayor the comments which he ought to submit to the Review Committee. Under this state of affairs, Mr Muhtar is being asked to adopt a position in respect of his own recommendations on matters of review.

It seems to me blatantly obvious that a real possibility of a conflict of interest exists between Mr Muhtar's role as a member of the Management Committee and his role as a member of the Review Committee. Mr Muhtar is acting as a member of the Review Committee from an already biased and prejudiced position, in the sense which these terms have in this context. The fiduciary duty and good faith required of Mr Muhtar in his capacity on the Review Committee oblige him to devote himself solely to the concerns of review. He cannot do so when the review itself relates to his own actions, inasmuch as a twofold fiduciary creates the real possibility of a conflict of interest. 'The reviewed cannot become the reviewer.' It is true that the conflict of interest now before us is not between a public and a private interest. It is between two governmental interests, but even such a conflict is prohibited. It may be presumed that Mr Muhtar will do his utmost to perform his two functions in an appropriate manner. However the law requires that he be prevented from being in a situation where he has to make critical recommendations about his own actions in order that he be not put to a test which he may well fail. Not only is the work of the Review Committee adversely affected thereby but also public faith in the review system is shaken. The public is bound to have no faith in the recommendations of the Review Committee when these have been formulated by those who are themselves subject to review. The conflict of interest in this case is not a one-time-only affair relating to an isolated action. The role of the Management Committee is to advise the Mayor. The actions of the Mayor and thus also the advice of the Management Committee are at the centre of both external and internal review and therefore the central interest of the Review Committee. In these circumstances there is no escaping the fact that, as a result of the conflict of interest, Mr Muhtar must cease to serve on the Management Committee or, alternatively, he must cease to be a member of the Review Committee or its chairman. The petition presented to us is directed at Mr Muhtar's membership of the Review Committee, and it is on this issue that Mr Muhtar made his defence. Since we have rejected his position, we have no alternative but to invalidate his membership of the Review Committee, so long as he serves on the Management Committee.

10. I have indicated that there are times when the actual substance of the material we are dealing with contains the elements of a conflict of interest and as a result the application of the rules may be modified. I do not think that this applies to the case before us. The very fact that we are dealing with an elected political body does not in any way prevent the application of the rules on conflicts of interest. All public servants must refrain from conflicts of interest and this is particularly so of publicly elected persons who are exposed to public scrutiny and must serve as a model to the public.

The function of the Review Committee, which is to consider reports and make recommendations, does not include anything which should restrict or prevent the application of the rules on conflicts of interest. On the contrary. It is particularly in the sphere of review as in that of adjudication that so far as is possible, the independence and impartiality of those engaged in the review needs to be safeguarded.

11. We have noted that the rules on conflict of interests may sometimes give way to the needs of the moment. It is true that sometimes there may be no alternative to public servants, serving on a Review Committee, being required to take a stance and reach conclusions in the area of review relating to their own governmental actions. Take, for example, the review findings concerning the actions of a municipality under the Planning and Construction Law, 5725–1965. This review will naturally relate to the actions of the local committee under the Planing and Construction Law. As is well known the Municipal Council is itself the Local Planning and Construction Committee (under section 18A of the Planning and Construction Law) and all the members of the Review Committee are also members of the local Planning and Construction Committee. In their capacity as members of the Review Committee they have to take a stance, reach conclusions, and make recommendations concerning their very own actions as members of the Local Planning and Construction Committee. This state of affairs is not at all desirable since there is a clear conflict of interest here. But it is unavoidable because the Municipalities Ordinance provides that the Review Committee should be elected from among council members. It is clear that consideration should be given to a change in the law. Such a change would stipulate—as is current practice in council committees in general (section 112 of the Municipalities Ordinance)—that people who are not Council members should also serve on the Review Committee and furthermore that it is they who ought to deal with the findings of any review relating to the actions of any council members who are also members of the Review Committee.

12. In the case before us we have found no suggestion of 'the needs of the moment', which might have necessitated ignoring the rules forbidding a conflict of interests. According to the Municipalities Ordinance, there is no reason why the allocation of committee duties among the council members should not be such that members of the Review Committee do not serve on the Management Committee. The law does not stipulate a minimum number for the two committees and they could be appointed without any overlap in personnel.

A statute has the power to override the application of rules dealing with the prohibition on conflicts of interest. In the opinion of Mr Barr, the learned counsel for the respondents, the provisions of the Municipalities Ordinance do, indeed, override the rules on conflict of interests where they relate to the appointment of Review Committee members. In his opinion, the Legislature has ruled on who is eligible and who not, for the purposes of appointment to the Review Committee. In this way a closed list of qualifications has been determined; the court cannot then extend the list of those unqualified merely by judicial decision. Those eligible for the Review Committee are the members of the council. Those ineligible are the Mayor and his deputies. For the purposes of chairmanship of the committee a member of the same political party as the Mayor is also ineligible. Mr Muhtar falls within the list of those eligible and not in the list of those ineligible. His appointment is thus lawful. According to Mr Barr, the prohibition in section 149(c) for the Mayor, his deputies, and members of his political party (for the purposes of chairmanship of the Review Committee) would indicate an endorsement of members of the Review Committee having other duties allocated to them. If the Legislature had intended to widen the prohibition on membership of the Review Committee and extend it to cover those serving on the management committee—asks Mr Barr—why did it not do so explicitly? Since there is no provision at all in this respect it seems that the Legislature intended to make it possible for a member of the Management Committee to serve also on the Review Committee.

As we have seen, the rules on conflict of interests sometimes exist as rules of interpretation and sometimes as parts of the substantive law. They can help in the interpretation of a law and they can also be used to fill gaps in legislation. If section 149c had made no provision at all concerning the composition of the Review Committee we would certainly not have presumed that the Legislature was prepared to tolerate the existence of a conflict of interest (see *Diamantman* v. *Appeal Tribunal* [11]); we would not have interpreted the silence as a negative provision but rather would have ruled that the Legislature was leaving the whole matter open in the expectation that the gap would be filled by Israeli case law on the question of conflict of interest (see *Elteger* v. *Ramat Gan* [12]). The argument of the petitioner is that, in this case, a statutory provision has been made, one on the question of conflict of interests that fills the gap, leaving no space open for judicial completion.

I cannot accept this argument. Under our case law, in order to override the application of the laws of natural justice, clear and explicit language is required. This principle also applies to any attempt to deny the application of the rules on conflict of interests, which themselves derive from the rules of natural justice. . . .

Are we to say that the mention of disqualification of the Mayor and his deputies implies that there are no other cases of disqualification? In my opinion, such a conclusion is not called for. The law's reference to the Mayor and his deputies is solely to give expression to its view that those office holders, as the central executive figures in the running of the municipality, are immediately disqualified from acting as members of the Review Committee without any need to refer to the general law. But this specific provision is not of itself sufficient to imply that other members of the council would be eligible to serve on the committee even if a real possibility of conflict of interest existed.

And if one asks, why did the law not mention the other members of the Council and stipulate them in its disqualifying provisions? The answer is simply that the other members of the Council have many and varied functions. Some are affected by conflicts of interest and some not. The Legislature considered it best to leave the matter to the general law.

The foregoing conclusion stems, in my opinion, not only from the interpretation of section 149c of the Municipalities Ordinance; it also falls in line with the legislative objective behind the setting up of a Review Committee. The aim was, on the one hand, to establish the office of the Mayor as the executive authority of the Municipality, and on the other hand to create a balancing supervision over his actions by way of strengthening the council's power of review. . . .

To realize this objective, it is necessary not only to ensure the independence and objectivity of the municipality comptroller, but actually to bolster the position of the Review Committee, engender public confidence in its actions and enable it to fulfil its balancing and supervisory role. This will not be achieved if members of the council who are connected functionally with the Mayor through the Management Committee can also serve as members of the Review Committee. The requirements of balance and supervision demand the separation of the two authorities.

13. * * *

I would accept the first part of the petition, that Mr Muhtar be disqualified from being a member or chairman of the review committee so long as he is a member of the Management Committee. I would reject the second part of the petition.

**Bechor J:**

I have read with interest the instructive judgment of my esteemed colleague Barak J, but I regret that I must differ with him. My colleague has presented all the legislative provisions and described the position in depth. The question is what conclusion should be drawn in this situation; I can, accordingly, be brief.

The Mayor of a municipality is the executive authority. Under section 147(a) of the Municipalities Ordinance, the Council may choose from among its members a permanent Management Committee whose function is to advise the Mayor. Under subsection (b), the Management Committee members will be those whom the council appoints including the Mayor and his deputies.

According to section 149c which was added to the Law in 1978, the council must appoint from among its members a Review Committee whose function is to consider all reports of the State Comptroller concerning review of the municipality and all reports made by the Municipality Comptroller. It is then to submit its summaries and suggestions to the council. The number of members on this Committee will not exceed seven and its composition should as far as possible match the political party composition in the Council. The Mayor and his deputies are not to be members of the Committee. The chairman of the Committee should be of a different party from that of the Mayor unless there is only one political party represented in the Council.

The practical work of review is done by the Municipality Comptroller on a continual basis alongside the review by the State Comptroller. The role of the Committee is to receive the reports on the reviews it has conducted, to receive also the comments of the Mayor on these reports, consider these, and submit its own summary conclusions and suggestions to the Council. The Review Committee constitutes a kind of filtering intermediate body which is required to assist the Council in its decisions on the problems raised both by the State Comptroller and by the Municipality Comptroller.

* * *

The Legislature has provided that the composition of the committee should match that of the political groups in the Council. Every Council member is eligible to serve on the Review Committee subject to the limitation that the Mayor and his deputies are not eligible. From this it can be understood that a Council member who is on the Management Committee can also be a member of the Review Committee. The Legislature has made a further restriction in that the chairman of the Review Committee should be of a different political group from that of the Mayor.

* * *

The Legislature has stipulated that all the Review Committee members should also be Council members, and has set out certain reservations by defining who can and who cannot become members of the Review Committee and also who cannot be its chairman. I do not think that we should add any further restrictions of our own. Safeguarding the rules of propriety and justice is of the highest importance. I hold however, that it is not for the Court to go too far in this case, when the law has detailed its provisions in a clear enough form.

* * *

Were my opinion to be accepted this petition would be rejected.

**H. Cohn, J:**

The difference of opinion which has arisen between my two esteemed colleagues who have sat with me in judgment on this petition is one that has divided adjudicators for a very long time. What is the point at issue? It is a dispute as to the ways of interpreting a law. One holds that there is nothing in the law except what is actually apparent and that is the language of the legislator. The other says that there is more in the law than meets the eye and that is the subject of the law and the intention of the legislator. One says, 'give the law a literal interpretation, following the exact and grammatical meaning of the text.' The other says, 'give the law a contextual interpretation; for the law's objective to be realized, go beyond the text to arrive at the legislator's estimated aim.' It goes without saying that both are right.

My own view is that one should interpret the law according to the exact and literal meaning of the text in criminal law cases. It has been said that 'the words used by the Legislator are a kind of Magna Carta for someone who is indicted for a crime'. You cannot convict him except on the basis of an explicit provision by the Legislature. You cannot impose a punishment on the basis of logical deduction, analogy, allusion in the text, by an *a priori* inference, or on what appears to the judges to be the intention of the Legislature. For myself (and sometimes I have found myself in the minority here), I support the approach of word-for-word interpretation even when the law provides the State authorities with a cause of action or serves as a source of authority to deny or limit the rights of a citizen. It is from this premise that the obligation on the citizen to make statutory payments to the State or fulfil some other obligation can only derive from the explicit wording of the law.

However this is not so in the case of laws which are intended to set limits on acts of government and to protect or otherwise favour the citizen. With such laws I adopt a 'generous' mode of interpretation. Thus if the subject or purported intent of the Legislature, or the objective of the law, or the principles of natural justice so demand, I am prepared to read into the law things which are not actually there but which should be there if the objectives of the law are to be realized in reasonable measure.

This mode of interpretation does not necessarily constitute judicial law-making or trespassing into the territory of the Legislature. The judge is still not making the kinds of rulings which he would make if he were the Legislature. All he does is to look, in the text of the law and between the lines of its provisions, for some indication of the Legislature's purpose and thus for the proper way to carry out his task.

The law in question is section 149c of the Municipalities Ordinance whose purpose is to add a Review Committee to the existing committee in the municipal council. The duty of the additional committee is to submit to the council a summary of the reviews conducted by the State Comptroller and the Municipality Comptroller and to make suggestions with regard to the conclusions to be drawn from the review and the actions necessary to make good any wrongdoing. Review is, by nature, a means of restricting the misuse of power by those in authority in the body being reviewed. Its purpose is to ensure that the Executive not only keeps within the parameters of its lawful authority but also that it be particular about the probity of its conduct of its affairs. In all respects, the review constitutes a form of protection for the citizen from the possible abuses by the reviewed body or at the very least a way of providing material necessary for the complete and efficient protection of the citizen.

The purpose of the Legislature in requiring each Municipal Council to set up a Review Committee was, as clearly stated in the law, to ensure that the reports of the Comptrollers do not 'fall on deaf ears' but are brought up for discussion in the Council, which will, in turn, give due consideration to the practical recommendations to be made to it by the relevant committee in the wake of the review. Thus the committee fulfils an important function in the review process. A great deal depends on its efficiency and competence.

Had the Legislature stipulated that every member of the Council was eligible to be a member of the Review Committee, I would have witheld my apprehensions in deference to its will. But not only did it not say so, but it specifically excluded certain members of the Council from being eligible candidates for the Committee, and excluded any member of the Mayor's political party from candidacy for the chairmanship. The reason for excluding the Mayor and his deputies is that they are the ones being reviewed. They are responsible for running the city's affairs and it is their actions and possible shortcomings which are the subject of the review. The Legislature is cognizant of human nature and knows that a person is partial to himself, does not see himself as in any way liable, and does not like to work for something only to lose it. It is only natural that a person will reject criticism of his own actions and will prefer to have it buried and forgotten. Even if there were five righteous people in the city who had the spiritual strength to welcome criticism of their actions, the Legislature would still decide that it is better not to put them to the test. Moreover, the law must be enacted for all, righteous or otherwise. The legislator is also only human and cannot diagnose people's intentions.

* * *

Within the designation of the executive in a municipality, there are some who have actual authority to act and others who have potential authority. This should be so—the changes of time and circumstance, coalition calculations as well as economic and strategic considerations, are liable to require the concentration of power in one quarter or the transfer to another, and the reverse. Nor is what is appropriate for one municipality necessarily so for another. Furthermore, while a deputy has no specific duty or task in the management of the city's affairs so long as certain powers have not been allocated him (except for when the Mayor is unable to perform his duties as under section 134 of the Ordinance), a member of the Management Committee has an important function, even before any authority has been allocated him, and that is 'to advise the Mayor in any matter relating to the execution of his duties'. The petitioners' counsel have argued correctly here that, in the matter of review, an advisor is no less sensitive, and may be more so, than the executive authority himself. The executive may try to distance himself from the action by making it the responsibility of the advisor. Be that as it may the actual duty to give advice to the Mayor, which rests with the Management Committee, brings its members under the wing of the executive authority in the municipality—its very name is witness to the fact that it is intended for management, and it does in fact engage in management.

* * *

To achieve the transparent purpose of the Legislature and realize the objective of the law we must interpret the phrase 'the Mayor and his deputies' (in section 149c(b) of the Municipalities Ordinance) as if it meant to include all the other members of the permanent Management Committee. Such a broad interpretation is intended purely for the purposes of protecting the interests of rate-paying citizens, in order to ensure that the review procedures on the affairs of their city be efficient and be seen to be objective, and that those whose actions are under review do not become the reviewers and do not set themselves up as judges of those who are reviewing their own actions.

Since the respondent, Mr Muhtar, is a member of the Management Committee he is disqualified from being on the Review Committee and even more so disqualified from being its chairman.

I also agree that the petition for an order to the Municipal Council to choose a chairman for the Review Committee from one of the opposition parties has no substance. There is no disqualification attaching to any member of the Council who is not on the Management Committee and is not of the Mayor's party group from being appointed chairman of the Review Committee.

It is decided by a majority decision to make the first part of the temporary injunction final, and to declare that the second respondent is disqualified from being a member or chairman of the Review Committee so long as he is a member of the permanent Management Committee.

It is decided unanimously to reject the second part of the petition and to cancel section (b) of the temporary injunction.

There is no order for costs.

Judgment given on 14 January 1980.

# SECTION 5: ADMINISTRATIVE TRIBUNALS

# 13

# *The 1992 Administrative Tribunals Law: An Introductory Note*

MOSHE LANDAU



## 1. Introduction

In these notes, I propose to focus on matters pertaining to the legal organization of administrative tribunals in Israel and to the rules of procedure and evidence to be applied in such tribunals. I shall do so in light of a recent piece of Israeli legislation, the Administrative Tribunals Law ('the Law') which the Knesset passed in February 1992. My subject is closely circumscribed: it does not include matters concerning substantive administrative law, as applied by administrative tribunals ('tribunals') in Israel, nor does it include the kindred subject of the internal review of administrative action by recourse to a higher echelon within the administrative hierarchy. These two subjects of administrative law have not as yet been dealt with by legislative enactment, but are still almost entirely within the domain of judge-made law.

The Administrative Tribunals Law provides for procedures to be followed by an administrative authority in legal disputes between an individual or entity and the authority. A fair and efficient administrative procedure is important because of the great proliferation of administrative agencies which hold great power over our lives. As in England, the extensive legislation of the modern welfare state has given rise to a plethora of tribunals, each of which entertains numerous appeals against administrative decisions based on the enabling legislation. The main achievement of the Law is that it clarifies the procedure to govern these challenges to administrative action—an area of the law which has been in a state of flux ever since the establishment of the State of Israel in 1948.

In Israel, as elsewhere, the rationale for removing administrative disputes from the jurisdiction of the ordinary court system is: (1) that the courts would be flooded by the sheer volume of this new kind of litigation; (2) that disputes of this nature often need expert knowledge not possessed by the courts; and (3) that ordinary court procedure is too cumbersome for the speedy resolution of such disputes.

## 2. The Administrative Tribunals System before 1992

In designing its system of administrative tribunals, Israel has generally rejected the option of establishing a separate set of administrative courts equal to and independent from the ordinary courts. It did establish, in 1965, a separate set of labour courts which deal with individual and collective labour disputes and disputes concerning benefits guaranteed by national insurance legislation. However, the decisions of the labour courts are subject to the supervisory jurisdiction of the Supreme Court sitting as a High Court of Justice, which, in recent years, has exercised its jurisdiction quite vigorously.

The solution generally adopted in Israel has been to set up separate tribunals under each of the statutes in question, usually, but not always, with a right to appeal against the tribunal's decision to the High Court. The tribunals set up under this system are of varying composition. Generally, they are presided over by a judge or magistrate who is either still in office or retired from the bench, or by a person qualified for judicial appointment. In cases which require special professional expertise, the chairman of the tribunal need not be a lawyer, but may be a person possessing such professional experience. The tribunal will often include two further members chosen because of their professional or public standing. The enabling statute always provides that the tribunal is not to be bound by the rules of procedure and evidence observed in the ordinary court system.

Early in the history of these new tribunals, it became apparent that the profusion of different tribunals resulted in inconsistencies in the application of the various statutes enacted on a given subject. Thus, proposals were advanced to consolidate existing tribunals, or alternatively to group together tribunals dealing with similar subjects, such as social benefits or fiscal matters. A unification of the various rules of procedure was also suggested. In light of some of these concerns, the Attorney General proposed legislation in 1958 which would have transferred the jurisdiction over administrative appeals from the existing tribunals to an administrative division of the District Courts, with a judge sitting alone or with two assessors. However, no action was taken on this proposed law.

A second attempt at reform came in 1975 when an Advisory Committee issued a report on administrative appeals. The Committee's main recommendation was to transfer to the District Courts the jurisdiction of tribunals presided over by a judge or magistrate under existing law, but without setting up a separate administrative division. Some thought that this recommendation represented a large step backwards, ignoring the arguments in favour of the need to remove disputes in administrative matters from the ordinary courts. However, the counter-arguments which prevailed in the view of the majority of the Committee were: (1) that no matter where the appeals were heard, additional judicial manpower was needed and could be provided by statute; (2) that the shackles of procedure and evidence in the courts could be removed just as easily by providing more flexibility for the court sitting in administrative disputes; and (3) that consolidating tribunals with the general courts would add to the prestige of those tribunals in the eyes of the public. The Advisory Committee recommended further that tribunals which were to be presided over by persons not learned in the law should be left outside the court system and should be put under the supervision of a Council of Tribunals, to be created along the lines of the Council set up in England following the recommendations of the Franks Committee on Administrative Tribunals and Inquiries in 1957.

While much work was done by the Ministry of Justice in drafting legislation to implement the recommendations of the 1975 Committee, the Committee's report encountered opposition in various quarters and thus it, too, remained stillborn. Nonetheless, traces of the recommendations may be seen in the provisions of the Administrative Tribunals Law 1992, to which I now turn.

## 3. The Administrative Tribunals Law of 1992

As seen against the historical background described above, the main merit of the Law is the fact that the former legislative inertia has at last been overcome. The approach finally adopted in the Law was to proceed gradually, instead of attempting to solve existing problems all at once.

The Law provides for optional arrangements. Under section 4, the Law applies in principle only to the tribunals enumerated in the Schedule appended to it, which are at present fifteen in number. Among the tribunals covered by the Law are the tribunals dealing with benefits for disabled soldiers and their families, certain disputes of a fiscal nature with local authorities, disputes under the Antiquities Law, and disputes under the Standard Contracts Law. So far,the list looks haphazard. The inclusion of further tribunals will depend on the co-operation of the government ministries responsible for the subject matters dealt with by the remaining tribunals.

Even for those tribunals specifically listed in the Schedule, many of the arrangements adopted by the Law for the organization and the operation of tribunals apply only when not in conflict with specific provisions in any existing statute. For example, section 5(f) of the Law enables the Minister of Justice, in consultation with the Council of Tribunals (discussed below), to determine the qualifications required of members of tribunals and the rules for appointing such members. However, the power of the Minister of Justice must be read subject to subsection (a) of the same section, under which the mode of appointments of members of a tribunal and their qualifications are to be governed by specific existing statutory provisions. Similarly, the rules of procedure for tribunals which the Minister of Justice may make under the Law, in consultation with the Council, are again to be read as being subject to existing rules of procedure for any particular tribunal (see section 55(c) of the Law and clause 2 of the Regulations). Under this arrangement, litigation is likely to focus on whether a lacuna exists in the specific enabling legislation of a tribunal, which may be filled in by the provisions of the Law. This will largely be a question of statutory interpretation.

One cannot, in this brief review, give a full account of the specific provisions of the Law. I will therefore present a cursory view of some of its primary features which may be of general interest. Most basically, the Law does not purport to interfere with the dichotomy which existed prior to its enactment between tribunals presided over by a judge or magistrate and those which can be presided over by a non-lawyer. Tribunals of the first category, whose internal administration is usually already part of the general court system, are now expressly made subject to the directions of the President of the Court or his Deputy (sections 5(d) and 6). By contrast, no such express supervisory authority exists for tribunals of the second category, which are left outside the court system.

Section 7 of the Law provides that the chairman presiding over the panel of a tribunal has to be a judge or a person eligible to be appointed as judge of a magistrates court. But again, under section 4 of the Law, this requirement will apply only to a tribunal included in the appended Schedule. The Law also contains detailed provisions on the nature of possible conflicts of interest which will disqualify a person from serving as a member of a tribunal generally, or from sitting on a specific appeal (sections 9 and 15).

In order to facilitate the determination of questions requiring particular expertise, the Law allows for the appointment of an expert who is to report to the tribunal after considering expert opinions submitted by the parties to the appeal (section 29). With the consent of the tribunal, the parties may then require the expert appointed by the tribunal to reply to written questions arising out of his opinion. Yet, the final decision will always lie with the tribunal itself, even on questions requiring expert knowledge. By adopting this procedure, the tribunal can arrive at its decision of such questions after an open discussion and with the full knowledge of the parties. This contrasts with a system in which experts sit as members of the tribunal itself, which often leaves the parties unaware of the considerations which may have led the expert members of the tribunal to arrive at their conclusions.

Section 20 of the Law specifies that in all matters of procedure for which there are no specific provisions in the Law or other enactment, the tribunal shall 'act in the way it considers best in the interests of justice'. This is designed to give the tribunal the necessary flexibility to adjust its procedure to the needs of the case and subject matter before it. Nevertheless, the Law and the Regulations insist on the observance of rules of 'natural justice', such as giving the parties a fair hearing and requiring the tribunal to give reasons for its decision in writing. Legal aid is provided in certain cases, such as benefits for disabled persons and for discharged soldiers. Litigants can appear before a tribunal in person, be represented by an advocate, or be represented by another person, as long as this other person does not receive a fee.

The proceedings of the tribunals are generally open to the public, but there are exceptions to this rule, such as the need to ensure the security of the State or its foreign relations, to protect the morals or welfare of a minor, or to prevent the intimidation of a witness before a tribunal (section 25).

A litigant before the tribunal is accorded a general right to inspect documents in the possession of the administrative authority which rendered the decision being appealed. Again, there are exceptions to the exercise of this right, such as requests to inspect documents privileged by law or containing an evaluation of the personal qualifications of the litigant for appointment to office. In general, the tribunal itself may require the documents in question to be produced and may then allow the inspection of documents which the administrative authority was unwilling to disclose to the litigant (section 30).

Of special interest are the provisions in the Administrative Tribunals Law regarding documents which an administrative authority refuses to produce on the ground that their disclosure would prejudice the security of the State, its foreign relations, or an important public interest. These provisions follow the solutions adopted by the Israeli law of evidence for the ordinary courts. As early as 1957, the Supreme Court of Israel refused to follow the English rule in *Duncan* v. *Cammel, Laird and Co.* ([1942] AC 642), which apparently allowed the Executive unfettered discretion to refuse disclosure of a document in court on the ground that its disclosure would be harmful to the public interest.[1] Instead, the Supreme Court of Israel provided for a special procedure which left the ultimate decision in the hands of the court. Under this procedure, the court may inspect the disputed documents *in camera* and, if it finds no grounds for withholding the documents, may order their production in court despite the objection of the Minister that the documents' disclosure would harm the public interest. In 1968, the Knesset extended this procedure to cases where a privilege was claimed for reasons of State security or harm to foreign relations. In such cases, the law now entrusts to a single judge of the Supreme Court the decision whether the claim of privilege should be upheld or disclosure of the document compelled in the interests of justice.

Sections 31 and 32 of the Law adopt this statutory arrangement for administrative tribunals. Thus, when a privilege is claimed on grounds of State security or harm to foreign relations, the dispute will come before a single judge of the Supreme Court, as would a similar dispute in the ordinary courts. If the only privilege being claimed is harm to an important public interest, the tribunal itself is empowered to decide the dispute.

Under section 45 of the Law, final decisions of administrative tribunals are subject to appeal to a single judge of the District Court. However, if the tribunal was presided over by a judge of the District Court, the appeal will lie to the Supreme Court. The Law does not limit appeals of administrative tribunals to points of law, thereby doing away with the thorny problem of distinguishing between points of law and fact. Here, it must again be remembered that the provisions of the Law may be overridden by a contrary provision in existing legislation applying to a particular tribunal. It is also important to note that, in addition to this appellate jurisdiction specified in the Law, there exists the supervisory jurisdiction of the Supreme Court sitting as High Court of Justice. The supervisory jurisdiction of the High Court of Justice covers all administrative decisions affecting a citizen, including decisions by a tribunal, even where there is no statute granting a right of appeal.

Finally, the Law gives the Council of Tribunals ('Council') a basis in statute, instead of its former existence *extra legem*. Under the Law, the Minister of Justice is empowered to appoint the members of the Committee. Of the appointees to the Council, at least one third must have legal qualifications and not more than one third may be public servants.

[1] Apparently, the force of *Duncan* has been whittled down considerably by subsequent judicial decisions.

The Council's functions are to advise Ministers on the desirability of establishing new administrative tribunals or of abolishing existing tribunals, and on matters relating to the organization of such tribunals. In addition, the Council is authorized to set rules of procedure and evidence for the administrative tribunals.

Under its advisory power, the Council may advise the Minister of Justice or any other Minister having the power to do so, to issue guidelines on non-judicial matters concerning administrative tribunals. This advisory function of the Council is important especially regarding the operation of tribunals which are left outside the courts system. Guidelines for such tribunals should stress that these tribunals are to operate independently of the administrative framework of the government department or other public authority whose decision is being appealed. Similarly, in matters of the tribunals' own internal administration and clerical services, there must be a clear separation between the tribunal and the department or the authority in question, in order to preclude any impression of departmental bias on the part of the tribunal.

In conclusion, despite the built-in limitations on the scope of the Law, it does constitute an important step forward in the necessary process of introducing clarity and uniformity into the organization and procedure of administrative tribunals.

# 14

# *Administrative Tribunals Law, 1992*

## Chapter 1: General Provisions

**Definitions**

1. In this Law—

'administrative tribunal',* or 'tribunal', means any judicial body set up by a minister or other administrative authority having power of adjudication, whether it be termed a tribunal, objections board or appeal committee or whether it has any other designation;
'the Council' means the Administrative Tribunals Council set up under this Law;
'a member of a tribunal' shall include the chairman of the bench of a tribunal;
'power of adjudication' means the power to decide on a dispute to which an administrative authority is party;
'objection' means an application, under a provision in any enactment, to a tribunal for it to exercise its power of adjudication;
'an appointing authority' means a minister or other administrative authority empowered under any enactment to appoint a member of a tribunal;
'judge' shall include a person who has served as a judge in any court under the Courts Law [Consolidated Version], 1984, or in a labour court under the Labour Court Law 1969.

**Establishment of a tribunal**

2. An administrative tribunal shall be established by statute.

**Judicial independence**

3. In judicial matters, a member of a tribunal is subject to no authority other than of the law.

* Some of the more technical sections have been omitted.

**Application**

4. (a) The provisions of this Law shall apply to any tribunal enumerated in the Schedule and also to any other judicial body in respect of which any statutory provision prescribes that the provisions of this Law shall apply to it.

(b) The Minister of Justice, in consultation with the minister in charge of implementing the enactment under which the tribunal was established, together with the Council, and with the approval of the Constitution and Law Committee of the Knesset may vary the schedule.

(c) Despite the provisions of sub-section (a), no provision of this Law shall apply to tribunal if there exists a provision as to the same matter applicable to the same tribunal in another Law.

## Chapter 2: Administrative Tribunals

### *Article A*: *Appointment and Term of Office*

**Chairman of the bench**

7. The chairman of the bench shall be a judge or a person eligible to be appointed as judge of a Magistrates' Court.

**Term of Office**

8. (a) The term of office of a member of a tribunal shall be three years.

(b) A member of a tribunal may be re-appointed for additional terms of office in the same way as he was originally appointed.

(c) A decision of a tribunal shall not be deemed void merely because the term of office of one of its members has ended, as long as no more than six months have elapsed since the end of the term of office.

**Conflict of interests on appointment**

9. (a) No person who is liable to find himself, directly or indirectly, in a permanent state of conflict of interests between his function as member of tribunal and any other interest of his shall be appointed as member of the tribunal, nor shall he serve thereon.

In this section—

'any other interest' shall include an interest of a relative of a member of a tribunal, or the interest of a body in which a member or his relative have a controlling interest;

'relative' means a spouse, parent, child or other dependant of a member of a tribunal.

'a controlling interest' means an interest of one of the following: a director or other responsible employee of the body; a person having a share greater than 10 per cent in the capital or in the right to receive profits in that body; a person who may appoint 10 per cent or more of the directors; a person having 10 per cent or more of the voting rights in that body.

(b) No person who has a permanent professional, business or other connection with the administrative authority against whose decisions an objection may be submitted to a particular tribunal shall be appointed as a member of that tribunal; for this purpose, a present employee or elected representative of the administrative authority, or one who has retired from the authority within the past year shall, *inter alia*, be regarded as having a permanent connection with that authority.

**Proviso as to conflict of interests**

10. Irrespective of the provisions of section 9, an appointment shall not be regarded as involving a conflict of interests if

(1) it stems from a statutory provision whereby—

a member of the tribunal is to be appointed from a particular interest group; or

(2) it is necessary to appoint a member of the tribunal with a particular expertise or special qualification, and another suitable candidate cannot reasonably be found.

## *Article B*: *Bench of the Tribunal*

**Conflict of interests in a particular case.**

15. (a) A member of a tribunal shall not participate in the bench of the tribunal if he is liable to find himself, either directly or indirectly, in a state of conflict of interests between his function as member of the tribunal and any other interest of his.

In this section—

(1) 'any other interest' shall include an interest of a relative of a member of a tribunal, or the interest of a body in which a member of the tribunal are the directors or responsible employees or the interest of a body in respect of which they participate in the share capital, the share capita, the right to receive profits, the right to appoint a director or the right to vote.

(2) 'relative' means a spouse, parent, child, brother or sister or any other person dependant on a member of a tribunal.

(b) Whenever it becomes clear to a member of a tribunal that he is precluded from participating in the hearing of a particular objection owing to a conflict of interests, he shall so inform his colleagues on the bench, and, where the hearing has already commenced, also the litigants concerned, and shall refrain from taking part in the hearing of that objection.

(c) Where a member of a tribunal has a doubt whether he is precluded from participating in the hearing of a particular objection owing to a conflict of interests, or where one of the parties submits that a member of the tribunal is so precluded, the matter shall be decided by the bench of the tribunal including that member, by a reasoned decision; where the member of the tribunal is a serving judge, he shall decide the matter.

(d) A submission by a litigant that a member of the tribunal is precluded from participating in the hearing of a particular objection owing to a conflict of interests shall only be entertained if put forward at the commencement of the hearing or immediately after the ground for the conflict of interests has been brought to the notice of the party.

(e) Where a member of a tribunal is precluded from continuing to participate in the hearing of an objection owing to a conflict of interests, the bench shall be regarded, for that particular purpose, as a curtailed bench in accordance with section 17.

(f) The provisos in section 10 shall apply to this section.

**An incomplete bench**

16. (a) Where a bench of a tribunal has been convened for a session and one member of the bench, not being the chairman, is absent from the session, the hearing at that session shall take place before those members of the bench who are present (hereafter—an incomplete bench). If the parties have not consented thereto or if the chairman of the bench decides not to hold the hearing, it shall be postponed to another date.

(b) A decision of an incomplete bench in which opinions differ shall be taken in accordance with the opinion of the chairman of the bench.

(c) A hearing held before an incomplete bench shall continue and be concluded before the same bench, unless the chairman of the bench considers that participation of the member who was absent will assist the hearing and will not cause injustice.

**A curtailed bench**

17. (a) Where one member of a bench, not being the chairman, is prevented from concluding the hearing, the hearing shall continue to its conclusion before the remaining members of the bench (hereafter—a curtailed bench), if the litigants agree thereto, unless the chairman of the bench decides to terminate the hearing or the litigants do not agree to continue the hearing before the curtailed bench; if the hearing is terminated, another member, or a new bench, shall be appointed.

(b) Where another member is appointed to an existing bench, the bench may continue the hearing from the stage it reached with its previous composition, if it considers, after having given the litigants an opportunity to put their case, that no injustice will be caused; where the bench decides to continue the hearing, it may treat the evidence it took under its previous composition as if it had taken it itself (with its new composition), or it may retake the evidence, in whole or in part.

(c) Where a new bench is appointed, it shall hold the hearing from its commencement.

(d) A decision of a curtailed bench in which there is a difference of opinion shall be taken in accordance with the opinion of the chairman of the bench.

**Chairman who is a judge**

18. The powers conferred on the tribunal under sections 26(b), 28(a), 29, 30, 33, 36, and 46 shall be vested in the chairman of the bench if he is a judge during the time that the tribunal is not in session.

**A member whose office is terminated or discontinued**

19. A member of a tribunal who has commenced a hearing when his term of office as a member of the tribunal comes to an end, or whose office is discontinued before its term is ended, shall be authorized to conclude the hearing within six months from the date on which his office is terminated or discontinued, unless the Minister of Justice reduces that period.

## *Article C: Procedure and Evidence*

**Procedure**

20. In all matters of procedure concerning which there are no provisions in this Law or in any other enactment, the tribunal shall act in the way it considers best in the interests of justice.

**Rules of evidence**

21. A tribunal shall not be bound by the rules of evidence, apart from the rules regarding privileged evidence under Chapter Three of the Evidence Ordinance [New Version], 1971; this provision is subject to section 31 or any other legal provision.

**Time limit for submitting an objection**

22. (a) An objection to a decision of an administrative authority shall be submitted to the tribunal within 45 days from the day on which the decision was served on the objector together with a notice as to the right to bring an objection and the time limit for submitting it.

(b) The head of the tribunal or the chairman of the bench may extend the time limit for submitting the objection for special reasons which shall be recorded.

**Pleadings**

23. (a) An objection shall be submitted in writing and shall include the arguments, and copies of the documents, upon which the objector intends to base his case.

(b) Where an objection is submitted to a tribunal, the administrative authority shall state in its reply the reasons for its decision and its response to the arguments put forward in the objection, and shall attach copies of the documents upon which it intends to rely.

(c) If any such document is not attached, the party concerned shall not be allowed to rely on it at the hearing on the objection, except with the permission of the tribunal for special reasons which shall be recorded.

**Striking out or dismissal *in limine***

24. A tribunal may strike out an objection *in limine*, either in whole or in part, if it is satisfied that the tribunal does not have jurisdiction or that the objection reveals no cause of action, or is vexatious or oppressive.

**Public hearings**

25. (a) A tribunal shall hold its hearings in public.

(b) A tribunal may hear a particular matter, in whole or in part *in camera*, if it considers this necessary, for reasons to be recorded, in any one of the following cases:

(1) to safeguard the security of the State or its foreign relations;
(2) to protect morals or the welfare of a minor;
(3) a public hearing is liable to deter a witness from testifying freely or testifying at all;
(4) a public hearing is liable to infringe a trade secret; or
(5) a public hearing is liable to infringe individual privacy.

(c) Where a tribunal has decided to hold a hearing *in camera*, it may allow a person or a category of persons to be present during the whole part of the hearing.

(d) A representative on behalf of the Council may be present during a hearing of a tribunal held *in camera*.

(e) Where the tribunal has decided on holding a hearing *in camera*, the provisions as to the prohibition on publication specified in the Courts Law [Consolidated Version], 1984, shall apply as if this were a hearing *in camera* before a court.

**Pleading before a tribunal**

26. (a) A litigant has the right to plead orally, to present his evidence before the tribunal and to sum up his arguments after bringing evidence, in the order and the manner to be determined by the tribunal, to the extent that they are not prescribed by regulations.

(b) A tribunal may decide that certain arguments or evidence should be submitted by a litigant in writing, by affidavit or in another manner to be determined by it.

(c) On the request of all the litigants, the tribunal may consider and decide on the objection on the basis of arguments and evidence submitted in writing only.

**Representation before tribunal**

27. A litigant may be represented before a tribunal by an advocate or by another person, as long as such other person does not represent litigants before the tribunal by way of business or for payment even if not by way of business.

**Power to summon witnesses and compel their appearance**

28. (a) A tribunal may, on its own initiative or at the request of a litigant—

(1) summon any person to come and give evidence or produce documents or other exhibits in his possession.

(2) compel the appearance of any person who, without an excuse that satisfies the tribunal, fails to obey a summons.

(b) The tribunal shall caution the witness that he must testify to the whole truth and nothing but the truth, and that he is liable to the penalties prescribed by statute if he fails to do so.

(c) The powers of a tribunal in the above matters, including the power to impose penalties for contempt, shall be the same as those of a court in a civil proceeding, *mutatis mutandis*.

(d) Where the tribunal decides to compel the appearance of any person, such person may appeal against the tribunal's decision to the District Court, sitting with a single judge, within whose area of jurisdiction the tribunal functions; where such appeal is brought, the tribunal or the court may stay the execution of the decision which is the subject of the appeal until the decision of the court on the appeal.

(e) (1) Where a tribunal decides to impose a penalty on any person for contempt:

its decision requires the approval of the District Court.

(2) Where a tribunal has so decided, it shall notify the fact immediately,

in writing, to the President of the District Court within whose area of jurisdiction the tribunal functions.

(3) The President, or another judge authorized by him, may after allowing the person concerned to put forward arguments, confirm the decision, confirm it subject to conditions, mitigate it or not confirm it.

(f) Where the chairman of the bench of a tribunal is a judge serving in the District Court, the appeal under sub-section (d) shall be brought before the Supreme Court, sitting with a single judge, and the notice under sub-section (e) shall be given to the President of the Supreme Court.

**Expert on behalf of a tribunal**

29. (a) The tribunal may appoint an expert on its own behalf; in regard to this matter the following provisions shall apply:

(1) the tribunal may, after giving the parties an opportunity to put forward their arguments, appoint an expert on its own behalf to give a written opinion on a matter at issue between the parties;

(2) where an expert has been appointed on behalf of a tribunal, the tribunal shall transmit to him all the expert opinions that have been submitted to the tribunal;

(3) a litigant who did not submit an expert opinion on his own behalf prior to the appointment of the expert on behalf of the tribunal shall be allowed to do so after such appointment;

(4) an expert opinion on behalf of a party submitted as provided for in paragraph (3) shall be transmitted to the tribunal's expert and to other parties;

(5) a litigant may, with the approval of the tribunal, put to the tribunal's expert questions in writing in order to clarify his opinion, at a time fixed by the tribunal.

**Inspection of authority's file**

30. (a) Any person entitled to submit an objection against the decision of an administrative authority shall have the right to inspect the documents in the possession of the authority relating to the decision (hereafter—the file), and to copy documents from the file.

(b) The right to inspect the file shall not apply to documents, or parts thereof, to which one of the following applies:

(1) they have no connection with the decision against which the objection is brought;

(2) they contain a professional or trade secret or confidential information within the meaning of any law;

(3) state security, foreign relations or an important public interest require that inspection thereof should not be allowed;

(4) they consist of privileged evidence under Chapter Three of the Evidence Ordinance [New Version], 1971, or under any other law; section 31 below shall apply to privileged evidence under sections 44 and 45 of that Ordinance;
(5) they contain internal material, such as records of internal discussions, reports to superiors, proposals and drafts of decisions;
(6) inspection thereof is liable to unlawfully prejudice the right of personal interest of another person;
(7) they deal with an appointment, the designation of a function, a personal evaluation, qualification for office or a person's attainments, including those of the objector;

provided that inspection shall not be prevented for any one of the reasons referred to in this subsection except to the extent necessitated by that reason.

(c) A tribunal may decide, on its own initiative or at the request of the objector, that the file be handed over to the tribunal, except for documents the handing over of which is liable to prejudice State security or foreign relations or other documents which in the opinion of the tribunal ought not in the circumstances be handed over to it.

(d) Where the objector requests inspection of documents submitted to the tribunal, inspection of which is denied him, excluding documents excluded for reasons to which sub-section (b)(3) applies, the tribunal may allow the objector to inspect the documents, in a way it determines, if it considers that the necessity for inspection in the interests of justice takes precedence over the reason for preventing the inspection.

(e) Where the objector requests inspection of documents the inspection of which is denied him for one of the reasons specified in sub-section (b)(3), the provisions of section 31 shall apply.

**Prevention of inspection for special reasons**

31. (a) The administrative authority is not bound to hand over any document, nor shall the tribunal receive it, if either the Prime Minister or the Minister of Defence expressed the opinion, by a certificate under his hand, that handing over the document is liable to prejudice State security, or either the Prime Minister or the Minister for Foreign Affairs expresses the opinion, by a certificate under his hand, that handing over the document is liable to prejudice the foreign relations of the State, unless a Justice of the Supreme Court, on the petition of the objector who requests discovery of the document, finds that the necessity to discover it in the interests of justice takes precedence over the interest in not discovering it.

(b) Where a certificate as specified in sub-section (a) is submitted to the tribunal, the tribunal may, at the request of the objector seeking discovery of the document, interrupt the hearing for a period to be determined by it so as to allow submission of a petition for discovery of the document, and if it deems fit, even until a decision is made on the petition.

(c) The authority shall not be bound to hand over a document, nor shall the tribunal receive it, if a minister expresses his opinion, in a certificate under his hand, that handing it over is liable to prejudice an important public interest, unless the tribunal hearing the matter, on the petition of the objector requesting discovery of the document, finds that the necessity to discover it in the interests of justice takes precedence over the interest in not discovering it.

(d) The hearing of a petition for discovery of a document shall be *in camera*; in order to decide on the petition, the Justice of the Supreme Court or the tribunal, as the case may be, may require that the document or its content be brought to his, or its notice, and he, or it, may receive explanations from the Attorney General or from his representative and from the representative of the authority, even in the absence of the objector.

**Interface with proceedings**

32. A tribunal may order the removal of any person who disturbs the proceeding of a tribunal or acts in a way which offends the tribunal's dignity.

## *Article D: Competence of the Tribunal*

**Stay of execution**

33. (a) Where an objection is submitted, the head of a tribunal may order the stay of execution of the decision in respect of which the objection was brought, for a period which it shall determine and on conditions it considers fit, where it considers this appropriate in the circumstances.

(b) Once the tribunal has convened to hear an objection, the power to stay execution shall be vested solely in the tribunal.

**Interim decisions**

34. The tribunal may give an interim decision if it considers it appropriate in the circumstances.

**Payment of a sum not in dispute**

35. The tribunal may, even before giving its decision, order payment of a sum not in dispute in whole or in part.

**Decision on a compromise**

36. The tribunal may give the effect of a decision to a compromise agreed upon by the parties.

**Powers as to objections**

37. The tribunal has the power to confirm the decision against which the objection is brought, to annul it and reach a different decision in its place, or to return the matter to the authority that made the decision, with instructions.

**Incidental competence**

38. Where an objection is duly brought before a tribunal, and a question arises incidentally the determination of which is required for consideration of the objection, the tribunal may determine such question for purposes of that objection even if the subject matter of the question is within the exclusive competence of a court or of another tribunal.

**Payment of costs**

39. (a) A tribunal may award a party costs, including advocate's fees.

(b) A witness summoned to testify or produce a document or other exhibit before a tribunal may be awarded travelling and lodging expenses and compensation for loss of earnings and, if he is an expert, also remuneration.

(c) A tribunal may charge the payment of costs or remuneration for witnesses to the parties, or to one or more of them, and determine the rate each of them is to pay.

(d) The chairman of the bench may require a party to deposit a sum for payment of costs or remuneration to witnesses.

## *Article E: The Decision*

**Decision in writing**

40. (a) The decision of a tribunal shall be reasoned, be made in writing, and be signed by the members of the tribunal.

(b) The decision shall be handed to the parties or shall be served on them by registered mail or in another manner to be determined by the chairman of the bench.

**Differences of opinion in the tribunal**

41. Where a tribunal hearing an objection consists of three or more members, and there are differences of opinion, the majority opinion shall prevail; if there is no majority for any one opinion, the opinion of the chairman of the bench shall prevail.

**Notice of right to appeal**

42. Where the decision of the tribunal is subject to appeal, the tribunal

shall signify in its decision the right to appeal, and the time limit for bringing the appeal if this is prescribed in an enactment.

**Correction of errors in decision**

43. (a) Where a tribunal discovers that an error has occurred in a decision it has given, it may within 21 days from the day it was given amend it by a reasoned decision, and it may hear the arguments of the parties on this matter; in this regard, 'error' means a linguistic error, an arithmetical error, a slip of the pen, a casual omission, a fortuitous addition, and similar phenomena.

(b) With the consent of the litigants, the tribunal may decide at any time on any amendment to the decision it has given.

(c) Where a decision is amended as provided in sub-section (a), the date of the amendment shall be regarded as the date the decision was given for purposes of appeal.

(d) An amendment under sub-section (a) is not subject to appeal except by appeal from the decision of the tribunal.

**Execution of a decision**

44. A decision of a tribunal shall have the same legal standing for purposes of execution as the judgment of a court; the decision of a tribunal, not amounting to annulment of the decision of the administrative authority, shall not derogate from the power to implement the decision of the administrative authority under the Taxes (Collection) Ordinance or under any other law.

## *Article F: Appeal*

**Appeal**

45. (a) A final decision of a tribunal is subject to appeal before a District Court sitting with a single judge.

(b) Where the chairman of the bench of the tribunal is a serving judge of a District Court, the appeal under sub-section (a) shall be brought before the Supreme Court and shall be heard by a single Justice or by a larger odd number of Justices, as determined by the President of the Supreme Court.

(c) The judgment of a District Court on appeal under sub-section (a) is subject to appeal before the Supreme Court if leave is granted by the President of the Supreme Court or by another Justice of the Supreme Court designated by its President.

(d) An interim decision or a decision to stay the execution of the decision of an administrative authority, given by a tribunal, is subject to appeal by leave before a District Court, sitting with a single judge, if leave is granted by a judge of the District Court.

(e) An interim decision or a decision to stay the execution of the decision of an administrative authority given by a tribunal headed by a serving judge of a District Court, is subject to appeal by leave before the Supreme Court, sitting with a single Justice, if leave is granted by a Justice of the Supreme Court.

**Stay of execution of decision of a tribunal**

46. A tribunal and, where an appeal has been brought, the court hearing the appeal, may order stay of execution of a decision of the tribunal until a date fixed by them and under conditions they see fit to impose, if they consider this appropriate in the circumstances.

## Chapter 3: The Council

**Appointment of the Council**

47. (a) The Minister of Justice shall appoint a Council for Administrative Tribunals.

(b) The Council, which shall number up to 15 members having the appropriate qualifications shall include the Director of Courts; at least one third of the members shall have legal qualifications and at least one third of them shall not be civil servants.

(c) The Minister of Justice shall appoint the chairman of the Council from among those members having legal qualifications.

**Term of office**

48. (a) The term of office of a member of the Council shall be three years.

(b) A member of the Council can be re-appointed for further terms of office.

**Functions of the Council**

49. The functions of the Council are as follows:

(1) to advise the Minister of Justice or any other minister concerned on all matters relating to tribunals, in general or regarding specific tribunals or specific matters, including the following:

- (a) establishment of new tribunals or the abrogation and merger of existing tribunals;
- (b) the composition of tribunals;
- (c) the making of regulations regarding tribunals, including rules of procedure and evidence;

(d) issuing guidelines on matters other than adjudication;
(e) preparation of accounts relating to the tribunals.

(2) to carry out research projects, to publish surveys and other materials and to provide information in all matters pertaining to tribunals.
(3) to consider accounts relating to tribunals and make its comments to the Minister of Justice or to the Minister concerned.
(4) to fulfil any other function imposed upon it by statute.

**Functioning of the Council**

50. (a) One third of the members of the Council including the chairman, shall constitute a quorum.

(b) The Council may appoint committees and include in them individuals who are not members of the Council.

**Reporting by the Council**

51. The Council shall submit an annual report to the Minister of Justice.

**Budget of the Council**

52. The budget of the Council shall be included in that of the Ministry of Justice.

**Extension of Applicability**

53. This chapter shall also apply to tribunals not enumerated in the Schedule.

## Chapter 4: Miscellaneous Provisions

**Implementation and regulations**

54. (a) The Minister of Justice is charged with implementing this Law and he may, in consultation with the Council, make regulations for that purpose.

(b) The Minister of Justice may, in consultation with the Council, make regulations for the following matters, generally, for specific tribunals or for specific matters:

(1) rules of procedure and evidence for tribunals, including the time and manner for submitting objections;
(2) rules of procedure for appeals from a tribunal to a court, including the time and manner for bringing an appeal;
(3) deliberations of the council under section 14;
(4) attachment of documents to pleadings;

(5) appointment of experts on behalf of tribunals and the mode of examining them;
(6) administrative proceedings for tribunals;
(7) prescribing rates or maximum rates of costs and remuneration, for litigants or witnesses;
(8) submission of reports to the Council on the activity of tribunals;
(9) fees.

(c) regulations under subsections (6), (7), and (9) require the approval of the Constitution and Law Committee of the Knesset.

**Transitional provisions**

55. (a) This Law shall not apply to a matter in respect of which the hearing began before the Law came into force.

(b) This Law shall not affect the appointment of the head of a tribunal or a member of a tribunal made before it came into force: the validity of such an appointment shall expire on termination of the periods of appointment, but no later than three years from the commencement of this Law.

(c) This Law shall not derogate from the validity of regulations concerning a particular tribunal which were made before the commencement of this Law.

## Schedule (section 4) (enumeration of tribunals and statutory provisions under which each was established)

1. Fallen Soldiers Families (Pensions and Rehabilitation) Law, 5710–1950
2. Invalids (War Against the Nazis) Law, 5714–1954
3. Invalids (War Against the Nazis) Law, 5718–1957
4. Commodities and Services (control) Law, 5718–1957
5. Invalids (Pensions and Rehabilitation) Law, 5719–1959 (Consolidated Version)
6. Local Authorities (Regulation of Guard Service) Law, 5721–1961
7. Property Tax and Compensation Fund Law, 5721–1961
8. Local Authorities (Sewage) Law, 5722–1962
9. Appellations of Origin (Protection Law), 5725–1965
10. Water Law, 5719–1959
11. Inspection of School Law, 5729–1969
12. Value Added Tax Law, 5736–1976
13. Antiquities Law, 5738–1978
14. Standard Contracts Law, 5743–1982
15. Restrictive Trade Practices Law, 5748–1988

# SECTION 6: ADMINISTRATIVE DECISIONS AND REASONS

# 15

# *The Administrative Procedure Amendment (Decisions and Statement of Reasons) Law: An Introductory Note*

JUDITH KARP



## 1. Historical Background

The Administrative Procedure Amendment (Decisions and Statement of Reasons) Law 1958[1] gives expression to the norms of fairness and propriety in the conduct of the administration. The basis of these norms was in fact laid down before the enactment of the Law, in the form of a government decision and in the judgments of the Supreme Court. From 1952 onward, all State employees (including chairmen of administrative committees) qualified to make final decisions in matters affecting the individual citizen were obliged to enter in the relevant office file the reasons for such decisions. This government ruling applies to all decisions of State employees be they positive or negative, at the initiative of the government or on the citizen's application. The ruling was an important basic step in the training of State employees. However, it only dealt with the requirement to set down reasons; it did not oblige the employee to reveal them to the

[1] Hereinafter the 'Statement of Reasons Law'. For the updated version of the Law, see this Ch. For a detailed analysis of the Law in its original version, see J. Karp, 'The Israeli Statement of Reasons Act, 1958' (1963) 12 *Am. JComp.L* 72.

interested party. The State Comptroller emphasized this duty in his report for 1951, remarking that:

for a proper relationship between the citizen and the authority, it is essential that the authority provide the citizen with a statement of reasons at the time the decision is communicated to him rather than on request.[2]

While the note of the State Comptroller was merely a note of criticism directed at proper administrative conduct, the requirement of publicizing the reasons for a decision gained legal status with a judgment of the Supreme Court in 1956. The Court noted that a legal norm existed according to which 'the respondent is required by law to provide reasons for any decision arising from the exercise of discretion which could potentially adversely affect the citizen',[3] and that the reasons should be given at the outset, when the decision is handed down, and should be made known to the applicant. The Court further held that considerations of administrative convenience cannot detract from the duty to give reasons unless there are particular reasons for non-disclosure, such as State security, or some other vital interest of the State which alone can justify a deviation from the general rule. It would seem that this statement actually derives from the general outlook of the Court as it emerged in the early years of the State, tying the duty to give reasons with the substance of the right being denied by the authority's decision. Thus in the matter of freedom of movement and the right to leave the country, the Court held that this involves an individual's natural right; it can therefore not be restricted without the existence of a justifying reason. The requirement to give reasons has been turned into a substantive duty, arising from the nature of the right and based on the prohibition under which a public authority may not interfere with the citizen's right in the absence of a reasonable justification.[4]

The Statement of Reasons Law originated as a private member's bill. It was designed, following the example set by the Court, to incorporate in legislation a duty on the part of the various arms of the administration to disclose the reasons for their decisions. The duty set out in the legislation is not as wide as that which can be deduced from the decisions of the Court. It does not apply to every decision which is dependent on administrative discretion and which adversely affects the citizen, but it does include a wide range of decisions where the citizen is interested in knowing the administration's reasons because he stands to be adversely affected by them. These are the decisions which involve a rejection of an application. The Statement of Reasons Law does not give the force of law to the

[2] The State Comptroller's Report no. 2, for the year 1950/51, 23 and 59; The State Comptroller's Report no. 6 for the year 1954/55.

[3] HC 143/56 *Ahjij* v. *The Inspector of Transport* (1957) 11 PD 371.

[4] HC 111/53 *Kaufman* v. *Minister of the Interior* (1953) 7 PD 534, 536.

government ruling creating the requirement to record in the relevant file of the administration the reasons for every administrative decision. From this it would seem that the main concern of the Law, which deals with a duty to disclose reasons but not a duty to record them, is essentially the relations between the citizen and the administration. The interest of the authorities themselves in maintaining a record of the reasoning at the side of the decision, as a requirement of proper administration, follows only indirectly from the duty to disclose reasoning. It is worth noting that, in addition to the Statement of Reasons Law, there are, among the laws of the State, particular provisions which expressly require certain administrative authorities to record in the relevant file the reasons for specific decisions. There are special statutory provisions, which make it compulsory to record the reasons in a file, and not just to disclose the decisions. These relate in the main to decisions of administrative committees, to decisions which deviate from accepted policy, or to decisions where, because of their substance, the Law accords them special importance; before such decisions are reached, the Law requires particular consideration and particular self-scrutiny on the part of the decision makers.[5]

The need for the Statement of Reasons Law was represented by the Knesset Member who initiated the bill as arising from the duty of the Administration to behave fairly and as rooted in the need to prevent the arbitrary exercise of the Administration's authority. It was designed to secure the confidence of the public in the Administration, to improve relations between the citizen and the ruling authority, and to strengthen the lot of the citizen when confronting the machinery of the government. The Law was further presented as being designed to advance the democratic process and prevent its demise, as well as to bring about an improvement in administrative decisions and in the exercise of administrative discretion. It also aimed to protect the public servant against unjustified criticism at the same time as increasing the public servant's awareness of his duty to serve the citizen. It was also presented as providing the basis for external review of administrative decisions, including judicial review.

It is interesting to note that, along with the above universal reasons, the initiator of the bill also set out various justifications for it, rooted in the uniqueness of Israeli society, its historical background, and in certain aspects of its culture. In talking about the improvement in the administrative process as a measure of the appropriate relations between the citizen and the State, the initiator of the bill referred to the tradition of scant respect for the citizen on the part of the Administration. This, according to him, was a legacy of the Mandate period when the Mandate government

[5] e.g. s. 15 of the Administrative Offences Law 1985 stipulates a duty to record the reasons for bringing an indictment in the event of an administrative fine for an offence that has been declared an administrative offence. See HC 5537/91 *Efrati* v. *Ostfeld* (1992) 46(3) PD 501.

behaved towards citizens as to 'natives'. On the other hand the initiator of the bill also referred to the complete absence of an administrative culture, grounded in respect for the rights of the citizen, amongst immigrants from Eastern Europe and the Arab States. These made up the majority of the Israeli population and also accounted for a large number of administrative officials.

It may seem paradoxical that it is precisely the absence of a proper administrative culture that gave rise to a Law which, in many respects, was highly innovative for its time. Its innovative nature becomes apparent when one looks at the record of developed countries with a long tradition of administrative rule.[6]

## 2. Duties under the Law

The Statement of Reasons Law imposes four duties on the public servant called upon in writing to exercise the authority conferred upon him by law.

A. The duty to make a decision on the application and to make an early reply to the applicant, no later than forty-five days from the date of the application.[7] The duty to reply to the citizen remains even when the authority regards the citizen's business as completed and his repeated approaches to the authority over the matter a nuisance.[8] The Law indicates certain exemptions from the duty to reply within the time stipulated and also the various duties associated with the exercise of these exemptions (section 2).

B. In cases of the rejection of an application, there is a duty to inform the applicant, in writing, of the reasons for the refusal.

C. The duty to inform the applicant that he has a right to appeal against the decision, if such a right is contained in the legislation (section 5).

D. When an application to exercise an authority is submitted to a public servant who does not have that authority, there is a duty to pass on the application to whoever the authority has been conferred on, and to notify the applicant of this, or to advise the applicant of the proper address to which the application should be directed (section 2B).[9]

[6] For a comparative analysis, see Karp, n. 1 above.

[7] In the explanatory notes to the Bill it states that the Law is intended to amend 'one of the Administrative problems which causes great inconvenience to the citizen, namely the time lag in getting a response to his application' and to provide the citizen with the means to speed up the decision of the public servant and to get a response to the applicant. The initial law provided for a time limit of three months. The limit of 45 days was a 1994 amendment initiated by a private member of the Knesset.

[8] CA 472/79 *Sharaf* v. *Director of Customs and Excise* (1981) 35(1) PD 509, 513.

[9] This duty was added in July 1994, again on the initiative of a private member of the Knesset.

The abovementioned duties apply to every State employee and every local authority employee, and likewise to any employee of any other public authority on which power has been conferred under the law (section 1).[10] The obligation to reply in time and the duties which have been imposed—notifying the right to appeal and the transfer of an application when it is received by the wrong authority—are general and all embracing. They apply whenever there is an application in writing for the exercise of administrative authority. The obligation to notify the reasons for the decision on the other hand only applies when the public servant refuses the request to exercise his authority. It does not apply when he accedes to a request or when he acts on his own initiative under the law. However the duty does apply to any rejection of an application, whether the decision is given in formal administrative proceedings or is a routine administrative decision, so long as it is authority exercised under law or regulation.

The scope and content of the reasoning which it behoves the relevant authority to give have not been defined in law and are to be derived from the nature of the decision. The reasoning may be general or specific. In order for it to be considered reasonable it need not be so specific to the circumstances of the particular case. The reasons could refer to a general set of circumstances which form the background to the Authority's decision in the case of the particular application.[11] In general the reasons should cover facts, the findings of the administrative body, and the considerations which support the decision. They should also relate to the details of the particular case and the substance of the affected right.[12]

## 3. Exemptions under the Law

Along with the duty to disclose the reasons for a decision, the Law also stipulates several exemptions (section 3B) as well as the requirements for exercising them (section 4). Exemptions from the obligation to state reasons are also set out as specific provisions in other laws. The Statement

[10] The duty to give reasons does not apply to a body like the Knesset or one of its Committees: EA1/88 *Neiman* v. *Chairman of the Central Elections Committee to the Twelfth Knesset* (1988) 42(4) PD 192–3 and the references brought there. See HC 142/70 *Shapira* v. *The Bar Association District Committee* (1971) 25(1) PD 325.

[11] HC 13, 58/86 *Shahyu* v. *Commanding Officer of IDF Forces in Judea and Samaria* (1987) 41(1) PD 197, 214.

[12] HC 111/53 *Kaufman* v. *Minister of Interior* (1953) 7 PD 534; HC 143/56 *Ahjij* v. *Inspector of Transport* (1957) 11 PD 371; HC 684/87 *Mahmud* v. *Minister of Education and Culture* (1989) 43(1) PD 767; HC 2/79 *Al Asad* v. *Minister of Interior* (1980) 34(1) PD 505; HC 5537/91 *Efrati* v. *Ostfeld* (1992) 46(3) PD 501.

of Reasons Law gives these provisions legal force by adopting the exemptions contained in them.[13]

According to the case law, the exemptions from giving reasons apply not only to the Authority actually making the decision but also to any intermediate administrative body which advises or makes suggestions to the Authority making the decision.[14] It appears that the exemption from disclosing reasons applies not only to the actual statement of reasons but includes also the facts and supporting arguments if disclosure of these would frustrate the effect of the exemption.[15] The Law (section 6) provides for two consequences of nonfulfillment of the statutory obligation to provide reasons:

1. The public servant incurs disciplinary liability.
2. In the course of an appeal against the decision, the burden of proof that the decision or action of the public servant was lawful, rests with the public servant.

These consequences apply also to non-compliance with sections 2B, 4, and 5, and also to the obligation to give a reply on time.[16] However, the Law provides specifically that non-compliance with the obligation to give reasons (or with an obligation under section 2B, 4, or 5) does not, of itself, invalidate the decision (section 6).

The case law of the Supreme Court has tended to interpret the exemptions narrowly. This reflects the development of judicial review of the public administration in the years following the enactment of the Statement of Reasons Law. During this period the Court extended the right to present one's case, the right of the public to know, and the right to examine public documents. The right to know the reasons for an administrative decision

[13] These laws are few, providing sweeping exemptions, being in the main laws from the Mandate period preceding the establishment of the State. They may be understood when set against the background of the undemocratic nature of the regime; see, e.g., s. 6 of the Import Licences Order, 1939. The Israeli laws which provide exemptions from the requirement to state reasons, on the other hand, do so because of certain specific difficulties associated with stating reasons, such as providing someone with medical information which would be likely to be harmful to him. An example is reg. 25 of the Social Security regs. See also HC 708/88 *Dadon* v. *State of Israel* (1990) 44(2) PD 224, regarding the prohibition on keeping the reasons for a decision from an applicant, where such reasons are based on medical information, without statutory basis.

[14] HC 190/80 *Bahbut* v. *Minister of Interior* (1981) 35(2) PD 415.

[15] HC 111/53 *Kaufman* v. *Minister of Interior* (1953) 7 PD 534; compare also HC 2/79 *Al Asad* v. *Minister of the Interior* (1980) 34(1) PD 501: disclosure of reasons carries with it also the duty to disclose the evidence supporting the reasons.

[16] S. 6(2) of the Law stipulates that non-compliance with the duty to respond in time is tantamount to a rejection of the application without providing reasons. It is worth noting that years before the introduction of the law, the Court ruled that it is incumbent upon anyone occupying a public position to deal with applications with the necessary speed and diligence and that unreasonable delay, according to the standards of proper administrative behaviour, was tantamount to an unjustified rejection of the application. See HC 56/54 *Dayan* v. *Ramat Gan Municipality* (1955) 9 PD 1237, 1239.

fits in easily with this trend. It is therefore natural that the Court would tend to construe more narrowly the exemptions from the obligation to give reasons. This tendency towards a narrow interpretation finds expression, *inter alia*, in the following stipulation by the Supreme Court:

1. The exemption from the obligation to give reasons on the grounds of the exercise of an authority which entails the use of 'discretion' (section 3(1)). A wide interpretation following a literal test, i.e. any authority which carries with it the exercise of discretion, would effectively negate the obligation to give reasons of any practical importance. This is because nearly all authority entails the exercise of discretion. Hence the narrow interpretation. According to this, the exemption from the obligation to give reasons only exists when the law conferring the authority expressly authorizes the administrative authority to use its discretion in the matter.

2. An exemption from the obligation to give reasons does not also imply an exemption from the duty to grant a hearing. The Court has ruled that not to give an opportunity to the claimant to state his claim before the decision is taken is a violation of natural justice and is liable to bring about an annulment of the authority's action even when the authority is exempt from the obligation to give reasons.[17]

3. Even when there is an exemption from the obligation to give reasons, it is generally accepted that the administrative authority must disclose the reasons for its decision when the legality of the decision is challenged before the Court. In such cases the Court will examine the legality of the decision in light of the reasons given and according to the usual tests of judicial review.[18]

4. Where the authority discloses its reasons to the Court, the exemption from stating its reasons does not exonerate it from disclosing the factual basis for those reasons. In spite of the exemption, the Court will not accept a declaration by the authority that it has evidence of facts which support its decision. The Court will examine the validity of the decision on the basis of those supporting facts.[19]

5. The absence of reasons is no bar to the Court examining the decision in light of the directives and criteria by which the authority would normally act in other cases of a similar type.[20]

6. There are cases when disclosure of reasons before the Court is liable adversely to affect State security or some other vital public interest. In such cases an administrative authority can rely on its exemption in order to refrain from giving reasons even before the Court. In such cases, however,

[17] HC 222/81 *Zizi* v. *Minister of Interior and Police* (1982) 36(2) PD 186, 192; HC 685/78 *Mahmud* v. *Minister of Education and Culture* (1979) 33(1) PD 767.

[18] See e.g., HC 680/88 *Shnitzer* v. *Chief Military Censor* (1988) 42(4) PD 617 (in Ch. 2); HC 1958/90 *Ben Shetah* v. *Minister of the Interior* (1991) 45(1) PD 324.

[19] HC 2/79 *Al Asad* v. *Minister of the Interior* (1980) 34(1) PD 505.

[20] HC 799/80 *Shallam* v. *The Registrar under The Firearms Law* (1982) 36(1) PD 317.

the administrative authority will usually notify the Court that it is prepared to disclose its reasons and all the evidence on which its decision was based, to the Court, though not to the other party in the proceedings. If the other party agrees, the Court is prepared to examine the reasons and the evidence in chambers and without the presence of the other party. In this event the Court decides whether the reasons and the evidence justify the decision which was taken, according to the accepted tests of judicial review of administrative decisions. This practice, which has developed without any express statutory provision, allows for a better balance between the exemption from the obligation to give reasons and the need to examine the legality of the administrative decision on its merits.

## 4. Suggestions for Additional Reform

It might be appropriate at this time to add to and improve the Law. There is good reason for this, particularly after the enactment in 1992 of two basic laws on the rights of the individual: Basic Law: Freedom of Occupation and Basic Law: Human Dignity and Liberty. These laws stipulate that the basic rights protected by them cannot be impaired unless such an impairment comes by virtue of legislation that reflects the values of the State of Israel and has a proper objective, and does not exceed what is absolutely necessary.[21] If a law does impair a basic right, the burden of proof then passes to the legislature to demonstrate that the conditions for such an impairment have been fulfilled. This requirement is even more apparent when applied to the impairment of a fundamental right by an administrative authority. It follows that there may now be no further place for the presumption of the legality of an administrative decision when the decision infringes a basic right. Instead, it could be argued that in every such case the administrative authority would be asked to show that the infringement was justified.[22] In line with this there is, perhaps, a need to amend the Statement of Reasons Law so that the obligation to give reasons applies to every decision, i.e. not only to a decision which rejects an application but to any decision initiated by an administrative authority if it infringes the basic right of the individual. It would seem that there is good reason to abolish the provision in the Statement of Reasons Law,

[21] S. 8 of Basic Law: Human Dignity and Liberty and s. 4 of Basic Law: Freedom of Occupation. On these Basic Laws see Ch. 3.

[22] See HC 3872/93 *Meatreal* v. *The Prime Minister* (1993) (not yet reported) where it was stipulated that though under law the refusal to grant an import licence is exempted from the obligation to give reasons, the reasons for the refusal should be in accordance with the Basic Law: Freedom of Occupation.

granting exemption from the obligation in cases when the Law, conferring powers on the authority, expressly provides that the powers will be exercised at the discretion of the authority.

## 5. Epilogue

On 6 June 1995, the Knesset amended the Statement of Reasons Law by providing that the exemption from the requirement to disclose arguments be cancelled even in those cases where the Law expressly stipulates that the authority is authorized according to its discretion. One can say that this recent amendment brings the law closer to the values of the State of Israel, reflected in the aforementioned Basic Law.

# 16

# *Administrative Procedure Amendment (Statement of Reasons) Law 1958*

**Definition**

1. In this Law*—

'public servant' means a State employee, an employee of a local authority, and any authority vested with any power under any law.

**Duty to reply in time**

2. (a) Where an application in writing has been made to a public servant to exercise any power vested in him under any law, he shall decide upon the application and shall reply to the applicant in writing as soon as possible, but not later than 45 days from the date of receipt of the application.

(b) The provisions of subsection (a) shall not apply—

(1) where the subject-matter of the application requires investigation under any law;
(2) where a different period is prescribed by law for the reply;
(3) where it appears, upon examination, that the subject matter of the application requires further examination or consideration;
(4) where the subject-matter of the application is governed by procedures under which the time for consideration is longer than that prescribed in subsection (a).

(c) In the cases referred to in subsection (b), the public servant shall notify the applicant in writing as soon as possible, but not later than three months from the date of receipt of the application, for which of the said reasons he refrains from replying in time, and shall bring the notification to the knowledge of his superior. Where the reason is one of those mentioned in paragraphs (2) and (4) of subsection (b), the notification shall also indicate the time allotted for the reply or consideration; and where the reason is that mentioned in paragraph (3) of subsection (b), the notification shall give details as far as possible.

* Passed by the Knesset on the 4 Tevet 5719 (15 Dec. 1958) and published in No. 264 of 13 Tevet 5719 (24 Dec. 1958), 7.

(d) The public servant shall notify his decision to the applicant immediately after making it.

**Explanatory Refusal**

2A. Where application as specified in section 2(a) has been made to a public servant and he refuses the application, he shall notify the applicant in writing of the reasons for the refusal.

**Transfer to Authorised Public Servant**

2B. (a) Where a public servant has been requested to exercise a power according to section 2, and that power has not been granted to him, he shall do one of the following:

(1) transfer the application to the public servant who, in his opinion, has such power, and notify the applicant accordingly, indicating the name and address of the second public servant;
(2) notify the applicant of his lack of power, and add his recommendation as to the identity of the person who in his opinion is authorized to deal with the application, including relevant details.

(b) Where the application has been transferred in accordance with subsection (a)(1), the time period referred to in section 2 will begin upon the receipt of the application by the authorized public servant.

**Exemption from duty of stating reasons**

3. Notwithstanding the provisions of section 2A, a public servant shall not be bound to notify the reasons for his refusal in any of the following cases—

(1) if the law which vests the powers in him provides that he is authorized to exercise it at his discretion or without giving reasons;
(2) if the security of the State or its foreign relations requires or require that the reasons for the decision be not disclosed;
(3) if the application refused by him was for the appointment of the applicant to a particular post or the assignment to him of a particular task;
(4) if the disclosure of the reasons might, in the opinion of the public servant, unlawfully prejudice the rights of any person, other than the applicant;
(5) if the disclosure of the reasons will, in the opinion of the public servant, involve the disclosure of a professional secret, or of secret information, within the meaning of any law.

**Objection**

4. Where a public servant refuses to exercise any power conferred on him under any law and does not notify the reasons for the refusal as provided in section 2A, he shall notify the applicant, in writing, which of the grounds enumerated in section 3 has prompted him to refrain from notifying the reasons for the refusal; and the applicant may, within thirty days from the day of receipt of a notification as aforesaid, lodge an objection—if the public servant is a State employee—with the Minister to whom the public servant is subordinate or—if the public servant is an employee of a local authority or if he is an employee of some other authority—with the Minister charged with the implementation of the law which confers the said power.

**Notification of right of objection**

5. Where a decision of a public servant is subject to an objection of appeal under any enactment, the public servant shall notify the person entitled to lodge an objection or appeal, in writing, of the right of objection or appeal and of the modes and times of lodging it in so far as they are prescribed in the enactment.

**Effects of noncompliance with the Law**

6. (a) A decision or act of a public servant shall not be invalid by reason only that he has not complied with the provisions of sections 2A, 2B, 4, or 5; however, in any proceeding before an objection committee or appeal committee or before the Court, a public servant shall have to prove that a decision or act in respect of which reply or notification as aforesaid has not been made, has been given or done lawfully. The provisions of this section shall not derogate from the disciplinary responsibility of a public servant for non-fulfillment of his duty under this Law.

(b) Where a public servant has not replied or made notification within three months, as provided in subsection 2(a) or (c), he shall, for the purposes of any law, be deemed to have given a decision refusing the application without stating reasons.

**Savings of Laws**

7. This Law shall not derogate from any other Law dealing with the statement of the reasons of decisions of administrative authorities.

**Amendments**

8. (a) In section 10(f) of the Co-operative Houses Law, 1952,[1] the words 'at his discretion' shall be deleted.

[1] SH No. 113 of 5713, 6; VII LSI 4.

(b) In section 3(c) of the Marriage Age Law, 1950,[2] the words 'at his discretion' shall be deleted.

**Application**

9. This Law shall not apply—

(a) to decisions under the Firearms Law, 1949,[3] if disclosure of the reasons might prejudice the well-being of an individual or the operations of the police;

(b) to decisions of the Minister of the Interior, or a person to whom his powers have been delegated, under the Entry into Israel Law, 1952,[4] but not including a decision to cancel a Permit of Residence of someone legally in Israel.

Yitzchak Ben–Zvi
*President of the State*

David Ben-Gurion
*Prime Minister*

[2] SH No. 57 of 5710, 286; IV LSI 158.

[3] SH No. 18 of 5709, 143; III LSI 61.

[4] SH No. 111 of 5712, 354; VI LSI 159.

# SECTION 7: ADMINISTRATIVE OFFENCES

# 17

# *The Administrative Offences Law: An Introductory Note**

ITZHAK ZAMIR



## 1. The Development of Administrative Offences

The Administrative Offences Law, 1985, has proven to be a major step towards strengthening the rule of law on the one hand, and towards decriminalization of many offences on the other.

Criminal law was traditionally concerned with crimes such as murder, rape, theft, or robbery, which were commonly stigmatized as being of real moral turpitude and, therefore, as *mala in se*. Although such crimes have constantly increased in number, they constitute today only a small fraction of the criminal offences on the statute books of Israel and many other countries. There are now many more statutory offences, numbered in the thousands, which differ greatly from traditional crimes. These are relatively new offences, which have been established by the modern State as part of its regulation of many social and economic spheres, such as employment, commerce, taxation, town planning, public health, safety at work and on

* The original version of this note was published as an introductory note to the Administrative Offences Law in (1986) 21 *Is.LR* 201. In turn, the introductory note was based partly on the Explanatory Note to the Administrative Offences Bill, 1985, written by Prof. Itzhak Zamir in his capacity as Attorney-General of the State of Israel and published in [1985] HH No 708, 62.

the roads, and the like. Such offences are regularly committed by people commonly regarded as law-abiding and honest, in the ordinary course of their life or business. In most cases, they are considered to be light offences and, accordingly, are subject to only light punishment. Moreover, they are not usually envisaged as involving real immorality. Indeed, they are frequently offences of strict liability, requiring no criminal intent; they are therefore referred to as *mala prohibita*. Examples of such offences are: smoking on a bus or in another public place; speeding; failure to furnish an administrative authority with a tax form or some other information; failure to renew a business licence or some other licence; failure to provide safety measures for a dangerous machine in a plant; and so on. Obviously, there are many more offenders of such infractions than there are of traditional crimes.[1]

Such offences have been made criminal mainly because the legislature has found it convenient to make use of the existing and seemingly efficient criminal machinery to enforce the many new norms imposed by modern regulatory legislation. Consequently, offences against regulatory provisions are in practice treated much as any other criminal offence; that is, such regulatory provisions are usually enforced through police investigation, ordinary prosecution, criminal proceedings in a court of law, and a conviction, which constitutes a criminal record, followed by a penalty of fine or imprisonment.

In principle, however, regulatory provisions are an integral part of administrative regulation, and their enforcement should be considered part of the administrative process, rather than the criminal process. Accordingly, offences against such provisions, which differ so greatly from traditional crimes, should be considered a distinct class of offence, which may be called 'administrative offences'. The establishment of such a classification for administrative offences was the primary purpose and effect of the Administrative Offences Law 1985.[2]

[1] The Penal Law, 1977 (Special vol. LSI) contains just over 500 sections and enumerates about 400 different offences. There are, in addition, other offences, prescribed in other laws, which are in the nature of serious crimes. Their number is estimated in the few hundreds. (Chairman of the Committee, Paul Sieghart), *A Report by Justice on Breaking the Rules—The Problem of Crimes and Contraventions* (Justice, London, 1980) gives the figures for Britain. According to this Report, out of 7,200 statutory offences, only about 750 require intent of deliberate dishonesty, deliberate physical injury, or sexual gratification, and about 3,750 require no criminal intent. See pp. 15–16, 21–2. It is believed that the comparable numbers in Israel are not very different. And as to the number of offenders against regulatory legislation, suffice it to note that minor traffic offences alone account for more than half of the total number of criminal cases tried by the courts in Israel. It should also be borne in mind in this context that most traffic offences do not reach the courts. In about 80% of the traffic offences without accidents, fines are paid without trial. See *Judicial Statistics 1984* (The Central Bureau of Statistics, Jerusalem, 1985), xvii, 6.

[2] In other countries they may be given different names. For example, in Austria they are called (in English translation) 'administrative transgressions'; in Italy 'administrative breaches'; in

## 2. Problems with Enforcement through the Criminal Process

The enforcement of administrative offences through the regular criminal machinery entails some serious disadvantages. The main disadvantages are the following:

(a) The regular criminal process is cumbersome and therefore, lengthy and expensive. Hence, it is not really suitable for the disposal of less serious cases, such as traffic violations and many other administrative offences. In such cases, the criminal process may not be the most effective manner of enforcement and, in any event, it is unduly expensive.

(b) The police force, being so limited in its resources, tends to give preference to the fight against serious crime rather than to direct its efforts to the enforcement of regulatory legislation. Consequently, the enforcement of many laws regulating various spheres of social and economic activity is badly neglected, sometimes to the point that there is no enforcement at all.

(c) The very heavy workload imposed on the prosecution and on the courts does not enable them to cope effectively with the enormous numbers of administrative offences and offenders.

(d) In many cases it is unjust to expose a person who has committed an administrative offence to the criminal process and to attach to him the stigma of a criminal record.

(e) The fact that so many administrative offences have been made part of the criminal law, and so many offenders against such offences have officially been made 'criminals', is bound to generate disrespect for criminal law.

In view of the disadvantages of the criminal machinery with respect to administrative offences, measures have been taken in various countries to devise new methods for the enforcement of regulatory legislation. In some countries, such as Austria, Switzerland, and Germany, special laws have been enacted which provide a complete and separate system for dealing with administrative offences. These laws typically entrust the enforcement of specified administrative regulations to administrative authorities by empowering officials of such authorities to impose fines on offenders, subject to judicial review. In many other countries, which have not enacted special laws to deal in a general way with administrative offences, other measures have been taken in specific spheres, such as income tax and customs or traffic offences, to enable officials of the competent administrative

Germany 'infringement of order'. See *Report by Justice*, n. 1 above, at 44–52. The *Report by Justice* suggests that in Britain they should be called 'contraventions' as distinct from 'crimes'.

authorities to enforce the law through the imposition of fines or the compounding of the offence.[3]

## 3. Israeli Methods

In Israel, too, a variety of methods have been developed over the years. The most familiar and important is the system for disposing of traffic offences, which are probably the most common among all administrative offences. At first, the law provided that a policeman could impose a fine on the offender, but the offender had the option either to pay the fine or to be tried in court. It did not take many years to discover that many offenders preferred not to pay the fine, and the overburdened courts could not deal quickly enough with all these cases. The great and growing delay in processing such cases served as an incentive for an ever-increasing number of people not to pay their fines. The system proved itself cumbersome and therefore ineffective.

Consequently the system for disposing of traffic offences has been reformed. Under the present system, if the offender decides to have his case tried by the court, it is not enough for him to abstain from paying the fine, but he must notify the court, on a special form attached to his ticket, that he prefers a trial. If he does not so notify the court within the prescribed period, the fine, which automatically increases with the passage of time, may be levied like any other criminal fine; even more importantly, his driving licence will not be renewed until the increased fine is paid.[4] Although the reform appears to be rather formal and minor, it has made a big difference, probably due to the mysterious workings of human psychology, and the new system has become a success. Most people now pay their administrative fines in time and only a few prefer criminal proceedings.

The system for traffic offences has subsequently been adopted for other offences, such as offences against the Tourist Services Law, 5736–1976,[5] or against the Maintenance of Cleanliness Law, 5744–1984.[6] Also, additional systems of administrative enforcement have been devised. The most widespread of these additional mechanisms is the compounding of the offence, under which an administrative authority may agree not to prosecute an offence, upon request of the offender, in exchange for a sum of money. This system has been used with considerable success, mainly with regard to offences against tax, customs, and currency control laws.

[3] For a brief description of the situation in this matter in various countries, see *Report by Justice*, n. 1 above, at 44–52.

[4] Criminal Procedure Law (Consolidated Version), 1982, ss. 221–30 (36 LSI 35, 72–5).

[5] 30 LSI 223.

[6] [1984] *SH* No. 1118, 142.

However, prior to the enactment of the Administrative Offences Law, the alternative systems described above remained exceptions, with the vast majority of administrative offences still being processed through the criminal machinery. Because of the strain upon the criminal machinery, this meant, in practice, that the enforcement of much of the regulatory legislation was deplorably and hopelessly poor. Clearly, general reform was needed.[7]

## 4. The Administrative Offences Law

The Administrative Offences Law 1985 ('the Law') represents an important first step towards reform. Although an original creation based to a great extent on experience in Israel, especially with the operation of the ticket system in traffic offences, the Law was also influenced by similar laws enacted in some European countries.

The main objectives of the Law, as stated in the Explanatory Note to the Bill,[8] are the following:

(a) to improve, in simple, expeditious and inexpensive manner, the enforcement of laws and regulations creating administrative offences;
(b) to lighten the workload of the prosecution and the courts; and
(c) to enable a person who has committed an administrative offence to undergo suitable punishment without incurring the stigma of a criminal conviction, unless special circumstances justify his being brought to trial.

To accomplish these goals, the Administrative Offences Law authorizes regulations, subject to approval by a Committee of the Knesset, to prescribe that offences against specified laws and regulations shall also be administrative offences. This does not mean that such offences cease to be criminal offences. A prosecutor may still institute criminal proceedings regarding such an offence if in his opinion the circumstances so justify. But now, most administrative offences will be punished under the Administrative Offences Law, by way of an administrative fine.

The Law allows for two alternative types of fines. Under one type, an administrative fine may be fixed by the regulations at a specified amount for a specific offence. Such a fine may be imposed by inspectors appointed

[7] See S. Ginossar, 'Autonomy of Corrective Law: A Projection of the Doctrine of Constructive Negligence', (1974) 9 *Is.LR* 24; *cf Report on Decriminalization* (Council of Europe, Strasbourg, 1980).

[8] [1985] *HH* No. 1708, 62.

by the minister responsible for the implementation of the relevant legislation or, with special authorization, by the head of the local authority concerned. Under the second type of fine, the amount of the fine may vary according to the circumstances of the case, at the discretion of the administrative authority. Such a fine may be imposed only by a registrar, who is to be a specially qualified official, appointed by the Minister of Justice.

The person fined under the Law may pay the fine within a prescribed period, in which case the offence shall be deemed expiated and the offender shall not be regarded as having been convicted. He may, however, notify the inspector or registrar (as the case may be) that he wishes to be tried for that offence, and he will consequently be tried in ordinary criminal proceedings. Alternatively, in a case in which the amount of the fine is fixed at the discretion of the registrar, he may appeal to the court against the amount fixed.

A Schedule attached to the Law enumerates the laws prescribing criminal offences which now also constitute administrative offences. The original Schedule listed thirty-four administrative offences, including offences in the fields of employment, taxation, safety at work, public health, agriculture, tourism, etc. Laws may be added to the Schedule with the approval of the Knesset Committee. Indeed, eleven laws have already been added in the fields of consumer protection, radio and television and sea ports, to cite a few examples.[9]

[9] Regs. have been made to implement the Law. See the Administrative Offences Regs., 1986 [1986] KT No. 4923, 774.

# 18

# *Administrative Offences Law, 1985*

## Chapter 1: Administrative Offences

**Administrative Offences**

1. (a) The Minister of Justice may determine by regulations that an offence against a provision enacted by any of the Laws enumerated in the Schedule or by regulations under any such Law, other than a felony, shall be an offence for which a fine may be imposed administratively (hereinafter referred to as an 'administrative offence'). The determination may be general or subject to conditions or restrictions.

(b) Regulations under subsection (a) shall require the consent of the Minister charged with the implementation of the Law creating the offence and the approval of the Constitution, Legislation and Juridical Committee of the Knesset (hereinafter referred to as 'the Committee').

(c) Where it is determined by regulations under subsection (a) that a particular offence shall be an administrative offence, the provisions of this Law shall apply also to an offence as aforesaid committed before the coming into force of the regulations, provided that, if an information has been filed, the trial has not yet begun.

**Administrative fines**

2. (a) Regulations under section 1 shall prescribe for each administrative offence the fine which may be imposed administratively (hereinafter referred to as an 'administrative fine'). An administrative fine may be determinate or indeterminate.

(b) A determinate administrative fine may be fixed (1) at a determinate amount; (2) at a rate calculated in such manner or by such method as may be prescribed by regulations (such rate hereinafter referred to as a 'rate'); (3) at a determinate amount or at a rate, whichever is the higher; (4) at both a determinate amount and a rate.

(c) A determinate administrative fine may be fixed at different amounts or rates in respect of bodies corporate, continuing administrative offences, and recurrent administrative offences. For this purpose, 'recurrent administrative offence' means an administrative offence committed by a person within a period prescribed by regulations with the approval of the Committee, since the day on which he previously committed the same offence and paid an administrative fine therefor or was convicted thereof; regulations as aforesaid may relate to administrative offences generally or to particular classes of offences or to particular offences.

(d) An indeterminate administrative fine is a fine for which a maximum amount or rate or a maximum and a minimum amount or rate is or are fixed; such amounts or rates may be fixed with reference to such circumstances in regard to the offence or the commission of the offence as may be specified by regulations.

(e) An administrative fine may be higher than the fine prescribed for the offence in an enactment or than the maximum fine which may be imposed therefor under section 63 of the Penal Law, 1977;[1] but it shall not be more than twice as high.

**Updating of administrative fine**

3. (a) The Minister of Justice may vary the amount of administrative fines in the like manner as he may vary amounts of fines under section 64 of the Penal Law, 1977.

(b) Where an administrative fine is varied under subsection (a), it shall be imposed under Chapter 3 and section 14, as updated to the date of the imposition, or, if an appeal is filed and the fine is not paid by the date of the decision thereon, as updated to the date of such decision.

**Variation of Schedule**

4. The Minister may add a Law to, and delete a Law from, the Schedule with the consent of the Minister charged with the implementation of that Law and with the approval of the Committee.

## Chapter 2: Inspectors and Registrars

**Appointment of inspectors**

5. (a) A Minister charged with the implementation of a Law named in the Schedule or a person empowered in that behalf by such a Minister shall appoint an inspector for such offence against provisions enacted by that Law or by regulations thereunder as are administrative offences. An inspector shall be a State employee or an employee of a body corporate established by Law.

[1] LSI Special Vol.

(b) A Minister charged with the implementation of a Law named in the Schedule may with the consent of the Minister of the Interior, by order, empower the head of a local authority to appoint an employee of that local authority to be an inspector for such offences against provisions enacted by that Law or by regulations thereunder as are administrative offences and are committed in the area of that local authority.

(c) Notice of the appointment of an inspector who is an employee of a local authority shall be given to the Minister of the Interior. The Minister of the Interior may, at any time, cancel or vary the appointment.

(d) An inspector shall not be appointed for administrative offences for which an indeterminate administrative fine, as referred to in section 2(d), has been fixed.

(e) Notice of the appointment of an inspector and of the administrative offences under his jurisdiction, and notice of the cancellation or variation of his appointment, shall be published in *Reshumot*.

**Appointment of registrar**

6. (a) The Minister of Justice shall appoint a registrar for the purposes of this Law.

(b) A person qualified to be appointed Judge of a Magistrates' Court is qualified to be appointed registrar.

(c) A registrar shall be a State employee.

(d) Notice of the appointment of a registrar and of the administrative offences under his jurisdiction shall be published in *Reshumot*.

**Letter of appointment**

7. An inspector or registrar shall be appointed by a letter of appointment in a prescribed form indicating the administrative offences under his jurisdiction.

## Chapter 3: Imposition of Administrative Fine

**Imposition of determinate administrative fine**

8. (a) Where an inspector or registrar has reason to believe that a person has committed an offence punishable by a determinate administrative fine under section 2(b) or 2(c), he may impose on him the administrative fine prescribed for that offence.

(b) A notice of the imposition of the fine shall, in prescribed form, be served upon the person fined and shall contain the following particulars:

(1) the name and address of the person fined;

(2) a brief description of the facts constituting the offence;
(3) an indication of the place and time at which the offence was committed as far as they can be ascertained;
(4) an indication of the relevant provisions of the enactment creating the offence;
(5) the fine imposed.

(c) The person fined may give the person who imposed the fine notice in writing that he wishes to be tried for the offence. The notice shall be served within thirty days after notice of the fine is served upon him. If he gives such notice, the provisions of sections 13 and 14 shall apply.

**Notice and answer in case of indeterminate administrative fine**

9. (a) Where a registrar has reason to believe that a person has committed an offence punishable by an indeterminate administrative fine under section 2(d), he shall serve upon him, in prescribed form, a notice containing the following particulars:

(1) the name and address of the recipient of the notice;
(2) a brief description of the facts constituting the offence;
(3) an indication of the place and time at which the offence was committed as far as they can be ascertained;
(4) an indication of the relevant provisions of the enactment creating the offence;
(5) the administrative fine prescribed for the offence;

(b) The recipient of a notice under subsection (a) may, within fourteen days from the day on which it is served, serve upon the registrar an answer indicating one of the following:

(1) that he admits all the facts constituting the offence; in this case, he may, in his answer, make submissions concerning the amount of the fine to be imposed upon him;
(2) that he admits none or only part of the facts constituting the offence; in this case, he shall be deemed to have stated that he wished to be tried for the offence, and the provisions applying to a person who answers as specified in paragraph shall apply to him;
(3) that he wishes to be tried for the offence; in this case, the provisions of sections 13 and 14 shall apply.

(c) If the recipient of the notice does not answer, he shall be deemed to have admitted all the facts constituting the offence and to have made no submissions concerning the amount of the administrative fine to be imposed on him.

**Decision as to indeterminate administrative fine**

10. Where a person makes an admission under section 9(b)(1) or is deemed to have made an admission under section 9(c), the registrar shall decide his case and shall serve notice of his decision on him.

**Objection**

11. (a) A person on whom an administrative fine is imposed under section 10 may, within such time and according to such procedure as may be prescribed by regulations, object to the amount of the fine.

(b) The objection shall be lodged with the court, within the meaning of section 12, which would be competent to try the offence if an information in respect thereof had been filed against the objector.

(c) In objection proceedings, the court may confirm or reduce the administrative fine, and it may order the objector to pay the costs of the objection in the amount fixed by it.

## Chapter 4: Criminal Trial of Administrative Offence

**Definitions**

12. For the purposes of this Law—

'court' means a magistrates' court, a court for local matters or regional labour court, as the case may be;

'prosecutor' has the same meaning as in section 12 of the Criminal Procedure Law (Consolidated Version), 1982.[2]

**Information**

13. Where a person states that he wishes to be tried for an offence under section 8(c) or 9(b)(3), or is deemed under section 9(b)(2) to have so stated, a prosecutor shall file an information against him unless, for special reasons which shall be recorded, he sees fit not to do so.

**Fine imposed in judicial proceedings**

14. Where a person against whom an information has been filed under section 13 is convicted, then, if a fine is the only penalty, it shall not be less than the administrative fine which was imposed on him under section 8 unless it appears to the court, for reasons which shall be recorded, that there are special circumstances justifying its reduction.

[2] 36 LSI 35.

**Power of Prosecutor**

15. The designation of an offence as an administrative offence shall not derogate from the power of the prosecutor to file an information in respect thereof if he is of the opinion that the circumstances justify his doing so for reasons which shall be recorded, provided that an administrative fine has not yet been paid for the offence.

## Chapter 5: Payment of Administrative Fine

**Time for payment of fine**

16. (a) An administrative fine shall be paid within thirty days after service of notice of its imposition under section 8(a) or 10 unless the person fined gives notice, within the time prescribed therefor, that he admits none or only part of the facts constituting the offence or that he wishes to be tried for the offence.

(b) The lodging of objection under section 11 shall not delay the payment of the fine. If the objection is allowed, the fine paid shall, as far as the judgment in the objection proceedings so requires, be returned with the addition of linkage differentials and interest as prescribed by regulations.

(c) A registrar who has imposed an administrative fine on any person may, on the application of that person, direct that the fine be paid in such instalments and within such period as are prescribed by him, provided that such period shall not exceed six months and that linkage differentials and interest, as prescribed by regulations, shall be added to the fine. The application shall be submitted to the registrar within the time and in the manner prescribed by regulations.

**Unpaid fine**

17. (a) Where a person does not pay an administrative fine within the time proscribed therefor, linkage differentials, as prescribed by regulations, and an arrears surcharge shall be added to it.

(b) The arrears surcharge shall be 1½ per cent of the amount of the unpaid fine in respect of every week of delay or fraction thereof. If the rate of the arrears fine prescribed by section 2(a) of the Taxes (Arrears Fine) Law, 1980,[3] is varied, the rate of the fine prescribed by this subsection shall be varied accordingly.

(c) An amount paid or collected on account of an administrative fine to which an arrears surcharge has been added shall first be credited against

[3] 35 LSI 39.

the arrears surcharge and thereafter against the linkage differentials or shall be credited as prescribed by regulations.

**Collection of fine**

18. The provisions of the Taxes (Collection) Ordinance[4] shall apply to the collection of an administrative fine not paid in time, including linkage differentials, interest, and arrears surcharge, as if it were a tax within the meaning of that Ordinance.

**Imprisonment in lieu of unpaid fine**

19. (a) Where a person does not pay an administrative fine imposed on him within six months from the date of its imposition, the court may, on the application of a prosecutor, order that imprisonment for a term not exceeding one year be imposed on him in lieu of the unpaid fine. The court shall not direct that the imprisonment shall be conditional.

(b) The provisions of section 71(c) to (e) of the Penal Law, 1977, shall apply *mutatis mutandis* to imprisonment under subsection (a).

**Cancellation of registration of licence**

20. (a) Where an administrative fine is imposed on a person for an administrative offence connected with an occupation or activity requiring, under law, registration in a register, or a licence or permit, and the administrative fine is not paid in time, a court may, on the application of a prosecutor, order the deletion of the registration of that person from the register, or the withdrawal, non-renewal, or non-extension of the licence or permit granted to him, until payment of the fine or until the expiration of one year, whichever is the earlier.

(b) The provisions of this section shall not derogate from the provisions of sections 17 and 19.

**Summons and warning**

21. (a) The court may make an order under section 19 or 20 even in the absence of the person to which it relates if it appears to it that such person has been served with a summons indicating the contents of the order applied for.

(b) An order under section 19 or 20 made in the absence of the person to which it relates shall not be carried out until he has been served with a warning bringing the contents of the order to his knowledge, as well as with notice that the order will be carried out unless he pays the fine within thirty days from the date of service of the warning.

[4] *Laws of Palestine* (English edn.), ii, 1399.

**Fine imposed by local authority or body corporate**

22. An administrative fine imposed by an inspector who is an employee of a local authority or of a body corporate established by Law shall be paid into the fund of the local authority or the body corporate, as the case may be.

## Chapter 6: Expiation of Offence; Other Sanctions

**Expiation of offence**

23. When a person has paid an administrative fine imposed on him, the offence shall have been expiated; but this shall not release him from any duty under any enactment.

**Forfeiture**

24. Forfeiture under any Law shall not prevent the imposition of an administrative fine but shall be in addition thereto.

**Restriction as to monetary composition**

25. The provisions of any enactment relating to monetary composition shall not apply in respect of an offence designated as an administrative offence.

**Restriction on power of Fines Committee**

26. Where an offence against a provision of an Agricultural Board Law has been designated as an administrative offence, a Fines Committee appointed under that Law shall not be competent to impose a fine for it. For this purpose, 'Agricultural Board Law' means any of the following:

(1) the Vegetable Production and Marketing Board Law, 1959;[5]
(2) the Egg and Poultry Board (Production and Marketing) Law, 1963;[6]
(3) the Fruit and Vegetable Products (Manufacture and Export) Boards Law, 1973;[7]
(4) the Fruit Production and Marketing Board Law, 1973;[8]
(5) the Ornamental Plants Production and Marketing Board Law, 1976.[9]

[5] 13 LSI 245. [6] 18 LSI 10. [7] 27 LSI 349. [8] 27 LSI 370.
[9] 30 LSI 273.

# Chapter 7: Amendment of Laws

**Amendment of Court Law**

27. In section 23 of the Courts Law (Consolidated Version), 5744–1984,[10] the words 'or to an administrative offence punishable by a determinate administrative fine' shall be added at the end.

**Amendment of *Dayanim* Law**

28. In section 25(b) of the *Dayanim* Law, 5715–1955,[11] the words 'or to an administrative offence punishable by a determinate administrative fine' shall be added at the end.

**Amendment of *Qadis* Law**

29. In section 23(a) of the *Qadis* Law, 5721–1961,[12] the words 'or to an administrative offence punishable by a determinate administrative fine' shall be added at the end.

**Amendment of Druze Religious Courts Law**

30. In section 28(b) of the Druze Religious Courts Law, 5723–1962,[13] the words 'or to an administrative offence punishable by a determinate administrative fine' shall be added at the end.

**Amendment of Knesset Members Immunity Law**

31. In the Knesset Members (Immunity, Rights and Duties) Law, 1951,[14] the following section shall be inserted after section 5A:

*Administrative Offences*

5B. The provisions of sections 4(a) and 5 shall not apply in respect of an administrative offence punishable by a determinate administrative fine and concerning which a member of the Knesset has stated that he wishes to be tried.

**Amendment of Labour Inspection (Organization) Law**

32. In section 8c of the Labour Inspection (Organization) Law, 1954,[15] subsections (b) to (g) are hereby repealed. This section shall come into force on the date of the coming into force of regulations made under section 1 in respect of an offence under section 8C(a) of the said Law.

**Amendment of Customs Ordinance**

33. Sections 231A and 231B of the Customs Ordinance[16] are hereby repealed.

[10] 38 LSI 277. [11] 9 LSI 74. [12] 15 LSI 123. [13] 17 LSI 27.
[14] 5 LSI 149, amended in 37 LSI 3. [15] 8 LSI 175. [16] 1 LSI (NV) 51.

**Amendment of Value Added Tax Law**

34. In the Value Added Tax Law, 1975[17]—

(1) section 122 is hereby repealed;

(2) in section 125, the expression '95 and 122' shall be replaced by the expression 'and 95'.

## Chapter 8: Miscellaneous Provisions

**Service of documents**

35. (a) Any notice or other document to be served upon any person under this Law shall be served in one of the following ways:

(1) by delivery into his hands or, if he cannot be found at his place of residence or business, into the hands of a relative living with him and appearing to be at least eighteen years of age, and in the case of a body corporate or body of persons, by delivery at its registered office or into the hands of a person duly authorized to represent it;

(2) by registered letter, with certificate of delivery, to the address of the person, body corporate or body of persons; the date of the certificate of delivery shall be regarded as the date of service;

(b) Where the addressee has an advocate, it shall be sufficient if service is made upon the advocate or his articled clerk or by depositing the document at his office.

(c) Service upon an inspector or registrar may be by delivery to an employee at his office.

(d) The Minister of Justice may, with the approval of the Committee, make supplementary regulations, even in deviation from the provisions of this section, concerning the service of documents.

**Restriction**

36. (a) Regulations under section 1 prescribing an indeterminate fine shall be for a period not exceeding three years from the coming into force of this Law.

(b) Where an administrative fine under regulations as referred to in subsection (a) is imposed on a person before the expiration of those regulations, the provisions of this Law shall continue to apply to the administrative fine even after the expiration of the said regulations.

[17] 30 LSI 46.

**Implementations and regulations**

37. The Minister of Justice is charged with the implementation of this Law and may, with the approval of the Committee, make regulations for its implementation, including regulations as to—

(1) procedure for the registration of administrative fines;
(2) practice and procedure to be followed by an inspector or registrar;
(3) procedure for the hearing of applications under sections 19 and 20.

**Commencement**

38. This Law shall come into force on 1 December 1985.

## Schedule

* * *

# SECTION 8: ADMINISTRATIVE CONTRACTS AND PROMISES

# 19

# *Administrative Contracts and Promises*

YOAV DOTAN



## 1. Administrative Contracts

As in other areas of Israeli administrative law, the basic principles governing administrative contracts were inherited from the English legal tradition. The law in England limits the power of any administrative authority to create contractual obligations involving its governmental powers.[1] The rationale for this rule is that contractual promises by an administrative authority as to its public functions would unlawfully fetter future executive action.

Quite early in Israel's history, the Supreme Court of Israel departed from the strict English rule. In its landmark decision of *Miller* v. *Minister of Transport* (included in this Section), the Court adopted a more flexible position, proclaiming that the very action of contracting by an administrative authority does not, in itself, create any illegality. Hence, the contract is *prima facie* valid and the authority will ordinarily be bound by its terms. However, in recognition of the special nature of administrative contracts, the law acknowledges the power of the authority to free itself from the contract when necessary to protect vital public interests.

This compromise position enables the Court to overcome the problems inherent in the strict approach, both on a theoretical and a practical level. On a theoretical level, the Court's position balances the importance of honouring contractual promises with the need to preserve future executive

[1] See *Rederiaktiebolaget Amphitrite* v. *R.* [1921] 3 KB 500.

discretion in appropriate cases. On a practical level, this approach enables the government to enter into the many contracts necessary for implementing its powers. The Court's approach also obviates the need to distinguish between 'commercial' and 'governmental' (or 'magisterial') contracts, since both types of contracts are equally binding on the authority, and equally subject to *Miller*'s rules for discharging the government from its contractual obligation in appropriate cases.[2]

The approach adopted by the Court in *Miller* raises two important questions: first, when is the authority entitled to free itself from its contractual obligation? Secondly, what are the consequences of such a decision? In particular, what remedies will be available to the other party when the government cancels its contractual obligation?

According to Sussman J's opinion in *Miller*, an administrative authority is entitled to cancel its contractual obligation only when its *essential needs* so require.[3] It is clear from this formulation and the accompanying discussion in *Miller* that the authority cannot terminate the contract merely because it later determines it can achieve 'a better deal' elsewhere. Similarly, an authority's financial difficulty in abiding by the contract will not be a sufficient ground for termination.[4] But how exigent must the public interest be for the authority legally to free itself from a contractual obligation?

In theory, the answer depends on the circumstances of each case and on the Court's balancing of the conflicting interests of the general public and of the other contracting parties.[5] In practice, however, the importance of honouring contractual obligations usually wins out. Indeed, the Court seems to regard the authorities' right to terminate their contractual obligations as an exceptional privilege which should rarely be indulged.

There remains the question of the remedies to which the contracting party is entitled in the event of a termination. Termination is not a breach of the contract, and therefore does not carry with it all the regular contractual remedies.[6] But this does not mean that the contracting party should be left with no remedies at all. Fundamental notions of fairness require that the party at least be compensated by the public authority for the costs he or she incurred as a result of the contract.

More difficult is the question of whether the contractor should be entitled to compensation for loss of foreseeable profits from the terminated contract. The difficulty lies in the fact that in some cases, compensation for foreseeable profits may frustrate the very benefit the public gains from the

[2] HC 311/60 *Y. Miller, Engineering (Agency and Export) Ltd* v. *Minister of Transport and others* (1961) 15 PD 1989 (in this Ch.).

[3] *Ibid.* 86.

[4] CA 250/88 *Kupat Holim of the Histadrut* v. *Municipality of Be'er Sheeba* (1989) 33(4) PD 488.

[5] HC 218/85 *Arbiv* v. *Attorney General of Tel-Aviv* (1986) 30(2) PD 393.

[6] See P. P. Craig, *Administrative Law* (3rd edn., Sweet & Maxwell, London, 1994), 705.

termination of the contract. The courts in Israel remain undecided with respect to this problem of compensation for future profits.[7]

## 2. Administrative Promises

Alongside this development in the law of public contracts, Israeli courts have developed a unique concept of *administrative promises.* This concept first appeared in Berinson J's decision in *Scitex et al.* v. *Minister of Trade and Industry* (included in this Chapter), where he held the government accountable for a promise made by the Minister of Trade and Industry, on behalf of the government, to subsidise a group of exporters. The promise was contained in a circular distributed by the Minister to various exporting companies.

*Scitex*'s concept of administrative promise is innovative for two reasons. First, under *Scitex*, the creation of such a promise does not depend on any of the legal formalities typical of governmental contracts. Secondly, the legal protection awarded to the promisee under *Scitex* does not depend on whether damages resulted from the promisee's reliance on the promise. This distinguishes the concept of 'administrative promise' from the principle of 'promissory estoppel' in English contract law.[8]

Berinson J proposed a four-part test to determine when an administrative authority's promise would legally be binding: First, the promisor must have the authority to make the promise.[9] Secondly, the promisor must have intended the promise to have legal force. Thirdly, the promisor must be capable of keeping the promise. And fourthly, there must be no legal grounds on which to change or revoke the promise.

While the Israeli courts have followed Berinson J's test for determining the enforceability of administrative promises, the test has been very difficult to apply in some instances. The first and probably the most serious difficulty is in determining the 'intention' of the administrative authority—the second prong of Berinson J's test. The authority will almost always

[7] Cf the position of the courts in France, which acknowledge the right of the contracting party to be compensated for foreseeable profits in some cases. See R. Chapus, *Droit Administratif General* (5th edn., Montchrestien, Paris, 1990), i, 817, 820; A. de Laubaere, F. Moderene, and P. Delvolve, *Traité de Contrats Administratives* (2nd edn., LJD, Paris, 1984), 669–70.

[8] This point was emphasized by Berinson J in *Scitex* (in this Ch.). Cf S. A. de Smith, *Judicial Control of Administrative Action* (4th edn., J. M. Evans (ed.), Sweet & Maxwell, London, 1980) 102–3.

[9] In later cases, the courts have held administrative authorities bound by a promise made by a senior official even though he (as an agent) acted outside the scope of his authority provided that the fulfilment of the promise is not *ultra vires* the public body itself. See HC 69/80 *Hiram* v. *Minister of Defence* (1980) 35(4) PD 505: HC 142/86 *'Dishon'* v. *Minister of Agriculture* (1986) 40(4) PD 523. Cf Craig, n. 6 above, 682.

argue that it did not intend its promise to be binding. When will the Court infer, against the explicit testimony of the administrative authority, that the authority had in fact intended to make a binding promise?

This difficulty in determining the intention of the administrative authority was evident in the facts of *Scitex* itself. The 'binding promise' found by the Court in *Scitex* was contained in an *information circular* which the Ministers of Trade and Industry distributed among various exporters. The circulars contained information about the Ministry's general policy in that field. There was nothing in the language of the circular to indicate that a specific promise was being made, rather than a simple summary of administrative policy. Administrative policies are always subject to change by the administrative authority which formulated them.[10] Reflecting the problematic nature of deriving a binding promise from the literature of an administrative authority, several post-*Scitex* courts have rejected attempts by other manufacturers and exporters to hold the government bound to policy statements.[11]

These difficulties have not, however, prevented a gradual and careful development of the *Scitex* concept into well established law. The 'administrative promise' is now an effective tool which may be used to achieve fairness and consistency in administrative behaviour. This is exemplified by the case of *Algebrali and Others* v. *Mayor of Rehovot and Others.*[12] In *Algebrali*, the mayor was held bound by his promise to transport pupils to their elementary school. This decision illustrates a recent trend in which the courts will hold administrative authorities accountable for representations made within the scope of their legal power.

[10] See HC 198/82 *Munitz* v. *Israel Central Bank* (1982) 36(3) PD 466; HC 580/83 *Atlantic Shipping & Fishing Co. Ltd* v. *Ministry of Industry and Trade* (1983) 39(1) PD 29. Cf in (CA), England: *Laker Airways Ltd* v. *Department of Trade* [1977] 1 QB 643. In fact, the *result* of the *Scitex* case can be fully explained on the ground of *retroactivity* of the government action at issue.

[11] HC 534/75 *Hotels' Association of Israel* v. *Minister of Tourism and others* (1976) 30(1) PD 837; HC 73/76 *Osem Export (1962) Ltd* v. *Minster of Finance and others* (1976) 30(3) PD 636; HC 594/78 *Uman Ltd* v. *Minister of Industry and Trade* (1978) 32(3) PD 469.

[12] (1981) 41(1) PD 236.

# 20

# *Y. Miller, Engineering (Agency & Import) Ltd* v. *Minister of Transport and others*

[H.C. 311/60]
[15 PD 1989 (1961)]

*Olshan P, Agranat DP, Goitein J, Sussman J, and Berinson J*

Israeli cases referred to:

[1] HC 125/57—*Anit Michal Ltd* v. *Minister of Finance*; 11 PD 1490.
[2] HC 35/48—*M. Breslov and Partners Ltd* v. *Minister of Trade and Industry*; 2 PD 330.
[3] HC 327/52—*Bondi Zamir* v. *Inspector of Road Transport Jerusalem*; 7 PD 358.
[4] *Motion* 180/56—*Yaakov Feinberg and another* v. *Givatayim Local Council*; 11 PD 209.
[5] CA 187/52—*Israel Halperin* v. *The Mayor, Municipal Council and Inhabitants of Tel Aviv*; 8 PD 219.
[6] HC 30/51—*Y. Balaban* v. *Tel Aviv Municipality*; 6 PD 257.
[7] HC 161/52—*Israel Distillery Co. Ltd* v. *Mayor, Municipal Council and Inhabitants of Rishon Le-Tzion*; 7 PD 113, 125.

English cases referred to:

[8] *Rederiaktiebolaget Amphitrite* v. *R.* [1921] 3 KB 500.
[9] *Robertson* v. *Minister of Pensions* [1948] 2 All ER 767; [1949] 1 KB 227.
[10] *Howell* v. *Falmouth Boat Construction Ltd* [1951] 2 All ER 278; [1951] AC 837.
[11] *William Cory & Son Ltd* v. *City of London Corporation* [1951] 2 All ER 85; [1951] 2 KB 476.
[12] *Commissioners of Crown Lands* v. *Page* [1960] 2 All ER 726.
[13] *York Corporation* v. *Henry Leetham and Sons Ltd* [1924] 1 Ch. 557, 131 LT 127.

American cases referred to:

[14] *Hudson County Water Co.* v. *Robert H. McCarter*, 209 US 349 (1908).

[15] *Stone* v. *State of Mississippi*, 101 US 814, 25 LEd. 1079 (1879).
[16] *Cincinnati* v. *Louisville & Nashville Railroad Co.*, 223 US 390 (1911).
[17] *W. B. Worthen Co.* v. *Thomas*, 292 US 426 (1934).
[18] *Atlantic Coast Line R.R. Co.* v. *Philipps*, 332 US 168 (1947).

## JUDGMENT

**Sussman J:**

This is the return to an order *nisi.*

The petitioning company has been engaged for over fifty years in importing machines and for over thirty years in importing motor vehicles; it represents in Israel, *inter alia*, the well-known Swedish firm of diesel truck manufacturers, 'Scania Vabis'. In 1957 'Scania Vabis' made a proposal to the Israel authorities to set up a plant here for assembling its trucks and to send all the necessary parts that could not be produced locally. These diesel trucks are very popular in the local market, and figures submitted by the petitioner show that one third of the trucks imported into this country in 1959 were produced by Scania Vabis. The petitioner did not demand exclusive rights to sell its trucks in Israel, but only a promise of a minimum sale of 200 trucks *per annum.*

The petitioner's proposal was not accepted and instead the Israel authorities commenced negotiations with another manufacturer, also with an international reputation, namely, the English firm of Leyland. The petitioner declares that it has no objection to its competitor, Leyland, being assured a certain proportion of the local market (40 per cent), since ample opportunities would still remain for its activity in Israel. Leyland, however, according to the contention of the petitioner, demanded 'exclusive and monopolistic marketing rights' amounting to 100 per cent of the market. At the request of the petitioner, this Court on 13 December 1960 issued an order *nisi* to the respondents to appear and show why they should not refrain from signing an agreement with Leyland granting that firm monopoly rights.

2. Following the negotiations with Leyland, terms of agreement (exhibit PG/1) were signed in London between Leyland and the Government of Israel on 28 October 1960. This agreement is evidenced in the reply of Mr Pinhas Ginsberg, Director-General of the Ministry of Transport, filed on behalf of the respondents. This agreement was intended, as stated in the recitals, to carry out 'the mutual desire of the parties, as expressed in the two letters described in the schedule to this agreement. This agreement provided that Leyland should set up a plant for assembling diesel trucks in Israel . . . and stages for producing them.'

The two letters referred to in the preamble to the contract are; a letter of Leyland addressed to Mr M. Tsur, Director-General of the Ministry of Trade and Industry, dated 6 March 1960, and the latter's reply of 8 March 1960. In paragraphs 4 and 5 of their letter of 6 March 1960, Leyland states as follows:

4. In view of the limited Israeli market for buses and heavy trucks, the Israeli Government will guarantee to Leyland Israel or whatever the Company may be named, a guarantee of exclusive import and foreign exchange facilities and also undertake to give preferential treatment to Leyland in respect of customs duties and import facilities.

5. It is recognised by the Israeli Government that such a progressive manufacturing scheme cannot prosper in the limited Israeli market unless such a preferential treatment is guaranteed to Leyland in order to justify the capital expenditure involved.

In his reply, Mr Tsur expresses his agreement, in principle, with the substance of the letter.

However, in drafting the terms of agreement signed in London on 28 October 1960, the parties limited the scope of the said condition, with clause 12(c) of exhibit PG/1 stating as follows:

(c) Government will not allocate to any person, firm or company, other than Leyland, the Plant Company or its agents, during a period of up to 3 years from the date of commencement of local manufacture and assembly under these Heads of Agreement, foreign currency for import into the State of Israel of any Diesel trucks of over 7 tons carrying capacity (and also of such less weight as may be determined by Government's import policy in connection with Diesel trucks) similar to the types of Comet, Super-Comet, Super-Beaver and Super-Hippo, and other types as and when approved by Government. This is provided that within the aforesaid period the reduction in the import value into Israel of the products shall reach a minimum of 30% of the invoice cost of the completed chassis.

The same provision shall apply for a further period of two years provided that within those further two years the reduction in the import value into Israel of the products shall reach a minimum of 50% of the invoice cost of the completed chassis.

Clause 12(c) constitutes in effect the main point of controversy between the parties, and I shall revert to this provision and consider it later. At this point I wish to remark that we were told by the learned Deputy State Attorney that Leyland has waived the 'exclusive import facilities' referred to in its letter of 6 March 1960. Leyland will be satisfied with the Government's undertaking concerning the allocation of foreign currency to them as per clause 12(c).

3. We learn from the affidavit of Mr Ginsberg that prior to the conclusion of the agreement with Leyland, all possibilities were investigated by a committee consisting of representatives of the government departments

concerned. This investigation revealed that the offer made by a German firm, Magirus-Deutz, was better than the other offers in that it placed the emphasis on gradual progress towards the manufacture of diesel engines in Israel. The other offers, including that of Scania Vabis, only proposed the setting up of an assembly plant without any prospect of such a plant going over in due course to the manufacture of engines in Israel. The proposal of the German firm did not, however, ripen into an agreement, and eventually the respondents entered into negotiations with Leyland and reached an agreement with them, as already mentioned.

The terms of agreement PG/1 were intended to pave the way towards the gradual production of diesel engines in Israel. It was intended to establish a plant to be connected with the name of Leyland which has acquired a reputation in the international market. Responsibility for the local plant would rest upon Leyland, with the obligation to reach a minimum production of the total vehicles in the country by a fixed time. Furthermore, Leyland was to place the network of agents and subsidiary firms, engaged in selling Leyland products abroad, at the disposal of the plant to be set up in Israel.

The respondents say that they made a similar offer to the petitioners. However, in effect this was no more than an offer for the establishment of an assembly plant alone, without all the advantages ensuing from the agreement with the English firm. Specifically, the petitioner's offer contains no prospect of reaching the stage of local manufacture of the engines themselves.

4. In paragraph 35 of the petition the petitioner attacked the agreement on thirty-three grounds, some of which were sub-divided; we can however summarize their objections under three points:

First, the agreement PG/1 accords Leyland a monopoly without any legal basis.

Secondly, the Government in clause 12(c) of the agreement bound itself not to allocate foreign currency for the purpose of importation of other trucks for a period of five years. This policy constitutes a fettering of discretion entrusted to the Government as it has waived its duty to consider future requests.

And thirdly, the agreement PG/1 does not assure the State any real advantages as against the petitioner's offer.

I shall consider the last argument first.

5. The reason the respondents preferred Leyland's offer to the others was that they saw in it a chance of achieving the manufacture of diesel engines in Israel as well as their repair. Mr Toussia-Cohen, on behalf of the petitioners, pleaded with great skill that the agreement PG/1 contained no substantial guarantee of attaining this goal but only expressed hopes and good intentions without any actual obligations.

I cannot accept this argument.

In my opinion, the citizen should be given more extensive protection of his rights than this Court can give as against the system of State control that has prevailed since the Second World War. However, so long as the protection of the citizen is entrusted solely to this Court, I see no possibility of extending the shield beyond the existing bounds. Supervision by this Court of the administration will of necessity be legal supervision only. In other words, this Court will be limited to inquiring whether the administration has exceeded its powers as laid down by law, or whether an error of law has been revealed in the exercise of its discretion. The effectiveness of the exercise of the discretion and the measure of its wisdom—as distinct from its legality—are not subject to judicial investigation, for the simple reason that it lacks the requisite ways and means thereof. Hence, I cannot arrogate to myself the task of determining whether the respondents are justified in their opinion that the agreement with Leyland serves the requirements of the State better than the arrangement put forward by the petitioner. In this matter we can do no more than rely on the good sense of the respondents and on the professional skill of their advisers.

6–9. [*Turning next to the question whether Leyland had been given a monopoly without legal authority, Sussman J finds that the preferences accorded Leyland in section 12(c) of the agreement do not amount to a monopoly.*]

10. From here I move on to the final question, whether the contract was defective because of the obligation of the Government not to allocate foreign currency to any other person, as stated in clause 12(c) of the contract.

Mr Toussia-Cohen's objection to the contract on this ground was based on the well-known judgment of Rowlatt J in *The Amphitrite* [8]. In that case, the court considered the validity of a promise given by the British authorities during the First World War that a certain Swedish ship arriving in England would be allowed to return to its home country. The judge gave his opinion as follows:

> Now . . . I have to consider whether there was a contract at all. . . .
>
> No doubt the Government can bind itself, through its officers, by a commercial contract and, if it does so, it must perform it like anybody else or pay damages for the breach. But there was no commercial contract in this case. It was an arrangement whereby the Government purported to give an assurance regarding its future executive action in relation to a particular ship arriving in this country with a particular kind of cargo. To my mind, a breach of this type of contract does not give rise to damages in a court of law. It is merely an expression of an intention to act in a particular way under certain conditions.
>
> My main reason for so thinking is that it is not competent for the Government to fetter its future executive actions, which must necessarily be determined by the needs of the community when the question arises. The Government cannot by

contract hamper its freedom of action in matters which concern the welfare of the state.

The Deputy State Attorney responded by citing the judgment of Denning J (as he then was) in *Robertson* v. *Minister of Pensions* [9]. Denning J differed from the view of Rowlatt J by concluding that it was not necessary to the decision in *The Amphitrite.*

Finally there is the House of Lords case of *Howell* v. *Falmouth Boat Construction* [10] which is the law of this country (see *Zamir* v. *Inspector of Road Transport* [3]). Though it does not deal directly with the question before us, the *Howell* judgment differs from the opinion of Denning J who relied on the precedent of the *Robertson* case.

11. Professor Mitchell, whose profound study, *The Contracts of Public Authorities*, aided me in writing this judgment, is not in agreement with Denning J's position (see *ibid.* 30). He is of the opinion that Rowlatt J was basically right, although the exact extent and significance of his ruling need clarification. With all due respect, I associate myself with this view for the following reasons:

First of all, what is the difference between 'commercial contracts' referred to by Rowlatt J in *The Amphitrite* and other 'arrangements'? All agree that the State has the ability to bind itself by contract and be subject to the contract rules at private law like any other person. Such contracts are made by the State not in its magisterial or sovereign capacity but—in Continental legal phraseology—as 'fiscus', or as they are referred to in *Feinberg* v. *Local Council of Givatayim* [4], 'commercial contracts'. In the realm of 'commercial contracts', Rowlatt J declared that if the State does not fulfil the contract it shall pay damages.

That said, the contract which we are considering here—at least as far as it is the subject of controversy—is not a 'commercial' (or civil) contract. The State bound itself under clause 12(c) in a matter in which it acts in a magisterial capacity. The subject matter of its obligation is a government act, the effect of which must be determined by public law.

12. In this matter there are those who adopt a stricter attitude and postulate that an act of responsibility by a government authority can never be the subject of a private contract. This is the opinion of Austrian jurists: see Adamovich, *Verwaltungsrecht*, 5th edition, p. 85, and Antoniolli, *Allgemeines Verwaltungsrecht*, p. 201. As against this orthodox view in administrative law, there is another opinion that such a contract is not to be invalidated outright but that there are limits to its legality and efficacy. This is the view of Professor Ruck of Switzerland as expressed in his book *Schweizerisches Verwaltungsrecht*, 3rd edition, p. 124, and in particular that of Professor Forsthoff, the author of the leading work on *German Administrative Law*, 9th edition, article 14. Professor Forsthoff cites a number of reasons which

fit the case before us. On the one hand, the contract enables the authority concerned to solve specific problems, by adjusting itself to each new situation. The law in the abstract, all-embracing and undifferentiating, is not capable of such flexibility. On the other hand, a contractual arrangement presents the danger that the contractual limits will hinder the State in the future in carrying out its governmental task so that it will no longer be free to consider each matter according to its circumstances and contemporary requirements. Furthermore, the contract may serve the authorities as a means for departing from the principle of equality of all citizens before the law, by granting a benefit to one person which the public as a whole does not enjoy.

The Supreme Court of the United States has adopted the rule that a contract made by an authority which concerns a governmental act is always subject to the power of the government to free itself of its obligation when the public interest so requires. This is true whether the origin of this power is in the 'police power' or in 'eminent domain', the boundary between these two being in any case ill-defined: see *Hudson County Water Co.* v. *McCarter* [14].

It follows from this that the Court will not invalidate a contractual bond between the State and a private individual, even if the subject matter is a governmental act—[as opposed to] a 'commercial' or civil matter—but that the contract is not final. Along with its obligation to perform the contract is the power vested in the State, for the public weal, to set aside the binding force of the contract and free itself from its obligations (See *Stone* v. *State of Mississippi* [15]).

In other words, the contract is effective but its enforcement is limited, since the State has the power to annul it whenever its essential needs require. Such needs supersede the sanctity of contracts. As was stated in *Cincinnati* v. *Louisville and Nashville Railroad Co.* [16]:

> Every contract, whether between the state and an individual, or between individuals only, is subject to this general law. There enters into every engagement the unwritten condition that it is subordinate to the right of appropriation for a public use.

13. This rule proposed by the American courts solves at least one of the problems raised by Professor Forsthoff. Without depriving the authority of the capacity to contract with a private individual even on matters of governmental or public import, the rule does not fetter the authority permanently and absolutely by the letter of the contract. Rather, the rule leaves the Government the freedom it requires to protect the vital needs of the State despite the existence of the contract. The right to rescind the contractual bond in these circumstances was referred to by Hughes CJ in *Worthen* v. *Thomas* [17] as a part of the 'prerogative of self-protection'.

14. A similar problem came before this Court in *Balaban* v. *The Municipality of Tel Aviv* [6]. The municipality refused to grant the owner of a certain plot of land a licence to build a cinema since it had declared its intention to expropriate the property concerned. The applicant opposed expropriation, relying on a contract made with his predecessor in title, by which the municipality expressly bound itself to refrain from such expropriation. Following *William Cory & Son Ltd* v. *City of London Corporation* [11], we decided that 'the obligation of the municipality is contrary to the public interest and is void *ab initio*'. The reason was that the legislature requires the municipality in certain circumstances to acquire and expropriate land needed for public purposes. In undertaking to refrain from expropriation, the municipality in effect undertook not to fulfil a task imposed upon it as a public body.

The same question was recently discussed in another context in the (English) Court of Appeal in *Commissioner of Crown Lands* v. *Page* [12]. At 458 of the report, Devlin J (as he then was) reiterated the notion expressed in *The Amphitrite* case [8]: in contracting with a private individual, the State does not undertake to bind its hands regarding the future use of its sovereign powers when it is required to make use of such powers for the public weal. At 459, Devlin LJ says:

> I need not examine the question whether, if the Crown sought to fetter its future action in express terms, it could effectively do so. It is most unlikely that in a contract with the subject, it would ever make the attempt.

Such an attempt, however, was made by the State in the case before us, and we have to determine whether or not it is lawful.

15. The Deputy State Attorney sought to confine our ruling in the *Balaban* case [6] to municipalities and similar public corporations and argued that this ruling does not apply to the State itself. As stated in *Page's Case* [12], at 458, there are in effect two grounds on which we might invalidate the obligation of a public authority not to exercise its powers. Such obligation can be invalidated for being *ultra vires* the authority or for reasons of public policy. In *Halperin* v. *The Mayor of Tel Aviv* [5] we compared the powers of a municipality as detailed in the Municipal Corporations Ordinance 1934, with the objects clause in a company memorandum under the Companies Ordinance. Under section 98 of the Municipal Corporations Ordinance 1934, the legislator accorded municipalities powers necessitating the acquisition of land. There is also a reference to the Land (Acquisition for Public Purposes) Ordinance 1943. Municipalities are established in order to fulfill public functions, not to refrain from doing so. It can therefore be maintained that if such a body undertakes not to fulfill one of its functions it acts *ultra vires* the powers granted to it. Moreover, such undertaking is also contrary to the public

interest, for if a public body renounces its duty who will supply the omission?

In the *Balaban* case [6] we stressed the public policy ground of invalidity, but both grounds co-existed in the obligation assumed by the municipality. The policy in question was also *ultra vires*, as can be seen from the *Cory* case [11] previously mentioned and also *York Corporation* v. *Henry Leetham and Sons Ltd* [13].

I agree with the Deputy State Attorney that an obligation of the State cannot be set aside as being *ultra vires* its powers. The State was not set up by an instrument—a statute or other documents—allocating to it certain functions and prohibiting it from fulfilling others. In respect of the acts of a particular civil servant, the question may arise whether he was authorized to do what he did or whether he exceeded his authority. Just as a particular transaction may be *ultra vires* the authority of the director of a company, so it may be *ultra vires* a particular civil servant who has carried it out. But that is another matter. A transaction can be *ultra vires* a company, a municipality, or any other corporation, but cannot be beyond the powers of the State, which are not defined or restricted.

On the other hand, I do not agree with the contention that an obligation given by the State can never be invalidated on the very same ground on which we declared invalid the obligation of the municipality in the *Balaban* case [6]. The notion that the public interest may require a contract not to be performed is a universal one and State contracts are no exception (see *Michal* v. *Minister of Finance* [1]). If, for instance, the State should undertake to pardon an offender in consideration of a payment in foreign currency, or if it should contract with a private individual to wage or not to wage war against another State, no one would have any illusions as to the fate of such an undertaking. The argument that the State is in need of foreign currency and that the contract contributes to the development of the economy will not save it from attack. It is unfitting that an undertaking to exercise or not to exercise any such sovereign power should be exchanged in return for money to a private individual.

16. I see no justification for us in Israel to adopt the strict view which I described above. Such a view would require us to find an exact criterion to determine whether each contract is subject to public law or to private law. It is unanimously conceded that the boundaries between public and private law are becoming increasingly blurred.

Also, the strict view stems from the attitude that it is not proper for the State to demean itself by negotiating and concluding a contract with a private citizen in respect of a governmental act. According to this view, the very matter would appear to be something unbefitting the status of the State, and for this reason it would be invalidated as contrary to the public interest. One learned authority at the beginning of the century said that 'the State commands', as a person in authority may command, but it does not meet the private individual and negotiate with him as an equal. This view is now outmoded, and according to the prevailing view such a contract does not demean the State. The legislator has now placed his view in the statute book that the State may enter into a contract with a private individual even where the subject is not a private civil matter. Take, for example, the agreement referred to in section 22(3) of the Land (Acquisition for Public Purposes) Ordinance 1943, made by the Minister of Finance with 'any person' on whose behalf he is about to requisition land. Note the agreement mentioned in section 9 of that Ordinance 'as to the amount of the compensation to be paid' for requisitioned property. These are not private agreements but rest on governmental acts; and yet the Minister of Finance is authorized to make them.

It may happen that the contract is contrary to the public interest, but as I have already stated, the Court will in such a case set the contract aside, irrespective of whether it concerns a civil ('commercial') matter or a public matter.

17. Apart from one important distinction, the principle established in the United States is similar to the law laid down in England in the *Amphitrite* [8] and *Page* [12] cases. The difference is that according to the English rule a contract whereby an authority undertakes to fetter its executive discretion is totally lacking in validity. Conversely, the Americans recognize the validity of the contract, but alongside the contractual obligation they preserve the authority's right to free itself from the restraints of the contract whenever its terms are inconsistent with a vital public interest. What is the difference between the two approaches? A person who makes a contract with the State, which the latter repudiates, may according to the American rule be entitled to damages. The scope of these damages is not necessarily the same as those payable for breach of contract, since the State was not in breach of contract but repudiated it lawfully. In contradistinction to this approach, the English rule denies the existence of a valid contract and thus precludes the possibility of State liability in damages. In the controversy between these two schools, I favour the American view. Rather than leaving the claimant powerless against the authority, the American approach gives him a certain guarantee against the all-powerful State. That said, I am not obliged to lay down a hard and fast rule for the purposes of the present case. The question of what rule governs the State of Israel in such an instance does not affect the petitioner and will not decide the fate of the petition. Moreover, it is not for this Court, as a High Court of Justice, to answer this question.

In my view, the American rule is more calculated to achieve the ends of justice. This rule does confine the activities of the authority concerned, and safeguards the public interest. The Court has the power to invalidate the contract if it is found contrary to the public interest and the State is entitled to repudiate it. These two facts are sufficient to guarantee that the public interest will not suffer. In stating that this rule should in my view serve us as a guiding principle, I do not mean that in every matter dealt with by the United States Supreme Court I would have decided as that Court. Thus, for instance, I do not think that an authority may, without legal authorization, release a particular person from a tax burden, as was decided in *Atlantic Coast Line R.R. Co.* v. *Philipps* [18].

The principle that all are equal before the taxing authorities cannot in my view be made subject to conditions and exceptions. I would declare such an exception invalid for reasons of public policy. However, I would adopt the American rule for the reasons stated above.

18. Before dealing with the last question, whether or not the obligation in this case is against the public interest, I feel obliged to express another doubt as to the standing of the present petitioner. When A comes to Court with a complaint that the authorities have unlawfully granted B a monopoly, this means that A's right to engage in a particular occupation or trade has been infringed and this Court will entertain the complaint. However, A's standing is less certain when its plea is that one of the contractual terms between the State and B is invalid for being contrary to the public interest. In such a complaint, it is not clear what particular right of the petitioner has been infringed.

Mr Toussia-Cohen maintains that it is virtually certain that when the petitioner applies to the respondents for an import licence it will be met with a refusal. The respondents will consider themselves bound by their contract with Leyland and will want to prevent competition with that firm. At this point I deem it necessary to clarify one thing. The need to safeguard Leyland's business, or any other commercial consideration, is not a matter for which the authorities were entrusted with the extensive powers that authorize them to determine which goods may be imported and which not. It follows that a contract made with Leyland can never provide the respondents with a ground for refusing the petitioner or any other applicant for licence; see *Israel Distillery Co. Ltd* v. *Mayor of Rishon Le-Tzion* [7]. If the petitioner desires to import trucks, and the needs of the country justify such import, then the respondents will be obliged to accede to the petitioner's request. On the other hand, the petitioner's application may be rejected because Leyland supplies all the country's requirements, and in such a case this Court is likely to uphold such rejection; see *B. Breslov & Partners* v. *Minister of Trade & Industry* [2] and other similar cases. In such an instance, however, the petitioner's case will not be prejudiced just because of clause 12(c) of the contract. For example, were clause 12(c) missing from the contract, and the respondents refused the petitioners application for the above reason, what difference would this make to the legal position?

19. Having expressed my doubts as to the status of the petitioner, I shall nevertheless consider the question whether the undertaking contained in clause 12(c) is contrary to the public interest. I think that while generally it is advisable for an authority to refrain from binding itself by contract as to how it will exercise its future discretion, in this case it was nevertheless necessary. The limitations of the small local market, as stated in paragraph 4 of the letter dated March 1960, mandated such a clause, for otherwise the value of the whole transaction would have been undermined. Unlike the two examples I cited in paragraph 15 above, this transaction was not one which ought not to have been effected. So what defect affects it? If it transpires that Leyland's products are unsatisfactory or that the transaction was a mistaken one which will not meet the requirements of the State, the respondents are likely to regard themselves bound. No foreign currency will be allocated to any person for the importation of trucks owing to the sanctity of the contract which was concluded and the public interest will be prejudiced.

I have already explained that in spite of the contract, the respondents, when exercising their discretion under the Defence (Finance) Regulations 1941, and the Import, Export and Customs Powers (Defence) Ordinance 1939, will be bound to ignore the fact that Leyland has acquired rights under the contract. The contract will not serve as an excuse to reject other applications. We have also seen that the respondents have the inalienable right to repudiate the contract and disregard it in order to carry out the tasks of government. In these circumstances, I cannot say that the said condition involves any injury to the public, and the order *nisi* should therefore be discharged.

**Berinson J:** I concur.

**Olshan P:**

[*After discussing the question of whether Leyland had been given an illegal monopoly, Olshan P states his agreement with Sussman J on the issue of 'fettering the (State's) freedom of action in the exercise of their powers in the future.'*

*However, Olshan P adds that he would not 'lay down in advance a rule on the question of the right of Leyland to claim damages in the event of the respondents not being able to fulfil their obligation regarding the exercise of their power in the future.*]

**Agranat, DP:**

[*Agranat DP concurs in the 'exhaustive and profound judgment of his colleague Sussman J', subject to a reservation on the monopoly issue.*]

Order *nisi* discharged.

Judgment given on 27 October 1961.

# 21

# *Scitex Corp. Ltd and others*
# v.
# *The Minister of Trade and Industry*

[H.C. 135/75, 321/75]
[30(1) PD 673 (1976)]

*Sussman DP, Berinson J and Manny J*

Israeli case referred to:
[1] HC 134/67—*Vanunu* v. *Ministry of Transport*; 21(2) PD 710, 716–17.

## JUDGMENT

**Berinson J:**

The petitioners in this case are manufacturing/exporting companies who seek to have the respondent [the Minister of Trade and Industry] honour his undertaking to them regarding special aid promised for their 1974 exports. The availability of such one-time aid to exporting industries was publicized in Circular 8/74, published by the Foreign Trade Section of the Ministry of Trade and Industry on 10 September 1974. . . . Such aid was promised only to manufacturers in the fields specifically mentioned in the circular and only where exports totalled more than 50 per cent of their 1973 sales. Such an enterprise was termed 'an eligible enterprise' [*and promised a grant of 25 agorot for each dollar of 1974 exports, up to that enterprise's 1973 exporting total*].

* * *

All the petitioners come under the category of 'eligible enterprise' as defined by Circular 8/74 and, in fact, have already received half of the special aid. However, before the second half of the aid came due, there was a financial crisis in Israel. On 10 November 1974 the Israeli Lira was devalued, raising the official dollar exchange rate from 4.2 Israeli Lira to 6 Israeli Lira. . . . From the day of devaluation and onwards, it was decided to grant all exporters, through indirect tax refunds, the [same] special aid previously bestowed only on eligible enterprises.

This move raised the effective exchange rate for all exporters to an average of 7.3 Israeli Lira, . . . effectively nullifying the special preference previously given to eligible enterprises. This new policy was contained in Circular 9/74, under which eligible enterprises could receive the second part of their aid in one of two ways: either as a grant, as in Circular 8/74, or under the new arrangement, described in Circular 9/74.

The petitioners have challenged this arrangement, contending that it is prejudicial to them and deprives them of the rights promised them under Circular 8/74 . . . While initially claiming that they were entitled to *both* the special aid promised in Circular 8/74 *and* the tax refunds and subsidies described in Circular 9/74, the petitioners have now restricted their claim solely to the special aid for their exports up until the day of devaluation (10 November 1974).

On this point, I believe the claim is justified. The basis of the petitioner's claim is that the respondent cannot retroactively rescind the promises made in Circular 8/74 and apply the new policy to the period before it was adopted, that is, before the devaluation. The petitioners argue that as far as this period is concerned, all of the elements of the well-known doctrine of 'promissory estoppel' are present: namely, a promise was made with the intent that others should act on it; the petitioners acted on it, and in fact worsened their situation as a result.

The claim that the petitioners worsened their position on account of the promise is a doubtful one. The promise, made in September 1974 and expanded towards the end of October 1974, applied to exports over the whole year, *including the nine to ten months that had already passed.* It is not claimed—and such a claim would indeed have been far-fetched—that in the relatively short space of time that passed from the issuing of Circular 8/74 (and its amendments) up to the devaluation, the petitioners entered into export commitments on the basis of the special aid, which were actually completed by the day of devaluation.

However, in my opinion, this point is unimportant as I do not base my decision on the doctrine of promissory estoppel. The matter is actually quite straightforward and does not raise any undue difficulty. An undertaking was made and there is no reason why it should not be honoured in full, at least for the period up to the devaluation. It is a cardinal precept in public law that a public administration must conduct itself in good faith, namely, by acting honestly and fairly in its dealings with its citizens. If, in private law, people must act in good faith in negotiating contracts and in honouring their contractual obligations (see sections 12(a) and 39 of the

Contracts Law (General Part), 1973), a public administration has a heightened duty to act fairly in its dealings with its citizens.

When a governing body makes a promise that comes within its legal authority and is intended to have legal force, and a second party accepts it as such, then public fairness demands that the promise be kept so long as the promisor is capable of keeping it. This is so whether or not the citizen has worsened his position as a result of the promise. The integrity of the Government in the eyes of the public is inestimably more important than the possibility that, in a given case, the Government might be allowed to rescind a promise or undertaking made within the scope of its legal authority and capable of practicably being fulfilled.

* * *

The respondents did not really dispute this principle, but rather contended that the (original) promise had been fulfilled by the terms of the new arrangement as outlined above. According to the respondents, the new exchange rate, together with the new tax refunds, offered much more than what the petitioners would have received for the export dollar in the second half of 1974, even including the special aid [promised under Circular 8/74]. . . . While this argument holds as far as the period *after* the devaluation is concerned, it does not apply to the period *before* it. [Were it not for the decision to apply the post-devaluation policy retroactively, the petitioners, during the period prior to the devaluation, would have benefitted from their preferred status as recipients of special aid.] After the devaluation, the status of all exporters was realigned so that the petitioners no longer benefited from their preferred status as recipients of special aid. Therefore, it cannot be said that this new arrangement offered adequate compensation for the petitioners' prior entitlement.

Clearly, the Administration may change its policies whenever it wishes. But it must honour its previous policy commitments. In the words of the judge in *Vanunu* v. *Ministry of Transport* [1], 'a public authority is free to change its policy at any time, but only prospectively and not retrospectively'.

We therefore order that the temporary injunction be made permanent and that the respondents pay the petitioners the special aid set out in Circular 8/74 for all of their exports up to 10 November 1974. The respondents will pay the petitioner in HC 135/75 and the petitioner in HC 321/75 their costs of a total of 5,000 Israeli lira.

Judgment given on 25 December 1975.

# PART III
# *Judicial Review*

# SECTION 9: JUSTICIABILITY AND STANDING

# 22

## *Standing and Justiciability*

SHIMON SHETREET*



The judgment in the *Ressler* case,[1] delivered nearly ten years ago, was a turning point in the development of judicial review of the Administration as regards questions of standing and justiciability. The judgment also complements developments concerning the plea of unreasonableness, an area which has broadened considerably in recent years.[2]

### 1. The Right of Standing prior to the *Ressler* Case

The traditional approach of the Supreme Court (sitting as a High Court of Justice) was to demand that, in order to establish a right of standing, a petitioner would have to show possible harm to a direct and material personal interest.[3] Over the years the circle widened. The Court recognized the

* The author is indebted to Ms Ayelet Yavin and to Mr Guy Pessach for their help in preparing the manuscript for print.

[1] HC 910/86 *Ressler* v. *Minister of Defence* (1988) 42(2) PD 441 (excerpted in this section).

[2] See S. Shetreet, *Justice in Israel* (Martinus Nijhoff, Dordrecht, 1994). Note the spread of judicial review of Knesset decisions and laws, *ibid.* 425–47. Note also the spread of judicial review of government and other executive decisions: *ibid.* 382–9.

[3] See HC 600/75 *Koren* v. *Minister of Defence et al.* (1975) 30(1) PD 514, 515; HC 287/69 *Meron* v. *Minister of Labour et al.* (1970) 24(1) PD 337, 343.

representative interest of an organization that wished to protect the interests of its members,[4] and likewise a material and direct interest that was common to the public as a whole rather than peculiar to the individual petitioner.[5] Similarly the Court extended the circle of interests that could be recognized as material interests of the petitioner.[6]

Despite these developments, however, in anything to do with a public petition, one that sought to fight the public battle rather than that of the individual petitioner, the Court for many years refused to recognize the right of standing of the public petitioner.[7] Moreover, the more public the particular petition, the more stringent was the Court's requirement that the petitioner be personally affected before being granted right of standing.[8]

Thus, for example, in the case of *Twick* v. *Director of Broadcasting Authority*[9] the Court did not recognize the right of standing of the 'broadcasting consumer' who demanded that the Broadcasting Authority publicize the source of an item of information put out on television. In the words of the Court:

> The petitioner . . . has failed to show any harm done to a material personal interest of his as a result of the non-disclosure of the source of the aforementioned item. He therefore has no right of standing to present a petition to this Court.

The decision of the High Court in the case of *Shiran* v. *Broadcasting Authority* marked the beginning of the movement towards recognizing the right of standing of the public petitioner. In that case, the petitioners claimed that 'The Pillar of Fire'—a historical documentary series filmed by the Broadcasting Authority on the history of Zionism—did not adequately present the contribution made by immigrants from Moslem countries to the development of Zionism. In this case, Shamgar J sought to adopt

> . . . a more liberal approach, if it transpires that the matter raised by the petition is of public import, with a direct bearing on furthering the rule of law and laying the ground for securing its continued existence in practice.[10]

There was sufficient in the nature of the duties of the Broadcasting Authority, a body intended to serve the public as a whole, to base recognition of the standing of the 'broadcasting consumer' before the Court.

[4] See HC 19/64 *Association of Insurance Brokers* v. *Inspector of Insurance* (1964) 18(3) PD 506.

[5] See HC 217/80 *Segal* v. *Minister of the Interior* (1980) 34(4) PD 429.

[6] Z. Segal, *The Right of Standing in the High Court of Justice* (2nd ed. University of Tel Aviv, Tel Aviv, 1993), 97–103.

[7] See HC 107/50 *Ariav* v. *Minister of Justice et al.* (1951) 5 PD 523; HC 40/70 *Becker* v. *Minister of Defence* (1970) 24(1) PD 238 (1970).

[8] See HC 40/70 *Becker* v. *Minister of Defence* (1970) 24(1) PD 238.

[9] HC 221/78 *Twick* v. *Director General of Broadcasting Authority* (10 Apr. 1978, not yet reported), 1.

[10] HC 1/81 *Shiran* v. *Broadcasting Authority* (1981) 35(3) PD 365, 374.

After the *Shiran* case, the trend of the Court was towards recognizing the right of standing of the petitioner, even when the petition was of a blatantly public nature. The Court recognized the right of standing of the public petitioner, *inter alia*, when a question of public import arose and when facts were presented to the Court that pointed to a material injury done to an individual's basic civil rights and to his freedom as an individual;[11] when the petition raised a clear constitutional problem,[12] and when the matter at hand was of an exceptional nature with a bearing on the principles of the rule of law.[13]

This new way of thinking on the question of the right of standing in public matters, which applies to this day in the High Court, was essentially developed in the *Ressler* case.

## 2. Lack of Justiciability prior to the *Ressler* Case

For many years the High Court refrained from dealing with matters that in its judgment did not warrant discussion or judicial ruling. These were of two kinds: first, matters over which the Court felt it lacked the means with which to make a judicial ruling; secondly, cases where the issue concerned was political-ideological, with distinct public overtones, which the Court felt disinclined to deal with because of concern for likely harm to the principle of the separation of powers and the invasion into the territory of another arm of government.

Thus, for example, the Court ruled that a petition seeking the banning of the entry of the German Ambassador to Israel on the grounds of his service in the German army during the Second World War, was not a legal but a clearly political matter, one which could not be dealt with along legal lines;[14] that questions relating to the organization, structure, equipping, and operation of the army were not justiciable;[15] and that the decision of

[11] HC 243/82 *Zichroni* v. *Management Committee of the Broadcasting Authority* (1983) 37(1) PD 757. Here the petitioner was protesting against the decision of the Managing Committee of the National Broadcasting Authority, ruling that it was forbidden to broadcast chance interviews with public figures identified with the PLO.

[12] HC 428/86 *Barzilai* v. *Government of Israel* (1987) 40(3) PD 505. In this case the Court dealt with a petition lodged against the decision of the President of Israel to grant a pardon to members of the General Security Service, suspected of responsibility for the deaths of some terrorists, even before their conviction for the crimes they were alleged to have committed.

[13] HC 852/86 *Aloni* v. *Minister of Justice* (1987) 41(2) PD 1. Here the question concerned the authority of the Minister of Justice not to extradite to the requesting country someone who had been declared 'extraditable' by a competent Israeli court.

[14] HC 186/65 *Reiner* v. *Prime Minister* (1965) 19(2) PD 485.

[15] HC 561/75 *Ashkenazi* v. *Minister of Defence* (1976) 30(3) PD 309.

the President of the State, giving the job of forming a government to a particular Member of the Knesset, was not justiciable.[16]

Towards the middle of the 1980s, there was a narrowing of the limitation of non-justiciability, at the same time as a broadening and deepening of the scope of judicial review of the actions of the various arms of government.

In a series of judgments, the High Court ruled that various decisions of the Knesset were justiciable and therefore subject to judicial review. In this way, it rules on decisions of the Speaker of the Knesset, a Knesset Committee, and even the House itself. Among these were the decision to prevent a party in the Knesset from submitting a Bill of a racist nature;[17] the decision to prevent a single-member party from tabling a no-confidence motion against the government,[18] and the decision of the House to deprive a Knesset Member of his parliamentary immunity.[19] At the same time, the Court ruled that it would exercise restraint when it came to judicial review of Knesset internal procedure. As the Court explained, out of respect for the Legislature, the Court would only intervene in actions of the Knesset when what was at stake was serious harm to the very fabric of the constitutional system.[20]

Against the background of these developments, judgment was given in the *Ressler* case, setting out the new view of the Court on the issue of non-justiciability, one that significantly restricted those areas where a claim of non-justiciability would be accepted.

## 3. The *Ressler* Case

The subject of the petition in *Ressler*—the deferral of the military service of rabbinic students—had been brought before the Court on several previous occasions. On all these occasions, however, the petition had been dismissed, without a decision on the merits of the case, on the basis of the preliminary arguments of lack of standing and non-justiciability.

In the *Becker*[21] case in 1970, the first of the petitions on this question, the Court dismissed the petition, ruling that the petitioner could not petition the Court on a matter that affected the public as a whole since he had not managed to show any personal and material injury.

[16] HC 65/51 *Jabotinsky* v. *President of Israel* (1951) 5 PD 801.

[17] HC 742/84 *Kahane* v. *Speaker of the Knesset* (1985) 39(4) PD 85.

[18] HC 73/85 *Kach Party Faction* v. *Speaker of the Knesset* (1985) 39(3) PD 141.

[19] HC 620/85 *Miari* v. *Speaker of the Knesset* (1987) 41(4) PD 169.

[20] For a comprehensive discussion of the intervention of the HC in parliamentary proceedings, see Ch. 10.

[21] HC 40/70 *Becker* v. *Minister of Defence* (1970) 24(1) PD 238.

A further petition[22] on the same matter, submitted about ten years later, was also dismissed when the Court ruled that the question whether or not to draft rabbinical students was, in the main, a political question, one over which there was much public debate and not therefore a question where a judicial ruling would be appropriate.

Such statements, on the lack of standing and non-justiciability, formed the background to the dismissal of other submissions and petitions over the question of the exemption of rabbinical students from the draft.[23]

In the final petition submitted by Ressler, on the question of rabbinical students not being drafted to the IDF,[24] a change took place: for the first time the Court dealt with the case on its merits instead of summarily dismissing it. The High Court recognised the right of standing of Ressler as a public petitioner, seeking to bring to the Court a matter of special public importance and making a *prima facie* case for the existence of serious faults in government practice. The Court also stated that the types of cases in which the right of standing of the public petitioner would be recognised did not constitute a closed list of categories, and that there were very possibly other types of cases where the Court would acknowledge the right of standing of the public petitioner.

On the issue of justiciability the major innovation of the Court in the *Ressler* case was in the distinction it made between cases of 'normative non-justiciability' and those of 'institutional non-justiciability'. Normative justiciability related to the question whether there were the legal means to deal with the dispute before the Court. Institutional justiciability on the other hand, dealt with the question whether it was appropriate or desirable for the Court to make a ruling in the dispute, or whether it was best left to the decision of another arm of government. On the question of normative justiciability, the Court ruled that it was generally possible to look at any action of government in terms of its constitutionality. In other words, in each case one could examine whether the action had been performed within the bounds of the enabling law and within the bounds of reasonableness. It followed that all actions of government were normatively justiciable.

As to institutional justiciability, the Court restricted the list of instances that were not institutionally justiciable, overruling the previous case law which had held it to be inappropriate for the Court to make a ruling on matters of a political or ideological nature. There were, however, differences of opinion between the judges in *Ressler* over the range of instances that were not institutionally justiciable. Barak J held that the claim of

[22] HC 448/81 *Ressler* v. *Minister of Defence* (1982) 36(1) PD 81.

[23] FH 2/82 *Ressler* v. *Minister of Defence* (1982) 36(1) PD 708 and also HC 179/82 *Ressler* v. *Minister of Defence* (1982) 36(4) PD 421.

[24] HC 910/86 *Ressler* v. *Minister of Defence* (1988) 42(2) PD 441.

non-justiciability should be restricted to certain exceptional cases, where the Court's handling of the matter would seriously jeopardize the public's faith in the Court. In practical terms this meant essentially that the Court would exercise restraint when it came to judicial review of the internal workings of the Knesset. Shamgar P, on the other hand, extended the range of cases that were institutionally non-justiciable to include all those where the issue was by and large political in nature, or where other aspects of the case led one to conclude that it would be preferable if a decision on the matter came from an arm of government other than the Court.

Despite this disagreement, it might be said that with respect to the scope of institutional non-justiciability, the Court would not now adopt the kind of sweeping approach adhered to in the past, whereby anything of a political—ideological nature which was highly controversial would be non-justiciable.

## 4. The Development of the Case Law in the Wake of the *Ressler* Case

Since the *Ressler* case, the general trend has continued towards recognizing the right of standing of the public petitioner and lowering the barrier of non-justiciability.

Support for recognition of the standing of the public petitioner has come in a number of cases. Thus, for example, in the *Ganor*[25] case, the standing of public petitioners was recognized. Their petition was against the decision of the Attorney General not to prosecute the banking executives and accountants suspected of offences that had led to a major crisis on the stock exchange. Likewise in the *Giergevsky*[26] case, where the Court was called upon by a petitioner to declare void a coalition agreement forged between two parties during the attempts to form a government, and where the Court reiterated its former ruling that on clear constitutional matters the Court would reject a claim of lack of standing. Further expression of this recognition of the standing of the public petition has come in the wave of judgments handed down on petitions submitted by organizations set up to protect and advance the cause of the rule of law.[27]

[25] HC 935/89 *Ganor* v. *Attorney General* (1990) 44(2) PD 485.

[26] HC 1635/90 *Giergensky* v. *Prime Minister* (1991) 45(1) PD 749.

[27] See HC 4267/93 *Amitai, Citizens for the Integrity of Government* v. *Prime Minister* (1993) 47(5) PD 441—a petition in which the Court was asked to order the Prime Minister to exercise his powers and remove from office the Deputy Minister of Religion, against whom the Attorney General had prepared a criminal indictment, but where the Knesset had decided not to remove his parliamentary immunity. See also HC 3094/93 *The Movement for Quality of Government* v. *The Government of Israel* (1993) 47(5) PD 404—a petition where the Court was asked to order the

With regard to justiciability, here also the trend towards lowering the barriers of non-justiciability has found expression in a series of judgments.

Thus, for example, in the *Giergevsky*[28] case, the Court ruled that a political agreement between two parties was justiciable. In the *Murkos*[29] case the Court rejected the argument that a petition, submitted at the outset of the Gulf war for an order to distribute gas masks to residents of the occupied territories, was non-justiciable since it involved security, military, and political considerations. Furthermore, in the *Nimrodi*[30] case the Court stated that judicial review of the actions of the Knesset would extend to declaring a law void where its passage had not followed Knesset regulations.

At the same time there is a limit to the readiness of the Court to extend the right of standing and relax the barrier of justiciability. Thus, for example, with regard to the barrier of justiciability the Court has ruled in a number of recent cases that it will not deal with questions of foreign policy or security policy where the political aspect of the case, rather than the legal aspect, is the dominant one. The Court ruled this way, for example, when it was asked to prohibit the Israeli Government from signing an agreement with the PLO,[31] when it was asked to rule on a petition relating to the peace talks with Syria and to order the Government to desist from any moves designed to remove areas of the Golan Heights from Israeli sovereignty,[32] and when a general petition was submitted, unrelated to any particular dispute, but simply aimed against the settlement policy of the Government in the territories.[33]

As regards the right of standing in a public petition, the Court of late has come out strongly against petitions that are insufficiently founded, brought in the main to attract public attention or to earn some personal publicity. To go by recent cases the Court could well refuse to recognize the standing of a public petitioner in a case where there exists a potential petitioner with a material and personal interest who has refrained from bringing his case to the court.[34]

Prime Minister to remove the Minister of the Interior from office after the Attorney General had decided to indict him on serious criminal charges.

[28] HC 1635/90 *Giergenski* v. *Prime Minister* (1991) 45(1) PD 74. See also the collection of articles on the subject of political agreements published in (1992) 26 *Is.LR* 407 ff.

[29] HC 168/91 *Murkos* v. *Minister of Defence* (1991) 45(1) PD 467.

[30] HC 975/89 *Nimrodi Land Development Ltd* v. *Speaker of the Knesset* (1991) 45(3) PD 154.

[31] HC 4877/93 *The Organisation for Victims of Arab Terror* v. *State of Israel* (not yet reported).

[32] HC 4354/92 *The Temple Mount Faithful Movement* v. *Prime Minister* (1993) 47(1) PD 37.

[33] HC 4481/91 *Bargil et al.* v. *Government of Israel* (1993) 47(4) PD 210.

[34] See HC 2148/94 *Gelbert* v. *The President of the Supreme Court and Head of Commission of Inquiry on the Hebron Massacre* (not yet reported); Z. Segal, *The Right of Standing in the High Court of Justice* (2nd ed. University of Tel Aviv, Tel Aviv, 1993) 251–3.

## 5. Observations

The doctrine of justiciability and the rules of standing are the means by which the High Court, amongst other things, seeks to set the boundaries between itself and other public and governmental bodies.

For many years I have supported the widening of the right of standing, both at the practical level of representing public petitioners[35] and also on the academic front,[36] in articles supporting a relaxation of the doctrine of justiciability and a widening of the scope of judicial review.

It seems to me, however, that the High Court has now arrived at an appropriate stopping point between itself, the Executive, and the Legislature. It would appear that the High Court itself is cognizant of this and has begun to show a degree of restraint,[37] seeking to leave the purely political field free to the Executive, and doing so without in any way detracting from the role of the Court as guardian of the rule of law. I would define this as a process of fine tuning, essential to a more precise definition of the demarcation between the Judiciary and the various other political bodies.[38]

I view this as an encouraging trend. Alongside the general relaxation of the doctrine of justiciability and opening up to public petitioners, the Court should seek to exercise restraint when the petition concerns matters that are blatantly political, devoid of any dominantly legal aspects.

The need for restraint in the Court's exercise of judicial review not only relates to the rules on standing and the doctrine of justiciability but also to the use by the Court of the plea of unreasonableness for the purposes of intervening in the discretion of the Executive or Legislature.[39]

We have, in my opinion, reached a point in the development of the doctrine of non-justiciability and the rules on the right of standing, where the High Court is approaching the outer limits of its powers in relation to the other arms of government, the Knesset and the Executive. This is therefore the appropriate time for a more precise demarcation of the divisions between these institutions—a form of fine tuning.

The attempt to express a more precise demarcation of these dividing lines is particularly essential in view of the current controversy regarding the appropriate role of the judiciary in Israel. Public voices are now

[35] In HC 1/81 *Shiran* v. *Broadcasting Authority* (1981) 35(3) PD 365, 374 and in HC 852/85 *Aloni* v. *Minister of Justice* (1987) 41(1) PD 2.

[36] Shetreet, n. 2 above, 382 ff., 425 ff.

[37] See cases in nn. 30–33 and the corresponding text.

[38] Shetreet, n. 35 above, at 519–20.

[39] S. Shetreet, 'Developments in Constitutional Law' (1990) 24 *Is.LR* 368; S. Shetreet, n. 35 above, 519–20. See also S. Shetreet, 'A Time for Self Restraint' *The Bar* (publication of the Israel Bar Association, Jerusalem, ed. G. Alon), 6–7 (Nov. 1993).

expressing the view that the current boundaries have perhaps been set in areas in which the Court has no legitimate place. The Court cannot act in a way that is totally detached from its social milieu and from the current political climate, since it is dependent on the public's continuing confidence.

The fine tuning we have spoken about is therefore essential and must be carried out by the High Court itself in the form of an exercise in self-restraint. It must be done, not so that the Court be made to climb down from the lofty stature built up over the years, but rather to encourage it to find an appropriate balance; the Court should be prevented from intervening whenever such judicial intervention seems likely to seriously disrupt the interrelations of the judiciary and the political arms of government.

Who is to determine what is a serious disruption? The Court itself. In the same way as the Court has constructed its own legal mechanisms and tests, by means of which it has managed to extend the scope of its own activity, such as the test of material harm to the rule of law, or the test of harm to the constitutional parliamentary fabric as grounds for intervention and as a basis for granting the right of standing, so also the Court is now bound to develop the notion of preventing a disruption in the interrelations of the Judiciary and the political arms of government as a rule for preventing judicial intervention. This will provide the kind of fine-tuning required in the demarcation of the boundaries between the various arms of government.

If the High Court were to act to develop the rules on standing and the doctrine of non-justiciability according to an approach of self-restraint based on protecting the proper balance between the various governmental institutions and preventing a serious disruption in the interrelations between the Judiciary and the other arms of government, it would then be possible to resist moves for intervention by the Legislature on the scope of intervention by the Judiciary. Various legislative initiatives that have appeared in recent times would seem to reflect the kind of trend I have just described. It would be far preferable if the Court were to prevent an intervention by the Legislature that might be construed as threatening the independence of the Court, by adopting its own brand of self-restraint according to judicial criteria that it developed itself.

This problem, the possibility of intervention by the Legislature in the powers of the Judiciary, is related to what I would call the 'Israeli paradox'. On the one hand the Court in Israel is more prepared to intervene in the actions of other arms of government than any Court in any other country, be it one with a constitution such as the United States, Canada, or Australia, or one without a written constitution such as England. On the other hand, in Israel a simple majority in the Knesset would have the authority to curb the powers of the High Court or have a deleterious effect on the terms of office of the judges; by a decision of the Knesset the salaries and rights of the judges could be impaired—at least until the passage of the Basic Law: Legislation, which is intended to grant superior status to the basic laws.

There is thus a paradox in Israel, a major widening of the judicial function, at the same time as there exists an absence of any constitutional protection for the courts, their powers, their status, and the rights of the judges themselves. Even today it is still possible to change the Basic Law: Judiciary by dint of the passage of a regular law, and the judges' salaries and terms may be changed merely by the decision of a Knesset Committee. Such a paradox highlights the importance of preventing any intervention by the Knesset in the status of the High Court, and of the judges themselves setting out the limits of their own powers of intervention.

Extending constitutional protection to the Judiciary is imminent, with the completion of the constitution itself and the passage of the Basic Law: Legislation. It is advisable that at the same time the Basic Law: The Judiciary be strengthened. Basic rights have been reinforced in Israel with the Basic Law: Human Dignity and Liberty and with the Basic Law: Freedom of Occupation. Likewise various forms of government have been reinforced, as with the Basic Law: The Knesset. It is, however essential also to reinforce the central provisions of the Basic Law: The Judiciary.

The need for self-restraint on the part of the High Court stems also from the 'solicited petitions'. Since the right of standing is now given more or less to anyone who wants it, the doctrine of justiciability has been extended to highly flexible limits, and the scope of judicial review on the grounds of reasonableness has also grown extensively, the Court finds itself involved in the political governance of the affairs of State to an extent unparalleled anywhere in the world. This new reality has led to the soliciting of petitions from both ends of the political spectrum—a further reason for the conclusion that the time is now ripe for the exercise of self-restraint.

# 23

# *Major (Res.) Yehuda Ressler, Attorney and others*
# v.
# *Minister of Defence*

[H.C. 910/86]
[42(2) PD 441 (1988)]

*Shamgar P, Ben Porat DP, and Barak J*

Israeli cases referred to:

[1] HC 40/70—*Becker* v. *Minister of Defence*; 24(1) PD 238.
[2] HC 731/86—*Micro-Daf* v. *Israel Electricity Company*; 41(2) PD 449.
[3] HC 287/69—*Meron* v. *Minister of Labour*; 24(1) PD 337.
[4] HC 217/80—*Segal* v. *Minister of the Interior*; 34(4) PD 429.
[5] HC 563/75—*Ressler* v. *Minister of Finance*; 30 PD(2) 337.
[6] HC 26/76—*Bar-Shalom* v. *Israel Lands Administrator*; 31(1) PD 796.
[7] HC 1/81—*Shiran* v. *Broadcasting Authority*; 35(3) PD 365.
[8] HC 29/55—*Dayan* v. *Minister of Religions*; 9 PD 997.
[9] HC 428/86—*Barzilai* v. *Government of Israel*; 40(3) PD 505.
[10] HC 609/85—*Zucker* v. *Mayor of Tel-Aviv–Yaffo*; 40(1) PD 775.
[11] HC 348/70—*Kfir* v. *Ashkelon Religious Council*; 25(1) PD 685.
[12] HC 852/85—*Aloni* v. *Minister of Justice*; 41(2) PD 1.
[13] HC 98/69—*Bergman* v. *Minister of Finance*; 23(1) PD 693.
[14] HC 148/73—*Kaniel* v. *Minister of Justice*; 27(1) PD 794.
[15] HC 152/82—*Alon* v. *Government of Israel*; 36(4) PD 449.
[16] HC 243/82—*Zikhroni* v. *Broadcasting Authority Executive Board*; 37(1) PD 757.
[17] HC 306/81—*Flato Sharon* v. *Knesset Committee*; 35(4) PD 118.
[18] HC 73/85—*'Kach' Party Faction* v. *Knesset Speaker*; 39(3) PD 141.
[19] HC 65/51—*Jabotinsky* v. *The President of the State of Israel*; 5 PD 801.
[20] HC 222/68—*Huggim Le'umiyim* v. *Minister of Police*; 24(2) PD 141.
[21] HC 561/75—*Ashkenazi* v. *Minister of Defence*; 30(3) PD 309.

[22] HC 802/79—*Samara* v. *Commander of Judea and Samaria*; 34(1) PD 1
[23] HC 186/65—*Reiner* v. *Prime Minister*; 19(2) PD 485.
[24] HC 89/83—*Levi* v. *Chairman of Knesset Finance Committee*; 38(2) PD 488.
[25] HC 302/72—*Hilu* v. *Government of Israel*; 27(2) PD 169.
[26] HC 742/84—*Kahane* v. *Knesset Speaker*; 39(4) PD 85.
[27] HC 669/85—*Kahane* v. *Knesset Speaker*; 40(4) PD 393.
[28] HC 321/60—*Lechem Chai Ltd* v. *Minister of Commerce and Industry*; 15 PD 197.
[29] HC 58/68—*Shalit* v. *Minister of the Interior*; 23(2) PD 477.
[30] HC 295/65—*Oppenheimer* v. *Minister of Interior and Health*; 20(1) PD 309.

Canadian cases referred to:
[31] *Thorson* v. *Attorney General of Canada* (*No 2*), (1974) 43 DLR (3d) 1.
[32] *Nova Scotia Board of Censors* v. *McNeil* (1976) 55 DLR (3d) 632.

English cases referred to:
[33] *Inland Revenue Commissioners* (*'IRC'*) v. *National Federation of Self Employed and Small Businesses Ltd* [1982] AC 617.

American cases referred to:
[34] *Poe* v. *Ullman*, 367 US 497 (1961).
[35] *Flast* v. *Cohen*, 392 US 85 (1968).
[36] *Baker* v. *Carr*, 369 US 186 (1962).
[37] *Cohen* v. *Virginia*, 19 US 120 (1821).
[38] *Goldwater* v. *Carter*, 444 US 996 (1979).

## JUDGMENT

**Barak J:**

Is the deferment of military service for yeshiva students lawful? This question—which has been submitted to this Court in the past—now arises before us again for renewed consideration. Should we examine this case on its merits or should the petition be rejected on the ground of lack of standing or non-justiciability? And if we address the merits—is the deferment of military service lawful?

### *The Facts*

1–5. * * *

6. Currently, the recruitment to military service of a yeshiva student 'whose religious study is his craft' and who is occupied full-time with his studies is deferred. The yeshiva student must study continuously from the

age of 16 in a recognized religious, secondary, or professional yeshiva. The deferment of military service is granted after the yeshiva student reports for registration, submits to tests that determine his physical fitness, and is found to be fit for service. The deferment of service is for one year only. Each year the yeshiva student must report anew. A yeshiva student who wishes to stop his studies, or whose studies are no longer his 'craft', is called to serve in the Israel Defence Forces. The length of service is then determined according to the age of the yeshiva student at the time he leaves the scheme of deferred recruitment, his physical fitness and his family situation. According to military data for the 1986–1987 working year, the number of yeshiva students in the deferred recruitment scheme was 17,017. With respect to the 1987 class of new recruits to the IDF, 1,647 yeshiva students requested and received a deferment of service.

## *The Legal Framework*

7. * * *

8. The Defence Service Law (Consolidated Version), 1959, was amended in 1971 (by the Defence Service—Amendment No 7, 1971). After its amendment, section 28 of the Defence Service (Consolidated Version) Law extended to exemptions from military service, as well as to reductions in the length of military service and deferments. The grounds for exemption, reduction, and deferment are all included in this provision. To this extent the change was technical in character, however a substantive change was introduced. The word 'similar' in the phrase 'or other similar reasons' was deleted. The language of the section's provision thus reads as follows:

> The Minister of Defence may, by order, if he sees fit to do so for reasons connected with the size of the regular forces or reserve forces of the Israel Defence Forces or for reasons connected with the requirements of education, security settlement, or the national economy, or for family or other reasons:
>
> (1) exempt a person of military age from the duty of regular service, or reduce the period of his service;
>
> (2) exempt a person of military age from the duty of reserve service . . .
>
> (3) on the application of a person of military age or a person designated for defence service, other than a person of military age, defer by order, for a period prescribed therein, the date of reporting for that person, under this Law or regulations thereunder, for registration, medical examination or defence service, or, if he has already begun to serve in defence service, the continuance thereof.

This provision became section 36 of The Defence Service (Consolidated Version) Law, 1986 (hereinafter 'The Defence Service Law'). This provision serves as the basis for examining the lawfulness of the respondent's actions in a specific petition.

## *Previous Petitions*

9–12. * * *

## *The Present Petition and its Arguments*

13–15. * * *

16. The petition before us poses three questions for our decision: first, whether the petitioner has standing in law to present the petition; secondly, whether the subject of the petition is justiciable; and thirdly, whether the decision of the Minister of Defence is lawful. That is, whether the Minister of Defence is empowered to defer the military service of yeshiva students and, if so, whether the Minister of Defence has exercised his power lawfully. We shall examine each of these questions separately, starting with the question of standing.

## *Standing in Law*

### A. The Premise

17. In the past, we have dismissed petitions relating to the deferment of military service for yeshiva students on grounds of the rules of standing. However, in my opinion, the present petitioners do have standing in law, and if their grievance is justiciable, it should be examined on the merits.

In order to support this conclusion, it is appropriate to discuss the status of the rules of standing in this Court. This inquiry is based on the provisions of section 15(c) and (d) of Basic Law: The Judiciary. Section 15(c) vests power in the High Court of Justice to hear matters in which it is deemed necessary to grant relief in the interests of justice, and which do not come under the jurisdiction of any other court. Section 15(d) authorizes the High Court of Justice to issue orders against governmental authorities 'to do or refrain from doing any act in the lawful exercise of their functions'. There is nothing in either of these two provisions that relates to the question of 'administrative right' or 'administrative duty', and neither of them refers, therefore, to the question of the standing in law of a person who claims that a right or duty has been violated.

The legislature created a court with jurisdiction, on the assumption—in the spirit of the accepted tradition in England—that by vesting such jurisdiction to hear specified matters, it also delegated the power to create judicial rules in cases coming within that jurisdiction. I referred to this connection between the judge and the law in *Micro-Daf* v. *Israel Electricity Company* [2]:

This connection between the legal rule and the judge, between the law and the court, characterizes both Israeli law in general, and Israeli administrative law in particular. The principal development of administrative law has occurred as a side effect of the jurisdiction of the High Court of Justice.

Within the framework of this power, the High Court of Justice has established appropriate rules concerning the manner in which it exercises its discretion. The rules of standing are one of these areas of judge-made law. There is nothing in Basic Law: The Judiciary which addresses the rules of standing. Unlike the United States, where the rules of standing grew out of a constitutional provision, our rules of standing developed without any statutory anchor. On the contrary: the statutory language appears broad and authorizes the High Court of Justice to deal, among other things, with any violation of law by a governmental authority, regardless of the status of the petitioner. Indeed, the rules of standing were developed as self-limitations on the exercise of the jurisdiction of the High Court of Justice. (See Bleckmann, 'The Aim of Judicial Protection: Protection of the Individual or Objective Control of the Executive Power? The Role of *Locus Standi*', in *Judicial Protection Against the Executive* (1971), iii, 19). In this respect, there is no substantial difference between common law countries and civil law countries, and the latter also have laws of standing (see Harding, '*Locus Standi* in French Administrative Law' [1978] *Public Law* 144). Thus, the Israeli High Court of Justice, too, has developed rules of standing that are intended to impose self-restraints on its discretion—though not on its jurisdiction—to grant relief to a petitioner who does not enjoy lawful standing. Within this framework one must examine the lawful standing of the petitioner before us.

**B. The Sources of the Problem**

18. The laws of standing in Israel are in flux, and have been for some time. Already in *Meron* v. *Minister of Labour* (hereinafter 'the *Meron* case'), Agranat P noted that 'a study of the local case law shows a development over time in this Court's approach to the question of standing, in a liberal direction'.[3] This development has continued ever since *Segal* v. *Minister of Interior* [4] (hereinafter 'the *Segal* case'). This is not peculiar to Israeli law. It is a principle also found in other modern western countries (see Wade, *Administrative Law* (5th edn., 1982). Witkon J related to this in *Ressler* v. *Minister of Finance* when he noted that 'in recent years there has been a discernible world-wide trend towards opening the doors of the court to every claimant'.[5] This trend in the modern world finds expression in the rulings of courts, as well as in the works of scholars and in proposals for legislative reform (see Tokar, 'Administrative Law: *Locus Standi* in Judicial Review Proceedings' (1984) 14 *Manitoba LJ* 209).

19. What is it that underlies this development and why have the rules of standing not found a place of rest? The answer to this question is not rooted in the failure of judges or scholars of jurisprudence to formulate clear rules of standing. This possibility exists and has been suggested more than once in the literature (see Davis, *Administrative Law Treatise* (2nd edn., 1983), iv, 208). In my opinion, the answer to this question is rooted in the lack of agreement as to the very nature of the rules of standing. One cannot formulate the rules of standing without having consolidated a conception as to the function of these rules in public law. In order to reach a consensus regarding the nature and function of the rules of standing, one must take a position as to the function of judicial review in the area of public law. 'The determination of a policy in the matter of standing is affected by a fundamental normative and substantive conception of the function of judicial review within the general structure of state authorities' (Segal, *The Right of Standing in the High Court of Justice* (1986), p. 5). Indeed, 'standing' within a model that views the proper function of judicial review as protecting the rights of the individual is different from 'standing' within a model that views it as maintaining the rule of law and the legitimacy of government.

Thus, in order to consolidate a conception as to the function of judicial review, one must take a position as to the general function of the judiciary in society and the status of the judiciary among the other governmental authorities (see Cane, *An Introduction to Administrative Law* (1986) 27, 165). There is a difference between a judge whose judicial philosophy is based solely on the conception that the judge's function is to resolve disputes between holders of existing rights and a judge whose judicial philosophy is rooted in the consciousness that the judge's function is to create rights and maintain the rule of law. In this light one can explain the confrontation between the position of Witkon J in *Becker* v. *Minister of Defence* [1] (hereinafter 'the *Becker* case') and Berinson J in *Bar Shalom* v. *Israel Lands Administrator* [6] (hereinafter 'the *Bar Shalom* case'). Witkon J held that 'the more public in character the subject of the grievance, the more stringent the requirement that the aggrieved party suffer substantial prejudice within his private sphere' ([1], at 247). The position of Berinson J is that 'the greater the importance of the matter from a public perspective, the greater the tendency of the court to recognize the petitioner's right even as an ordinary citizen, to bring the matter before it' ([6], at 802). It is true that the theory of standing developed 'in an empirical manner' (as *per* Witkon J in the *Becker* case [1], at 245), but action is based on theory, and theory is based on a world view as to the function of adjudication in society. It is not surprising, therefore, that different judges have taken different positions on the rules of standing. They thus expressed their different approaches to the function of judicial review in public law and to the function of the judge in a democratic society.

**C. 'The Classic Approach'**

20. I have already mentioned the liberalization of the rules of standing over the past decades. This liberalization has not aggravated the judicial difference of opinion; on the contrary, it has resulted in its contraction. It seems to me that there is a consensus among the judges as to the outer limits of the problem of standing, and the controversy focuses mainly on the areas that approach those limits. The following two propositions seem to be accepted by the majority of the judges in this Court who have addressed the question of standing, and may be said to represent a 'classic' judicial position. First, in order to acquire standing in law, the petitioner is not required to point to a violation of any legal right of his. . . . That is, a petitioner does not have to be a 'Hohfeldian petitioner' in order to acquire standing (the *Segal* case [4], at 440). It is sufficient if the petitioner can indicate prejudice to an interest of his. Moreover, such interest does not have to be special to the petitioner; standing of a petitioner whose interest has been prejudiced will be recognized, even if that interest is common to him and many others (see the *Segal* case). Ben Porat J addressed this point in *Shiran* v. *Broadcasting Authority* when she held '[i]t is not necessary, to establish a right of standing, that the claimed prejudice be limited to the petitioner alone rather than to a group of persons among whom he is included.'[7] Finally, in laying the evidentiary foundation for the claim of a prejudiced interest, the petitioner does not have to show that his interest has been prejudiced as a matter of certainty. It is sufficient for the petitioner to show a reasonable likelihood that his interest will be prejudiced. We do not concern ourselves with prophecy but with a simple evaluation of probability. For this reason, the rulings of this Court have emphasized that it is sufficient for the petitioner to prove a 'fear' of prejudice to his interest (as *per* Silberg J in *Dayan* v. *Minister of Religions* [8]). The petitioner can also show that a governmental action 'might be prejudicial' (*per* Agranat P in the *Meron* case [3], at 343), or that the petitioner 'might be prejudiced' (per Witkon J in the *Bar Shalom* case [6], at 806).

The second proposition accepted by the majority of the judges who have dealt with the laws of standing is that Israeli law does not recognize the standing of every citizen who claims that the government has violated the law. The *actio popularis*, as such, is not recognized in Israel (Agranat P in the *Meron* case [3], at 350; the *Segal* case [4], at 443; Shamgar P in *Barzilai* v. *Government of Israel* [9] ('this does not constitute any general acknowledgement of the existence of *actio popularis*'); D. Levine J in *Zucker* v. *Mayor of Tel Aviv–Yaffo* [10]). Ben Porat referred to this in the *Shiran* case [7] at 426, when she noted that 'there is general agreement that one should not allow the individual to demand satisfaction for a public affront or to fight a public dispute in an *actio popularis*'.

**D. The Accepted 'Exceptions'**

21. In view of the agreed parameters, the controversy focuses on special situations ('exceptions') in which the standing of a petitioner will be recognized without his indicating any prejudice to an interest of his. On this matter, there is agreement among the majority of the judges in several areas. First, the standing of a petitioner will be recognized where he raises an argument that, on the merits, indicates corruption on the part of the governmental authority. As Landau J stated in *Kfir* v. *Ashkelon Religious Council*:

> Thus it is possible that in a grave case in which the public interest appears to be decisive, as, for example, where it is feared that those in charge of monetary expenditures in a local authority have been acting with actual corruption, the Court will overcome its reluctance and will agree to hear the merits of a complaint brought before it, by a taxpayer, as such ([11] at 692).

Therefore, if a public authority acted arbitrarily or out of a conflict of interests, the standing of a disinterested petitioner will be recognized.

Secondly, this Court will recognize the standing of a petitioner who raises before it a problem of 'salient constitutional character' (*Aloni* v. *Minister of Justice* [12]). This framework has included questions relating to elections and political party funding (*Bergman* v. *Minister of Finance* [13] and *Kaniel* v. *Minister of Justice* [14]), the establishment of commissions of inquiry under the Commissions of Inquiry Law, 5729–1968 (*Alon* v. *Government of Israel* [15]), the duty of the Broadcasting Authority to observe principles of freedom of expression (*Zikhroni* v. *Broadcasting Authority* [16]), as well as other issues that concern 'the very essence of the democratic regime or the constitutional structure of our society' (Elon J in the *Aloni* case [12], at 68).

**E. Liberalization of the 'Exceptions'**

22. The scope of the principal controversy is delimited by the characterization of those 'exceptions' in which we have recognized the standing of 'the public petitioner'. Three questions arise in this context: first, whether the 'corruption' exception is limited to an argument of corruption, or whether it should be extended to include any argument that indicates a grave defect in administrative action. Secondly, whether the 'salient constitutional' exception is limited to constitutional matters or whether it should be extended to include any matter of public character that directly concerns the rule of law. Thirdly, whether there is room to recognize additional exceptions, or whether there are only these two. The opinions of the judges appear to be divided on each of these questions. As far as I am concerned, I accept a 'liberal' stance on each of these questions. My opinion is, therefore, that the first exception is not limited solely to governmental

corruption and that it should be extended to any case in which a petitioner points to a grave defect in administrative action. Likewise, the second exception is not, in my opinion, limited to constitutional matters alone, but extends to all cases in which, as my colleague Shamgar P has phrased it, 'the matter raised in the petition is of a public character that directly concerns the promotion of the rule of law and the delineation of guidelines to ensure its observance in actual practice' (the *Shiran* case [7], at 374). The exception similarly extends to 'issues of extraordinary legal substance that concern the principles of the rule of law' (the *Aloni* case [12], at 23).

Finally, my opinion is that the exceptions to the rule against the *actio popularis* are not confined to the two exceptions that I have noted. We should beware of creating rigid categories of exceptions and should allow the matter to remain flexible, leaving the door open to recognize additional situations in which the standing of a disinterested petitioner might be acknowledged. For example, there are cases which by their very definition do not affect any personal interest according to the accepted tests. In such situations it is sometimes necessary to recognize the standing of the 'public petitioner' (the *Segal* case [4], at 443; the *Aloni* case [12], at 28). In this spirit there have been consistent judicial rulings in Canada which broadened the rule of standing (see [31] and [32]). . . .

* * *

I therefore accept the approach of Dr Segal, who maintains that the 'public petitioner' should be recognized, when he points to a matter of special public importance, or to what appears to be an especially grave defect in the action of the authority, or when he challenges an action of special importance (Segal, *op. cit.*, at 235). The premise that guides me has its source in the basic principle, which Berinson J stated twenty years ago, that 'this Court is the safest and most objective stronghold of a citizen in discord with the government' (at 362) and that the function of the High Court of Justice is to assure the realization of the principle of the rule of law. Closing the doors of the court to a disinterested petitioner who gives warning of an unlawful governmental action is detrimental to the governance of the law, since where there is no judge—there is no law. The possibility of applying to the court is the cornerstone of the rule of law (see Pieris, 'The Doctrine of *Locus Standi* in Commonwealth Administrative Law' [1983] *Public Law* 52, 89). Lord Diplock addressed this in the case of *IRC* v. *National Federation of Self-Employed and Small Businesses Ltd*, stating:

> It would, in my view, be a grave lacuna in our system of public law if a pressure group, like the Federation, or even a single public-spirited taxpayer, were prevented by outdated technical rules of *locus standi* from bringing the matter to the

attention of the court to vindicate the rule of law and get the unlawful conduct stopped.[33]

23. According to my approach, the courts in a democratic society are bound by a duty to preserve the rule of law. The meaning of this, among other things, is that they must impose the law upon governmental authorities and make sure that the government acts lawfully. This conception of the judicial function is not inconsistent with the principle of the separation of powers and the role of the judiciary within the framework of that principle. On the contrary, this approach draws its strength from the principle of the separation of powers. The modern meaning of this principle is that there exists a system of checks and balances among the various authorities (see *Flato Sharon* [17]). I addressed this matter in the *Kach* case [18] noting that:

> An enlightened democratic regime is one of separation of powers. That separation does not mean that each branch of government exists in and of itself, without any consideration of the other branches. Such a conception would deeply violate the foundations of democracy itself, as it would imply a dictatorship of each branch within its own sphere. To the contrary, the separation of powers implies reciprocal checks and balances among the various branches. There are no walls between the branches, but rather checking and balancing bridges.

These checks and balances mean, among other things, that within the framework of a legal dispute, the Court must ensure that all the governmental branches: the Legislature, the Executive, and the Judiciary, act within the bounds of the law.

For these reasons, I cannot accept the following words of Elon J (in *Aloni* [12]) that as a rule, there is no standing where there is no interest:

> It is counter-productive to open the doors of this Court 'to transform the world', as has been stated time and again in this Court's decisions and in scholarly works:
>
> A. The Court would be flooded with matters calling for principled discussion, and it would not be freed to fulfil its principal function, which is to see that law and justice are done between litigants claiming violations of their rights;
>
> B. This might result in a detriment to the principle of the separation of powers by dragging the Court into questions of public character which ought properly be dealt with in the house of representatives or in the executive branch.
>
> C. Last but not least, this would constitute a deviation from the principal and primary function of the judicial branch, to hear and resolve actual disputes between two citizens or between a citizen and the government, when both are 'litigants' and one claims that he has been prejudiced by the other.

In my opinion, the principle of the separation of powers does not mean that a problem of public character must be resolved by the legislative and executive branches rather than by the Judiciary. Under the doctrine of separation of powers, the Legislature may, in the absence of constitutional constraints, determine the legal framework within which a problem of public character will be regulated, and the Executive may solve a problem of public character within the legal framework determined for its actions. But once that legal framework has been determined, the Court must determine whether it has been preserved in actual practice. There is nothing in the principle of the separation of powers that allows any authority to act in contravention of the law. Likewise, there is nothing in the principle of the separation of powers that requires the judicial branch to refrain from dealing with actions of public character, in so far as it focuses on the lawfulness of the action. As Lord Diplock stated in *IRC* v. *National Federation of Self-Employed and Small Businesses Ltd* ([33] at 644):

> It is not, in my view, a sufficient answer to say that judicial review of the actions of officers or departments of central government is unnecessary because they are accountable to Parliament for the way in which they carry out their functions. They are accountable to Parliament for what they do so far as regards efficiency and policy, and of that Parliament is the only judge; they are responsible to a court of justice for the lawfulness of what they do, and of that the court is the only judge.

Indeed, examination of the lawfulness of any action, be it of public character or not, is the function of the Judiciary, and is a realization of its designated role in the general scheme of the separation of powers. I therefore do not accept the approach presented by Elon J that the principal and primary role of the Judiciary is to resolve disputes that centre on an argument of one party being prejudiced by the other. The source of this conception is in private law, where the litigants are persons whose rights have been prejudiced. Even in private law this approach has its exceptions, such as the standing of shareholders to vindicate the company as against a third party by means of the derivative action.

This approach is not at all accepted in public law. The 'classic' laws of standing are based on the interest of a prejudiced person, and they do not require the interest-holder to point to an actual violation of a right as a condition for judicial intervention. The well-known exceptions are not in any way based on an argument of prejudice. Professor Wade addressed this in *Administrative Law* (5th edn., 1982), 577, noting that the approach whereby only a person whose rights have been violated may move the court to intervene, is not appropriate in public law:

> In private law that principle can be applied with some strictness. But in public law it is inadequate, for it ignores the dimension of the public interest. Where some particular person is the object of administrative action, that person is naturally entitled to dispute its legality and other persons are not. But public authorities have many powers and duties which affect the public generally rather than particular individuals. If a local authority grants planning permission improperly, or licenses indecent films for exhibition, it does a wrong to the public interest but no wrong

to anyone in particular. If no one has standing to call it to account, it can disregard the law with impunity. An efficient system of administrative law must find some answer to this problem, otherwise the rule of law breaks down. . . . The law must somehow find a place for the disinterested citizen in order to prevent illegalities in government which otherwise no one would be competent to challenge.

It is generally known and accepted that the court is an institution that decides disputes and does not act in the absence of a dispute, and that it is not permitted to create a dispute of its own initiative. But where a dispute presents itself before the court, there is no ground to confine the judicial function only to those disputes in which one of the parties argues that he has been prejudiced by the other.

* * *

It is true that 'there is no quarrel where there is no aggrieved person', but why should the aggrieved person have to claim that his right or interest has been violated, and not simply that a law has been violated? What is the moral foundation of the approach that allows a person who claims that his money has been stolen unlawfully to approach the court, but denies a person who claims that public funds have been stolen unlawfully to do the same? What principled argument is there, founded in case law or in the theory of the separation of powers, to justify this distinction? In my opinion, this distinction has no justification. The requirement that there be a right or interest as a condition for standing in law is philosophically unfounded, is not anchored in the separation of powers, nor supported by any moral ground, and is detrimental to the rule of law.

### F. The Solution: A Pragmatic Balance

24. This conception of the function of the court should, as a matter of principle, lead to recognition of the *actio popularis* as a general rule and not only in exceptional cases. I have noted, that I do not accept this result. In principle, there is no reason why the 'public court' should not open its doors to the public petitioner. The impediment against 'generally open doors' is not rooted in legal theory or the separation of powers, but is based primarily on considerations of judicial policy (see Scott, 'Standing in the Supreme Court—A Functional Analysis', 86 *Harv. LR* 645 (1973) ). The fear was that the court would be flooded with 'public petitions'. Consequently, precious judicial time would not be properly allocated, and the hearing of litigants claiming a violation of their individual rights would be delayed. It has also been argued that the requisite factual foundation would not properly be presented by a party who does not have an interest in the outcome of the litigation (see *Judicial Review of Administrative Action* (4th edn., 1980), 410).

These and other arguments do not have a principled dimension, but invoke a practical dimension that varies from petition to petition. Some are more founded, others less. Their cumulative effect might present a practical problem. A solution to such problems will be found in the proper balance between the principled conception and the practical problem. The 'exceptions' in which the standing of the 'public petitioner' has been recognized, and the judicial view that expounds an empirical and flexible approach are expressions of such balance. Hence, the greater the defect that is claimed to attach to the authority's action, the more prominent the public character of the dispute. Due to the general public character of the problem, there are very few holders of individual rights and interests. In such instances, the considerations in favour of recognizing the 'public petitioner' are especially high. As noted by Berinson J (in the *Bar Shalom* [6] case, at 802):

> Instead of rigid rules, the approach is empirical, one that is flexible and not strict or stringent. The test does not necessarily require a cardinal interest or either direct or indirect personal relevance, but rather the sincerity and seriousness of the application and its public importance or material merit. The greater the significance of the matter in terms of the public interest, the greater the tendency of the Court to acknowledge the right of an ordinary citizen to bring it forth.

My opinion is that we should maintain the approach that does not recognize the standing of the 'public petitioner' as such, but demands 'something more', as set forth in the 'liberal' approach to the exceptions.

25. I am aware of the fact that this flexible 'liberal' approach presents several difficulties. First, it creates uncertainty because the court must apply the 'expert feel of lawyers' in deciding the question of standing (see Shamgar P in the *Shiran* [7] case, at 373). As for myself, I am not at all sure that this uncertainty is greater than that inherent in defining the concept of 'interest'. Be that as it may, one may assume that this uncertainty will lessen with the passage of time, as the distinction between persons with and without standing becomes more clearly defined. Moreover, I fail to find any defect in this lack of clarity. In my view, the rules of standing are practical rules designed to ensure the efficiency of the court's activity and not to create 'dead areas' in which, in the absence of standing, the government can act unlawfully. Governmental authorities must assume that every petitioner has standing and plan their actions lawfully.

Secondly, I understand that there is a practical difficulty in distinguishing between those 'public petitioners' who apply to the court for mere purposes of self-advertisement (whose petitions will be dismissed) and those who apply out of a true desire to guarantee the rule of law (whose petitions should sometimes be heard). The fear is, therefore, that undeserving petitioners would be heard, and thus the time of the court would be wasted. Moreover, the court might find itself swamped with frivolous petitions.

This is a real problem and one must find ways to deal with it. However, I do not regard the problem of the vexatious petitioner as a serious one. In response to this problem, Professor Scott asserts (at 674) '[t]he idle and whimsical plaintiff, a dilettante who litigates for a lark, is a spectre which haunts the legal literature, not the courtroom.'

I also consider the problem of flooding, both in the instant context as well as in others (see Maher and Evans, ' "Hard" Cases, Floodgates and the New Rhetoric' (1985) 8 *University of Tasmania LR* 96), to be marginal for the reason that there is no empirical evidence that the argument has any substance. Experience in other countries that were prepared to recognize the public petitioner within specified limits has not shown any flooding within those limits (see Segal, at 170). Professor Davis said in this connection (*Administrative Law Treatise* (2nd edn., 1983), iv, 227–8):

> A reason sometimes asserted against the central principle is that it opens the gates to floods of litigation. The fear has no foundation. New York and Massachusetts have often allowed 'any citizen' or 'any resident' to challenge the legality of governmental action. . . and the result has been trickles, not floods. The D.C. Circuit has pointed out that 'the dockets . . . have not increased appreciably as a result of new cases in which standing would previously have been denied'. The various statutes of the 1970s that allow standing to 'any interested person' or 'any person' have not resulted in an unusual amount of litigation.

This also seems to have been the experience of the High Court of Justice in Israel. The 'liberalization' in the laws of standing that has taken place over the past few years has not resulted in the flooding of the Supreme Court with actions brought by 'public petitioners'. The 'public petitions' continue to be few in number, with only a few brought by vexatious petitioners.

That said, one should prevent, even in those few cases in which public petitioners apply to the court, frivolous actions by vexatious petitioners. The courts have had much experience in examining whether a litigant has made a sincere application to the court. A similar examination can be done with respect to the public petitioner. The imposition of court expenses is a proper measure of deterrence. While one must pay due attention to this practical problem, which troubles many judges and prevents them from taking a liberal stance on the question of the public petitioner's standing, the practical consideration ought not be decisive. We cannot allow the Court's workload to close the Court's doors in the faces of petitioners who complain about grave violations of the law in matters of public concern.

Thirdly, I agree that there is difficulty in determining criteria for whether or not the matter raised in the petition is of a public character, and whether or not the defect in the administrative action is a grave one. This lack of clarity regarding the grounds for standing could lead to inconsistent decisions. This initial uncertainty, however, will surely be clarified over the years. I agree that the argument that the law has been violated and the rule of law prejudiced is not sufficient in itself to grant lawful standing. A violation of the rule of law is a necessary condition, but it is not sufficient to support the standing of the public petitioner. Even the fact that the petitioner regards the matter as one of public character is not sufficient. Elon J noted correctly that 'it is not sufficient that the petitioner seeks in his petition to insist on the rule of law, even if the matter is, in his view, essential and central' (the *Aloni* case [12], at 66).

In addition to a violation of the rule of law there must be an indication of something more, according to objective standards. This could include: a grave deficiency in the administration's actions, a matter of public character, or a matter that pertains to the principles of the rule of law where there is no interested petitioner. We have seen that this list is not closed, and there is thus inevitable uncertainty as to both the content of the list and its limits. However, I consider this approach to be preferable to that which ties the hands of the court in such instances. Even the 'strict' approach acknowledges certain 'exceptions', which create similar uncertainties as those noted above. In my view, these tests are no more certain than the more 'liberal' constructions that I expound, and I am not prepared to regard the uncertainty that is inherent in the two kinds of tests as justification for a 'strict' approach.

### G. From the General to the Particular

26-29. [*Applying these rules to the instant petition, Barak J finds that the petitioners have standing to challenge the deferment granted to yeshiva students. In the view of Barak J, the claimed injury to the petitioners' interest in a lighter and more equitable burden of military service is sufficient to give the petitioners standing, even under the classical approach. Alternatively, Barak J holds that the petitioners fit into the established exception for problems of 'salient constitutional character'. Finally, Barak J holds that the petitioners would have standing even were the above grounds not present. Under this approach, the petitioners have standing because the problem is of a public character, which directly affects the rule of law, and which would evade review if the petitioners' standing were not recognized.*]

* * *

## *Justiciability*

### A. The Parties' Assertions

30–31. * * *

### B. Different Meanings of the Concept of Justiciability

32. The opposing arguments as to the justiciability or non-justiciability of the subject of the instant petition raise anew the general question of

justiciability. The problem of justiciability is a difficult one. It has been contemplated by this Court ever since its establishment. It has arisen in the rulings of courts outside Israel, where it is viewed as a question that is not given to 'scientific verification' (*per* Frankfurter J in *Poe* v. *Ullman* [34]; quoted with approval in the '*Kach*' case [18], at 161). Witkon J devoted an in-depth study to the question of justiciability in general, and the justiciability of political matters in particular (*Politics and Law* (1965); *Law and Adjudication* (1988), 55), and he concluded by confessing with admirable honesty that 'we went in search of a guide for the perplexed, but I am afraid that we are still stupefied' (*Politics and Law*, 69).

The emphasis of the rulings, both within and without Israel, is that the doctrine of justiciability is unclear, 'defies precise definition of its elements' [18] (the '*Kach*' case, at 161), and is 'a concept of uncertain meaning and scope' (*Flast* v. *Cohen* [35]) . . .

33. . . . It seems to me that many of the problems in understanding the concept of justiciability have their source in the fact that this concept has manifold meanings (Marshall, Justiciability', in *Oxford Essays in Jurisprudence* (1st Series (ed. Guest, 1961), 265). It appears, therefore, that the first task to be undertaken is to separate the different meanings of the concept of justiciability in the light of modern developments in the area of public law.

It should be mentioned at the outset that our examination of the concept of justiciability is based on the notion that, whatever its content, it does not concern the jurisdiction of the court but the manner in which its judges may exercise discretion. At first, this Court took the approach that lack of justiciability entails lack of jurisdiction (*Jabotinsky* v. *President* [19]; hereinafter 'the *Jabotinsky* case'). The error was subsequently corrected by emphasizing that 'there is a difference between jurisdiction and justiciability' (Witkon J in *Huggim Le'umiyim* v. *Minister of Police* [120]), and that justiciability is an independent matter that 'should not be confused with the matter of jurisdiction' (Kahan DP, at 125).

Likewise, standing should not be confused with justiciability. The right of standing concerns the power of the petitioner to move the court to hear his petition; justiciability concerns the suitability of the petition for judicial hearing. 'We must distinguish between two separate issues: on the one hand, the question of the petitioner's *right of standing*, according to which this Court will decide whether to listen to his particular voice, as if he were litigating his own quarrel. On the other hand, there is the separate and distinct problem of *justiciability* which poses the question whether the court should deal with the merits of the issue raised before it' (Shamgar P in *Ashkenazi* v. *Minister of Defence* [21]; hereinafter 'the *Ashkenazi* case').

34. In principle, there is room to distinguish between two different

meanings of the concept of justiciability (*Samara* v. *Commander of Judea and Samaria* [22]). One can be termed 'normative justiciability', and the other 'institutional justiciability' (cf the excellent article by Bendor, 'Justiciability in the High Court of Justice' (1987) 17 *Mishpatim* 592, which distinguishes between 'material' and 'organic' justiciability; see also Galligan, *Discretionary Powers* (1986) 241). Normative justiciability involves the question whether there exist *legal standards* for resolving the dispute before the court. Institutional justiciability answers the question whether the court is the *appropriate institution* for resolving the dispute, or whether the dispute might not be more properly resolved by a different institution, such as the Legislature or the Executive. These two meanings of justiciability are different and ought not to be confused.

* * *

## C. Normative Justiciability (or Non-Justiciability)

35. A dispute is justiciable in the normative sense if there exist legal standards for its resolution. A dispute is not justiciable in the normative sense if there do not exist legal criteria for its resolution. Normative justiciability thus deals with the capacity of the law and the court to decide a dispute. The question is not whether the dispute *ought* to be decided in law and by a court, but whether it *can* be decided in law by court (emphasis added by the report editor). Normative justiciability does not deal therefore with the desirable but with the possible. It was this aspect of justiciability that Brennan J referred to in *Baker* v. *Carr* [36], when he noted that a dispute is non-justiciable because it raises a 'political question'. In such cases there is 'a lack of judicially discoverable manageable standards for solving it'.

This meaning of the concept of justiciability was also propounded by Sussman J, both in his rulings from the bench and in other writings. In *Reiner* v. *Prime Minister* [23] (hereinafter 'the *Reiner* case') the petitioner sought to prevent the ambassador for West Germany from entering Israel because of the ambassador's service in the German army during the Second World War. The High Court of Justice dismissed the petition. Sussman J said, in relation to the question of diplomatic relations with Germany (at 487), that 'the matter is not a legal matter but a political matter *par excellence*; it cannot be examined according to a legal standard'. As for the confirmation or disqualification of this or that ambassador, Sussman J was of the opinion that it was a matter of diplomacy.

> This is not a legal matter that by its nature can be clarified in a court. The considerations are not legal considerations but ones of foreign policy and the suitability of a candidate for the position, which this Court is neither authorised nor able to decide (*ibid.*).

* * *

On the other hand, we have ruled that a question is justiciable if it raises 'a manifest legal matter' (Goldberg J in *Levi* v. *Chairman of Knesset Finance Committee* [24], at 496), that can be solved 'according to the ordinary legal standards with which we examine the powers exercised by a statutory authority' (Shamgar P in the *Aloni* case [12], at 37).

* * *

36. The theoretical premise for examining normative justiciability (or non-justiciability) is the notion that the law is a system of prohibitions and permissions. Every action is either allowed or forbidden in the world of the law. There is no action to which the law does not apply. There is no 'legal vacuum' where actions are carried out without the law taking any position in their respect. The law extends to all actions. At times it prohibits and at other times it permits, while often creating either an assumption of permission ('all is allowed to the individual unless it is forbidden') or of prohibition ('all is forbidden to the government unless it is permitted'). Even where there exists a legal 'lacuna', the law provides ways to fill the gap. According to this approach, it is impossible for a situation to arise in which there is no legal norm to apply. In this respect, it does not make any difference what the action is, whether it is a matter of politics or policy. Every action, be it a matter of politics or policy, is caught in the world of the law, and there is always a legal norm that takes a position on whether it is allowed or forbidden.

The argument that 'the matter is not a legal matter but a political matter *par excellence*' confuses two distinct issues. The fact that a matter is 'a political matter *par excellence*' does not change the fact that it is also 'a legal matter'. Everything is 'a legal matter' in the sense that the law always takes a position on whether it is permitted or prohibited. For example, the government decision in the *Reiner* case [23] to establish diplomatic relations with West Germany was a classic 'political' decision. Nevertheless, the law also takes a position on it. Specifically, the law takes a position on the question of which state organ is authorized to decide to establish diplomatic relations with West Germany. It is unthinkable to argue that this is a political and not a legal matter. The question of authority is a legal matter that has political implications. It is also a political matter that has legal implications. Likewise, if such organ accepted bribes, it would be unthinkable to argue that the matter was political and not legal. The law takes a position on the action of taking bribes, regardless of its political aspects. It follows that the political level and the legal level are not two separate spheres.

Of course, the political character of the acting body and the action performed by it will sometimes affect the content of the legal rules regulating the action. For instance, the political character of a body might affect the scope of the considerations that it may take into account and the options available to it. 'The dimensions of the zone of reasonableness are determined in consideration of the status of the governmental authority and the character of its powers' (Shamgar P in *Barzilai* [9], at 505), but this is a far cry from the approach that political character leads to non-justiciability. The political material might, indeed, affect the formulation of the content of the legal material. Furthermore, the political material might sometimes even result in a situation in which a certain rule of public law does not apply to specific actions that carry political implications. But in all these situations a legal norm does still exist. The content of this legal norm does not prohibit but rather permits such political action. A petition will be dismissed in such cases not because of a preliminary argument of normative non-justiciability but rather on the merits of the case, i.e. there is no cause of action.

Note that I am not maintaining that the political character of the action always affects the content of the legal rules which regulate it. On the contrary, my view is that in most cases the political aspects of the action do not affect its normative evaluation. For this reason we were of the opinion that even the Knesset, for instance, is subject to the rules of reasonableness and fairness when it acts to remove the immunity from one of its members. There can, however, be exceptional cases. For example, it might well be the case that the ordinary rules of the law of administrative discretion ought not be implemented in relation to a decision to make peace or to start a war. In such exceptional cases a petition will be dismissed, not because of the absence of a legal norm, but because of the absence of a prohibitive norm and the existence of a permissive norm, that is to say, the absence of a cause of action. The action is not non-justiciable. It is justiciable but lawful.

It appears that the cases which have examined this type of justiciability (or non-justiciability) did not dwell on the absence of a legal norm, but rather emphasized the absence of legal standards and criteria for resolving the dispute. It seems to me that it is not possible to speak in one breath of the existence of a legal norm and the absence of legal standards. If the norm exists, this means that legal standards also exist. If legal standards do not exist, this means that the norm in question does not exist, and another norm applies. I fail to see how one can speak of the existence of a legal norm without the circumstances and conditions of its application. It might, of course, be difficult to comprehend the content of the norm and the circumstances and conditions of its application. Every legal norm requires interpretation. The interpretation might be complicated and difficult. But at the end of the interpretive process there exists a legal norm, which by its very nature also includes the criteria for its application. A legal norm without criteria for its application is like a body without a shadow or a form without content, and this phenomenon does not exist in the world of law, which is composed entirely of bodies and shadows, of forms and contents.

37–40. * * *

41. In essence, the argument as to material [or normative] non-justiciability is an argument as to the absence of a cause of action. When the court accepts an argument of material non-justiciability it does not abstain from dealing with the legality of the action. On the contrary: the court takes a position as to its legality and holds that it is lawful. Witkon J noted that:

> there is no actual difference between such 'non-justiciability', which does not save a hearing on the matter and might reveal itself only in the course of the hearing, and the usual reasoning that the matter is given to the discretion of the administrative authority, and that it acted lawfully and reasonably (the *Huggim Le'umiyim* case [20], at 166).

In my opinion, normative non-justiciability is nothing but the absence of a cause of action in law. Professor McCormick wrote in this respect (McCormick, 'The Justiciability Myth and the Concept of Law', 14 *Hast. Cont. LQ* 595 (1987) ):

> To say that a 'case' before the court is non-justiciable is to say that the plaintiff has no judicially enforceable right. To say that the plaintiff has no judicial right is to make a conclusive statement about the nature of the 'law' on which the plaintiff is relying; it is necessarily an exercise in interpretation and application of that law to say that the law applied by the court does not protect the plaintiff. Masking the holding in language that purports to decide only a 'preliminary' or 'threshold' issue hides a decision on the merits without elaborating the reasons behind the decision. Justiciability, like any other decision for or against a claimed 'right', is a label that expresses a decision on the conflicting interests of the parties and the constraints that operate on each.

42–45. * * *

46. One might ask whether a decision of a governmental authority is justiciable in every case. For example, whether a decision to start a war or make peace is also 'justiciable' and can also be 'imprisoned' in a legal norm and a judicial hearing. My answer is in the affirmative. Even in matters of war and peace one must determine which organ is authorized to make a decision, and what is the nature of its considerations (for example, a prohibition against personal corruption). One might, of course, determine that other rules of administrative discretion do not apply, although that difficult question remains open. In such a case, however, a petition would be dismissed not because of its non-justiciability but because of the legality of the challenged action.

To summarize, I regard the doctrine of normative justiciability (or non-justiciability) as a doctrine that does not have independent existence. The argument that a matter is normatively non-justiciable is nothing more than an argument that the action is not governed by a prohibitive norm, and is therefore permitted. This approach is based on the conception that every governmental action is covered by a legal norm, and that it is always possible to formulate standards and criteria within the framework of the applicable norm to determine the conditions and circumstances of lawful action. This certainly pertains to norms that determine authority and proper considerations for exercising such authority. It also applies where the operative norm is that which requires reasonable governmental conduct. Within the framework of that norm it is always possible to formulate principled standards for examining the reasonableness of the conduct. The action of the authority will be examined on the merits according to those standards without resorting in any way to an argument of normative justiciability (or non-justiciability).

**D. Institutional Justiciability (or Non-justiciability)**

47. A dispute is institutionally justiciable when it is appropriate for it to be resolved according to law in a court. A dispute is not institutionally justiciable when it is not appropriate for it to be resolved according to legal standards in a court. Institutional justiciability deals, therefore, with the question whether the law and the courts are the proper framework for resolving the dispute. The question is not whether the dispute can be resolved according to the law in a court, for the answer to that question is in the affirmative. The question is rather whether it is desirable to resolve a dispute that is normatively justiciable according to legal standards in a court of law. Brennan J addressed this aspect of justiciability, in addition to normative justiciability, in *Baker* v. *Carr* ([36] at 217), where he notes that a dispute is non-justiciable if there exists in relation to it:

> a textually demonstrable constitutional commitment of the issue to a co-ordinate political department; . . . the impossibility of a court's undertaking independent resolution without expressing lack of the respect due co-ordinate branches of government; or an unusual need for unquestioning adherence to a political decision already made; or the potentiality of embarrassment from multifarious pronouncements by various departments on one question.

These words have been cited several times by the Justices of the Supreme Court of Israel (see the *Huggim Le'umiyim* case [20], at 135; *Hilu* v. *Government of Israel* [25]; *Flato Sharon* [17], at 133; and the '*Kach*' case [18], at 162). These judges reflect an unclosed list of considerations when the Court takes a position on whether it ought to resolve a dispute before it. In all these cases the Court will ask itself if it might be proper for it 'to refrain from fulfilling its ordinary judicial function' (Agranat P in the

*Huggim Le'umiyim* case [20], at 215) and whether 'the matter is suitable for judicial resolution' (Witkon J in *Hilu* [25], at 182). For example, we ruled that the Court will not examine a petition that raises an argument as to alleged illegal activity in administering the internal affairs of the Knesset, unless the decision in question entails a substantive detriment to the web of parliamentary life and the structural foundations of the constitutional regime (the '*Kach*' case [18]; *Kahane* v. *Knesset Speaker* [26]; *Kahane* v. *Knesset Speaker* [27]).

48. If we study the different matters mentioned by Brennan J in *Baker* v. *Carr* [36] as examples of the principle of institutional non-justiciability, it appears that they are not at all simple. Take, for example, the first non-justiciable matter, in which resolution of the matter is vested in a political authority. When a given provision vests power in a governmental authority, it also vests power in the court to interpret it, to determine the limits of its scope, and to decide whether it has been exercised lawfully. That is to say, where resolution of a given action is in the hands of a governmental authority, this does not mean that the question of the legality of such action is also in the hands of that authority. To the contrary:

> The final and decisive interpretive decision as to the law in effect at any given time is in the hands of the court, and, with respect to issues that are raised within the legal system, in the hands of the highest judicial [court] (Shamgar P in *Flato Sharon* [17]).

Hence, a legal decision as to the lawfulness of an action, the performance of which is in the hands of a governmental authority, ought not be regarded as non-justiciable.

49. The second matter mentioned by Brennan J is the non-justiciability of a dispute which is impossible to decide judicially without expressing lack of consideration for governmental branches of equal rank. This matter, too, is questionable, since when the Court examines whether a governmental authority has acted lawfully, it does not thereby express lack of consideration for that governmental authority.

> The role of the court is to interpret the law, and it often happens that its interpretation is different from that rendered by another state organ. It is inconceivable to say that preference for the judicial interpretation over that of another organ (executive or legislative) amounts to lack of respect for that organ. How can we intervene in the acts of the executive branch if we take the approach that we offend its honor when we interpret the law differently? . . . There is no lack of respect due to other branches when the judiciary exercises its constitutional function and acts in accordance with its legal imperative. When the court interprets the law it performs its function, and if its interpretation differs from that deemed proper by other branches, it is seen as correcting their error without implying any lack of due respect (the '*Kach*' case [18], at 163).

In fact, when the Court points out the error of the other branch and prevents it from violating the law, it restores the lost honour of that branch. The important issue is respect for the law. I fail to see how insisting on respect for the law by a governmental branch could offend that branch or disrupt its relations with other branches of government.

50. It is usually assumed that the matters mentioned in *Baker* v. *Carr* [36] are mere examples of a general approach, according to which institutional non-justiciability should properly exist in relation to disputes of 'political' character (see Zemach, *Political Questions in the Courts* (1976) ). The argument is that the resolution of political disputes should be done by political organs and not by the Judiciary, and that the involvement of the Judiciary in such disputes is detrimental to the principle of the separation of powers, the democratic regime, in which political decisions are made by political authorities, and the court itself. These are weighty arguments. The judge's natural instinct is to veer clear of decisions that have a political aspect. Witkon J correctly noted that 'judges' reluctance to deal with sensitive political matters has gained currency in legal consciousness as well as in public opinion' (*Politics and Law*, at 70). We shall deal briefly with the elements of this argument: the element of separation of powers, the element of democracy, and the element of the public's faith in the court system. We shall start with the first element.

51. Is it proper to say that, by virtue of the principle of the separation of powers, a problem of political character ought to be decided by a political organ and is therefore institutionally non-justiciable? In my opinion, this argument is fundamentally erroneous. According to the modern conception of separation of powers, there is reciprocity between the governmental branches, within which it is legitimate for a political decision of a governmental body (the Knesset or the Government) to be subject to judicial review. Indeed, the modern conception does not separate the branches in a manner that makes them independent of each other. The modern approach creates a balanced connection between the branches, so that the judicial branch exercises judicial legal review over the other branches. It is only natural for a political authority to weigh political considerations, and it is only natural for the judiciary to examine whether such political consideration is lawful. Shamgar P elaborated upon this modern conception of the principle of separation of powers in the *Flato Sharon* case ([17] at 141), as follows:

> The separation of powers does not necessarily mean the creation of a barrier that absolutely prevents any contact between the branches, but finds principal expression in a balance between the powers of the branches in actual practice, which affords independence together with defined reciprocal control.

Shamgar addressed this principle again in the *Ashkenazi* case ([21], at 319):

The presence of efficient review of each of the branches is a fundamental feature of every governmental system that subscribes to the separation of powers, and it also guarantees, among other things, the balance among the powers that is an essential component of any democratic regime.

Shamgar expressed a similar view in the *Aloni* case ([12] at 38):

All are obliged to respect the law, and judicial review extends to the legality of all actions by any authority. The separation of powers establishes the independence of the branches, but it does not *in itself* block judicial review. This is the fundamental conception of Israeli law and the source of the rule of law, which finds support *inter alia* in the exercise of section 15 of Basic Law: The Judiciary with respect to the actions of various arms of the executive branch.

It follows that there is nothing in the principle of the separation of powers to justify the negation of judicial review of governmental actions, regardless of their character and content. On the contrary: it is precisely the principle of separation of powers that justifies judicial review of governmental actions, including those of a political character, since it guarantees that every branch acts lawfully within the bounds of its authority, and thus ensures the separation of powers.

52. A democratic regime is one that finds a proper balance between the rule of the majority and the rights of the individual. The first principle (majority rule) is intended to ensure that government acts in accord with the opinion of the majority. This means, among other things, that political decisions are made by political organs that are elected, whether directly or indirectly, by the people. The second principle (individual rights) is intended to ensure that the majority, acting through the political organs, does not violate fundamental rights of the individual. Judicial review ensures that the political organs act within the scope of the powers vested in them by the democratic regime, and is therefore consistent with this democratic conception. Indeed, it is judicial review which safeguards the proper action of the democratic formula. On the one hand, it ensures that the majority opinion will find its proper expression within the legal framework provided by the regime (the constitution, statutes, secondary legislation, orders) and will not exceed those limits. On the other hand, it ensures that the majority will not violate rights of the individual unless it is lawfully empowered to do so.

* * *

53. What remains is the argument that institutional non-justiciability with respect to political matters is justified because it protects the Court against 'the politicization of adjudication' and impairment of the public's confidence in judicial objectivity. As for myself, this argument seems most

problematic. Even when the court deals with political standards, it does not examine them according to political standards. The Court examines the legality of the political decision. As we have seen, the political level and the legal level are not different. In adjudicating, the Court examines the legal aspects, not the wisdom, of politics. Therefore, when a judge examines the legality of a political resolution he does not endorse, in the affirmative or the negative, the merits of such resolution. He does not become part of the political decision. He does not examine its internal logic. He merely examines its lawfulness according to legal standards. In doing so he fulfils his classic role. I find it difficult to regard this as an action that ought to be avoided.

Even when the object of the resolution is an ideological political problem, judicial review is always performed according to legal standards. The judge does not express his personal ideology but rather his legal conception of the lawfulness of the ideology in question. It is legitimate for the judiciary to deal in this manner with ideology. Witkon J referred to this in the *Shalit* case ([29] at 532), as follows:

> Sometimes the court must take a position on an ideological question, and there is no room for the fear that it is not capable of doing so, or that its prestige will be harmed thereby. In terms of both positive law and desirable law, there remains little substance to the usual argument that such questions exceed the scope of the judiciary.

In this context, it is worth quoting the words of Agranat P in the *Shalit* case ([29] at 600):

> Justice does not require us to take a position on the ideological issue at hand, when it is clear that there is no consensus among the enlightened public in this respect and that our position will be based solely on our own private opinions and personal predilections. For surely the principle of the rule of law means that the judge must distance himself as far as possible from preferring his personal views over the requirements of justice in deciding the dispute before him, since if that were not the case one might suspect that instead of interpreting the law he acted arbitrarily in rendering judgment. . . . If a problem of world view arises before us, as to which the opinions of the enlightened public are fundamentally divided by a deep abyss—and more so when such controversy excites the passions—then it is better for the judge to restrain himself from expressing his personal opinion on the issue, so long as there exists a judicial outlet that does not require him to do so.

I agree with this statement. The judge must always restrain himself from expressing his personal opinion. But this does not mean that an ideological controversy that has a legal aspect is not justiciable.

In truth, I am less afraid of the possibility of 'the politicization of adjudication' than I am of the Court's reluctance to deal with 'political matters', which will lead to violation and shattering of the public's faith in the rule of law. The following words of Landau J in the *Oppenheimer* case ([30] at 334) are pertinent in this respect:

> On the matter of 'justiciability' I concur with the opinion of my esteemed colleague, the Deputy President. The matter on which we have been asked to rule falls within the scope of section 7(b)(2) of the Courts Law, 1957. The State Attorney suggested that we act with a measure of 'judicial restraint'. That is, indeed, a good virtue, but I am not persuaded that it should, in the instant case, come between the word of the law and its operation in actual practice. I do not believe that there is any danger of disrupting the relations of the governmental branches, as suggested by Mr Bar-Niv; but there is a danger of disrupting the faith of the citizen in the rule of law if we disclaim the power vested in us. When the Knesset delegates important legislative powers to the executive branch, the proper balance among the governmental powers of the various branches requires that the judiciary retain its power of review over secondary legislation.

These words are pertinent not only with respect to the Court's review of secondary legislation enacted by the administration. They are also relevant with respect to any governmental action by the administration. If the court were to extricate itself from its power of review, merely because the dispute at hand had a 'political' aspect it would harm the governance of the law and the public's confidence in its rule.

The outcome of institutional non-justiciability, like that of lack of standing in law, is to create an area in which there is no law and no judge. This result is problematic in terms of the separation of powers, the democratic regime, and the rule of law.

> We must beware of two prohibitions in relation to the separation of powers: one, that we do not exceed the bounds of our jurisdiction, and the other that we do not hesitate to exhaust it fully (Witkon J in *Lechem Chai Ltd* v. *Minister of Commerce and Industry* [28], at 208).

A similar idea was expressed as early as 1821 by Marshall CJ in *Cohen* v. *Virginia* [37]:

> We have no more right to decline the exercise of jurisdiction which is given, than to usurp that which is not given. The one or the other would be treason to the Constitution. Questions may occur, which we would gladly avoid; but we cannot avoid them. All we can do is, to exercise our best judgment and conscientiously to perform our duty.

I am afraid that we would transgress these two prohibitions and violate our unwritten constitution if we were to recognize institutional non-justiciability.

54–55. * * *

56. What conclusion arises from our analysis of institutional justiciability (or non-justiciability)? In my opinion, the conclusion is that this doctrine is most problematic; that its legal foundations are shaky, and that it is based to a large extent on 'irrational reasons'. This issue should be

approached with due caution as there will be room to consider its use only in special cases, where the fear of harming the public's confidence in the judges surmounts the fear of harming the public's faith in the law. The list of such cases is not closed, but will be decided, ultimately, according to the experience of judicial life and the expert feel of the judge.

**E. From the General to the Particular**

57. I have already noted that the doctrine of justiciability (or non-justiciability) does not enjoy independent status. The law and its standards exist in all places. Indeed, the instant dispute comes within the scope of several legal provisions, some statutory and some judicial, from which legal standards to decide the dispute may be derived. The question of the power to defer military service is related to the interpretation of section 36 of the Defence Service Law. This is an ordinary interpretive problem that can be decided according to the accepted standards of interpretation (cf. the words of Brennan J in *Goldwater* v. *Carter* [38], according to which the question of the President's power to declare war is justiciable because 'the issue of decision-making authority must be resolved as a matter of constitutional law, not political discretion.') It is inconceivable to say that the question whether or not a governmental authority is functionally empowered to perform a governmental action is normatively non-justiciable. This question can always be decided by a legal norm and legal standards.

The question of discretion in the deferment of military service is determined according to the accepted tests of the theory of administrative discretion. As we shall see below, we will need to examine whether the considerations of the Minister of Defence were material or extraneous, and whether his decision meets the test of reasonableness. Such examination is performed entirely according to the regular legal standards, and there can be no question of the existence of legal tools for its performance. Thus, for example, the question of reasonableness is determined according to the accepted standards that pose the question whether a reasonable Minister of Defence might have made the decision as to the deferment of service. In this respect, there will be room to examine the weight given to the various considerations. This examination is also performed according to the accepted standards of judicial review over administrative acts.

58. In my opinion, the theory of institutional non-justiciability does not apply to the instant petition. It is true that 'the question whether or not to recruit yeshiva students is fundamentally a public issue that should be left in the hands of the political bodies whose duty it is to decide the matter' (*Kahane* [26], at 88). However, the question whether or not it is lawful to grant deferment to yeshiva students is a legal question that should be left in the hands of the legal bodies whose duty it is to decide the matter. The politicians will decide the legal question and will weigh political

considerations. The judges will weigh the legal considerations.

We are not deciding the question whether or not it is proper to defer the service of yeshiva students. We do not take any position on that question. We are merely addressing the following questions: whether the Minister of Defence has authority to defer the service of yeshiva students, whether he weighed the pertinent material considerations, and whether his decision is reasonable. In doing so we do not take any ideological position on the public issue. We merely take a legal position on the legal question.

* * *

For these reasons, it appears to me that the instant petition is justiciable in both the normative and institutional sense.

* * *

*Powers of the Minister of Defence*

59–66. * * *

*Considerations of the Minister of Defence*

67–71. * * *

*Additional Arguments*

72–73. * * *

*Conclusion*

[*Addressing the merits, Barak J holds that the petition must be dismissed 'because the Minister of Defence has authority to defer the military service of yeshiva students, and it has not been proven that the exercise of his discretion in the circumstances was unreasonable'. Barak J stressed that he is not in any way expressing his or the Court's opinion as to the desirability of such deferment.*]

**Shamgar P**: [*Concurring*]

**Ben-Porat DP:** [*Concurring*]

Decided according to the judgment of Barak J.

Judgment given 12 June 1988

# SECTION 10: JUDICIAL REVIEW OF STATUTES AND PARLIAMENTARY PROCEEDINGS

# 24

## *The Supreme Court and Parliamentary Supremacy*

DAVID KRETZMER



One of the fundamentals of the Israeli constitutional system was long thought to be the principle of parliamentary supremacy.[1] In the early years of the State, attempts were made to persuade the Supreme Court to review primary legislation passed during the British Mandatory period that had been received into the Israeli legal system under a provision in the first legislative act passed after independence.[2] These attempts rested on the theory that legislation that was inconsistent with the spirit or letter of Israel's Declaration of Independence, or that was undemocratic in nature, was not valid in the new state. The Supreme Court was not receptive to these arguments. Following the English model, it held that deciding on the validity of primary legislation was a matter for Parliament, and the Court was not competent to deal with the issue. In later years the Court adopted the same approach when attempts were made to challenge primary legislation of the Knesset itself.[3]

[1] See A. Rubinstein, *The Constitutional Law of the State of Israel* (4th edn., Schocken, Tel Aviv, 1991) 135 (Hebrew).

[2] See *Ziv* v. *Gubernick* (1948) 1 PD 85; *Leon* v. *Gubernik* (1948) 1 PD 58.

[3] See e.g. *Azuz* v. *Ezer* (1963) 17 PD 2541, 2547; *Manor* v. *Minister of Finance* (1970) 24(2) PD 442, 445; *Rogozinsky* v. *State of Israel* (1972) 26(1) PD 129.

In theory the principle of parliamentary supremacy is still intact. However, a number of significant inroads have been made on the principle.

## 1. Supra-constitutional Principles

Israel's elections are based on the proportional representation system. Each voter votes for a list of candidates submitted by a faction in the outgoing Knesset or by a specified number of registered voters. Every list which receives at least 1.5 per cent of the votes is entitled to a share of the 120 seats in the Knesset proportionate to its share of the votes.

The statute dealing with the elections originally made no provision for disqualification of a list that met the formal requirements for participation in the elections. The issue in the *Yeredor* decision was whether there was any inherent non-statutory power to disqualify a list.

The background to the case was the formation in the early 1960s of a nationalistic movement of Arabs in Israel called *el-Ard* (the Land) which identified with the Nasserite movement, then the leading political force in the Arab world. The authorities, who took the view that this movement endangered the security of the State, employed various measures to crush it. The final measure was a declaration by the Minister of Defence, under the British Defence (Emergency) Regulations 1945, that *el-Ard* was an unlawful association.

Half of the candidates on one of the new lists submitted to the Central Elections Committee in 1965 had been members of the *el-Ard* movement. The Committee decided to disqualify the list on the ground that it was an unlawful association that identified with Israel's enemies. The question before the Supreme Court in the appeal against the Committee's decision was whether the Committee had the power to disqualify a list.

With Haim Cohn J dissenting, the Court upheld the decision to disqualify the list. While Agranat J based his opinion on a somewhat convoluted statutory interpretation which allowed disqualification of subversive lists, Sussman J held that there are 'supra-constitutional principles of law' that allow a court to act in defence of the State, even in the absence of statutory powers.

The notion of supra-constitutional principles was never followed by the Court in later cases.[4] In 1984 the Court gave a restrictive interpretation to

[4] In *Israel Electricity Corporation Ltd* v. *Ha'aretz* (1978) 32(3) PD 337, 343, Landau J expressly dismissed the notion that there are 'supra-rights' in the Israeli legal system that are superior to parliamentary legislation. He stated that to the best of his knowledge Sussman J's opinion in the *Yeredor* case is the only mention of this notion in the decisions of the Sup. Ct.

the *Yeredor* precedent and refused to extend the power to disqualify lists to lists that were racist or anti-democratic.[5] In response to this decision the Knesset amended the law, and made express provision for disqualification of lists in certain defined cases.[6]

## 2. Interference in Parliamentary Proceedings

Until the early 1980s very few attempts were made to persuade the Court to review parliamentary proceedings and those that were made met with a cool reception.[7]

The first case in which the Court entertained a petition relating to a Knesset decision other than legislation involved a decision by the Knesset Committee to suspend a member who had been convicted of a criminal offence.[8] The Court held that as the decision was a quasi-judicial decision relating to the basic rights of a Knesset member and those who had elected him, it was competent to hear the case and that the issue was justiciable. It proceeded to interpret the statutory provision that defines the power of the Knesset Committee to suspend a member and to decide that the Committee had exceeded its statutory power.

The *Sarid* case was the first decision in which the Court displayed willingness to examine the legality of a decision relating to internal parliamentary proceedings that were not of a quasi-judicial nature. Barak J stated that, in deciding whether to review the legality of such proceedings, the Court faces a clash between the interest in the rule of law and the interest in the autonomy of Parliament. Neither of these interests has supremacy and a judicial balance needs to be struck between them 'based on self-restraint of the judiciary, which does not amount to being totally bound'. That balance rests on the 'extent of the alleged harm to the fabric of parliamentary life and the scope of its effect on the foundations of our constitutional regime'.

In the *Sarid* case itself the Court relied on the said balancing test in order to justify its decision not to interfere with a decision of the speaker to delay the hearing of a non-confidence motion by a few hours. However, in a number of subsequent cases the Court relied on the same test in order to justify intervening in internal parliamentary decisions. In one such case it ruled that the Knesset Presidium had acted illegally when it refused to

[5] See *Neiman* v. *Chairman of Central Elections Committee to Twelfth Knesset* (1985) 39(2) PD 225.

[6] See S. 7A, Basic Law: The Knesset.

[7] The progression of the Court's decisions is discussed in D. Kretzmer, 'Judicial Review of Knesset Decisions' (1988) 8 *Tel Aviv Studies in Law* 95.

[8] See *Flatto-Sharon* v. *Knesset Committee* (1981) 35(4) PD 118.

allow the one-man faction of Meir Kahane to table a motion of non-confidence;[9] in another it held that under the existing House Rules, the Presidium did not have the power to refuse to table a private member's bill (also submitted by Kahane) on the grounds that it was racist.[10] In response to this decision the Knesset amended the House Rules so as to give express power to the Presidium to reject private members' bills that are racist in essence. The Court subsequently refused to rule that this amendment was invalid.[11]

Judicial review of parliamentary proceedings has become an accepted facet of political life in Israel. In the majority of cases the Court has in the end refused to interfere in the proceedings. In most of the cases in which it has intervened it has done so in order to protect vulnerable political minorities.[12] Attempts by the largest parties in the Knesset to enlist the Court's help in parliamentary battles have been unsuccessful.[13]

On two occasions the Court has invalidated decisions of the Knesset plenum itself. In both cases the decisions related to lifting parliamentary immunity. In the first case the Court held that the immunity against arrest and search had been lifted for an improper purpose—to punish the Knesset member, rather than to prevent a future danger.[14] In the second case, it held that in dealing with the request of the Attorney General to lift immunity of a member so that he could be charged with a felony, the Knesset plenum had not been provided with sufficient information so as to allow it to fulfil its quasi-judicial task in a proper fashion.[15]

## 3. Judicial Review of Legislation

### *A. Compatibility with Basic Laws*

The Declaration of Independence states that Israel will have a formal constitution to be drawn up by an elected constituent assembly. The said assembly was duly elected, but it transformed itself into the First Knesset,

[9] See *Kach Faction* v. *Knesset Speaker* (1985) 39(3) PD 141.

[10] See *Kahane* v. *Knesset Speaker* (1985) 39(4) PD 85.

[11] See *Kahane* v. *Knesset Speaker* (1986) 40(4) PD 393.

[12] See Kretzmer, n. 7 above.

[13] See e.g. *Sarid* v. *Knesset Speaker* (1982) 36(2) PD 197 (petition brought by Labour party) (contained in this Ch.); *Reisser* v. *Knesset Speaker* (1988) 42(3) PD 142 (petition brought by Likud); *Ratz Faction* v. *Knesset Speaker* (1990) 44(2) PD 31 (petition brought by Ratz and Labour parties).

[14] See *Miari* v. *Knesset Speaker* (1987) 41(4) PD 169.

[15] See *Pinkhasi* v. *Knesset Speaker* (1993) (not yet reported). This decision was reached by a majority of 3–2. The minority, which included the President of the Court, Shamgar J, was of the opinion that even if there had been a flaw in the proceedings no substantive injustice had been caused and the Court should therefore refrain from intervening.

Israel's parliament. In a debate on the need to frame the formal constitution, the Knesset decided in 1950 that the said constitution would be drawn up gradually in a series of basic laws that would eventually form the complete constitution. On the strength of this resolution, basic laws have indeed been enacted dealing with most of the institutional aspects of Israel's constitutional system. In 1992 two basic laws dealing with protection of fundamental rights were also enacted.

Most of the basic laws are not entrenched, but some of the non-entrenched laws include one or two entrenched provisions. The most important entrenched provision is section 4 of the Basic Law: The Knesset, that was considered in the *Bergman*[16] case. This section, which stipulates the principles of the electoral system, provides that it may not be changed except by an absolute majority in the Knesset (i.e. at least sixty-one of 120 members).

In the *Bergman* case, the petitioner challenged the validity of primary legislation passed in the Knesset on the grounds that the said legislation infringed one of the principles laid down in section 4, namely that the elections shall be equal, and that it had not been passed by an absolute majority. This petition raised a number of fundamental constitutional questions: whether the basic laws have special status; whether the Knesset indeed has the power to bind itself; whether the Court is competent to decide on the validity of primary legislation and whether the petitioner had standing to challenge the legislation in court. Surprisingly, however, since the Attorney General asked for a ruling on the merits, the Court left these questions in abeyance. It reached the conclusion that the said legislation did indeed infringe the principle of equal elections and that, as it had not been enacted by an absolute majority, it was inoperative. This decision has been followed in a number of cases in which the Court has struck down legislation passed with an ordinary majority that offended the principle of equal elections.[17]

The constitutional questions left in abeyance in the *Bergman* precedent were for a long time not fully considered by the Court. However, the enactment of two basic laws on human rights considered in Chapter 3 have pushed these questions to the fore and the Court has recently pronounced on them. According to the majority view, legislation enacted after the basic laws on human rights came into force that does not meet the standards required under these basic laws is invalid and the courts have power to declare it so. Two of the justices also expressed the view that all basic laws have superior normative status and that legislation which is substantially inconsistent with them may also be declared invalid. These rulings have

[16] HC 98/89 *Bergman* v. *Minister of Finance* (1969) 23(1) PD 693, included in this section.

[17] See *Agudat Derekh Eretz* v. *Broadcasting Authority* (1981) 35(4) PD 1; *Rubinstein* v. *Knesset Speaker* (1982) 37(3) PD 141; *Tenuat Laor* v. *Knesset Speaker* (1990) 44(3) PD 529.

opened a new era in Israeli constitutional law, in which judicial review of Knesset legislation will become an accepted feature of the system.

## *B. Compatibility with Fundamental Values*

In a few cases, decided before the cases dealing with the basic laws on human rights, the Court intimated that it was not as committed as it was in the early years to confining judicial review of primary legislation to compatibility with entrenched clauses in basic laws. In one case a petitioner attempted to challenge parliamentary legislation on the ground that it offended the principle of equality before the law.[18] Following the traditional approach, the Deputy President of the Court, Ben-Porat J, remarked that even if the legislation violated the equality principle it could not be invalidated. However, the President of the Court, Shamgar J did not seem to think that the issue was as clear as all that. He rejected the argument that the legislation in question violated the equality principle and added that he would therefore 'not deal with the broad constitutional question whether judicial review by this Court extends to primary legislation of the Knesset, over and above the review connected with the entrenched clauses in basic laws'.[19]

In a dissenting opinion in another case, Barak J discussed the argument that the Court could invalidate legislation that offended the entrenched equality of elections principle but that had been passed with required special majority.[20] Barak J spelled out three propositions that determine the parameters of the Court's willingness to entertain the notion of judicial review of legislation:

1. On the theoretical level of principle, a court in a democratic country may declare invalid a law that offends basic tenets of the constitutional system even if these tenets are not enshrined in a rigid constitution or in an entrenched basic law;
2. According to the accepted social and legal approach in Israel, the Supreme Court does not assume the power to declare invalid a law that is inconsistent with basic tenets of our system;
3. At this stage of our national life, change in the judicial approach should be made by the people and their representatives, and the Court should therefore not abandon its traditional approach.

The obvious implication of these propositions is that the Court's traditional approach could be modified at some future stage, especially if the general notion of judicial review of primary legislation were to receive legitimation from 'the people and their representatives'. Such legitimation was

[18] See *Cohen* v. *Minister of Labour and Welfare* (1987) 41(2) PD 540.

[19] *Ibid.* 543.

[20] See *Tenuat Laor* v. *Knesset Speaker*, n. 16 above.

indeed provided in the Basic Law: Freedom of Occupation and the Basic Law: Human Dignity and Liberty that are discussed in Chapter 3. As noted above, the Supreme Court has ruled that the courts have indeed been granted the power to review whether legislation is compatible with the basic laws. It is not yet clear, however, whether the legitimation provided for a defined field of judicial review will cause the Court to abandon other avenues of review that it was prepared to entertain in the past, or whether it will provide political legitimation for a general theory of judicial review of primary legislation that goes beyond compatibility with basic laws.

# 25

# *A. Bergman*
# v.
# *Minister of Finance and State Comptroller*

[H.C. 98/69]
[23(1) PD 693 (1969)]

*Agranat P, Sussman J, Landau J, Berinson J, and Manny J*

Israeli case referred to:
[1] EA 1/65—*Yeredor* v. *Chairman of the Sixth Knesset Elections Committee*; 19(3) PD 365.

American case referred to:
[2] *Opinion of the Justices to the House of Representatives*, 197 NE2d 691 (Mass., 1964).

## JUDGMENT

**Landau J**:

On 30 April 1969 this Court issued an order *nisi* against the Minister of Finance, to show cause why he should not refrain from any expenditure under section 6 of the Knesset and Local Authorities Elections (Financing, Limitation of Expenses and Audit) Law 1969 (hereafter 'the Financing Law'); and against the State Comptroller to show cause why he should not refrain from any act which he is directed or authorized to implement pursuant to sections 11 and 12 of the Financing Law. The order *nisi* was issued on the petition of Advocate Dr A. Bergman on two principal grounds: one related to the manner in which the Financing Law was initiated and the other related to the manner in which the Law was passed in the Knesset.

The first argument is that since the Financing Law imposes a monetary burden on the Treasury, it could only have been initiated by the Government. In fact, the Law was initiated by six Knesset members as a private bill (see HH 807). The petitioner bases his argument on the English constitutional practice that finds expression in section 87 of the Standing Orders of the House of Commons 1958 (Halsbury-Simonds, vol. 28, 442). The petitioner argues that these directives embody an important and necessary constitutional principle that the legislative branch may not decide on monetary expenditure on its own initiative, as it does not bear the responsibility for finding sources of revenue to balance the new expenditure.

The petitioner's second argument is that the passing of the Financing Law was invalid and was a violation of the principle of the equality of elections as provided in section 4 of the Basic Law: The Knesset (hereafter 'the Basic Law'). According to Section 46, which was added to the Basic Law in 1959:

> The majority required under this Law to amend sections 4, 44 or 45 will be required for resolutions of a plenary meeting of the Knesset at every stage of the legislation, other than the debate upon a motion for the agenda of the Knesset. For the purpose of this section 'amendment' [means] either expressed or implied [amendments].

And section 4 of the Basic Law reads:

> The Knesset shall be elected by general, national, direct, equal, secret and proportional elections, in accordance with the Knesset Elections Law; this section shall not be varied save by a majority of members of the Knesset.

The first reading of the Financing Law was passed by the Knesset by a majority of twenty-four to two (DH, Sixth Knesset, Fourth Session, 1377), that is, by less than a majority of the number of Knesset members [*ed. note*: there are 120 members in the Knesset, thus a majority vote requires sixty-one votes]. As for the third reading, the Knesset records (*ibid.* 1674) state merely that the Law was 'adopted', without a recorded count of the votes. The petitioner argues that this session too was not attended by a majority of the Knesset members, and the Attorney General, who appeared for both the respondents, did not dispute that. In any event this is immaterial, since section 46 of the Basic Law requires a 'special' majority at every stage of legislation.

This petition raises potentially weighty preliminary questions of a constitutional nature, relating to the status of the Basic Laws, and to the justiciability before this Court of the issue of the Knesset's actual compliance with a self-imposed limitation in the form of an 'entrenched' statutory provision, such as section 4 of the abovementioned Basic Law. However, the Attorney General relieved us of the need to deliberate on this matter by stating on behalf of the respondents that they 'do not take a position on the question whether the legal validity of a legislative enactment is a justiciable matter before this Court, since they are of the opinion that the petition must fail on its merits'. The Attorney General stated this in his preliminary arguments and repeated it in his oral argument. When asked what position he would take if the Court found that the petition was substantiated, he replied that in such an event he would put himself at the court's disposal in making his submissions on the question of justiciability. It is therefore up to the Court to decide whether it wishes to examine the question of justiciability of its own accord. We have decided not to do so because, for obvious reasons, the substantive problems raised here require urgent resolution, whereas clarification of the preliminary constitutional questions would entail separate, lengthy deliberation. We therefore leave the question of justiciability open for further consideration and, clearly, nothing in this judgment should be taken as an expression of opinion on that matter. Additionally, the respondents have not disputed the petitioner's standing to file the petition, so that question does not arise before us.

We now return to the petitioner's two arguments. The first can be answered briefly. Whatever the law in England—and we find it unnecessary to delve into that question—our law has no statutory provision to prohibit members of the Knesset from initiating a private bill that imposes a monetary burden. Indeed, the Knesset Rules adopted by this body under section 19 of the Basic Law: The Knesset indicate the contrary. In the seventh chapter of the Rules, entitled 'Debate on Bills of Knesset Members', rule 105 (a) provides: '[e]very member of the Knesset may propose a bill'. There is no limitation on the content of the bill. Section 5 of the Law and Administration Ordinance 1949 provides that '[t]he budget of the Provisional Government shall be fixed by an Ordinance of the Provisional Council of State' and again nothing is said on the manner of initiation of such budgetary legislation on the part of the legislature. The Financing Law considered here is *sui generis*: it is not a budgetary law in the technical sense, since it does not *authorize* the government to expend money but rather *obliges* the Minister of Finance to put certain sums at the disposal of the Chairman of the Knesset. There are no special provisions in our positive law as regards the procedure for enacting a statute of this kind. The Minister of Finance will have to find sources of finance for the monetary expenditure involved in the implementation of this Law, and if he encounters difficulty in doing so that is a matter which, constitutionally speaking, pertains to the relations between the legislative branch and the executive branch, and does not concern this Court.

That leaves the principal question: does the Financing Law contradict section 4 of the Basic Law? First, however, we wish to make it clear that this Court ought not involve itself in the debate conducted in the Knesset and by the general public concerning the system of State financing of the general activities of the political parties and their specific activities in the electoral campaign. Much has been said and written about the deficiencies of this system from the public perspective, while respected members of the Knesset representing a large majority of the House, including the initiators of the Law, have defended this system as necessary in our political reality. They stress, on the one hand, the improvements brought about by this Law compared to the previously prevailing state of affairs, especially with regards to limitations on election expenditures and their auditing—two subjects that have no necessary connection with the matter of State funding. On the other hand, they endeavour to appease the critics by pointing to the experimental character of the entire Law, which is intended to apply only to the Seventh Knesset elections.

This entire public debate falls outside the range of our judicial interest; the problem before us is confined within its legal framework. What is the petitioner's legal argument? He argued, half-heartedly, that 'it is doubtful whether the allocation of funds to political parties is an allocation for purposes of State', citing an opinion of the Massachusetts Supreme Court that such an allocation is not an expenditure for a 'public purpose' in the sense of that state's constitutional law [2]. We have no similar provision in our law, which suffices to dispose of this argument.

For us, therefore, the question is framed within the context of section 4 of the Basic Law alone. In this respect the learned Attorney General argued that there is no contradiction between equality in the elections as secured under section 4 of the Basic Law and the provisions of the Financing Law. He contended that section 4, in its entirety, deals only with the electoral system in its technical sense, as evidenced by the marginal heading of the section, and that the principle of equality embodied therein means only that each voter has one vote, all votes being equal in weight—that and no more. In support of this argument he referred us to the legislative history of this provision, which finds its origins in the Mandate period, in rule 4 of the Knesset Israel Elections Regulations of 1 March 1930, and also to the constitutions of other countries in which the principle of 'one man, one vote' finds explicit recognition. He argued that this technical principle should not be confused with the fundamental principle of equality for all before the law, which is likewise expressed in various constitutions. However, we do not have a written constitution. It is true that we, too, recognize the equality of citizens before the law as a fundamental principle of our constitutional regime, yet the principle has not been embodied in a written constitution or even in a provision of a basic law that requires a special majority for amendment. Hence there is nothing to prevent the legislature from deviating from this principle even in a law passed by an ordinary majority. The Financing Law should be seen as part of the Elections Law, and Section 4 of the Basic Law itself says that the Knesset shall be elected 'by general elections in accordance with the

Knesset Elections Law'. In any event, if the Financing Law deviates at all from the principle of equality, it is but a minor deviation which is to be accepted so that other important goals are achieved, such as preventing the undue fragmentation that could result from too rigid an application of the equality principle in financing.

With all due respect we must dismiss this argument because it does not answer adequately the petitioner's main complaint: that the limitation of funding to parties represented in the present Sixth Knesset exclusively is prejudicial to equality of opportunity for those new parties that seek to take part in the campaign for the Seventh Knesset elections but were not represented in the Sixth Knesset.

We do not accept the argument that Section 4 of the Basic Law merely prescribes technical directions regarding the conduct of the elections. We are prepared to assume that the draftsmen of this Section envisaged primarily the principle of 'one man, one vote' when they prescribed that the elections should be 'equal'. However, we do not believe that this exhausts the full meaning of the provision in the Basic Law. Each of the adjectives 'general, national, direct, relative' has two facets: they address both the right to elect and the right to be elected, and there is no reason why the word 'equal' should not be given the same broad meaning. This is indicated by the order of the Sections: first comes Section 4 with its general significance, and then the more specific provisions in Section 5 regarding the right to vote, and in Section 6 regarding the right to be elected. Were it otherwise, and the word 'equal' referred only to the right to vote, it would have been more natural to include the idea of 'one man, one vote' in Section 5.

If the principle of equality in Section 4 extends to the right to be elected, it must also find expression in an equality of opportunity for the various candidates who contend the Knesset elections. In our electoral system the election candidates join in candidates' lists that are submitted either by a party group of the outgoing Knesset or—in the case of a new list—by 750 voters (section 4 of the Knesset Elections Law (Consolidated Version) 1969). In this way, the individual candidate aspires to achieve his set goal, and by the same token the will of the individual voter is realized in voting for the list.

This interpretation of the equality provision in Section 4 is consistent with the fundamental principle of the equality of all persons before the law. To be more precise, it applies the general principle as an emanation thereof in the specific area of the law of elections. However, it can also exist independently without resting upon a provision in a written constitution that expressly declares the principle of the equality of all persons before the law. We do not have such an express provision, either in a written constitution or in an 'entrenched' provision of a basic law, nevertheless this unwritten principle is the soul of our entire constitutional regime. It is therefore proper—precisely in the borderline cases where a statutory provision can be construed in two ways—that we prefer the construction that upholds the equality of all persons before the law over one that sets it at naught. This fortifies our construction of the equality provision in Section 4.

After all, what is the simple meaning of the words 'equal elections'? What would we say, for example, about a statutory provision that allowed only one list of candidates? Could such elections be called 'equal' because each voter still has one vote? Or, assuming the Financing Law determined that only the largest party was entitled to State funding; we would certainly regard that as a glaring violation of the equality principle in Section 4. In other words, this Section has the potency to prevent violations of equality also beyond the narrow confines of 'one man, one vote'.

Before we examine the Financing Law in light of the abovementioned comments, we wish to note three preliminary points:

First, a Law of the Knesset is presumed to be valid as adopted. Therefore this Court's primary inclination must be to uphold the law and not to strike it down, even when the argument against it is that it contradicts an 'entrenched' statutory provision (and it is stressed again that everything said here presupposes that the matter is justiciable before this Court).

Secondly, we are in an area that is far removed from the idea of equality before the law in its simple classic meaning, that is, equality of rights for the citizen as an individual. There is no better example of this classic meaning than the rule of 'one man, one vote'. This equality must be guarded without compromise. However, as we draw away from this fundamental meaning of the principle of equality before the law, so it clashes with other important principles to which it must defer. Thus, for example, in the *Yeredor* case [1] this Court affirmed a decision to disqualify a list of candidates whose purpose was to undermine the existence of the State of Israel. Likewise, with regard to the matter of State funding for the elections: all agree that the political parties should not be absolutely equated with one another by being allocated equal funds regardless of the party's size, although the campaign needs of a small party might require as much of these means as a larger party. Furthermore, all agree that the principle of equality in financing should not be applied in such a way as to encourage the submission of candidates' lists that would not have formed at all were it not for the temptation that they would receive an advance against the funding.

Inequality in the general election laws does exist, primarily in the minimum percentage of votes required in order to gain representation in the Knesset, and similarly the requirement that a new list must deposit a bond, as well as the fact that its representatives do not participate in the election committees except as observers after publication of the list. All these restrictions inevitably derogate from absolute equality. It was not argued here that for this reason they are invalid.

Thirdly, and related to the preceding point, the issue before us—State financing of elections—is complicated and complex by its very nature and its legislative solution entails diverse practical considerations that require special expertise which this Court lacks.

Taking all these factors into consideration, we have concluded that the absolute denial of funds to new lists of party candidates substantially prejudices these lists' equality of opportunity, thus violating the equality principle in Section 4 to an unjustifiable degree that goes beyond a minor deviation from that principle. We have already mentioned the provision in the Knesset Elections Law that allows any 750 voters to submit a candidates' list. This opens the doors of the Knesset to new party groups. Such opportunity is one of the hallmarks of our democratic regime, particularly the electoral system. It might be argued that the situation of a new list in the elections to the Seventh Knesset is no worse than it was in the elections to the Sixth Knesset, since such a list can still finance its election expenditures from private sources. We would answer that this is not the correct comparison to make; rather the *current* situation of such a list should be compared with the *current* situation of the existing party groups, and, if so, it is clear that the new list is at a real disadvantage compared to the others, because existing party groups are entitled to receive substantial sums from the State coffers to finance their expenditures whereas the new list is denied that right.

In the Knesset debates on the Financing Law, the merits of a method of finance based on the balance of party power in the outgoing (Sixth) Knesset was contrasted with a method based on the new party balance in the incoming (Seventh) Knesset. The Knesset preferred the first method based on the reasoning that there was a danger that short-lived lists would be formed due to the temptation to receive an advance on the funding allocation. This danger can be countered without causing the inequality that we have found to be unlawful, by promising a new list funding without an advance payment and only funding it retroactively after it has stood the test of the elections and gained at least one seat. All this on the condition that the list has consented in advance to the audit by the State Comptroller in accordance with the Financing Law, and has met all the other conditions specified in the Law. It appears to us that provisions of this nature could still be added to the Financing Law without undue difficulty, without changing the existing provisions as regards the parties represented in the Sixth Knesset and without overturning the entire situation, so as to avoid the apprehended inequality. It goes without saying that in making this suggestion we in no way intend to encroach upon the sovereignty of the Knesset as the legislative authority.

The Knesset, accordingly, has two courses of action from which to choose: it can re-enact the financing provisions in the Financing Law, despite their inherent inequality, if the majority required under Sections 4 and 46 of the Basic Law is attained; or it can amend the Law so as to remove the inequality, and we have indicated above a possible way of doing so.

We therefore make absolute the order *nisi* in the sense that the first respondent, the Minister of Finance, is to act pursuant to section 6 of the Financing Law only if the financing provisions in the Law are re-enacted with the required majority, or if the Law is amended so as to remove the inequality contained therein. We see no need to issue any order against the State Comptroller. Respondent no 1 shall pay the petitioner his costs in the petition.

Judgment given on 3 July 1969.

# 26

# *M. K. Yossi Sarid*
# v.
# *Speaker of the Knesset, Menachem Savidor*

[H.C. 652/81]
[36(2) PD 197 (1982)]

*Ben-Porat J, Barak J, and D. Levin J*

Israeli cases referred to:

[1] HC 222/68—*'Huggim Leumi'im' Society* v. *Minister of Police*; 24(2) PD 141.
[2] HC 306/81—*Flato Sharon* v. *Knesset Committee*; 35(4) PD 118.
[3] CA 228/63—*Azuz* v. *Azar*; 17 PD 2541.
[4] HC 188/63—*Batzul* v. *Minister of Interior*; 19(1) PD 337.
[5] HC 108/70—*Manor* v. *Minister of Finance*; 24(2) PD 442.
[6] HC 98/69—*Bergman* v. *Minister of Finance*; 23(1) PD 693; 8 SJ 13.
[7] HC 246/81—*'Agudat Derech Eretz'* v. *Broadcasting Society*; 35(4) PD 1; 8 SJ 21.
[8] HC 563, 566/75—*Ressler* v. *Minister of Finance*; *Zivoni* v. *Speaker of Knesset Finance Committee*; 30(2) PD 337.
[9] HC 637/79—*Yitzhak* v. *Minister of Agriculture*; 34(2) PD 442.
[10] HC 248/80—*Cohen* v. *Speaker of the Knesset*; 34(4) PD 813.
[11] HC 217/80—*Segal* v. *Minister of Interior*; 34(4) PD 429.
[12] HC 65/51—*Jabotinsky* v. *President of the State of Israel*; 4 PD 801.

American cases referred to:

[13] *Baker* v. *Carr*, 369 US 186 (1962).
[14] *Joint Anti-Fascist Refugee Committee* v. *McGrath*, 341 US 123 (1951).
[15] *Powell* v. *McCormack*, 395 US 486 (1969).
[16] *Poe* v. *Ullman*, 367 US 497, 509 (1961).

# JUDGMENT

**Barak J**:

1. On Tuesday, 1 December 1981, at 11.40 a.m., the [Labour] Alignment faction submitted a motion of non-confidence in the Government. The Speaker of the Knesset decided that the no-confidence motion would be debated on Wednesday, 2 December 1981, and that the sitting would convene at 5.00 p.m. Knesset Member Yossi Sarid petitioned the Court against the scheduling of the sitting in the afternoon hours. He argued that under rule 36(a) of the Knesset Rules, a motion of no-confidence is required to be debated 'at the next regular sitting', and that sitting had long since been scheduled for Wednesday at 11.00 a.m. The petitioner contended that the delay in convening the sitting was designed to allow several Knesset Members, who support the Government, to return to the country in time for the vote, and that this consideration, which motivated the Speaker of the Knesset, is not legitimate, since the Speaker thus became 'an instrument in the hands of the Government'. The petitioner did point out that the reason given by the Speaker for his decision was that a memorial for the late David Ben Gurion would be held on Wednesday, but the petitioner claimed that this reason was not genuine.

2. The petition was brought before a judge of this Court on Tuesday evening, who referred it to a panel of three judges for a hearing on Wednesday morning, while also summoning a representative of the Attorney-General to appear. On Wednesday there appeared before us the petitioner and his counsel, and also Ms Beinish, on behalf of the Attorney-General. Due to the urgency of the matter Ms Beinish did not have time to prepare an affidavit. In her opening remarks she submitted that the petition should be dismissed as non-justiciable. . . . [Moreover, she argued] that the change in the scheduling of the sitting on Wednesday from 11.00 a.m. to 5.00 p.m. was made by the Speaker [of the Knesset] by virtue of his authority under rule 27(c) of the Knesset Rules, according to which 'the Speaker of the Knesset may change the scheduled time of a sitting'. The primary reason for the change was the memorial for the late Mr Ben Gurion. Nonetheless, there was also an additional reason, namely that, because of the Prime Minister's illness and in view of the nature of the matter, the Government's reply to the no-confidence motion was to be given by the Minister of Defence, who was in the United States, and would be returning to Israel at the earliest for the afternoon sitting.

3. A factual dispute arose, therefore, regarding the considerations of the Speaker of the Knesset. The dispute could not be resolved at that stage, since Ms Beinish's statements with respect to the Speaker's considerations

were delivered orally and were not supported by an affidavit. In these circumstances, counsel for the petitioner declared that he would accept Ms Beinish's factual declarations as if they had been made by affidavit. He contended that even on these facts the Speaker's decision was invalid, since according to Rule 36(a) of the Knesset Rules—and this specific provision prevails over the provision in Rule 27(c)—the Speaker should have scheduled the sitting for 11.00 a.m. According to this reasoning, the only way to change the opening time of a regular sitting is by resolution of the Knesset Committee under Rule 148, which provides that 'the Knesset shall not deal with any matter in a manner contrary to the rules, or to precedents, unless the Knesset Committee has considered the matter, and decided thereon'. The difficulty is that the Knesset Committee, before which the matter was brought, 'refused to intervene in the Speaker's decision on the ground that the matter fell within the scope of his authority, and the Committee should not deal with it'.

As against these arguments, Ms Beinish submitted that the Speaker's decision was made lawfully, within the scope of his authority under section 27(c) of the Rules, and on the basis of material considerations. Ms Beinish concentrated in the main on the argument that the decision of the Speaker was not justiciable and that the Court, therefore, should not hear the petition on its merits. She contended that the working procedures of the Knesset were non-justiciable, since they fell within the sovereign power of the Knesset, and were of a clearly political character. Mr Shachal, counsel for the petitioner, argued in reply that the Speaker's decision was based on law and is of a purely administrative nature, so that it is subject to review by this Court. Such review, he argued, is important to ensure that the Knesset Speaker observes the law.

4. The question arises whether it is proper for the High Court of Justice to entertain a petition concerning the authority of the Knesset Speaker in regard to Knesset working procedures. I said, 'whether it is proper' to entertain the petition, because the question posed to us is not one of jurisdiction, but one of discretion (see *Huggim Leumi'im Society* v. *Minister of Police* [1]). This Court's jurisdiction to hear the petition stems from section 7(b)(2) of the Courts Law 1957, under which the High Court of Justice is empowered to issue orders to State authorities which 'exercise any public functions by virtue of law'. The Knesset Speaker is a State authority, and in deciding to change the time of the sitting he exercised a public function by virtue of 'law'—that is, the Knesset Rules, which were adopted by the Knesset under section 19 of the Basic Law: The Knesset (see also the definition of 'law' in section 1 of the Interpretation Ordinance (New Version)). Indeed, the provisions of the Rules relating to the working procedures of the Knesset form part of the constitutional law practised in the State (see E. Likhovski, 'On the Working Procedures of the Knesset' in *Legal Studies*

*in Memory of Abraham Rosenthal* (ed. Tedeschi, Magnes, 1964), 380). This Court, therefore, is empowered to hear the petition (see *Flato Sharon* v. *Knesset Committee* [2]). The question still remains, however, whether the Court should hear the petition on its merits in light of the special character of the Speaker's decision which concerns 'internal parliamentary proceedings' (in the words of Shamgar J [2], at 142).

5. The Knesset is 'the house of representatives of the State', and is required to perform many varied functions. It enacts the Basic Laws and the ordinary Laws; it sometimes participates—in the plenum or in the various committees—in the process of subsidiary legislation; it supervises the actions of the Government, which holds office for as long as it enjoys the confidence of the Knesset, by means of parliamentary questions, motions of non-confidence and similar motions; it fulfills, in the plenum or in committees, several *quasi-judicial* functions, such as deciding on election appeals, withdrawing immunity, and, in special cases, suspending a Knesset member, or removing him from office (see A. Rubinstein, *The Constitutional Law of the State of Israel* (3rd edn., Schocken, 1981) 81, 291, 296; C. Klein, 'On the Legal Definition of the Parliamentary Regime and Israeli Parliamentarian' (1974) 5 *Mishpatim* 308).

The wide variety of Knesset functions leads to a corresponding range in the scope of the court's judicial review of the manner in which the Knesset performs its duties—in the plenum, or in committees, or through other functionaries. Indeed, the scope of judicial review of the Knesset's actions and decisions cannot be exhausted in a simple formula, but often varies according to the nature of the function under review. Take, for instance, the Knesset's legislative function. While a statute is not generally subject to review of the legality of its content (*Azuz* v. *Azar* [3]; *Batzul* v. *Minister of Interior* [4]; *Manor* v. *Minister of Finance* [5]), this Court has reviewed the legality of a statute with regard to an entrenched provision in a Basic Law (*Bergman* v. *Minister of Finance* [6]; *'Agudat Derech Eretz'* v. *Broadcasting Society* [7]). It is true that in so doing, the Court left the question of its power to act in this way open for further consideration, but the very hearing and decision are in themselves:

> at least some intimation of this Court's approach to the question of the boundaries of its constitutional powers. Had the Court believed that the separation of powers forbade it from dealing in any way with a petition concerning the Knesset and its committees, it would have raised that question on its own initiative. In other words, the Court's readiness to explore the issue on its merits has, in itself, implications as to the interpretation of the powers of the different state authorities.

(*Per* Shamgar J in *Flato Sharon* [2], at 141.)

Against this limited review of the legislative process there stands the Court's ordinary review of quasi-judicial decisions of the Knesset and its committees, such as the removal from office or suspension of a Knesset member [2]. Likewise, judicial review is exercised over decisions of the Knesset—in the plenum, or in committees, or by other organs of the Knesset—relating to subsidiary legislation, or which are of an administrative nature concerning, for example, party funding (see *Ressler* v. *Minister of Finance*, *Zivoni* v. *Chairman of Knesset Finance Committee* [8]; *Yitzhak* v. *Minister of Agriculture* [9]; *Cohen* v. *Knesset Speaker* [10]). In summary, all that can be said, by way of generalization regarding judicial review of decisions of the Knesset, is that the scope of this review differs according to the nature of the decision reviewed. A 'legislative' decision is different from a 'quasi-judicial' decision, and both of these differ from a decision relating to the Knesset's supervision of Government actions.

6. The petition before us concerns a decision of the Knesset Speaker relating to the working agenda of the Knesset, in regard to the control exercised by the Knesset over the Government by means of the vote of non-confidence. What is the scope of the judicial review of such decisions of the Speaker? These decisions are not embodied in a *statute*, nor are they even *judicial* decisions, or decisions made in the framework of subsidiary legislation. We are dealing here with a decision of an administrative character, taken in the course of intra-parliamentary proceedings concerning the reciprocal political relationship between the Knesset and the Government. Is a decision of this kind subject to judicial review?

7. This question is by no means simple, since its solution involves a conflict between two opposing considerations. On the one hand there is the principle of the rule of law which means, in its formal sense, that all the organs of the State must obey the law. The principle of the rule of law is addressed to both individuals and governmental organs, and applies to the legislature itself, in the sense of 'the rule of law in the legislature' (in the words of Silberg J in his book *Principia Talmudica* (2nd edn., Hebrew University Law Faculty Publications, 1964), 70). If, therefore, the Knesset Rules contain provisions governing the conduct of the *internal* proceedings of the House, by the different Knesset authorities, these authorities must act in accordance with the Rules. Just as this Court exercises its jurisdiction in any case of failure to obey the law by the governmental authority, so too must it act in regard to a failure to implement the provisions of the Rules concerning the administration of the House, for were that not so, we might find the legislature itself in violation of the law. The provisions of the Rules express the law regarded by the Knesset as appropriate for the conduct of its parliamentary life, and for allowing its members to fulfill their political mission. Breach of the Rules frustrates these objectives, and judicial review is essential to prevent such, for where there is no judge there is no law, and where the Court fails to intervene, the principle of the rule of law is violated (*Segal* v. *Minister of Interior* [11], at 441).

On the other hand, there is the principle that the working rules of the legislature are its own internal affair and, on the basis of the separation of powers, belong to the legislative authority itself, which also has the tools to examine itself and to scrutinize its own decisions. It is proper, therefore, that the judiciary respect the internal affairs of the legislature, and refrain from interfering in them. Moreover, decisions of the Knesset with respect to its reciprocal relations with the Government are usually heavily laden with political content from which the judiciary should properly distance itself so as to prevent, as far as possible, the 'politicization of the judicial process' (in the words of Witkon J in *Politics and Law* (The Hebrew University of Jerusalem, 1965), 58). It follows that:

> Paramount considerations relating to the separation of powers, the independence of parliament and the mutual respect which should prevail between state authorities, require that the Knesset enjoy freedom of action in managing its proceedings as it deems fit, without having its acts scrutinized by outside authorities. Were the Court to sit in judgement over the propriety of Knesset proceedings, this body would be unable to function properly, and the Court too would be flooded with litigation turning it into a perpetual arena of political and procedural conflict.

(Y. S. Zemach, 'The Problem of Non-Justiciability in Parliamentary Proceedings' (1973) 3 *Iyunei Mishpat* 752, 753.)

Indeed, the need to respect the status of the Legislature, on the one hand, and to protect the Judiciary on the other hand, justify judicial restraint and forbearance from reviewing the administration of the Legislature, as regards its reciprocal relations with the Government.

8. These opposing considerations are of great weight, and we should properly take them into account. It appears to me, therefore, that there is no room to lay down a comprehensive rule as to the scope of the Court's intervention in the working procedures of the Knesset. Indeed, the accepted approach in England, that parliamentary proceedings are excluded from the range of judicial review, has not been adopted in Israel, and this Court has held that:

> There is no reason why this Court should not exercise its power as against a Knesset decision taken in violation of the law or the principles of natural justice (save in cases where the matter dealt with by the Knesset is non-justiciable).

(*Per* Kahan DP in *Flato Sharon* [2], at 132).

However, that ruling concerned a *quasi-judicial* decision, whereas we are concerned with a decision that is not *quasi-judicial*, but administrative, concerning intra-parliamentary affairs. True, the decision of the Knesset Speaker to delay the time of the sitting until the afternoon is *justiciable* in the sense that its legality can be judged by legal standards, but that, alone, does not exhaust the principle of non-justiciability, which also addresses the reciprocal relations and mutual respect owed by the legislature and the judiciary to one another (see *Baker* v. *Carr* [13]).

9. It seems to me that these opposing considerations of the rule of law, on the one hand, and respect for the Knesset's special standing on the other hand, require a judicial balance, which is based on restraint, yet does not yield to complete impotence. This self-restraint must be based on a standard which will define those areas in which the Court will not interfere out of respect for the uniqueness of the Knesset as the people's elected body, and those in which the Court will intervene to preserve the rule of law in the legislature. The determination of this standard is a difficult task that requires use of that 'expert feel of lawyers' referred to by Frankfurter J in *Joint Anti-Fascist Refugee Committee* v. *McGrath* [14], and in which Smoira P found 'an excellent definition of limits of judicial power' (*Jabotinsky* [12]).

In my opinion, the proper balance between the need to secure 'the rule of law in the legislature' and the need to respect the special standing of the Knesset in its decisions concerning its internal affairs, will be assured if we adopt a standard that takes into account the degree of the apprehended harm to the fabric of parliamentary life, and the extent of its influence on the fundamental structure of our constitutional regime. When the alleged violation of the intra-parliamentary process is minor, and would not affect the foundations of our parliamentary regime, the consideration of the independence and uniqueness of the Knesset outweighs that of the rule of law, and the judiciary would be justified in refraining from hearing a matter that is essentially political. The matter would be different when the violation complained of is manifest and impairs substantive values of our constitutional regime. In such circumstances, the need to secure the rule of law prevails over all other considerations, much as that need prevails where we are concerned with a violation of the right of a Knesset member as an individual in a quasi-judicial proceeding (see *Flato Sharon* [2], and also *Powell* v. *McCormack* [15]). In determining the proper standard, which takes into account the degree of harm and the interest affected, we commend a flexible criterion which, by its very nature, defies exact definition, and the content and scope of which will be determined by the Court according to the needs of the time, and the matter involved (cf *Poe* v. *Ullman* [16]).

10. In view of these standards, it appears to us in the instant matter that even if the Knesset Speaker departed from the provisions of the Rules—and in this respect we are not expressing any opinion on the merits—it was of minor significance and must be resolved through the intra-parliamentary process itself. We do not have before us any substantial violation, such as might have occurred if the possibility of the no-confidence vote in the Government had been entirely precluded or seriously jeopardized which would have justified our intervention. Grievances of the kind raised in this

petition ought to be resolved in the house of representatives itself, through the frame of its own institutions, as part of its internal administration. This petition does not warrant our intervention.

For these reasons we dismissed the petition on 2 December 1981.

Judgment given on 1 March 1982.

# 27

# *Unreasonableness, Balance of Interests and Proportionality*

ITZHAK ZAMIR*



In recent years, the Supreme Court of Israel has developed three separate grounds for reviewing administrative action: 'unreasonableness', 'balance of interests', and 'proportionality'. While balance of interests and proportionality were once considered mere instances or sub-categories of the more inclusive standard of unreasonableness, this approach no longer reflects the law in Israel. Balance of interests and proportionality have developed into separate grounds of review. This article considers the distinct features of each of these three grounds of review.

## 1. Unreasonableness

Unreasonableness is an established ground of review which has been developed and defined through the case law. An administrative decision is unreasonable, according to the case law, if it is capricious or arbitrary, manifestly unjust, made in bad faith, or oppressive. The case law has stated, by way of definition, that an administrative decision can be found unreasonable if it is so unreasonable that no reasonable authority could

* An earlier version of these notes appeared in (1992) 11 *Tel Aviv University Studies in Law* 131.

ever have reached it.[1] Such a tautological definition, though perhaps guiding the 'expert feel of the lawyer', does not adequately delineate the bounds of unreasonableness nor does it sufficiently explain its nature. A more meaningful understanding of unreasonableness may be reached through an analysis of the doctrine's application in recent decisions of the Supreme Court of Israel.

As a starting point, it is important to understand the difference between unreasonableness and other grounds for the review of administrative discretion, such as 'irrelevant considerations' and 'improper purposes'. Irrelevant considerations and improper purposes concern the propriety of the administrative process. The question asked under these doctrines is whether the administrative authority made a specific mistake during the administrative process by taking into account an irrelevant consideration or directing its mind to an improper purpose.

By contrast, unreasonableness, according to the traditional view, does not examine the process, but rather the end result. Accordingly, the question to be asked under the unreasonableness doctrine is whether the administrative decision as it stands, regardless of the process, is unreasonable. The Court can hold the decision unreasonable without pointing to any specific mistake in the administrative process—indeed, the Court need not even examine whether any specific mistake has occurred. This is a convenient course for the court. It affords substantial leeway to correct administrative action which is obviously wrong or undesirable. However, at the same time, because it is so vague, the doctrine of unreasonableness may be unpredictable and dangerous. Therefore, the court is usually very cautious in employing this ground of review, and will only rarely strike down an administrative decision as unreasonable. This, in turn, may diminish its utility as a means of control.

The traditional view, according to which the unreasonableness of the decision, and not the propriety of the process, is examined should be reconsidered. It may be assumed that a decision will not be unreasonable unless some mistake or defect occurred in the process. Usually this mistake or defect will be an irrelevant consideration or an improper purpose. In such a case, unreasonableness is not the defect but rather the result or the symptom of the defect. If a decision appears to be unreasonable, this in itself

[1] See *Kruse* v. *Johnson* (1898) 2 QBD 91, 99; *Associated Provincial Picture Houses Ltd* v. *Wednesbury Corporation* [1948] 1 KB 223, 230. On unreasonableness, see generally, H. R. Wade, *Administrative Law* (7th edn., Clarendon, Oxford, 1994), 387 ff.; S. de Smith, *Judicial Review of Administrative Action* (5th edn., Stevens and Son, London, 1995), 549 ff. The definition of unreasonableness offered by these cases was adopted and extensively applied by the Sup. Ct. of Israel. See e.g. HC 21/51 *Binnenboim* v. *Municipality of Tel Aviv* (1952) 6 PD 375; CA 311/57 *Attorney General* v. *M. Dizengoff and Co.*, (*Navigation*) *Ltd* (1959) 13 PD 1026. In the last case, the Court held that the ground of unreasonableness should be applied to subordinate legislation even if made by a minister.

gives rise to a suspicion that some mistake or defect occurred in the process. Such suspicion may be a sufficient ground for the Court to issue an order *nisi* (as is the practice in Israel) or grant leave to apply for judicial review (as is the practice in England). In the course of review it may be discovered that the decision is tainted with irrelevant considerations or improper purposes. In such a case, the decision can be invalidated on those grounds, and need not, therefore, be invalidated for unreasonableness.

In other cases, the review may lead to the conclusion that the decision is based on relevant considerations and proper purposes and is not therefore defective in this respect. However, the review may disclose that the authority attributed undue weight to an otherwise relevant consideration. For instance, it might have turned a marginal consideration into a central and decisive one. Clearly, an authority vested with discretion must have freedom to ascribe to any relevant consideration such weight as it sees fit in the circumstances of the case. Yet, as the Supreme Court of Israel has held, this discretion is not without limits. There is, in each case, a range of reasonableness, or a margin of appreciation, within which the authority has discretion regarding the weight to be attached to any relevant consideration. If the weight given in a particular case remains within the limits of this range, the Court will refrain from intervention, whether or not it agrees with the decision. If, however, the authority steps outside the limits of this range, the decision may be invalidated for unreasonableness.

In this context, unreasonableness means undue weight given to a relevant consideration. Such an approach to reasonableness is consistent with a focus on the administrative *process*, rather than the *outcome*. At the same time, this approach treats reasonableness as a separate ground of review and not merely as a symptom of another ground, such as irrelevant considerations or improper purposes. There is now ample case law to support this view of unreasonableness.[2]

For example, in *Ganor* v. *Attorney General*,[3] the Supreme Court examined the decision of the Attorney-General not to bring criminal charges against the officers of Israel's major banks. These officers were suspected of having unlawfully manipulated the bank shares, thereby causing a crisis on the stock exchange. The Attorney General decided, nevertheless, that there was no public interest justifying the prosecution of the bankers. Explaining his position, he stated, *inter alia*, that it was not only the bankers but also other official authorities who shared responsibility for the

[2] e.g. HC 156/75 *Fausi Daka* v. *Minister of Transportation* (1976) 30(2) PD 94, 105; HC 389/80 *Dapei Zahav, Ltd* v. *Broadcasting Authority* (1981) 35(1) PD 421, 444–6; HC 910/86 *Ressler* v. *Minister of Defence* (1988) 42(2) PD 441, 503–6; on unreasonableness as a ground of review, see also M. Shaked, 'Comments on Judicial Review of Reasonableness of Administrative Action' (1982) 12 *Mishpatim* 102 (Hebrew); E. Zamir, 'Unreasonableness—A Ground for Judicial Intervention in Administrative Law' (1982) 12 *Mishpatim* 291 (Hebrew).

[3] HC 935/89 *Ganor* v. *Attorney-General* (1990) 44(2) PD 485.

manipulation of the bank shares, that the bankers had already been sanctioned by having been forced to resign from their positions in the banks, and that much time had elapsed since the collapse of the bank shares. The Supreme Court agreed that all of these were relevant considerations to be taken into account by the Attorney-General. However, the Court held that the Attorney-General had given excessive weight to these considerations, and had given insufficient weight to other considerations, such as the severity of the offences attributed to the bankers, the grave consequences of these offences and the need to deter potential offenders. Accordingly, the Court held the decision of the Attorney-General to be unreasonable and invalid. Following the decision of the Court, the Attorney-General reconsidered his decision and ordered that the bankers be prosecuted.[4]

## 2. Balance of Interests

Administrative decisions are usually the product of a balance of different interests. If the balance is patently wrong, the decision may be considered unreasonable, and invalidated as such. The Supreme Court of Israel has long invalidated administrative decisions for an improper balance of interests under the rubric of unreasonableness.[5] However, it seems that recently the court has, in effect, elevated the balance of interests to the rank of a distinct ground of review. Indeed, it has lately become such a popular ground of review that it threatens to overshadow unreasonableness.

Like unreasonableness, the balance of interests relates to the weight attributed by the administrative authority to relevant considerations. Unreasonableness examines the weights given to a specific consideration. Balance of interests, on the other hand, examines the relative weight given to various considerations, and thus better reflects the reality of the

[4] Excerpts from the decision of the Sup. Ct. opinion are reproduced in this section. In the same vein, the Sup. Ct. invalidated, as unreasonable, a decision of the government to appoint someone with a criminal record as director-general of a ministry. As the Court held, the government did not give due weight to the criminal record of that person and, therefore, had made an unreasonable decision. *See* HC 6163/92 *Aisenberg* v. *Minister of Housing* (1992) 47(2) PD 229. Similarly, the Sup. Ct. invalidated, as unreasonable, the decision of the Prime Minister not to remove from office a minister whom the Attorney-General decided to prosecute on serious charges. See HC 3094/93 *Movement for Good Government in Israel* v. *Government of Israel*, (1993) 47(5) PD 404. On the same ground, the Court held that the Prime Minister was bound to remove from office a deputy minister, against whom there was *prima facie* evidence of the commission of certain offences. See HC 4267/93 *Amitai* v. *Prime Minister* (1993) 47(5) PD 441.

[5] e.g. HC 73/53 *Kol Ha'am* v. *Minister of the Interior* (1953) 7 PD 871 (see Ch. 4). In this celebrated decision the Sup. Ct. laid down the rule safeguarding free speech against restrictions imposed to protect public order. The rule was based on a balance of interests. The Court stated that only near certainty of a substantial damage to the public order could justify restriction upon free speech.

decision-making process, which necessarily involves the balancing of different interests. Usually, the weight to be given to a specific consideration in a case depends on the nature of the other considerations involved in that case. The decision ultimately depends on the relative weight given to all relevant considerations. Balance of interests is thus a more sophisticated and realistic version of unreasonableness.

In some circumstances, the Court has gone beyond merely declaring that the balance of interests in a given case is wrong, and has specified a criterion to be applied by the authority in balancing the conflicting interests in a given category of cases. Such a criterion may help to establish the proper relationship between the relevant interests in those cases.

The main area in which the Court has specified such a criterion is the field of human rights. For instance, in cases involving the restriction of freedom of speech or freedom of demonstration on the ground of public order or national security, the Supreme Court has repeatedly held that the freedom concerned, be it freedom of speech or another freedom, is a relevant consideration for the authority. The authority must weigh this consideration against other relevant considerations. Moreover, the Court has stated that the proper balance of free speech and the other considerations in this area allows for restriction of free speech only if there exists 'near certainty' that 'substantial damage' will result to public order or national security.[6]

However, the Court has indicated the importance of flexibility in balancing the relevant considerations, with the balance varying according to the conflicting interests concerned. Where, for instance, a conflict exists between free speech and the judicial process, as in the case of *sub judice* publications, a more lenient standard will suffice. In such a case, the Supreme Court has held that free speech may be restricted if there exists a 'reasonable possibility' that substantial damage will be caused to the judicial process.[7] The standard established by the Court reflects the relative importance attributed to each of the competing interests. Once established, the standard serves as a guideline in the future exercise of administrative discretion, as distinct from a retrospective examination, which is characteristic of review for unreasonableness. This gives balance of interests a great advantage over unreasonableness as a means to control administrative discretion.

[6] e.g. HC 14/86, *Laor* v. *Board of Censorship for Films and Plays* (1987) 41(1) PD 421 (freedom of speech); HC 153/83 *Levi* v. *Commander of the Southern District of the Police* (1984) 38(2) PD 393 (freedom of demonstration). See also A. Barak, 'Freedom of Expression and its Limits' (1991) 40 *Hapraklit* 5, 14 ff. (Hebrew).

[7] Cr.A 696/81 *Azulai* v. *State of Israel* (1983) 37(2) PD 565.

## 3. Proportionality

The concept of proportionality is a basic element of fair administration. Administrative power should not be exercised in a manner which inflicts injury on private interests disproportionately to public needs. In such cases, administrative action may be invalidated for unreasonableness. Proportionality may thus be considered one of several categories of unreasonableness. This seems to be the prevailing view in England.[8] In some other jurisdictions, however, proportionality is recognized as a distinct and important ground of review.[9]

As a distinct ground of review, proportionality may take judicial review one step beyond reasonableness and balance of interests. The balance of interests may justify a certain course of action by the administrative authority, such as the imposition of restrictions on free speech. At this point the concept of proportionality becomes relevant to instruct the authority that the restriction should not be disproportionate to the needs or risks involved, for example, to public order or national security. Thus, screening a movie may be restricted if there exists 'near certainty of substantial damage' to public order. This, however, does not necessarily justify a total ban on the movie. Rather, it may be sufficient in the circumstances of the case if, for example, minors are excluded from the cinema house, or certain scenes are cut out, or criminal proceedings (instead of prior restraint) are instituted.[10]

Proportionality in this sense has been applied by the Supreme Court to scrutinize and invalidate administrative decisions. Thus, a decision to cancel an import licence in order to protect a consumer interest was invalidated by the Court where that interest could have been safeguarded effectively by adding certain conditions to the licence.[11] In another case, the Court invalidated emergency regulations made by the Minister of Housing, where the Minister could have, and in the circumstances of the

[8] See Wade, n. 1 above, 403; J. F. Garner, *Administrative Law* (7th edn., Butterworths, London, 1989), 203–4; de Smith, Woolf and Jowell, *Judicial Review of Administrative Action* (5th ed. 1995), 593 *et seq.*

[9] See, as to Germany, M. P. Singh, *German Administrative Law in Common Law Perspective* (Springer Verlag, Berlin, 1985), 88–92; France—L. N. Brown and J. S. Bell, *French Administrative Law* (4th edn., Clarendon, Oxford, 1993), 218–20; the European Communities—L. N. Brown and F. G. Jacobs, *The Court of Justice of the European Communities* (3rd edn., Sweet and Maxwell, London, 1989), 295–8. See also J. Schwarze, *European Administrative Law* (Sweet and Maxwell, London, 1992), 677 ff.

[10] The *Laor* case, n. 6 above, 437–8. See also the *Levi* case, n. 6 above, 406–12.

[11] HC 344/89 *Ch. S.H. International Trade, Ltd* v. *Minister of Industry and Commerce* (1990) 44(1) PD 456. The Sup. Ct. held that in the exercise of power there should be a proper relationship between the purpose and the means, and that, in the circumstances of the case, the means employed, namely, cancellation of the import licence, were too extreme and therefore unnecessary and unjustified.

case should have, achieved his purpose through ordinary (as distinct from emergency) legislation.[12] Similarly, the Court has stated that it may examine whether security measures taken by a military commander in the territories occupied by Israel fit the severity of the situation.[13] Thus, only in exceptionally severe cases can a military commander order a house to be demolished, rather than confiscated or boarded up.[14]

In these and other cases the Supreme Court did not specifically refer to the doctrine of proportionality as the ground for review. However, in a recent case, proportionality finally won the recognition of the Court as a distinct ground of review.[15] In that case, the Court was asked to examine an order to demolish a house in which a terrorist convicted of murder resided. The order was issued by a military commander pursuant to his power under the Defence (Emergency) Regulations of 1945. However, another family also resided in that house. In the circumstances of the case, the Court was of the opinion that the demolition of the house would inflict disproportionate harm on that family. Therefore, the military commander was bound to pursue a less drastic course; he could not demolish the whole house, but could only board up part of it.[16]

Proportionality is an effective means to control administrative discretion and reduce the abuse of power. Now that it has been formally recognized by the Supreme Court as a ground of review, it may be expected to gather momentum and become one of the main instruments for judicial review of discretionary powers.

[12] HC 2994/90, *Knesset Member Poraz* v. *Government of Israel* (1990) 44(3) PD 317.

[13] HC 358/88 *The Association for Civil Rights in Israel* v. *Commander of the Central Command* (1989) 43(2) PD 529, 540.

[14] HC 361/82 *Hamri* v. *Commander of the Region of Judea and Samaria* (1982) 36(3) PD 439, 443; HC 5667/91, *Gabarim* v. *Commander of the Region of Judea and Samaria* (1992) 46(1) PD 858.

[15] HC 5510/92 *Turkman* v. *Minister of Defence* (1994) 48(1) PD 217.

[16] On this case, see Z. Segal, 'Security Measures, Administrative Proportionality and Judicial Review' (1992–3) 1 *Mishpat Ummimshal* 477 (Hebrew). See, also, Segal, 'Disproportionality in Administrative Law', 39 *Hapraklit* (1991) 507 (Hebrew). For recent decisions invalidating administrative decisions on the ground of disproportionality, see HC 987/94 *Euronet Golden Lines (1992) Ltd* v. *Minister of Communications* (1995) (as yet unpublished); HC 3477/95 *Ben Atya* v. *Minister of Education, Culture and Sport* (1995) (as yet unpublished).

# 28

# *Uri Ganor, Advocate and others*
# v.
# *The Attorney General*

[H.C. 935/89]
[44(2) PD 485 (1990)]

*Shamgar P, Barak J, and S. Levin J*

Israeli cases referred to:

[1] HC 910/86—*Ressler et al.* v. *Minister of Defence*; 42(2) PD441.
[2] HC 98/69—*Bergman* v. *Minister of Finance et al.*; 23(1) PD 693.
[3] HC 148/73—*Kaniel* v. *Minister of Justice*; 27(1) PD 794.
[4] HC 152/82—*Elon* v. *Government of Israel*; 36(4) PD 449.
[5] HC 463/86—*Barzilai* v. *Government of Israel*; 40(3) PD 505.
[6] HC 852, 869/86—*Aloni et al.* v. *Minister of Justice*; 41(2) PD 1.
[7] Cr.A 1/48—*Sylvester* v. *Attorney General*; 1 PD 5.
[8] HC 156/56—*Shore* v. *Attorney General*; 11 PD 285.
[9] HC 506/89—*Beeri* v. *Head of Prosecutions, Investigations Section, National Police Headquarters*; 44(1) PD 604.
[10] HC 650/82—*Beeri* v. *Attorney General et al.*; 37(4) PD 216.
[11] HC 665/79—*Weinograd* v. *Attorney General et al.*; 34(2) PD 634.
[12] HC 241/60—*Kardosh* v. *Registrar of Companies*; 15 PD 1151.
[13] FH 16/61—*Registrar of Companies* v. *Kardosh*; 16 PD 1209.
[14] HC 742/84—*Kahane* v. *Speaker of the Knesset*; 39(4) PD 85.
[15] HC 953/87, 1/88—*Poraz et al.* v. *Mayor of Tel Aviv-Yaffo*; 42(2) PD 309.
[16] HC 844/86—*Dotan* v. *Attorney General*; 41(3) PD 219.
[17] Cr.A 639,656/79—*Aflalu et al.* v. *State of Israel*; 34(3) PD 561.
[18] Cr.A 532/71—*Bahmutski* v. *State of Israel*; 26(1) PD 543.
[19] HC 218/85—*Arviv* v. *District Attorney's Office, Tel Aviv et al.*; 40(2) PD 393.
[20] Cr.A 192/79—*State of Israel* v. *Katsenstein Adler & Co. Ltd*; 34(2) PD 397, 412.
[21] HC 223/88—*Sheftel* v. *Attorney General et al.*; 43(4) PD 356.
[22] FH 10/69—*Boronovski* v. *Chief Rabbinate of Israel et al.*; 25(1) PD 7, 35.

[23] HC 425/89—*Tsofan et al.* v. *Chief Military Prosecutor*; 43(4) PD 718.
[24] HC 156/75—*Dakah et al.* v. *Minister of Transport*; 30(2) PD 94, 105.
[25] CA 243/83—*Municipality of Jerusalem* v. *Gordon*; 39(1) PD 113, 137.
[26] HC 389/80—*Dapei Zahav Ltd* v. *Broadcasting Authority*; 35(1) PD 421, 444.
[27] HC 14/86—*Leor et al.* v. *Council for the Censorship of Films and Plays*; 41(1) PD 421, 434.
[28] HC 292/86—*Haetzni* v. *State of Israel*; 42(4) PD 406.
[29] HC 74/69—*Anon.* v. *Disciplinary Court for State Employees et al.*; 23(2) PD 421, 427.
[30] HC 853/78—*Sharaf* v. *Central Committee of Tel Aviv Bar Association*; 33(1) PD 166, 168.
[31] HC 134/62—*Greenberg* v. *Attorney General et al.*; 16 PD 2896, 2897.
[32] HC 340/72—*Niniv* v. *State of Israel et al.*; 27(1) PD 325, 329.
[33] HC 119/59—*Reichbach* v. *Attorney General*; 13 PD 1486.
[34] HC 4/64—*Wagner* v. *Attorney General*; 18(1) PD 29, 31.
[35] HC 746/80—*Anon.* v. *State of Israel*; 35(2) PD 453, 455.
[36] HC 248/81—*Wallis* v. *Bar Association District Committee et al.*; 37(3) PD 533.
[37] HC 372/88—*Fuchs* v. *Chief Military Prosecutor et al.*; 42(3) PD 154, 155.
[38] HC 652/81—*Sarid* v. *Knesset Speaker*; 36(2) PD 197.
[39] HC 680/88—*Schnitzer et al.* v. *Chief Military Censor et al.*; 42(4) PD 617, 638-9.
[40] Cr.A 185/59—*Mataanah* v. *Attorney General*; 14 PD 970.
[41] HC 676/84—*Time Inc.* v. *Attorney General et al.*; 38 (4) PD 561, 566.
[42] HC 329/81—*Nof* v. *Attorney General et al.*; 37(4) PD 326, 334.

Australian cases referred to:

[43] *The Queen* v. *Collins* (1976) 50 Aust. L.J. 471.

American cases referred to:

[44] *Wayte* v. *United States*, 470 US 598, 608 (1985).

## JUDGMENT

**Barak J:**

On 12 November 1989, the Attorney General, Mr Yosef Harish, decided that 'I do not see a public interest in returning and once again imposing on the public the cost and the nuisance and the strain of yet another round in the bank shares affair.' Thus, it was decided, regarding the accountants, to bring the matter before the Accountants' Council in order to ensure a full and comprehensive investigation. Is there a legal basis for this decision or should it be invalidated? These are the questions to be decided in the petition before us.

## *The Conflict*

1. At the beginning of October 1983 a major crisis hit the Tel Aviv–Jaffa Stock Exchange. Investors rushed to sell off their bank shares but the banks did not have the financial wherewithal to absorb such a run on their shares. Consequently, trading on the Stock Exchange was brought to a halt. A severe crisis threatened the whole banking system and investors stood to be seriously harmed. Following Government intervention, an arrangement was worked out between the Government and the banks whereby the Government undertook to buy up these shares, at various fixed intervals, for their value at the point when trading on the Stock Exchange had been interrupted. In this way the value of the bank shares was secured. However, an immense financial burden was placed both on the Government and on the general public.

* * *

These events were the subject of a report which the State Comptroller presented to the Knesset Committee on Reviewing State Affairs. Following section 14(b) of the State Comptroller (Consolidated Version) Law, 1958, the Committee decided to set up a commission of inquiry, to be headed by Beiski J. The Beiski Commission submitted its findings a year later. It set out the various factors leading to the bank share crisis, named those responsible, and made recommendations for the future regarding both individuals and institutions. According to its findings, the crisis was the direct, or at least the probable result of a phenomenon referred to as the 'rigging' of bank shares. The 'rigging' referred to here was described as a series of transactions made either directly or indirectly by the banks, aimed at turning bank shares into much sought-after, valuable securities, without reflecting the true financial state of the banks. Among other things, the banks avoided disclosing details of the rigging process and even, in certain instances, included misleading information in their financial reports. Clerks gave advice to the public in such a way as to serve the 'rigging' interests of the banks, prevailing upon customers to take out credit to purchase bank shares, or making the granting of credit conditional on buying bank shares.

* * *

Based on its findings, the Beiski Commission indicated that the activities of the banks and their officers had been in apparent breach of the law. On the strength of this, the Commission's report was passed on to the Attorney General ('the respondent'). The respondent approached the Israeli Police with a request to check those areas requiring investigation. At the end of the police inquiry and after several months on the case, the respondent decided not to prosecute the relevant banks and bank officials. As to the accountants responsible for preparing and approving the bank reports, the respondent decided that the matter ought to be referred for investigation to the Auditors' Council.

* * *

At the root of the respondent's decision lay the consideration that it was not in the public interest to prosecute the banks and bank officials. In the opinion of the respondent, the absence of a public interest arose from a number of secondary considerations: that the bank officials concerned had already been made accountable for their actions; that responsibility for the share rigging did not only lie with the banks and the bank officials but also with the State authorities, the Securities Authority, and the Stock Exchange (all of whom had known what the banks were doing but had remained silent nevertheless, thus allowing the situation to deteriorate); and finally, that the amount of time that had elapsed since the crimes attributed to the banks and bank officials reduced any reopening of the discussion of the share rigging to arriving, inevitably, at 'that same punitive end'.

Hence the petition. The petitioners argue that the respondent's decision should be invalidated because of its inherent unreasonableness. The respondent argues, *inter alia*, that the petitioners do not have standing in this case.

2–21. * * *

## *The Questions of Law*

22. There are three main questions of law here: first, do the petitioners have standing? Secondly, was there a flaw in the considerations of the Attorney General in arriving at his decision? In examining this question we shall have to look at the extent of the Attorney General's discretion: what factors he is bound to take into consideration and the weight to be given to each of these factors and hence, in this particular episode, whether the appropriate factors were in fact taken into account. If we determine that they were not, then our third question arises: the extent of this court's intervention in the discretion of the Attorney General. In dealing with this

question we shall have to examine the grounds for the High Court of Justice intervening in the discretion of the Attorney General, and the redress this Court grants the petitioner who shows proper grounds for such intervention.

## *Standing*

23. Dr Cheshin has argued here that the petitioners are without legal standing in this case, and that therefore their petition should be dismissed. The argument was not raised by the Attorney General, and is, in any case, unfounded. The petitioners do have legal standing, satisfying both the 'classic' rules for standing, the approach that would accept recognized exceptions to the classic rules, and also the 'liberal' approach to standing. (For an analysis of these approaches see *Ressler* v. *Minister of Defence* [1]). . . .

* * *

First under the classic rules: some of the petitioners owned bank shares which were subject to the rigging process and whose value was severely affected by the crisis. In this, it would seem to me, the petitioners have the necessary 'interest' to support standing in its classic sense. Secondly, under the recognized exceptions to the classic rules, whereby the standing of a petitioner is recognized when his petition raises a problem of a 'clear constitutional nature': it would seem to me that just such a problem has been raised in the petition before us. The question of the public interest in applying the criminal law, on the one hand, and the proper value to attach to a recommendation by a commission of inquiry, on the other, are questions of a 'clear constitutional character', as the principle has been interpreted and applied in the case law. (See *Bergman* v. *Minister of Finance* [2] (on the question of the funding of political parties); *Kaniel* v. *Minister of Justice* [3] (funding political parties); *Elon* v. *Government of Israel* [4] (setting up commissions of inquiry under the Commissions of Inquiry Law); *Barzilai* v. *Government of Israel* [5] (on the President's power to grant pardons).) And finally under the 'liberal approach', one instance where a petitioner's right of standing will be recognized is when his petition raises a matter of a public nature with a direct bearing on the rule of law. Under this approach, the standing of a petitioner (without an 'interest') is not limited solely to his being able to pinpoint a problem of a 'clear constitutional nature'. It will be recognized whenever 'the matter raised in his petition is of a definite public nature with a direct bearing on the advancement and preservation of the Rule of Law', and indeed in all matters 'of an exceptional legal character touching the very foundations of the rule of law' (my colleague President Shamgar in *Aloni* v. *Minister of Justice* [6], at 25–6 and 23). The present petitions come within this category. The problem of the Attorney General's discretion as it relates to filing criminal charges for the alleged crimes in the share rigging episode—an episode that led to the setting up of a commission of inquiry under the Commissions of Inquiry Law—unquestionably gives rise to a problem which both is public in nature and has a direct bearing on the rule of law.

Thus, however one looks at it, the petitioners before us have the necessary standing. I would add that under the Criminal Procedure Law (Consolidated version), 5742–1982, anyone may submit a complaint to the police regarding commission of a crime (section 58), and a decision not to prosecute may be subject to an appeal to the Attorney General (section 64); having been granted 'standing' before the Attorney General, such a potential appellant would automatically have standing before this Court. We may now, therefore, enter 'the chamber where crime and punishment are adjudicated' (President Zmoira in *Sylvester* v. *Attorney General* [7], at 19), and examine the first question of law before us (that of the discretion of the Attorney General). Thereafter we shall examine the second question of law here (that of the scope of review of the High Court of Justice), and ask whether, in the light of this latter question, we should not in fact step back out, back from the chamber into the ante-chamber.

## *Prosecutor's Authority and Discretion in the Decision to Prosecute*

24. The criminal law is designed to maintain and preserve appropriate forms of societal existence and public order as well as the values and principles upon which these are based. In the vast majority of cases the very existence of such societal norms, and the presence of those values and principles on which they are founded, are sufficient in themselves to ensure that the precepts of the criminal law are adhered to. In addition there is the power of deterrence in the sanctions that follow from a breach of the criminal law. When an individual is deemed to have broken the criminal law, there is a resultant conflict between such an individual and organized society in the form of the State. It is then felt necessary to release the hitherto mere potential of a deterrent force into the realm of the concrete and the real, all of which:

> in order to protect the social fabric, endangered by the possible repetition of the crime by this criminal or other, potential criminals, who, in addition to the warning embodied in the law itself, need the more palpable warning of actual punishment imposed on the criminal who has broken the law. (S. Z. Feller, 'The Foundations of Criminal Law' (The Harry Sacher Institute for Legislative Research and Comparative Law, Vol. 1, 1974–5, 108).

In this way it is also possible to ensure that, in addition to the deterrent aspect of punishment (both general and individual), other, more concrete, goals may be realized, such as the treatment and rehabilitation of offenders, as well as giving vent to the legal-moral sensibilities of the general public.

25. The criminal law is effected by means of the criminal process. The accuser and the body responsible for bringing charges is the State (The Criminal Procedure Law (Consolidated version), section 11), represented by a Prosecutor. The Chief Prosecutor is the Attorney General (section 12(a)(1) ). This was underlined by Agranat J in *Shore* v. *Attorney General* ([8], at 301) when he noted that:

> To protect the public interest, control over the criminal process, in terms of its continued operation or interruption, will always lie with the sovereign power, viz., its representative, the Attorney General, who has been entrusted with safeguarding that interest.

The Prosecutor's authority to prosecute stems from section 62 of the Criminal Procedure Law (Consolidated version) which states:

> If the Prosecutor to whom the results of the investigation have been passed, considers the evidence sufficient to convict a particular individual, then he shall proceed with the prosecution, unless he determines that there would be no public interest in a trial.

According to this section, the filing of a criminal indictment is dependent upon two separate conditions, a 'positive' condition, and a 'negative' one. The 'positive' condition is that the Prosecutor considers there to be sufficient evidence to convict. The evidence referred to here is *prima facie* evidence, viz. evidence that is admissible and which, in the Prosecutor's view, has the capacity to bring about a conviction of the accused. The 'negative' condition is that the Prosecutor does not consider an absence of public interest in a trial. This latter condition presupposes the existence of *prima facie* evidence and concerns itself with a lack of public interest in convicting and sentencing the accused. Hence the existence of *prima facie* evidence is a prerequisite, but not in itself sufficient, to proceeding with a criminal prosecution.

> The prosecutor is not always obliged to press charges whenever there is *prima facie* evidence of a crime having been committed. It is left to his discretion. He can decide not to prosecute if he considers that to do so would not be in the public interest. (*Beeri* v. *Head of Prosecutions* [9])

The decision of the Attorney General in the matter before us concerned both these conditions. Nevertheless, from the wording of his decision and from the explanations presented before us, it is clear that the central thrust of the Attorney General's remarks concerned the question of the 'public interest'. I therefore propose to deal first with the whole question here of the authority of the Attorney General under section 62 of The Criminal Procedure Law (Consolidated version). Thereafter, I will examine the decision of the Attorney General as it concerns the existence of *prima facie* evidence.

## *Prosecutorial Discretion on the Question of 'the Public Interest'*

26. Section 62 of The Criminal Procedure Law (Consolidated version), which makes the presenting of a criminal charge conditional on the Prosecutor determining that there would be no public interest in going to trial, confers on the Prosecutor governmental power, involving the exercise of some discretion. The scope of this discretion is 'extremely broad' (Kahan P in *Beeri* v. *Attorney General* [10], at 218). It has been described as an 'almost absolute discretion' (Witkon J in *Weinograd* v. *Attorney General et al.* [11], at 637). And yet, despite it being very broad indeed, it is *not* absolute discretion. As Powell J rightly remarked in *Wayte* v. *United States* [44], '[a]lthough prosecutorial discretion is broad, it is not "unfettered" '.

In a democratic State no arm of government can be said to have absolute discretion. All governmental discretion is limited. (See *Kardosh* v. *Registrar of Companies* [12]; *Registrar of Companies* v. *Kardosh* [13]; *Kahane* v. *Speaker of Knesset* [14], at 91.) It is limited to the purposes and goals for which it was instituted. Indeed, 'the law's finest hour is when it sets limits to governmental discretion' (*Poraz et al.* v. *Mayor of Tel Aviv–Yaffo* [15], at 325). Nor is the Prosecutorial Office an exception here. Prosecutorial discretion is governmental discretion, having a judicial aspect and limited to the confines of the Criminal Procedure Law (Consolidated version) (see *Dotan* v. *Attorney General* [16], at 226). In addition to the Criminal Procedure Law, and acting in tandem with it, the exercise of this discretion is governed by the general provisions of administrative law. It therefore behoves the prosecutor, in arriving at his decision, to take only relevant factors into consideration. He is bound to act in good faith, fairly, reasonably, and without prejudice.

What are the parameters of that discretion which must guide the prosecutor and how should it be properly exercised? These are the questions which we must deal with now.

## *The Purpose of 'the Public Interest'*

27. What are those parameters within which the consideration of 'the public interest' can act to stop the course of a criminal prosecution, despite the existence of *prima facie* evidence? Our starting point must be the substantive provisions of criminal law. These

reflect the need of the organised society to protect those values essential to its proper functioning and development in keeping with whatever beliefs govern it at any given time. (S. Z. Feller. *op. cit.,* at 1).

Society has seen fit to establish a set of prohibitions so that anyone transgressing these can then expect the sanction meted out by that society. These prohibitions are intended to direct the day-to-day life of the individual. When the individual breaks them, the prohibitions then serve as the basis for the sanctions that are bound up with them. Implementing such sanctions is done by means of the rules of criminal procedure which are designed to put into effect the substantive provisions of criminal law.

The criminal process is in fact a set of norms, arranged and coordinated so as to put into effect the substantive provisions of criminal law. (*Aflalu et al.* v. *State of Israel* [17], at 575)

In theory, one could argue that every one of the provisions of the substantive criminal law is vital to protect the values of our society, and that, consequently, any breach of these would justify setting in motion the entire machinery of the criminal process—viz: investigation, prosecution, and finally the court's ruling on the guilt or innocence of the accused. This is not our approach. The law recognizes the fact that not all the provisions of the criminal law are of the same level of importance nor are all crimes carried out in similar circumstances. The law accepts that prosecuting because of the harm done to certain interests sometimes involves harming other interests. The law takes account of the fact that criminal investigation and prosecution can have far-reaching consequences for the lives of both suspect and complainant. The law also understands that the machinery of law enforcement must work under various constraints, which greatly hampers the full implementation of the substantive criminal law.

In view of all of the above, the law has empowered the prosecutor not to prosecute a suspect, despite the existence of *prima facie* evidence of his having committed a crime, if, in the opinion of the prosecutor, such a prosecution would not be in 'the public interest'. In this way an element of flexibility has been incorporated into the process. Nor is this a bad thing. For it allows the prosecutor to take into account all the circumstances of the case and to determine whether pressing ahead with a criminal charge would best serve those ends which the criminal law was designed to achieve. (See C. D. Breitel, 'Controls in Criminal Law Enforcement' 27 *UChic.LRev.* 427 (1960).) Thus, there would be no 'public interest' in proceeding with a prosecution where the good that might accrue from such a prosecution to the values and principles which the criminal law was designed to protect, is outweighed by the harm that would be inflicted on those same values and principles from such a prosecution. Looking at it from the point of view of the suspect, we might say that there would be no 'public interest' in prosecuting where the harm that would be inflicted on the public interest (comprising both that of the general public as well as that of the particular suspect), in the event of a prosecution, outweighed the possible good that might accrue to the public interest (which would also include that of the suspect himself) from such a prosecution. (See A. Ashworth, 'The Public Interest Element in Prosecutions' [1987] *Crim.LRev.* 595, 598.)

Our essential starting point must therefore be, that once the law has determined that a certain type of behaviour is to be regarded as criminal, there exists a definite public interest in prosecuting the suspect of such a crime. This is in order to protect those values and principles which the State wishes to protect and which the suspect has allegedly violated, and to prevent such a violation from happening again. There may be circumstances, however, which point to the harm that would be inflicted on other interests and values (which the law is no less concerned about), if the suspect were to be prosecuted. It is only when the public interest in not prosecuting outweighs the public interest in proceeding with a prosecution that the prosecutor is entitled to infer a definite public interest in not prosecuting.

28. The term 'public interest' here does not refer to the interest the general public may show in the matter of a particular prosecution. It is a normative rather than a descriptive term. It denotes an evaluation of the good that will accrue to the social fabric as a result of prosecuting, as set against the harm that might ensue from this, and the good that might result from not prosecuting. Thus, only when the prosecutor is absolutely convinced that prosecuting would bring about a harm to those interests and values which society wishes to protect, so great as to outweigh whatever good might accrue from a prosecution to the interests and values which the criminal law is intended to serve, does there exist a definite public interest in not prosecuting a suspect.

In the Report of the Lawyers' Committee on the Powers of the Attorney General ('The Agranat Committee'), on page 7, we read:

> The term 'the public interest' in this context means that the prosecutor is bound to take the following into account before making a decision on whether to prosecute an individual:
>
> (a) The general good requires, as a matter of course, that whoever breaks the law be punished, whether because of the damage he may have caused or because of the consideration that 'one crime leads to another'.
> (b) Opposed to this is the public consideration—closely linked with the private interest of the individual—not to allow groundless accusations to be brought.
> (c) Justice sometimes requires that, because of the special circumstances of a particular case, we refrain from punishing an individual who has committed a crime, even when to do so may not accord with the exact letter of the law.

(d) In certain circumstances, in a matter which contains elements of state security and public policy, it may be necessary not to proceed with a prosecution.

The prosecutor is thus in the business of calculating net gains and losses. He must weigh all the considerations pointing to the existence of a public interest in proceeding with a prosecution against those considerations pointing to a public interest in refraining from a prosecution. Only when the scales are tipped in favour of not prosecuting can it be said that there exists a definite public interest in not prosecuting a suspect. The starting point should always be that, once an act has been designated a crime, the interest of the public lies in prosecuting one suspected of having broken the law. However, there may be other considerations which may tip the scales towards a position where, in the particular circumstances of the case, the interest of the public lies in not prosecuting. In all of this, the following factors, *inter alia*, should be borne in mind: the gravity of the crime, the personal circumstances both of the accused and of the victim, and also the institutional considerations of the Prosecutor's office and the courts. I will deal with these briefly.

The first of these is the gravity of the crime. The more serious the crime attributed to the suspect, the greater the public interest in prosecuting. As the crime becomes less serious, so the public interest in prosecuting diminishes. The seriousness of a crime may be measured by a number of different factors. For example, the seriousness of the crime as set out in the statute, measured by the punishment set down in the statute, serves as an indication of how seriously the law views such an act. In addition, the circumstances in which a particular crime was committed will have a bearing on the seriousness of the crime. We should look at the extent of the damage the crime may have caused to the general public or a part of it, and also at how common such criminal behaviour may be. The destructive effect of the crime, on the fabric of society and on its proper governance, will also serve as an indicator of its seriousness. In this context we should look, on the one hand, at the period of time over which the criminal acts went on and, on the other, at the amount of time that has elapsed since the crime was committed. The longer the crime went on the stronger the case becomes for prosecuting. On the other hand, while the crime may have been a serious one at the time it was committed, over the course of time its particular seriousness may have become dulled.

The second consideration—often equally as important as the first—is the individual circumstances of the suspect. In this regard the following should be considered: the age and state of health of the suspect; his criminal record and attempts made at his rehabilitation; what he may have endured prior to and since committing the crime; how far he has co-operated in the investigation; administrative actions brought against him in the past and the sanctions levelled against him. All the above will provide some indication of the effect criminal proceedings will have on the suspect. When that effect is perceived as negative or destructive, there may be grounds for a public interest in not proceeding with a prosecution. A further set of considerations relates to the victim of the crime. The more serious the injury inflicted on him, and the less reparable the harm, the more weighty will be the public interest in prosecuting. On the other hand when the harm suffered by the victim is slight, or when the victim adopts a conciliatory view, or when some satisfactory arrangement has been worked out between suspect and victim, in such circumstances one would be inclined to infer a lack of public interest in prosecuting. A further set of considerations are unconnected to the seriousness of the crime or the circumstances of suspect or victim, but relate instead to other vital interests of the State. As has been rightly observed:

> In certain circumstances, where matters of state security or public policy are involved it may be necessary not to proceed with a criminal prosecution. (from 'Report of Lawyers' Committee on the Powers of the Attorney General')

Similarly, there will be times when proceeding with a prosecution, designed to safeguard those values and interests which the criminal law seeks to protect (such as judicial integrity or faith in the judicial process), will actually do harm to other values and interests important to society (such as freedom of speech). At such times, society's general interest is likely to lessen the force of the public interest in proceeding with a prosecution.

Finally, there are the institutional considerations—the Prosecution and the courts. The public interest in convicting one person is likely to provide the grounds for a different public interest in not prosecuting someone else, or for prosecuting for a lesser offence. Hence the interest to the public in plea bargaining or in the phenomenon known as 'state witnesses'. (See *Bahmutski* v. *State of Israel* [18]; *Arviv* v. *District Attorney's Office*, *Tel Aviv et al.* [19].) Another institutional consideration relates both to the Prosecutor's Office and to the courts. The manpower available to the Prosecutor's Office is limited. It should be used advisedly, taking into consideration the incidence of crime as a whole. And a list of priorities should be agreed upon. (See *State of Israel* v. *Katsenstein Adler & Co. Ltd* [20], at 412; *Sheftel* v. *Attorney General et al.* [21].) In a similar vein, there is a shortage of time required for adjudicating cases. Judicial time is limited and, consequently, priorities must be determined for its proper use.

The proper weight to be given to these considerations will depend on the weight given to others. For example, when the crime is a serious one, the harm inflicted on the victim is also serious and the individual circumstances of suspect and victim unexceptional, then public interest demands that the suspect be prosecuted, and the Prosecutor's Office will then have to find the necessary manpower, and the courts the necessary time, for such a prosecution.

### *Exercising Judgment on the Question of 'the Public Interest'*

29. I have dealt with the various factors the Prosecutor must take into consideration when deciding on the 'public interest' in prosecuting. The decision is not a difficult one when all considerations point to one end. In that event the way is clear for the Prosecutor to determine the existence or otherwise of a 'public interest' in proceeding with a prosecution. Often, however, the various considerations will point in different directions. Thus, for example, the seriousness of the crime is likely to point to the existence of a public interest in prosecuting, while the personal circumstances of the suspect point to the opposite. Here the Prosecutor is faced with having to decide between competing considerations. The decision must be made in line with standard administrative law doctrine on the use of judgment. The Prosecutor must reach his decision by first weighing the relevant factors, and these alone. His decision must be made in good faith and not be arbitrary or show prejudice of any kind; and it must be made fairly and reasonably. I would like to deal with three of these administrative law rules over which various pleas have been raised before us here. They are: extraneous factors, non-prejudice, and reasonableness.

### *Extraneous Factors and the Independence of Judgment*

30. The Prosecutor does not have absolute discretion on the question of the 'public interest'. This means, *inter alia*, that in exercising his judgment he is not entitled to consider whatever consideration he chooses. Alongside those factors which he may take into account and which determine the parameters of his discretion, there are others which are outside these parameters. For example, he may not take into consideration anything relating to the suspect's political, religious, or ethnic affiliation.

The prosecutor who holds back from laying criminal charges against a suspect merely because the latter's political views appeal to him is taking extraneous factors into account, which he is prohibited from doing. The same would be true if the prosecutor decided to prosecute a suspect merely because he did not like the suspect's political views. Furthermore, in exercising his judgement, the Prosecutor must be free of any external influence. Even when he has to consult with different government bodies before deciding whether or not to prosecute, the final decision must be his and his alone. Thus, for example, before deciding whether or not to prosecute, the Attorney General may and sometimes must consult with the Justice Minister or with the Prime Minister on the proper use of his authority. But the final decision will be his.

## *Impartiality in Exercising Prosecutorial Authority*

31. In using his discretion, the Prosecutor must be completely impartial. Equality is a value of fundamental importance to any democratic society, a value 'which, out of justice and fairness, the Law of any democratic society aspires to affirm.' (President Agranat in *Boronovski* v. *Chief Rabbinate of Israel et al.* [22], at 35). In a previous case, I dealt with the reasons for the importance of this value, explaining as follows:

> The individual becomes a part of the general fabric, and plays his part in building his society, knowing that others are doing the same. The need to ensure equality is a natural thing, stemming as it does from such factors as justice and fairness. One who would have others recognise his right must in turn recognise the right of others to seek similar recognition. The need to maintain equality is essential to society and to the consensus on which society is built.
>
> Equality prevents arbitrariness in government. There can be no force more destructive to society than the feeling of its members that they are being arbitrarily dealt with. The sense that people are being treated unequally is one of the most difficult to bear. It undermines those forces that unite society, and the self identity of the individual. (*Poraz* [15], at 332)

The above statement is especially true of the exercise of prosecutorial authority in filing criminal charges. The proper implementation of the criminal process derives from the trust that the public has in the prosecuting authorities and the belief that equality underlies their decisions. Instituting criminal proceedings in anything but an impartial fashion harms the public's trust in the prosecuting authorities, raising severe difficulties for a democratic regime. These difficulties are threefold: one, a non-impartial exercise of prosecutorial authority undermines those assumptions which are behind the granting of prosecutorial discretion. Two, inequality in the filing of criminal charges undermines the trust that the public have placed in the Prosecutor in particular, and in the authorities in general, and leads to a complete breakdown of the complex web of consensus that unites the members of a society. Three, an unequal implementation of prosecutorial authority undermines the deterrent force of the criminal law. These considerations were encapsulated in a directive issued by the Attorney General, Directive 50.050 of 1 January 1972, quoted by agreement by Beiski J in *Tsofan et al.* v. *Chief Military Prosecutor* [23], at 735:

> damage to the public interest does not necessarily mean that a particular criminal, who is not to be prosecuted, is going to commit another crime. It also connotes the harm done to the public faith that justice is being done and that the authorities are not acting arbitrarily (the rule that not only must justice be done but it

must also be seen to be done is not only a rule of thumb in the professional parlance of lawyers, it is a practical and essential yardstick for the people's representatives responsible for implementing the law). The object of implementing the law is not just the punishing of criminals, it is also the prevention of further crimes, and there can be no such prevention or deterrence when the public have lost their faith in the activities of the authorities responsible for implementing the law.

Hence the importance of determining in advance prosecutorial policy with regard to filing criminal charges and to the 'public interest' in not filing them. This would provide clear indications as to the position taken by the Prosecutor and would ensure not only an impartial implementation of prosecutorial authority, but also that such impartiality would be seen to exist.

## *Reasonableness of Judgement*

32. As with the discretion of any government body, the exercise of judgement by the Prosecutor in deciding whether or not to prosecute must be reasonable. The concept of reasonableness is neither a physical nor a metaphysical concept; it is a normative one. Reasonableness means weighing all the relevant factors, giving each proper weight. Shamgar J underlined this point in *Dakah et al.* v. *Minister of Transport* [24], when he said:

There may be situations when the ministerial body has not taken any extraneous factors into account and has confined itself solely to relevant factors, yet there has been such a distortion and a lack of proportion in the weight given to these that the final result cannot possibly hold up and is, therefore, completely unreasonable.

We are used to resolving the question of reasonableness by referring to the 'reasonable man' or the 'reasonable man in government'. We have indicated at times that the reasonable man is none other than the court itself. (*Municipality of Jerusalem* v. *Gordon* [25]; see also Y. Shachar, 'The Reasonable Man and the Criminal Law' (1989–90) 39 *Hapraklit* 78). These are merely metaphors for reasonableness. Reasonableness is not a personal attribute here but a substantive thing. It is not the reasonableness of the person making the decision that makes a decision reasonable, but rather it is the reasonableness of the decision that makes the decision-maker reasonable. The reasonableness or otherwise of a decision is determined by the inner weight given to the central factors that formed it (see *Dapei Zahav Ltd* v. *Broadcasting Authority* [26]). Professor MacCormick underlined this point when he wrote:

What justifies resorting to the requirement of reasonableness is the existence of a plurality of factors requiring to be evaluated in respect of their relevance to a common focus of concern (in this case a decision). Unreasonableness consists in ignoring some relevant factor or factors, in treating as relevant what ought to be ignored. Alternatively, it may involve some gross distortion of the relative values of different factors, even though different people can come to different evaluations each of which falls within the range of reasonable opinions in the matter in hand. (MacCormick, 'On Reasonableness', in C. Perelman and R. Vander Elst (eds.), *Les Notions à Contenu Variable en Droit* (1984) 131, 136)

We may see, therefore, that there is no such thing as reasonableness 'in and of itself'. As Landau P has correctly noted, 'One cannot set up pre-arranged determiners for reasonableness by which a decision taken after the exercise of administrative discretion might be measured . . . since the test of reasonableness does not provide . . . a hard and fast rule' (M. Landau, 'On Judiciousness and Reasonableness in Administrative Law' (1989) 14 *Iyunei Mishpat* 5, 11, 12). Reasonableness will always be a function of the relevant factors and of the appropriate relative weight to be given to each. The concept of reasonableness presupposes a pluralistic approach, one which accepts the existence of a number of appropriate factors and which seeks to balance these by attributing the right weight to the inner relations that exist between each factor (see G. Fletcher, 'The Right and the Reasonable', 98 *Harv.LRev.* 848, 980. (1985) ). The 'appropriateness' of the weight to be given the relevant factors is determined by their capacity to further the goals that are at the heart of the action (or decision) whose reasonableness is under scrutiny. This 'proper weight' is not some natural phenomenon inherent in the relevant factors. Nor can it be established by logical deduction. As Professor Stone has correctly indicated, the concept of reasonableness is a legal category of indeterminate reference, for, in its application, facts alone are insufficient; we require evaluations and the attributing of the appropriate weight to competing factors (see J. Stone, *Legal System and Lawyer's Reasonings* (Stanford, 1964), 263). Thus 'the proper weight' is an evaluation to what extent the various factors serve to advance the goals which the action (or decision) is designed to achieve (see *Leor* v. *Council for the Censorship of Films and Plays* [27], at 434). I dealt with this point in *Dapei Zahav* ([26], at 445) when I stated:

The Administration must balance the different interests in line with the general norm, as set down by the Law. This balancing is reasonable, if the relevant Authority attributes the appropriate weight (i.e. the weight that is warranted by an interpretation of the legal norm which the Administration is putting into effect) to the different interests that are to be taken into account.

Sometimes the goals, which the action is designed to achieve, can be advanced in different ways. At such times there are likely to be a number of different 'weights' appropriate to the inner relation that exists between the relevant factors behind the action. As a result we would find a situation where a number of actions may be deemed reasonable, without any one of them having priority over the others, leading to what may be termed 'a range of reasonableness', i.e. a number of options, each one reasonable in itself, fulfilling the conditions that only relevant factors are to be considered, and that each factor is to be given its proper weight in relation to the others (see *Dapei Zahav* [26], at 445). In such circumstances an action will be deemed unreasonable only when the weight that it gives to certain factors is so distorted that the action or decision cannot possibly further the goals it was intended to.

33. What is a reasonable decision in the realm of 'public interest'? The answer: the decision which takes account of all the relevant factors, and which attributes to these the weight likely to mean that the good that will accrue from the decision to the values and principles which the criminal law is intended to serve, outweighs the harm that might be caused to those values and principles. Mansfield and Peay outlined this point as follows:

> Decision-making on grounds of public interest recognises that competing values within any complex society must be reconciled. Thus the prosecutor's extra legal considerations involve the balancing of different types of harm: the harm done, or avoided as a result of prosecutorial action or inaction. The balance striven for may be characterised as pursuit of a society's 'net interest' in whatever issue is under consideration. (G. Mansfield and J. Peay, *The Director of Public Prosecutions* (1987) 27)

It is only natural that in this area there are going to be a number of possible options, all of them reasonable. A decision will be unreasonable here only when the prosecutor attributes so distorted a weight to the factors involved that, in any of the possible options that follow from the objectives central to the 'public interest' requirement, the harm likely to result to the values and principles which the criminal law seeks to serve outweighs the good likely to accrue to such values and principles. We find, therefore, a 'range' of options, all of which are reasonable, for the existence or absence of a 'public interest'. Addressing the question of the 'public interest' in *Haetzni* v. *State of Israel* [28], at 412, Bach J correctly pointed out that it is 'a flexible quantity allowing different and sometimes opposing approaches, each one legitimate'.

Hence the opinion of Agranat J that the concept 'the public interest' was 'extremely broad' (see *Shore* [8], at 300). And yet the range of possible legal options is not unlimited; there are decisions which fall outside it. For example, in *Tsofan* [23], where an army officer suspected of having given an order (allegedly exceeding his powers in doing so) likely to endanger human life and in gross violation of the law, the Prosecutor decided not to prosecute, principally because the officer concerned had been forced to resign from the army as a result of the incident. This Court decided that the Prosecutor's decision showed extreme unreasonableness and was, furthermore, inherently distorted. In that particular calculation of net gains and losses therefore, the decision of the Prosecutor not to prosecute produced a harm to those interests and values which the criminal law sought to protect, not equal to the good that might have accrued to those interests from the decision.

## *From the General to the Particular*

34. Against this background of general principles, we must now examine the decision of the Attorney General. I will begin with the question of extraneous considerations and unlawful external influence. After having studied all the material, I am satisfied that the Attorney General did not take extraneous considerations into account. On this question the Attorney General himself remarked, on page 3 of his decision:

> As for myself, I can only say that in reaching my decision I was guided solely by considerations related to the matter at hand, considerations of justice being done and being seen to be done, and considerations related to the public good. In arriving at my decision I was compelled to make an enormous effort to ignore completely the criticism and pre-judging that filled the print and electronic news media. These, rather than dealing with the issue at hand—an unexceptionable activity—busied themselves instead with personality issues such as the status of the Attorney General and the measure of his resolve.
>
> By contrast, even if a word here or there reached my ear, with hints and implicit suggestions on behalf of the potential accused parties, the overall effect was insignificant. In short, I have never been guided other than by the duties of my mission which I have always endeavoured to fulfil considering both the good of the issue at hand, and the individual and public interests. I have never been in the least impressed by either the position or the financial status of the banks, the heads of the banks or their associates. Had the issue at hand involved the humblest and the poorest of the nation, I would have arrived at the same decision. And while I abhor the kind of base calumny directed at myself, clothed in ordinary criticism which on its own is quite legitimate, there was nothing in such attacks to influence in any way the view I took of the issue at hand and the various considerations involved.

No evidence has been brought before us that would refute the above. The Attorney General was faced with a particularly difficult question. He took into account the relevant considerations and refrained from considering any extraneous factors. The independence and integrity of the Attorney General's discretion remained constant throughout.

35. What of the principle of equality in the Attorney General's decision? No data have been brought before us as to similar incidents of this type. The distinct impression we have formed, however, is that there cannot have been many cases in which the suspects (the banks and bank officers), having allegedly committed serious offences in circumstances such as these and over an extended period of time (particularly as regards the securities

related offences), causing immense harm to thousands of private investors and to the State Treasury, would not in the end be prosecuted. From this point of view the case before us is exceptional. In fact it is hard to avoid the impression that, while the banks and bank officers, who allegedly committed the most serious offences and caused almost incalculable harm, are not to be prosecuted, persons suspected of far lesser offences causing far less real harm are being brought to trial daily. Such an impression leads one to conclude that the application of the authority to prosecute is inequitable. It is an impression that is strengthened in the light of the conclusions of the Beiski Commission, whose practical bottom line is a recommendation to prosecute. Now, while a recommendation from a Public Commission cannot of itself bring about a prosecution, there is, nonetheless, the uncomfortable feeling that remains of inequity. Such a feeling is a difficult one for a society to bear and is perilous to the confidence the public has in the authorities in general and in the Prosecutor's Office in particular. However, in the absence of sufficient data on similar cases, we will refrain from affirming that the decision of the Attorney General showed unlawful discrimination.

36. In our view the real fault in the decision of the Attorney General lies in the inherent unreasonableness of its conclusion that there was no 'public interest' in prosecuting the banks and the bank officers. It would be true to say that the Attorney General did not take any extraneous factors into account and only considered relevant factors. Nevertheless the weight given to the various factors oversteps the range of reasonableness and, as a result, a decision was reached on the absence of a 'public interest' that grossly distorts the appropriate weight to be given to those factors. The offences attributed to the banks and bank officers—and I am thinking here particularly of the securities related offences—are extremely serious ones given the circumstances of the case. The criminal activity attributed to them continued over an extended period of time. It was carried out in secret. It resulted in grievous harm being inflicted on many thousands of ordinary citizens, who lost their savings, and on the State Treasury which was compelled to make vast amounts of money available as part of the arrangement reached with the banks, the effect of which on the country's economy was severe. All this creates the weightiest of considerations for prosecuting. The public interest in punishing those responsible and in providing a proper deterrence for banks, bank officers, and other forces in the financial markets is very great. If the earthquake produced by the share rigging episode does not lead to a prosecution, when *will* there be justification for prosecuting banks and bank officers allegedly responsible for securities related offences? The different considerations which the Attorney General cited do not adequately balance the picture. We shall now examine these in turn.

37. The Attorney General, in his decision that there was no 'public interest' in prosecuting, gave great weight to the fact that the suspects had already paid for their acts at the administrative and public levels, as evinced by the fact that the decision of the Beiski Commission had 'imposed severe sanctions on them, involving dismissal from office and being thrown out of the banking profession'. Furthermore, the Attorney General noted, the Beiski Commission itself had brought the unlawful practices to public notice and, in doing so, had punished the banks and provided the necessary deterrence. Such considerations are faulty as they relate to the banks themselves. No sanctions were imposed on the banks, neither dismissal from office nor being thrown out from anywhere. In our view, these considerations are partially correct with regards to the bank officers, but their weight, in the circumstances, cannot be significant. A sanction imposed at the administrative level may well lessen the weight of public interest in prosecuting when the offence is not a serious one and when the result of such a sanction is sufficient deterrence against the individual suspect and against other potential offenders. However, the administrative sanction is incapable of lessening significantly the public interest in prosecuting, when the alleged offences are serious ones given the circumstances of the case, and when the deterrent effect of such a sanction on the broader public is not significant. Beiski J underlined this point in *Tsofan* [23], at 732, in dealing with the departure of an officer from active military service as a consideration for not prosecuting:

> His departure [from the military] was called for not as a punishment for the offence he had committed but on quite a different level—because the IDF (Israel Defence Force) requires that its camp be untainted and that one committing such acts not find a place in the IDF and be immediately removed from service.
>
> But the respondent still owes his debt to society and to the rule of law for the offence attributed to him. Do we say that this debt has in fact been paid, since the IDF does not want him in its service? This may well prove an argument for leniency if the respondent is convicted of the alleged offences, if and when the court comes to pass sentence. But the criminal offence is not blotted out by his departure from the IDF, which no longer wants him as a result of the act concerned. If we were to say otherwise we'd find that an offender, however serious his offence, only ran the risk of possible dismissal from service and disciplinary action.

The same is true in the matter before us. The bank officers owe a debt to society and to the rule of law for the criminal offence attributed to them. This debt has not been paid. There exists a profound public interest in prosecuting them, particularly in order that others may take note, and in order that such an episode does not repeat itself. The judicial process, which determines the facts of a case and attributes criminal responsibility where necessary, is intended to reinstate acceptable norms of behaviour and express the public interest in imposing legal responsibility, on the one hand, and in providing a deterrence for potential offenders, on the other. Not prosecuting the bank officers in these circumstances and sufficing with some public-administrative sanction, means, in effect, not carrying out the law as warranted against those suspected of having caused grievous harm to society. It also means that we do not provide the deterrence that is crucial to the continued functioning of society. In fact the opposite is true. Such inaction serves as an invitation to potential offenders to take similar risks in the future.

38. The Attorney General gave significant weight to the consideration that responsibility for the share rigging did not solely rest with the banks and the bank officers but also rested with the State authorities responsible for the Stock Exchange and the running of the economy. These knew about the share rigging and yet did nothing to prevent it. This consideration should certainly be taken into account. However, in the particular circumstances of the case, its weight cannot be significant, for two reasons: one, in so far as senior office holders in the State authorities are implicated in the offences attributed to the banks and bank officers or in other such offences, prosecutions against such people should also be considered. As far as can be gleaned from the material before us, there is nothing to suggest evidence of offences by office holders in the State authorities; the main part played by such public office holders in this episode was in not preventing the share rigging. In this regard, there can be no comparison between the degree of responsibility that rests with one who did not prevent the thing happening and the responsibility of the one who actually originated it and caused it to happen. The Beiski Commission reiterated that 'the banks were the ones who brought about the share rigging after making a decision to act in this way' (the Commission Report at 225), and that it was the act of share rigging by the banks that had led to the crisis (*ibid.* at 305). Two, knowledge on the part of office holders in the State authorities of the share rigging related to the phenomenon as a whole. In practice, that is a far cry from having knowledge of the actual criminal offences that were committed. The existence of share rigging was something known to many at the time, but the specific crimes which the banks and bank officers are alleged to have committed were not. The Beiski Commission reiterated several times that in anything relating to the details of the share rigging, the banks and bank officers had acted in secret. On page 74, the Beiski Commission Report states:

> The need to circumvent extreme states of either supply or demand in the share market, either of which would have been calamitous for the banks, required that they impose a veil of secrecy over any of their actions connected with the share rigging, and that they avoid revealing facts which, by law, ought to have been revealed. This was done to prevent speculators from cashing in on such extreme states and, in addition, to avoid arousing the fears of the general public over the

inability of the banks to carry the financial load involved. Revealing all of the facts would have placed a strain on the share rigging process and might even have forced the banks to put a stop to it. The need for secrecy in the banks' share rigging activities was one of the factors behind the banks' opposition to the creation of Stock Market regulations, required by the law for the ordering of fair trade.

The 'veil of secrecy' which the Commission dealt with at length (104) was intended both for the Authorities and for the general public. It was also directed at branch managers and investment consultants. The Commission states (at 142):

The banks presented a wonderfully plausible explanation, for the benefit of their investment consultants, branch managers and anybody else coming into contact with the general public, of all the possible benefits of the bank shares; each bank in relation to its own shares. Their success, in imparting a sense of calm and security in anything related to investing in bank shares, was complete. Not only did the public come to regard these shares as a safe and reliable investment, the branch managers and investment consultants did too. The veil of secrecy, as with the imparting of incomplete or misleading information, was aimed at branch managers and investment consultants in exactly the same way as it was aimed at the general public.

Referring to the claim of the banks and bank officers that the authorities had known about the rigging process, the Commission notes, *inter alia*, that:

the veil of secrecy which the banks imposed on their share rigging activities prevented full knowledge and understanding of everything connected with the rigging process. (*ibid.* at 223)

Thus the knowledge on the part of the public and the authorities of the general existence of the share rigging phenomenon cannot be regarded as a factor of any real significance and cannot detract from the force of the other factors, which point to a genuine public interest in the filing of criminal indictments.

39. In his written decision, the Attorney General gave considerable weight to the length of time that had elapsed since the committing of the offences attributed to the banks and bank officers. He affirmed:

I see no public interest in setting about imposing on the public either the expense, the worry or the chore of rolling back the curtain on the share rigging episode, solely for the purposes of achieving that same punitive end (at 11).

These are considerations worth taking into account. And yet, in the circumstances, they ought not to be given any significant weight. As to the amount of time that elapsed, this was partly due to the fact that the Attorney General himself knowingly put off making a decision, out of a desire, as he put it, 'to maintain a distance from matters which, in his experience, were capable of tipping the scales one way or another' (at 4). Without going into the question whether such a 'distance' was justified, it certainly cannot be seen as a factor in support of not prosecuting the banks and bank officers. But there is a further point here. The share rigging episode and the crisis that followed caused such a trauma in Israeli society that the passage of time, which the Attorney General placed such emphasis on, could not lessen the impact of those events or detract from their severity, and could not justify not bringing the law to bear against those responsible. As to the consideration of possible harm being done to the efficient working of the system—this is an important consideration when lesser crimes are concerned. It should not be given any significant weight in the circumstances of the case before us, where the offences were serious ones and the harm caused was immense. Furthermore, even if, out of considerations of expediency, it becomes necessary to concentrate on the main perpetrators and to ignore the minor ones, an indictment of some sort cannot be avoided on grounds of administrative expediency alone.

40. I noted earlier that a decision on the question of 'the public interest' in submitting an indictment is reasonable, when the good that accrues from it to the values and principles which the criminal law serves to protect outweighs the harm caused to them. According to this yardstick, the Attorney General's decision that there existed no 'public interest' in prosecuting the banks and bank officers was unreasonable. The harm it has caused to the values and interests which the criminal law comes to protect has been immense. Suspects who committed serious offences in the circumstances of the case have not been prosecuted. The perpetrators embarked on a venture described as a 'business failure of such colossal proportions, that, at least in Israel it would be hard to find its equivalent' (The Commission Report, at 226). In the course of this venture, under the cloak of secrecy, a whole string of criminal offences are alleged to have been committed—these perpetrators are not being made to bear any criminal responsibility. An object lesson of deterrence has not been learned. The principle that all are equal before the law has been badly dented. The capacity of the criminal law to regulate societal behaviour has been damaged. The trust placed by the general public in the authorities has been shaken. Behaviour that had such a destructive effect on commercial and social life has gone unpunished. This harm cannot possibly be outweighed by the good that might have accrued to societal and individual interests from not prosecuting the banks and bank officers. One must, it is true, take account of what the bank officers have endured since the crisis broke, the price they have paid in the light of the recommendations of the Beiski Commission, and the good that will accrue to them from not being prosecuted, bearing in mind that this good also represents a public interest. One must also consider the good that will accrue to the public from not burdening the prosecution ser-

vice with the onerous task of submitting indictments and conducting trials. And yet, even in its aggregate, this good can still not measure up to the harm caused to the public interest by not prosecuting the banks and bank officers. It is not a question of the scales being evenly balanced; prosecuting and not prosecuting are not two viable possibilities here. The gap between the harm caused to the public if the banks and bank officers are not prosecuted and the possible good that might accrue from this decision is so great as to lead one to the inevitable conclusion that, in relation to the weight given in this decision to the various factors, 'there has been such a distortion and a lack of proportion . . . that the final result cannot possibly hold up and is, therefore, completely unreasonable.' (Shamgar P in *Dakah* [24].)

41. My conclusion on the unreasonableness of the Attorney General's decision gains added force when one considers that no weight at all was given in his decision to the fact that a commission of inquiry, acting under the Commissions of Inquiry Law, did recognize a 'public interest' in prosecuting. As is well known, a commission of inquiry may add its own recommendations to any report on the results of its inquiry (section 19(a)). Such recommendations, as their name suggests, are not binding. The government body which makes its decision in the wake of the recommendations of the commission of inquiry does not have to follow them (see *The Queen* v. *Collins* [43]). At the same time, it cannot ignore them entirely. It must examine the recommendations and give them due consideration (see Y. Zamir, 'The Commission of Inquiry from a Legal Standpoint' (5743–4) 35 *Hapraklit* 323). Such consideration derives from the objective, professional, and official character of the commission of inquiry, as well as from the depth of its investigations, the integrity of its discussions, its impartiality and breadth of scope, the seriousness of its recommendations, and the general expectation of the public that its recommendations will be carried out (see Z. Segal, 'The Power to Probe into Matters of Vital Public Importance' (1984) 58 *Tul. LRev*. 941, 943). These recommendations gain particular weight when the very question to be decided is the existence or not of a 'public interest' in submitting a criminal indictment. Thus the recommendation of a commission of inquiry—whose actual setting up derived from the existence of an interest of crucial public importance—is bound to have some weight in such a decision. As Ben-Porat J correctly noted in *Elon* ([4] at 459):

> In the absence of well supported arguments to the contrary, one should not leave the suspicions raised by the Commission's Report to roam about without proper legal investigation, being the only way of establishing and endorsing facts.

I should emphasize, I am not affirming here that the fact that the authority making the decision did not follow the recommendations of the commission of inquiry is an indication in itself of the unreasonableness of the decision. Nor am I affirming that, once a commission of inquiry has established the existence of a 'public interest' in submitting an indictment, the Prosecutor must perforce do likewise. My view is that the finding by a commission of inquiry on the existence of a 'public interest' in submitting an indictment represents a consideration which the Prosecutor must take into account. It can support the weight of other factors pointing the same way. I am therefore supported in my finding that, in the overall balance of factors, those supporting the prosecuting of the banks and bank officers have the upper hand; a finding borne out, *inter alia*, in the light of the recommendations of the Beiski Commission.

42. With regard to the accountants involved, the Attorney General made two decisions: one, that they are not to be prosecuted, for 'several of the considerations which led me to affirm that the public interest does not require the prosecution of the banks and bank officers' (at 12); two, that an investigation of their actions should be instituted before the Auditors' Council (as per section 12 of the Auditors' Law). The object of such an investigation would be to examine:

> whether the accountants concerned, in their preparation of financial reports etc., followed accepted accounting practices, as upheld by the best and most respected of the accounting profession, or whether the public interest, which demands that their reports reflect a full, true, and accurate account of the financial activities of the audited bodies, was, in this case, shunted aside in favour of the business or other interests of those bodies (at 12).

The investigation would also need to find:

> whether, out of regard for the sanction against those found to be in breach of professional etiquette, or out of regard for the honour and integrity of the Accounting profession, the measures as stipulated by the Auditors' Law, 1955, should not be instituted (at 13).

43. In my view, and based on the material before him, the Attorney General's decision regarding an investigation by the Auditors' Council was well founded. As he noted, the Beiski Commission affirmed that the accountants involved had not exposed the share-rigging process in full in their audits. However, the Commission refrained from affirming whether, as a result, the accountants should bear criminal or disciplinary responsibility. The Commission recommended to the Attorney General that he determine 'whether there is room for disciplinary or legal action in this matter' (Commission Report at 365). In this light, we hold that the Attorney General acted properly in deciding to hand over the findings of the police inquiry—bearing out, as I said, those of the Beiski Commission—for investigation by the Auditors' Council. However, we do not believe that the Attorney General acted properly in deciding in advance

that there was no 'public interest' in prosecuting the accountants, whatever the outcome of the investigation by the Auditors' Council. A proper weighing up of the various factors involved would surely require that the Attorney General wait until the decision by the Auditors' Council, and then make his own decision on that basis. Thus, for example, it may well happen that, based on the findings of the Auditors' Council, the Attorney General would decide that, not only were the accountants in breach of their professional obligations, they were also in breach of the norms set out in the criminal law. If *prima facie* evidence exists, where is the justification for stipulating in advance that there is no 'public interest' in the matter of the accountants? In this regard we should emphasize that the Attorney General himself noted in his written opinion:

> If it is a formidable task to exonerate the banks and their directors from anything to do with the share rigging phenomenon and its most insidious aspects, and for the way they duped one and all, how much more difficult will it be to exonerate the accountants, should it be found, after thorough investigation, that they deviated from the professional standards that are a *sine qua non* of their profession (at 11).

If, therefore, it becomes apparent to the Attorney General as a result of the investigation that, in his view, the accountants did in fact deviate from 'the professional standards that are a *sine qua non* of their profession', he will then have to weigh whether there exists a 'public interest' in prosecuting them. It is completely unreasonable to decide in advance that, even if it becomes apparent that the accountants were in breach of their obligations, they should not be prosecuted. Such a finding would not even follow from the reasoning of the Attorney General himself. He notes in his decision:

> Unlike the bank officers and certain other office holders, who were removed from office after the findings of the Beiski Commission, the accountants all remained where they were; their professional status was not impaired. If therefore, they are found to have violated their professional code, should it not then follow that they are to be uniformly dismissed? (at 13).

The above, said in connection with the disciplinary investigation, holds true also for a criminal indictment. How much more then, does the Attorney General's decision not to prosecute the accountants because of a lack of 'public interest', jar with our finding that there exists a definite public interest in prosecuting the banks and bank officers. The Attorney General will therefore have to take the whole picture into consideration, weigh, impartially, the relevant factors, and give each consideration its proper weight. Moreover, he must do so in the light of the findings of the Auditors' Council, without such findings being necessarily binding.

44. In the course of its investigation, the Auditors' Council will examine the question raised before us by the accountant, Mr Haft (respondent

no 14). There is, as we have seen, some discrepancy between the factual findings of the Beiski Commission on this matter and the affidavit of Mr Haft before us. It would be inappropriate for us to conclude any finding on this factual dispute which should properly be brought before the Auditors' Council. We do note, however, that according to the affidavit of Mr Haft, the Attorney General looked at all the material before him and could find nothing to justify an indictment for perjury and that consequently, the matter was also not passed on for police investigation.

## Prima Facie *Evidence*

45. The Attorney General's decision not to prosecute the banks and bank officers was based on two considerations: one, the main consideration, the absence of a 'public interest' in prosecuting; two, the secondary consideration, the doubt in the mind of the Attorney General as to the existence of *prima facie* evidentiary material. The Attorney General notes:

> It is not only on this consideration—the doubt as to the actual occurrence of the elements of the crime involved—that I have based my decision, it is on a combination of factors, as I have set out below (at 5).

In our decision here, we have found that the reasoning of the Attorney General on the absence of a 'public interest' cannot stand. Given this, it would be appropriate to allow the Attorney General to re-examine the evidence before him, based, this time, on the premise that there *is* a 'public interest' in prosecuting the banks and bank officers. Such a re-examination has not been conducted by the Attorney General and he should be allowed to form his own position on the matter. In this regard it should be noted that the Attorney General is not solely confined to those charges included in draft indictments previously submitted to him. He is at liberty to consider afresh whether, from the evidence arising from the police investigation, there is a *prima facie* case that the banks, bank officers, or others committed criminal offences. It would also be appropriate to consider whether certain offences are not proscribed under the law of limitations, and, as is common practice for a prosecutor, to select those aspects of an indictment for which the public interest demands a prosecution.

## *The Scope of Intervention by the High Court of Justice*

46. We have found that the decision of the Attorney General was unreasonable. Its unreasonableness does not merely stem from a slight deviation from that which would have been the appropriate weighing of the different factors. It stems from a complete aberration in its whole approach, making its ultimate finding totally untenable and, consequently, wholly un-

reasonable. On the one hand this unreasonableness brings about an annulment of the Attorney General's decision and, on the other, it justifies the intervention of this Court. It is now accepted practice in the Supreme Court that such extreme unreasonableness warrants the intervention of the High Court of Justice. It is true that, initially, the scope of this Court's intervention was limited to instances where it was claimed that there had been a lack of good faith in the Attorney General's decision (see *Shore* [8]; *Anon.* v. *Disciplinary Court for State Employees et al.* [29], at 427; *Sharaf* v. *Central Committee of Tel Aviv Bar Association* [30], at 168; *Weinograd* [11]) or 'something bordering on a lack of good faith' (*Greenberg* v. *Attorney General et al.* [31], at 2897; *Niniv* v. *State of Israel et al.* [32] at 329). In time, however, it was widened to include claims of arbitrariness (*Reichbach* v. *Attorney General* [33]), defective reasoning (*Wagner* v. *Attorney General* [34], at 31), and illegitimate considerations (*Anon.* v. *Attorney General* [35], at 455). In *Wallis Bar Association District Committee et al.* [36], at 540, Shamgar DP noted that the list was not a closed one, but reflected:

> a trend of general principle, while highlighting typical causes of action. Thus, for example, this Court might decide to intervene in the judgment of the complainant, if his decision reveals an extreme unreasonableness that touches at the very core of the matter, even when there is no indication of a lack of good faith.

Subsequently it was held that this Court would intervene in a decision of the Attorney General if it was 'absolutely clear that there had been a mistake which touched at the very heart of the matter, or if some other gross distortion were apparent that required putting right' (Shamgar P in *Fuchs* v. *Chief Military Prosecutor et al.* [37], at 155). In *Haetzni* [28], at 411, Bach J noted:

> The capacity of this Court to intervene on a decision of the Attorney General is not limited to those instances where it has been proven to us that the decision was made in bad faith. . . . In my view there is also scope for our intervention if we are convinced that the decision was reached from spurious or extraneous considerations and the decision itself, appearing to be completely illogical, provides ample indication of this. The absence of evidence as to a lack of good faith cannot 'save' such a decision from annulment or change.

Hence the finding of Beiski J in *Tsofan* [23], at 729 that the scope of this Court's intervention:

> was not confined solely to a lack of good faith, integrity, or illegitimate motives, but would include, *inter alia*, inherent distortion, extreme unreasonableness that went to the very heart of the matter at hand, unlawful discrimination or some consideration that was antithetical to the public interest.

In the same case, Kedmi J reiterated this approach (736), remarking that the criteria for this Court's intervention on a prosecutor's decision (in that case it was the Chief Military Prosecutor) were twofold:

The first, an objective criterion, whose principle concern is the 'reasonableness of the Chief Military Prosecutor's decision whereby inherent unreasonableness—which includes, *inter alia*, inherent unlawful discrimination, a mistake at the heart of the matter at hand and other gross distortions—will bring about the annulment of the decision; the second, a subjective criterion, whose principle concern is the good faith of the Chief Military Prosecutor, whereby a lack of good faith—including, *inter alia*, integrity, honesty and purity of purpose—will bring about an annulment of the decision.

In the same case, D. Levin J also remarked (at 742) that he was in agreement with the approach, by which:

we will intervene in the discretion of the Chief Military Prosecutor only in extreme circumstances where it is absolutely clear that a mistake has been made which touches at the very heart of the matter at hand, or if some other inherent distortion becomes apparent which requires being restored, i.e. instances where one can point to a lack of good faith on the part of the decision maker, or where impure or illegitimate motives lay at the heart of the decision or where the decision shows inherent and extreme unreasonableness.

It is therefore generally accepted that extreme unreasonableness which goes to the very heart of the matter at hand may justify the intervention of this Court. Such a fault is to be found in the decision of the Attorney General in the case before us. It is therefore not simply that we have the authority and power to intervene in this decision; we are bound to do so, in our capacity as guardians of the rule of law.

47. Behind the rules on this Court's intervention in the decisions of the Attorney General, lie three basic premises: one, that the Attorney General possesses wide discretionary powers in a decision over whether or not to prosecute a suspect. Such discretion means the power to choose from a number of legitimate decisions. The choice is directed, as we have seen, by attributing the proper weight to the different factors being taken into account in deciding whether or not there exists a 'public interest' in prosecuting. In determining this weight, there is a good deal of room for manœuvre. The process depends, *inter alia*, on weighing up day-to-day as well as normative realities, and on a general world view. It is inevitable that different Attorneys General will attach different weight to the various factors that go into formulating a criterion for 'the public interest'. However, provided that the weight which the Attorney General attaches to particular factors falls within the ambit of his discretionary powers, the decision will be a legitimate one. It follows that different Attorneys General are likely to arrive at different and contrary decisions, on the existence or otherwise of a 'public interest', where all such decisions are legitimate. In such a scenario the High Court of Justice will not intervene in the decision of the Attorney General. The rationale is not some special immunity the

Attorney General may have from judicial review by the High Court of Justice, but rather because the Attorney General's decision is legitimate and there are therefore no grounds for the intervention of this Court. It is true that the High Court of Justice may affirm that, had it possessed the decision making power, it would have reached a different decision from that reached by the Attorney General. The Court is then liable to call the Attorney General's decision 'misguided'. But that would not make it an illegitimate decision. The Court does not put itself in the position of the Attorney General, as some 'higher' Attorney General. It examines the legitimacy, not the wisdom, of the Attorney General's decisions. Since a decision which is 'misguided', i.e. one that chooses a legitimate option, which the Court itself, were it acting as the Attorney General, would not have chosen—is also capable of being quite legitimate, the High Court of Justice will not intervene, as there are no grounds for it to do so. The Deputy President, Shamgar J underlined this point in *Wallis* [36], at 541, when he remarked:

> To warrant the intervention of this Court, it is not sufficient that the body exercised its discretion in a way that appeared to the Court as misguided, so long as there was nothing to indicate the required degree of illegitimacy and fault referred to above.

Bach J reiterated this view, in *Haetzni* [28], at 411–12, as follows:

> The mere fact alone that a decision appears to us wrong or misguided, cannot of itself warrant our intervention. Even when we are convinced that we would have reached an entirely different conclusion from that reached by the Attorney General, were the authority to have resided with us, that still cannot be grounds for accepting a petition lodged against the Attorney General's decision.
>
> What so distinguishes our capacity for intervention in the decisions of the Attorney General on applying the legal process from our capacity for intervention in the acts and administrative decisions of most other public bodies is not just the fact that the Attorney General's decisions are often grounded in complex legal and factual considerations, but that there is generally another aspect to his decisions—the consideration of the public good. This is, by definition, highly flexible, allowing for different and even opposing views where each one is legitimate.

We find, therefore, that non-intervention stems from the fact that there are no grounds for intervention, since the Attorney General has chosen a legitimate option. Orr J reiterated this same principle in *Sheftel* [21], at 371, as follows:

> Since we are dealing with considerations which are many and varied, it follows that there may be a number of different possible decisions in the same circumstances, each one of which is legitimate. Thus the question to be dealt with in examining whether to intervene in the discretion of the Attorney General is not whether the Court believes the Attorney General should have made a different decision. A

pre-condition of such intervention is that a fault, of the type that would warrant this Court's intervention, is to be found in the decision. It is not sufficient that this Court believes that the Attorney General made a mistake.

We turn now to the second premise on which, in fact, the ruling of this Court is based. This states that when the Attorney General has chosen an option that is illegitimate, rendering his decision both misguided and unlawful, then this Court will intervene. A basic tenet of this Court is that, subject to submissions against the admissibility of a petition such as lack of good faith, unwarranted delay, etc., the causes of action for annulling a decision of the Attorney General and the grounds for the intervention of this Court must coincide. Without the grounds for annulling a decision of the Attorney General, the grounds cannot exist for the intervention of this Court. If, however, the grounds do exist for annulling such a decision, then there will be grounds for this Court's intervention. The Attorney General has, therefore, no special immunity from the intervention of the High Court of Justice. The Court cannot countenance a situation where there might be grounds for annulling a decision of the Attorney General and not, at the same time, grounds for judicial review. Were such immunity from judicial review to exist, it would represent a severe blow to the rule of law. Only in very special instances have we recognized the possibility of immunity from judicial review, and these have concerned the Legislature itself (see *Sarid* v. *Knesset Speaker* [38]). There have also been other special cases, which we have characterized as 'non-justiciable' (see *Ressler* [1]). The case of the Attorney General does not belong to either category. His decisions are justiciable and he is not part of the Legislature. He also carries considerable governmental power. 'Such unbridled discretion contains within it the danger of misuse, corruption and unlawful discrimination' (Netanyahu J in *Dotan* [16], at 226). Judicial review is therefore essential to the proper exercise of the Attorney General's governmental powers, as it is essential to the exercise of any governmental power. I underlined this point in a recent case as follows:

> There is no reason why an Administrative Law court should not scrutinize for legality, the full gamut of administrative discretion. If it did not, large areas of administrative discretion would be left immune from judicial review, leading, in the end, to lawlessness; for, without a judge there can be no law. Indeed, it is worth looking at administrative discretion from the perspective of the laws that determine the legal bounds of that discretion. Once it is perceived, under the doctrine of administrative discretion (both substantive and procedural), that the exercise of some discretion is at fault, then it is only right that the Administrative Law Court should be in a position to review the legality of the exercise of such discretion. There is no basis for saying that certain areas of administrative discretion are not subject to judicial review (subject of course to submissions as to lack of standing,

non-judiciability, and other similar submissions of non-admissibility). (*Schnitzer et al.* v. *Chief Military Censor et al.* [39])

The above also holds true for the scope of judicial review on acts of the Attorney General. When a decision of the Attorney General has been found to be defective under the doctrine of administrative discretion, then the Court will intervene to determine the nature of the illegality of the decision, provided that the petitioner has fulfilled the relevant requirements of admissibility. Such judicial review is essential to the rule of law and to the freedom of the individual in this country.

48. The obvious corollary of these two basic premises is that the key issue here is the scope of the Attorney General's discretion and not the scope of the court's intervention. The real issue is the existence of grounds for the annulment of the decision rather than grounds for the court's intervention. What concerns us is the question of the authority and discretion of the Attorney General rather than the question of the authority and discretion of the court. Indeed, the scope of the court's intervention is a function of the scale of the illegality of the Attorney General's decision. Subject to submissions on admissibility, the scope of the court's intervention coincides exactly with the causes of action against the illegality of the Attorney General's decision. The decisive question is therefore the following: what are the grounds, in substantive administrative law, for finding fault with the Attorney General's exercise of discretion? Are these to be regarded as causes of action which would suffice for 'regular' administrative discretion but not for that of the Attorney General? Study of the judgments of the Supreme Court will show that on this question there is no special law for the Attorney General. In fact, the trend of this Court is to maintain uniformity in accepting causes of action that would annul the exercise of administrative discretion. There is no hierarchy in the way public office holders are subject to judicial review. Those causes of action which would lead to an annulment of some administrative act apply across the board of governmental authority. Thus we have ruled that even a decision of the President of the State should be measured by the regular doctrine of administrative discretion (see *Mataanah* v. *Attorney General* [40]; *Barzilai* [5]). The same causes of action, therefore, which would undermine the exercise of discretion by some governmental body in general would also undermine the exercise of discretion by the Attorney General.

Finally, we will examine the third premise behind the ruling of this Court. This is the equal application of administrative law rules to all causes of action against the exercise of administrative discretion. In the same way as any administrative discretion is defective, if exercised from the consideration of extraneous factors, unlawful discrimination, dishonesty, or lack of good faith, so will the discretion of the Attorney General be defective if tainted in this way. Just as any administrative discretion may be found to be defective as a result of its extreme unreasonableness, so too may the discretion of the Attorney General be found to be defective as a result of the extreme unreasonableness that attached to it. I am in accordance with the view that to invalidate the discretion of the Attorney General it will not be sufficient merely to point out some slight unreasonableness. It must be shown that its unreasonableness is either inherent or extreme. This view does not derive from some special immunity of the Attorney General. No governmental body's discretion will be invalidated merely as a result of some slight unreasonableness. To invalidate administrative discretion we require substantive unreasonableness. I emphasized this point in *Dapei Zahav* [26] as follows:

> When we say that the act of an administrative body was unreasonable, we mean that this act deviated from the accepted standard of reasonableness pertaining to an administrative body in those circumstances. In the nature of things, such a deviation may be slight or serious. In civil law, in the Law of Torts, any deviation from the standard of reasonableness brings with it liability for negligence. I do not believe that the same principle should apply to Administrative Law, where our focus is on the administrative decision rather than on compensating the injured party. Invalidating an administrative act is a very serious matter, likely to have far reaching effects on the expectations, interests and rights of a number of people. . . . We should not, therefore, invalidate an administrative act merely because of some slight deviation from the standard of reasonable behaviour . . . or deviation over some side issue. For the deviation from the accepted standard to lead to the invalidating of the administrative act, there must be a substantive deviation that goes to the very heart of the matter in hand.

I am therefore of the view that the grounds for invalidating the exercise of administrative discretion in general are the same as those for invalidating the exercise of discretion by the Attorney General. It would indeed be unreasonable for us to set up a separate set of rules for dealing with the legitimacy of a decision by the Attorney General. We could not possibly countenance an approach whereby the discretion of an 'ordinary' prosecutor were subject to regular causes of action, while that of the Attorney General was subject only to special causes of action (compare *Time Inc.* v. *Attorney General et al.* [41], at 566). In a State governed by the Rule of Law, one cannot justify an arrangement whereby the discretion of the person at the head of the prosecutorial system is to be subject to special standards of review (see D. Freedman, 'Judicial Discretion in Criminal Prosecutions' (1983) 35 *Hapraklit* 155, 163). I should emphasize that this does not mean changing the discretion of the Attorney General for that of the Court, nor does it mean invalidating a 'misguided' decision of the Attorney General, i.e. one that chooses an undesirable, if legitimate option. All it means is equality before the law for all branches of government. Hence my position in *Nof* v. *Attorney General et al.* [42]:

> As for the scope of this Court's intervention, there is no difference between the Attorney General and any other holder of public office. Both must exercise their discretion with honesty, integrity, reasonably and without arbitrariness or unlawful discrimination, taking into consideration only relevant factors. Both are subject to judicial review. And just as there is no special law for the Attorney General as regards the authority of the court, neither is there any special law for the Attorney General as regards the scope of review by the court.

Based on the above, I am of the opinion that there is scope for the intervention of this Court in the decision of the Attorney General in the petition before us. The decision was not merely unreasonable in some 'ordinary' way, betraying some slight unreasonableness. It was inherently and substantively unreasonable, and thus defective under the doctrine of administrative discretion. Its defectiveness, invalidating the decision at the substantive level, automatically gives this Court the power to declare it invalid and to order its annulment.

We therefore rule that the temporary injunction become permanent, in the sense that the Attorney General's decision not to prosecute the banks and bank officers because of a lack of 'public interest' is annulled. We are returning the matter to the Attorney General to decide whether *prima facie* evidentiary material exists to prosecute the banks and bank officers. We also order that the Attorney General's decision not to prosecute the accountants because of a lack of 'public interest', be annulled. After the Auditors' Council has completed its investigation, the Attorney General will re-examine the material, and decide whether there is *prima facie* evidence for prosecuting the accountants.

**Shamgar P:**

1. I am in full agreement with the conclusions of my honoured colleague, Barak J, as I am with the method by which he arrived at his decision.

2. Our legal system creates a direct nexus between the criminal process and the public interest that underlies it. How is this so?

It is true that we have not taken on the continental law model of legality, which formally requires that criminal proceedings be undertaken whenever a crime has been committed. However, this does not mean that there are wide and general powers of discretion to filter cases, to select, from the pile of criminal investigations with *prima facie* evidence, those we intend to bring for trial. Under our system of law there is a rule to which there are also exceptions. The rule states that, where a crime has been committed and there is *prima facie* evidence, we commence legal proceedings (or, in less serious cases where fines are concerned, legal inquiries or administrative fine procedures), unless the Attorney General, or the competent authority under the Law of Criminal Procedure, is convinced that in a particular case there is no public interest in commencing proceedings. In other words, the selecting process does not go on in those cases where there *is* a public interest in prosecuting, but between those where there is a public interest and those where there is no such public interest, whether because of the possible outcome of criminal proceedings or the individual circumstances of the alleged offender.

3. Needless to say, there is no standard weight to attach to all the types of factors relating to a particular crime, nor is there any uniformity in the degree or severity of the different crimes. Each case is, in no small sense, a world unto itself. Hence our belief in the very individual nature of punishment. As the famous dictum of Roscoe Pound puts it:

> In law, some situations call for the product of hands not of machines, for they involve not repetition, where the general elements are significant, but unique events, in which the special circumstances are significant. (R. Pound, *An Introduction to the Philosophy of Law* (New Haven, Conn., 1954), 70).

Yet this does not mean that we cannot develop methods for prosecution work that, as far as is possible, follow standard and general lines. In this way we may provide ourselves with the means for comparing similar offences, in terms of their import and significance. We should look at whether people who have committed similar or even identical offences receive similar or identical treatment on the part of law enforcement agencies. I expressed this point in a Directive issued many years ago—Directive 50.-050 of the Attorney General, 1 January 1972, as follows:

> Damage to the public interest does not necessarily mean that a particular criminal, who is not to be prosecuted, is going to commit another crime. It also connotes the harm done to the public faith that justice is being done and that the authorities are not acting arbitrarily [the rule that not only must justice be done but must also be seen to be done is not only a rule of thumb in the professional parlance of lawyers, it is a practical and essential yardstick for the people's representatives, responsible for implementing the law]. The object of implementing the law is not just the punishing of criminals, it is also the prevention of further crimes, and there can be no such prevention or deterrence when the public have lost their faith in the activities of the authorities responsible for implementing the law.

4. The authority to decide on the lack of a public interest in a particular case should be exercised, therefore, according to fixed principles, ones that take into account the general interest that a reasonable and fair policy be instituted, free from bias and prejudice. This policy should aim at creating the belief and trust in the public mind that:

(a) All are equal before the law.

(b) The State is actively involved in dealing with the prime movers behind criminality.
(c) The State is actively concerned in protecting the individual, the victim of an offence.
(d) The State is cognizant of measures aimed at preventing future criminality.

The feeling that there is a lack of equality in the application of the law serves to undermine that trust which the public places in the legal authorities.

There is, furthermore, a definite correlation between paying adequate attention to the above guidelines, and the reasonableness of a decision made by the prosecutorial service. In line with the guiding principles of this Court, we are not wont to intervene in the decision of a statutory body solely because it has not chosen an option from those which this Court would have chosen, were it in the position of the statutory body. In the case of a gross deviation from the path of reasonableness, however, this Court has no option but to intervene.

**S. Levin, J:** I concur.

Decided according to the ruling of Justice Barak.

Given today, 5 May 1990.

# 29

# *Judicial Review of Administrative Action in the Territories Occupied in 1967*

EYAL BENVENISTI



## 1. The Jurisdiction of the High Court of Justice

The Supreme Court of Israel, in its capacity as the High Court of Justice, adjudicates complaints of Palestinians concerning the acts of the Israeli authorities in the territories occupied since the June 1967 war.[1] Initially the Court was hesitant, as a matter of law, to extend its jurisdiction over the acts of the military authorities in the territories. Indeed, in the cases in which it reviewed public acts, the Court emphasized the government's

[1] On the status of these territories see M. Shamgar (ed.), *Military Government in the Territories Administered by Israel 1967–1980—The Legal Aspects* (Hebrew University of Jerusalem, Faculty of Law, Harry Sacher Institute for Legislative Research and Comparative Law, Jerusalem, 1982); E. Cohen, *Human Rights in the Israeli-Occupied Territories 1967–1982* (Manchester University Press, Manchester, 1985); E. Benvenisti, *The International Law of Occupation* (Princeton University Press, Princeton, NJ, 1993). On the Israeli–Palestinian Declaration of Principles of 13 September 1993 and its implications on the status of the Territories see E. Benvenisti, 'The Israeli–Palestinian Declaration of Principles: A Framework for Future Settlement' (1993) 4 *European J Int. L.* 542. See also vol. 28 of the *Israel Law Review* (1994) dedicated to the peace process.

acquiescence in having its measures scrutinized.[2] In subsequent decisions, however, the Court made it clear that its jurisdiction to review occupation measures was mandated by law, and could be exercised independently of the government's consent.[3]

The jurisdiction exercised by the Supreme Court is unique. Although the legality of occupation measures has been examined by many national courts on various occasions,[4] never have these measures been scrutinized by the occupant's own judicial system. Indeed, the Supreme Court's willingness to permit judicial review of occupation measures stands in marked contrast to the attitude of the U.S. courts, which refused to entertain claims of Panamanian citizens and firms against the U.S. military, following the occupation of Panama in December 1989.[5]

The Israeli Government's readiness to have its measures scrutinized, and the Court's acceptance of this challenge, seem to have been motivated both by humanitarian concerns and by a desire to strengthen ties between the local residents and the Israeli system. It was hoped that providing Palestinians with a judicial forum for their complaints would encourage them to have faith in the Israeli legal system, and also have the concurrent effect of legitimizing the administration's actions through judicial approval.

The legal status of the different territories, a question hotly debated among scholars and politicians, has not been discussed by the Court. The Court has long refrained from explicitly declaring the *de jure* applicability of the law of occupation to the territories. The Israeli Government has never raised an objection before the Court, and thus the Court has not found it necessary to resolve the matter,[6] although it did recognize the *de facto* applicability of the Hague Regulations[7] to the West Bank and Gaza.[8]

[2] See, e.g. the Government's position in one of the earlier cases, *Hilou et al.* v. *The Israeli Government et al.* (1973) 27(2) PD 169, in which the Court examined the merits of the petition and relied on the Government's acquiescence.

[3] See *Abu Aita et al.* v. *Commander of Judea and Samaria et al.* (1983) 37(2) PD 197, 7 SJ 1 (1983–7); *Jamayat Askan* v. *Commander of IDF Forces in the Judea and Samaria Region* (1983) 37(4) PD 785, reprinted in this Ch.

[4] Benvenisti, n. 1 above, 192–202.

[5] *Industria Panificadora, S.A., et al.* v. *United States*, 763 FSupp. 1154 (D, DC, 1991); *Goldstar (Panama)* v. *United States*, 967 F2d 965, 968 (4th Cir., 1992). See also J. Semmelman, 'International Decisions', 87 *Am.JInt'lL* 288 (1993).

[6] For the Court's refusal to adjudicate this issue see *Ayyub* v. *The Minister of Defence* (1979) 33(2) PD 113, 127 (the *'Beit-El* case', English translation appears in *Military Government*, n. 1 above, 371); *Dweikat* v. *The Government of Israel* (1980) 34(1) PD 1, 13 (The *'Elon-Moreh* case', English translation appended to this Ch.). According to some of the justices' comments, had the Government raised its claim to sovereignty over the territories in court, the Court would have ruled the issue not justiciable: *Elon Moreh*, at 29; *Rouweidi* v. *The Military Court in the Hebron District* (1970) 24(2) PD 419, 423.

[7] Respecting the Laws and Customs of War on Land, annex to the Hague Convention Respecting the Laws and Customs of War on Land, No. IV of 1907.

[8] See *Jamayat Askan* v. *Commander of IDF Forces in Judea and Samaria* (1983) 37(4) PD 785

In 1988, however, the question came squarely before the Court, when a petitioner argued that, with the signature of the 1979 Peace Treaty with Egypt, the Israeli military administration in the Gaza Strip had ended, and therefore the local Commander lacked powers to order the petitioner's deportation. Shamgar P rejected this claim, holding that the law of occupation did apply to the Gaza Strip, simply because Israel had continued to control it.[9] The necessary and sufficient condition of that law's applicability, according to Shamgar P, was the effective control over the territory.[10]

## 2. The Applicable Law

In reviewing the actions of the military administration in the territories, the High Court considers international customary law and Israeli administrative law.

The international norms of customary law are embodied in the Hague Regulations of 1907. These regulations set forth a number of powers and limitations upon the occupying forces. The gist of these provisions is found in Article 43, which states:

> The authority of the legitimate power having in fact passed into the hands of the occupant, the latter shall take all the measures in his power to restore and ensure, as far as possible, public order and [civil life], while respecting, unless absolutely prevented, the laws in force in the country.

Since Article 43 requires the occupant to use the local laws, 'unless absolutely prevented', the authorities are subject to judicial review as to whether or not their actions are within the powers recognized by the local law. It should be noted, however, that the occupant may amend the local laws, and in such cases the Court would examine whether the change was justified under international law.

The Court does not review the administration's conduct under the Fourth Geneva Convention of 1949, since it views the Convention as a treaty whose norms have not gained international recognition as customary international law. The courts in Israel have held that only customary

(reproduced in this Ch.). ('Judea and Samaria [the West Bank] are administered by Israel by way of belligerent occupation . . . The Military Commander's powers and duties stem from the norms of public international law, whose concern is belligerent occupation.')

[9] *Afu* v. *Commander of the IDF Forces in the West Bank* (1988) 42(2) PD 4, 49 (reproduced in this Ch.). According to the 1978 Camp David Accords, negotiations were to be held regarding the future status of the Gaza Strip as well as the West Bank.

[10] In a previous decision (11 Jan. 1987), Shamgar J reiterated with approval (although in *obiter dicta*) the Government's interpretation of Art. 2 (i.e. the inapplicability of the Fourth Geneva Convention of 1949 to the West Bank and Gaza): *Shaheen et al.* v. *Commander of the IDF in the Judea and Samaria Region et al.* (1987) 41 PD 197, 207–8.

international law, such as the Hague Regulations, is part of the internal Israeli law.[11] Nevertheless, the Court refers on occasion to the Geneva Convention in order to show that the authorities act within the limits prescribed in the Convention. Moreover, following the Israeli Government's declaration that it will abide by the 'humanitarian provisions' of the Geneva Convention,[12] two justices noted the possibility that this undertaking might be enforceable in Court.[13]

In addition to international customary law, Israeli administrative law is also applied because the officials who perform their duty in the territories remain part of the administrative system, and therefore their actions are subject to judicial review.[14] This body of law imposes duties on the authorities which are independent of their duties under international law. Israeli administrative law also serves as a basis for judicial review of the local laws in the territories. Thus, for example, the Court determined that the power to demolish houses under local law could not be exercised without providing a right of hearing to its dwellers according to the standards recognized under Israeli administrative law.[15]

## 3. Rejection of 'Avoidance Doctrines'

The Act-of-State doctrine (in the British or American sense), the sovereign immunity doctrine (local or foreign), and questions of justiciability and standing have proved to be high hurdles for claimants in other jurisdictions who had sought to apply international customary law against officials.[16] The use of these doctrines prevented the application of the otherwise applicable international customary law.

While counsel for the Israeli Government has argued for the introduction of certain avoidance doctrines into the legal system, the Supreme Court has flatly and consistently rejected these arguments. Thus, for example, the Court refused to find that the legality of particular land acquisitions in the occupied territories for the purpose of the establishment of Jewish settlements was a non-justiciable political question.[17] Similarly, the Court refused to accept the Government's claim and adopt the British Act-of-State doctrine to prevent judicial review of acts of the Israeli Defence

[11] *Afu*, n. 9 above.

[12] See Shamgar, n. 1 above, at 42.

[13] Barak J, in *Jamayat Askan*, below, this Ch. and Bach J, in *Afu*, below, this Ch.

[14] *Jamayat Askan*, n. 8 above.

[15] *The Civil Rights Association in Israel* v. *The Commander General of the Central Area* (1989) 43(2) PD 529.

[16] See E. Benvenisti, 'Judicial Misgivings Regarding the Application of International Norms' (1993) 4 *European JInt.L.*

[17] *Ayyub* v. *Minister of Defence* (1979) 33(2) PD 113, at 124–5.

Forces in Lebanon during the 1982 war.[18] The Court never explicitly declared that the Government's interpretation of international law should be given 'great weight' and its opinions reflect independent elaboration.[19] Indeed, the rejection of the avoidance doctrines by the Court has led to its adjudication of issues that sharply divided the Israeli public. Cases involving considerations of national security and political issues, such as the settlement policy, are good examples. The Court, despite its concerns over public reaction, has not hesitated in expressing its view on the legality of such highly contested public acts.

## 4. The Interpretation of International Law

The Court has interpreted the relevant provisions of the Hague Regulations in the course of examining the lawfulness of administrative acts. The fact that the Hague Regulations reflect an outdated approach to public administration in general and to modern conditions of warfare and occupation in particular, coupled with the lack of modern case law on the subject by other national courts, required the Court to develop a modern approach to such situations. The protracted nature of the occupation has also created difficulties in applying the Hague Regulations, since these Regulations had been intended for a short-term occupation. The case of *Jamayat Askan* demonstrates both the challenge presented to the courts in applying the Regulations and the courts' ability to find solutions to the challenges.[20]

Although the Fourth Geneva Convention of 1949 could not have been invoked in Israeli courts,[21] the courts have at times referred to provisions of this convention. The *Afu* decision[22] provides an elaborate, and controversial,[23] incursion into international law (and especially into the meaning of Article 49(1) of the Fourth Geneva Convention concerning the legality of deportations).

[18] *Tsemel et al.* v. *Minister of Defence et al.* (1983) 37(3) PD 365, 379; *Al-Nawar* v. *Minister of Defence et al.* (1985) 39(3) PD 449, 461.

[19] Compare the practice in other jurisdictions: Benvenisti, n. 16 above.

[20] See the case, below, this Ch.

[21] See n. 10 above.

[22] See Y. Dinstein, 'Deportations from Administered Territories,' (1988) 13 *Iyunei Mishpat* 408 (in Hebrew).

[23] See the case, below, this Ch.

## 5. Judicial Review and National Security

One important trait of the High Court's case law in this area is its policy of deference to the discretion of the military authorities whenever the latter invokes security considerations. In such cases, the Court's scrutiny is usually confined to an examination of whether the act is *ultra vires*, and whether the reasons for cited security measures are actually a cover for irrelevant or illegal considerations.[24]

This policy is consistent with the Court's decisions regarding internal Israeli matters which involve claims to security considerations cited by authorities within Israel.[25] However, due to the continuing state of war in the region, terrorist activities, and, during the *intifada*, frequent clashes between soldiers and demonstrators, security reasons have been much more frequently invoked as the reason for measures taken in the Territories. Since the fact-finding procedure in the High Court of Justice is usually based only on affidavits, it is difficult to challenge the motives put forward by the authorities.[26] Rarely has the Court declared that security concerns were not the real motive behind the administrative acts, and therefore invalidated the action.[27]

During the *intifada*, the Court stood guard to prevent abuses of power by individual members of the security forces.[28] Although it did not seriously question the legality of the harsh security measures themselves, such

[24] See the *Beit-El* case, n. 6 above, at 126; the *Elon Moreh* case, n. 6 above at 20, 21.

[25] *Abu-gosh* v. *The Military Commander of the Corridor to Jerusalem* (1953) 7 PD 941, 943.

[26] This supervision of the High Ct. can be further curtailed when the Minister of Defence issues a Certificate of Privileged Evidence declaring the evidence which formed the basis of the administrative decision privileged for security reasons. In such a case, a J of the Sup. Ct. may decide to reveal the evidence, despite the Minister's declaration, in cases where the former finds that the interests of justice override the concern that led to the declaration: *Evidence Ordinance* (*New Version*), para. 44A. The tendency to defer to the authority's judgement in security matters would imply that the decision to reveal the evidence despite the stated security interests would take place only where no real security concerns existed and the Minister has misused his powers. In order to review the merits of a case despite the Certificate, a practice has developed in which the panel that is assigned the case examines the privileged evidence *ex parte*: I. Zamir, 'The Rule of Law and Control of Terrorism' (1988) 8 *Tel-Aviv Studies in Law* 81, 88–90.

[27] It did so in two cases only: *Elon Moreh*, and *The Electricity Company of East Jerusalem Case* (*No 2*) *Electricity Co. for the District of Jerusalem* v. *The Minister of Energy* (1981) 35(2) PD 673.

In *Samara* v. *The Commander of Judea and Samaria* (1980) 34(4) PD 1, the refusal to issue permission for the petitioner's husband to reside in the West Bank was rejected by the Court since the authorities did not claim to have had security reasons for the act (see 5).

[28] See e.g. *Khamdan* v. *The Minister of Defence* (1988) 42(3) PD 337; *Nasman* v. *The IDF Commander in the Gaza Strip* (1990) 44(2) PD 601. The Court was especially critical of the IDF Attorney-General's decision not to prosecute a high-ranking officer for ordering the brutal beating of Palestinian detainees, and demanded that criminal proceedings take place: *Tsufan* v. *The IDF Attorney General* (1989) 43(4) PD 718.

as deportations or the demolition of homes, it sometimes reprimanded specific acts as being 'unreasonable' or 'disproportionate'.[29]

With regard to procedural due process in military tribunals in the Territories, the Supreme Court has been strict in insisting that the procedural rights of individuals be respected, whether the tribunal is a military court,[30] the Appeals Committee,[31] or the Advisory Committee established under the Emergency Regulations (1945).[32] Indeed, despite the *intifada*, the Court ordered the Israeli Defence Forces ('IDF') to give hearings prior to making decisions regarding the demolition of houses, a procedure that did not exist under the local emergency regulations.[33] The Court ordered that hearings be held unless pressing security interests exist, such as a clear threat to the life of soldiers.[34]

## 6. Conclusion

In exercising its power of judicial review, the Court paid clear deference to security considerations. Most of its decisions overruled the petitioner's requests. Moreover, the military authorities, being the primary legislator in the territories according to international law, could at times effectively curtail the Court's supervision.[35] However, in assessing the Court's contribution, one should also keep in mind the petitioners' requests that were granted, and the cases in which the Court issued recommendations that were followed by the authorities.[36] There were also numerous other cases in which the Government contemplated and reconsidered its acts in view

[29] *Tourkman* v. *Minister of Defence* (1994) 48(1) PD 217; *Jabarin* v. *Commander of the IDF in Judea and Samaria* (1992) 46(1) PD 858. On the applicability of the regular tests for lawfulness of administrative acts to the acts of the occupation administration, see *Jamayat Askan*, n. 8 above.

[30] See *Al-Gazawi* v. *The Panel of the Military Court in Gaza* (1980) 34(4) PD 411.

[31] See *Shmalawi* v. *The Appeals Committee* (1985) 39(4) PD 598.

[32] See *Kawasme* v. *The Minister of Defence* (1981) 35(3) PD 113.

[33] See *The Civil Rights Association*, n. 15 above.

[34] *The Association for Civil Rights in Israel* v. *Commander of the Southern Command* (1990) 44(1) PD 626. The same consideration was approved in the case concerning the deportation of more than 400 residents of the West Bank and Gaza, suspected as members of Islamic terrorist groups, to Lebanon, without prior hearing: *The Association of Civil Rights in Israel et al.* v. *Minister of Defence et al.* (1993) 47(1) PD 267.

[35] Thus, e.g., following the *Elon Moreh* case (in which an order seizing land in order to erect a settlement was declared illegal) the Government changed its method of land acquisition, and the Court was effectively divested of supervisory powers in this crucial respect. When in another case, concerning a confiscation of private lands for 'public purposes', it was found out that notices to the owners had not been served according to the law, the authorities changed the law retroactively to legitimize the confiscation, and to prevent the Court from declaring the confiscation illegal: *Tabib* v. *The Minister of Defence* (1982) 36(2) PD 622.

[36] See e.g. for the recommendation to establish a military court of appeal: *Arjub et al.* v. *Commander of IDF Forces in Judea and Samaria* (1988) 42(1) PD 353.

of existing and potential petitions. One may assume that the possibility of judicial review was a key consideration for the administrative authorities. Thus, in retrospect, it may be concluded that the supervisory powers of the Court provided a meaningful check over the acts of the Israeli authorities in the territories.

# 30

# *Izat Muhamed Mustafa Dwaikat and others* v. *The State of Israel and others (the 'Elon Moreh Case')*

[H.C. 390/79]
[34(1) PD 1 (1980)]

*Landau DP, Witkon J, Asher J, Ben-Porat J, and Bechor J*

Israeli cases referred to:

[1] HC 58/68—*Shalit* v. *Minister of Interior*; 23(2) PD 477.
[2] HC 258/79—*Amirah* v. *Minister of Defence*; 34(1) PD 90.
[3] HC 606, 610/78—*Saliman Tufik Oyev* v. *The Minister of Defence* (*The 'Beit-El Case')*; 33(2) PD 113.
[4] HC 302, 306/72—*Abu Helou* v. *State of Israel* (*The 'Rafiah Salient Case')*; 27(2) PD 169.
[5] HC 392/72—*Berger* v. *Haifa District Planning Commission*; 27(2) PD 764, 773.
[6] *Kardosh* v. *Registrar of Companies*; 15 PD 1151.

English cases referred to:

[7] *Liversidge* v. *Anderson* [1942] A.C. 284.
[8] *Ridge* v. *Baldwin* [1964] A.C. 40.

## JUDGMENT

**Landau DP:**

This is a petition regarding the legality of the establishment of a civilian settlement at Elon Moreh, situated on land approaching the city of Nablus. Arab residents own this land privately. . . .

The sharpness of this dispute continues to be of concern internationally; what is more, it has intensified its hold on domestic Israeli politics, and is presently reflected in the decision to establish a civilian settlement at Elon

Moreh. Adopted by a majority vote of the Israeli Government, this move has caused acute public agitation.

In *Shalit* v. *Minister of Interior* [1], I spoke of 'the depressing result . . . when the Court abandons its proper place, as it were, which is to remain above the disputes which divide the public; instead, the judges themselves descend into the arena'. Furthermore I went on to explain, as one of the minority judges, that without a valid basis for its decision the Court must refrain from adjudicating this dispute. I added that 'there may be cases where a judge could perforce have to decide a disputed issue with a personal answer to a question of general outlook on life'. This time we have valid sources for deciding and no need (we are, in fact, prohibited whilst sitting in judgment) to interpose our personal views as citizens of the State. It is, however, still necessary to be cautious in order that the Court not appear to be abandoning its proper place and descending into the arena of public debate; this is particularly important because its decision will be received by one part of the public with acclamation and by another part with utter emotional rejection. In light of this possibility I regard myself to be bound by the obligation to decide in accordance with the law in every matter duly brought before the Court, though I know well from the outset that the public at large will pay attention only to the final conclusion, not to the legal reasoning. Therefore, the institutional status of the Court is likely to be prejudiced in taking a stand appropriate to it, that is, beyond the disputes which divide the public. But what else can be done? This is our task and our duty as judges.

On 7 June 1979, Israeli citizens, with the assistance of the Israeli Defence Forces, began a settlement project at Elon Moreh.

* * *

In his affidavit, the Chief of the General Staff ('CGS') explained that he generally believed that the establishment of this particular civilian settlement at this particular place was required for security reasons. His position concerning the importance of the area regarding security and the establishment there of a settlement was brought to the attention of the Ministerial Defence Committee. The Committee decided at its sessions on 8 and 10 May 1979 to approve the requisitioning of the area with an Order for the establishment of the settlement. As a result of this decision, approved by the Government *in plenum* at a meeting on 3 June 1979, the Commander of the Judea and Samaria Region issued the said Requisition Order. Lt. Gen. Eitan further expanded upon the important contribution of civilian settlements to the defence of the country's Jewish population. He stressed that even before the State was set up, as well as during the War of Independence, such settlements fulfilled security purposes in regional defence and in connection with IDF organization. This was the case in times of both tranquillity and emergency.

* * *

The CGS explained the special importance attaching to a civilian settlement, particularly in comparison to a military base. During fighting the force at a base goes out on mobile and offensive missions, while the civilian settlement remains where it is; properly armed and equipped, the settlement controls the surrounding area for assignments such as observation and protecting nearby lines of communication from the enemy's control. This is particularly true during a general mobilization of the reserves at the outbreak of war; in the case of Elon Moreh, the region of concern is the eastern front. At such time the forces must move to their fixed places of deployment, and control of the lines of movement to ensure speedy and uninterrupted passage increases in importance. Nablus and its surroundings form a junction that has no alternative route. Therefore it is especially important to control the adjacent roads. Elon Moreh commands a number of these roads, the Ramallah–Nablus Road, the Nablus–Jordan Valley Road via Jiftlik, and another road to the Jordan Valley via Akraba and Majdal which crosses nearby to the south.

There can be no doubt that Lt. Gen. Eitan holds these views with utter sincerity and profound inner conviction, for this is a matter falling within his great experience as a military professional. He does not conceal, however, the fact that others dispute his conclusion about the decisive importance of establishing a civilian settlement at the place chosen for Elon Moreh. In paragraph 23(d) of his affidavit he states:

I am aware of the view of respondent No. 2 who, whilst not contesting the strategic importance of the said region, thinks that security needs can be realized by means other than establishing a settlement at the said place.

The second respondent is the Minister of Defence. Thus an extraordinary situation has been created in which the respondents have different views of the petition's subject matter.

* * *

I have no intention of involving myself in the debate. It is sufficient for me to reiterate here what we said in *Amirah* v. *Minister of Defence* [2] (the *Matityahu* case):

In a dispute such as this on professional military questions, as to which the Court has no well-based knowledge of its own, we shall presume that the professional reasons set out in the affidavit made on behalf of the respondents and speaking for those actually entrusted with preserving security in the Administered Territories and within the Green Line, are correct. Very convincing evidence is needed to rebut this presumption.

In the same case it was also said that:

In matters of professional military assessment, the Government will certainly be guided first and foremost by the advice tendered to it by the Chief of the General Staff.

* * *

At the commencement of the present hearing—unlike in *Beit El* [3]—two settlers at the Elon Moreh site, who are members of the secretariat of the settlers' nucleus, were given leave to be joined as respondents to this petition. Kahan J, who dealt with the application, found that they have a real interest therein. In their affidavit and submissions these additional respondents opened up a vista far wider than that of the original respondents. An affidavit by one of them, Mr Menachem Reuven Felix, explained that the members of the nucleus had settled at Elon Moreh because of the Divine commandment to inherit the land given to our forefathers and that 'the two elements of our sovereignty and our settlement are therefore intertwined'. Furthermore, 'the act of settling the People of Israel in the Land of Israel is an act of real security, the most effective and the most genuine. Settlement as such . . . does not, however, stem from security reasons or physical requirements but from the force of destiny and by virtue of the return of Israel to its land.' Mr Felix further declares:

Elon Moreh is the very heart of the Land of Israel in the profound sense of the word; geographically and strategically, to be sure, but before all else it is the place where the first acquisition was made by the father of the nation after whom this land is named—the Land of Israel. . . . Consequently, reasons of security have their proper place and their truth, there is no doubt, but we are indifferent to them.

After citing *Numbers* 33:53—'And you shall take possession of the land and dwell therein, for unto you I have given the land to inherit it'—he goes on to say:

Whether or not the Elon Moreh settlers will be integrated into the regional defence system according to IDF plans, it is settlement in the Land of Israel—which is the mission of the Jewish people and of the State of Israel—that forms the security, the peace and the well-being of the nation and the State.

As regards the petitioner's arguments based on international law, including various international treaties, the deponent adopts the explanation given by his counsel. According to them, international law is totally irrelevant, since the dispute is an internal one between the Jewish people returning to its land and the Arab residents of the land of Israel. Furthermore, says Felix, what is involved is neither 'conquered territory' nor 'occupied territory', but the very heart of the Land of Israel, our right to which is beyond doubt. Additionally, in historical fact Judea and Samaria were part of the British Mandate and conquered with the force of arms by our eastern neighbour—a conquest and annexation which were never recognized by anyone (other than England and Pakistan). This is the substance of the affidavit.

Even those who do not share the views of the deponent and his group will respect the profound religious belief and self-sacrifice spurring them on. We, however, are judges of law in a state where the *Halakha* (religious law) is applied only in so far as secular law allows it. In this case, we must apply the secular law of the State. As to the deponent's view concerning title to land in the Land of Israel, I assume that he does not mean to say that according to the *Halakha* one may forthwith deprive non-Jews of their private property. The Bible says explicitly: '[t]he stranger that sojourneth with you shall be unto you as the home-born among you, and thou shalt love him as thyself for ye were strangers in the land of Egypt' (*Leviticus* 19:34). I find in the collection of literature submitted by counsel for the additional respondents that Chief Rabbi Y. Z. Hertz, of blessed memory, mentioned this verse when the British Government requested his opinion on the Balfour Declaration draft text. In reply he said that mention of the civil and religious rights of the non-Jewish communities in the draft declaration were simply a translation of this basic principle from the Torah (D. Ingrams, *Palestine Papers 1917–22 Seeds of Conflict* (John Murray, London, 1972), 13). The authentic voice of Zionism insists on the Jewish people's right of return to its land, a right recognized also by the other nations, as stated in the preamble to the Mandate on Palestine. The right to return, however, has never sought to deprive the residents of the country of their civil rights.

* * *

Here one should recall earlier petitions to this Court, where the important argument which Israel has voiced in the international arena was enunciated. The argument is based on the fact that when the IDF entered Judea and Samaria, this area was not occupied by any sovereign whose occupation was generally and internationally recognized. Mr Rahamim Cohen powerfully reiterated this argument. In *Beit-El* [3], I said that, '[w]e have not been asked to deal with this problem in this petition. We are therefore reserved in judging it, in combination with the group of reservations which I spoke of in *Abu Helou* v. *State of Israel* [4] and which remain open in this Court.' I think the previous situation is similar to that of the petition before us since the present petition can only be decided in accordance with the presumptions underlying the Requisition Order. These presumptions demarcate the boundaries of this hearing for the additional respondents as well.

We must therefore inquire into the legal force of the said Requisition Order according to international law, from which the Military Commander who issued it derives his powers. We must also inquire as to the legality of the Order's issue under municipal Israeli law since—as in the *Rafiah Salient* case [4] (at 176)—we assume here as well that the warrant for this inquiry exists against office holders in the Military Government personally, as individuals who exercise any public functions by virtue of law and are subject to the supervision of this Court, under section 7(b)(2) of the Courts Law 1957. Substantively, we must inquire whether according to Israeli domestic law the Requisition Order was lawfully issued according to the powers given to the Government and the military authorities under Basic Law: The Government and Basic Law: The Army.

* * *

I excluded Article 49(6) of the Geneva Convention altogether from consideration because it belongs to conventional international law, which does not legally bind an Israeli court, but I joined in the view of my distinguished colleagues regarding the justiciability of the question within the bounds of the Hague Rules, which bind the Military Government in Judea and Samaria as customary international law. Here also I shall proceed in similar fashion and refrain from dealing with the issue before us, as prescribed by the boundaries of Article 49(6) of the Geneva Convention. However, in so far as private property rights are concerned, the matter cannot be resolved by arguing the 'relativity' of the right, for in our legal system the right to private property is an important value protected under both civil and criminal law. Furthermore, it is immaterial whether land is cultivated or barren when contemplating the legal protection of property awarded the land-owner.

The principle of protecting private property applies also in the law of war, as expressed in Article 46 of the Hague Rules. A military government wishing to affect the individual's property rights must show legal warrant therefore and cannot exempt itself from judicial review of its act by pleading non-justiciability.

* * *

The question therefore remains as follows: have the respondents shown sufficient legal warrant to seize the petitioners' lands? The Requisition

Order was issued by the Military Commander who began by stating, as will be recalled, that the Order is being issued 'by virtue of my authority as Commander of the Region and my being of the opinion that the Order is required for military needs'. It should be mentioned here that in this Order the Regional Commander chose from the outset a more vague formula than that of the *Beit-El* matter. In that case, the Requisition Order stated that the area where the Beit-El camp stands as well as its environs would be seized only after eight years via the establishment of a civilian settlement 'required for essential and urgent military needs'. There, we justified the establishment of a civilian settlement based upon Article 52 of the Hague Regulations, which enables possession of land to be taken 'for the needs of the occupying forces'. At that time I cited Oppenheim who maintains that temporary use of private land is permissible if it is essential to 'all kinds of purposes demanded by the necessities of war'. I mentioned also the British *Manual of Military Law*, according to which the temporary use of land and buildings in private ownership is justified for 'military movements, quartering *and the construction of defence positions'*. We rejected Mr Khoury's contention that the notion of 'the needs of the occupying forces' must be understood as including only the immediate needs of the forces themselves, and we pointed out that 'the main function assigned to the army in occupied territory is "to safeguard public order and security", as provided in Article 43 of the Hague Regulations. What is required for achieving this purpose is *ipso facto* required for the needs of the army in occupation, within the meaning of Article 52'.

Up to this point I am at one with Mr Bach [the State Attorney] that the seizure of private land for the establishment of a civilian settlement can also be justified under Article 52 of the Hague Regulations. We have found no contrary precedent in international law. This, however, holds true only when it is proved on the facts of the case that it was army needs which actually led to the decision to establish a civilian settlement at the site in question. I emphasize once again that there should be no doubt in relation to the fact that according to Lt. Gen. Eitan's professional opinion, the establishment of the civilian settlement at the site is compatible with the needs of regional defence, the special importance thereof being to ensure the lines of movement during the deployment of the reserve forces in time of war. But generally I have come to hold that a professional assessment by the CGS would not in itself have led to the taking of the decision to establish the Elon Moreh settlement. The additional reason which impelled the Ministerial Defence Committee and the Government *in plenum* to do so was the strong desire of the members of Gush Emunim to settle in the heart of Eretz-Israel as close as possible to the town of Nablus. We were unable to go into the deliberations of the Ministerial Committee and the Government by inspecting the minutes. Regardless, we have sufficient indications in the evidence before us that both the Ministerial Committee and the Government majority were decisively influenced by Zionist views on the settlement of the whole of Eretz-Israel. That view emerges clearly from the statement made by Mr Bach on behalf of the Prime Minister during the court hearing on 14 September 1979 in reply to paragraph 6 of the affidavit of the additional respondents, to which I had drawn attention at the hearing of the previous day. I took down Mr Bach's statement verbatim because of its importance and the standing of the person in whose name Mr Bach was speaking:

> I spoke with the Prime Minister and he authorized me to state, after the subject came up in yesterday's session, that on many occasions both at home and abroad the Prime Minister has stressed the Jewish people's right to settle in Judea and Samaria but this is not necessarily connected with discussions in the Ministerial Defence Committee about concern over national defence and state security, when a specific question of requisitioning one or the other side for security needs comes up for discussion and decision. In the Prime Minister's view there is no inconsistency here, because in actuality two separate matters are involved. Regarding what was said about the Prime Minister's intervention, this took the form of bringing up the matter for discussion by the Ministerial Defence Committee, the Prime Minister being the Committee's chairman and paragraph 27(a) of the Rules of Government Procedure providing that, as regards the Committee's deliberations, the Prime Minister fixes the agenda on his own initiative or by application of a member of the Committee. He took part in the Committee's discussion and expressed his clear and unequivocal opinion in favour of issuing the Requisition Order for the establishment of that settlement. This, as I have said, was having regard *inter alia* to the opinion of the CGS.

The view about the right of the Jewish people, mentioned at the outset of the above statement, rests firmly on Zionist doctrine. But the question still remains for this Court in this petition whether that view justified the taking of private property situation in an area subject to rule by military government—and, as I have tried to explain, the answer to that depends upon the correct interpretation of Article 52 of the Hague Regulations. I strongly suggest that the military needs referred to in that Article cannot, in any reasonable interpretation, include national-security needs in the broad sense I have just mentioned. Allow me to quote Oppenheim, *ibid*, paragraph 147, 410:

> According to Article 52 of the Hague Regulations, requisitions may be made from municipalities as well as from their inhabitants, but so far only as they are really necessary for the army of occupation. They must not be made in order to supply the belligerent's general needs.

Military needs within the meaning of Article 52 can therefore include the needs of which the CGS spoke in his affidavit of reply. These are the needs of regional defence and of the defence of the lines of movement facilitating the uninterrupted deployment of reserve forces in time of war. In its discussions the Ministerial Defence Committee decided in a manner 'having regard *inter alia* to the opinion of the CGS', as Mr Bach put it. The Ministerial Committee's decision on 7 January 1979, cited above, assured Gush Emunim that the Government would decide on the time and place of the settlement 'in accordance with the appropriate considerations', and that when determining the area of settlement the Government would take into account the wishes of the Elon Moreh settlement nucleus as much as possible. I shall not err if I assume that what Mr Bach stated in the name of the Prime Minister reflects the spirit of the discussions in the Ministerial Committee. I do not doubt that the opinion of the CGS indeed figured among the Committee's various considerations, but in my view that is not sufficient to bring the decision within the bounds of Article 52. The following are my reasons:

(a) When military needs are involved, I would have expected the Army authorities to initiate the establishment of the settlement precisely at that site. Therefore, it would be a CGS initiative to put the Army's request to the political echelon so that the settlement's establishment could be approved if no political reasons to prevent it were found. The affidavit of the CGS does indeed indicate that this was the standard decision-making process. Had the settlement's establishment been pursued in this manner, I would say that the very course of the events attests to the fact that professional military consideration was dominant in the discussions at the political level. But the bigger picture obtained after the CGS replied to interrogation and the additional documents submitted by Mr Bach show clearly that the process was otherwise. The initiative came at the political level which asked the CGS to give his professional opinion, and then the CGS expressed a positive view in accordance with the belief he has always held. These points are clearly expressed by the CGS, in response to the interrogation, paragraph 2:

> (a) To the best of my knowledge the body that initiated the establishment of the settlement in Nablus area was the Ministerial Defence Committee.
> (b) I did not approach the political echelon with a proposal to establish a settlement at Elon Moreh. . . .
> (c) No plan existed, approved by an authorized military element, for the establishment of a civilian settlement at the given site.

(b) Further as to military necessity, I cited above the text of the Ministerial Defence Committee's decision at its meeting of 7 January 1979, as set out in the Government Secretary's second affidavit. The discussion at that meeting, it will be recalled, took place as a result of a demonstration by Gush Emunim members on a road near Nablus. The decision stated that '[w]hen determining the area of settlement for Elon Moreh the

Government will as far as possible take into consideration the wishes of this nucleus', and, as if in consideration of this assurance, the Elon Moreh members were required to return to the camp they had come from (that is, to desist from unlawful demonstration). This I regard as clear proof that it was pressure by the Gush Emunim that impelled the Ministerial Committee at that meeting to deal with the subject of civilian settlement in the Nablus area. Subsequently, the matter went to the Ministerial Settlement Committee. That committee sent its representatives on a preliminary survey for selecting feasible sites for the establishment of a settlement for the Elon Moreh nucleus in the vicinity of Nablus. The representatives chose five sites, from which the IDF approved the site presently at issue. It follows that the IDF had no part in determining these five sites but faced the choice of selecting one of five sites determined at the political level. This procedure is inconsistent with the language of Article 52 which, in my view, calls for demarcation of certain lands precisely because they are required for military needs; and, as I have said, it is natural that the initiative for this should come from military experts in Army needs and advance planning.

On this matter, Mr Bach submitted that the Army must consider whether there are candidates for civilian settlement prepared to go to the place where their settlement is militarily required. I agree, but again provided that military planning approved by competent authority precedes the search for candidates for settlement on the given site. Here the reverse occurred. The wish of the members of the Elon Moreh nucleus to settle as close as possible to the town of Nablus instigated the plan; then, as a result of the pressure they exerted, approval came at the political level and eventually at the military level. Political considerations were therefore the dominant factor in the Ministerial Defence Committee's decision to establish the settlement on that site, although I assume that the Committee and a majority of the Government were convinced that its establishment *also* serves military needs. I accept the declaration of the CGS that on his part he did not take into account political considerations, including the pressure of the Gush Emunim people, when he came to submit his professional opinion at the political level. But a secondary reason, such as the military reason supporting the decisions of the political level that initiated the settlement's establishment, does not comply with the precise requirements laid down by the Hague Regulations in giving priority to military necessity over private property rights. In other words: would the decision at the political level to establish the settlement at that site have been adopted, had it not been for the Gush Emunim pressure and the ideological-political reasons contemplated at the political level? I have been convinced that were it not for the latter the decision would not have been adopted in the circumstances then prevailing.

I wish to add a few words about the dominant as against the subordinate reason for the decisions taken by government authority. In *Berger* v. *Haifa District Planning Commission* [5] Kahan J mentioned the discussion of 'plurality of purposes' in the third edition of de Smith's *Judicial Review of Administrative Action*, 287 ff., and of the five tests proposed there he chose one: did the invalid consideration or invalid purpose really effect the authority's decision? For my part I am prepared to adopt the more lenient test proposed by de Smith at 289:

> What was the dominant purpose for which the power was exercised? If the authority is seeking to achieve two or more purposes when one is permitted, expressly or impliedly: the legality of the act is judged according to the dominant purpose.

(c) I have still not dwelt upon an additional ground impelling the invalidation of the decision to seize possession of the petitioners' land—a reason which can stand without regard to the others I have already specified. Previously, in *Beit-El* [3] the serious question arose how it is possible to establish a permanent settlement on land seized only for temporary use. There we accepted Mr Bach's answer that the civilian settlement can only exist in that place so long as the IDF occupy the area by virtue of a Requisition Order. This occupation can itself come to an end eventually, as a result of international negotiations, leading to a new arrangement that will take effect under international law and will determine the fate of this settlement and of other settlements existing in the occupied territories.

In that case, the settlers themselves made no submissions because they were not joined as parties. In the case at bar, the solution is not acceptable. The affidavit on behalf of the settlers states openly in paragraph 6:

> To base the Requisition Order on security grounds in the narrow technical sense and not on the basic and embracing sense, as explained above, means one thing—the temporary nature of the settlement and its transitoriness. This frightening conclusion we reject altogether. Nor is it consistent with the Government's decision concerning our settling in the place. In all our contacts with the Government Ministers and the many assurances we received from them and above all from the Prime Minister himself—and the said Requisition Order was issued on the intervention of the Prime Minister himself—all regard the Elon Moreh settlement as a permanent Jewish settlement, no less than Deganya or Netanya.

It should be noted that this passage is comprised of two parts. The first relates to the view of the settlers; the second to what they heard from Ministers. We were not asked to permit an affidavit in reply to be submitted on behalf of the Government or any of its Ministers to refute the statements attributed to them in the second part of this passage. They may, therefore, be taken to be wholly true. Since that is so, the decision to establish a permanent settlement destined from the outset to remain indefinitely—even beyond the duration of the military government established in

Judea and Samaria—comes up against an insurmountable legal obstacle. No military government can express military need which is designed *ab initio* to persist even after the end of the military rule, which is an unascertainable period of time. It is a patent contradiction, apparent also on the evidence before us in this petition, that the decisive consideration which moved the political level to allow the establishment of this settlement was not military. In these circumstances the legal form of only taking possession and not expropriating ownership cannot change the substantive situation, namely, the indefinite ownership implied in taking possession.

In view of the foregoing, the order *nisi* should in my opinion be made absolute in respect of the petitioners' land seized under Order No. 16/79.

**Asher J:** I concur.

**Ben-Porat J:** I concur.

**Witkon J:**
I am also of the opinion that the law is with the petitioners. As in *Beit-El* [3], here we must also examine the acts of the authorities both from the aspect of 'internal' law ('municipal' law according to the accepted terminology in this context) and from the aspect of international law. These are two separate matters, and as I said in *Beit-El*: '[t]he act of a military government in occupied territory may be justified from the military-security aspect and yet possibly be defective from the international law aspect.' The internal law to be dealt with is the law contained in two Orders, which the Commander of the Judea and Samaria Region issued by virtue of his powers as Commander of occupied territory (Orders 16/79 and 17/79). In these Orders the Commander stated that he 'is of the opinion that the matter is required for military needs', and declared that the areas were requisitioned 'for military needs'. There is indeed no dispute in point of internal law and in fact also of customary international law (the Hague Convention) that the validity of the Orders depends upon their being made for 'military needs'.

We have already expanded upon the nature of 'military necessity' and the extent to which we may interfere with the discretion of the military elements: *Abu Helou* v. *The Government* [4] and *Beit El* [3]. Repeatedly we have emphasized that the bounds of our interference are limited. . . . In those cases, we were satisfied that the requisitioning for establishing a civilian settlement did in fact serve a security purpose. Here I am not satisfied that this was the purpose.

How does the present case differ from the previous cases? The most important difference is that in the present case, even the experts entrusted with the security of the State disagree on the necessity of settlement at the site. The security authorities similarly submitted affidavits for the purpose of persuading the Court of the military-security need for requisitioning land and establishing thereon civilian settlement, but previously the evidence was uniform and unequivocal. With regard to Elon Moreh, however, it emerges from the evidence before us that the main issue, military need, is disputed by experts.

* * *

The petitioners averred in their petition that 'as far as they know from the news media, respondent No. 2 (the Defence Minister) has declared that there is no military or security need for the area of land'. Generally we do not take account of hearsay but here confirmation of the differing opinion of the Defence Minister is provided by the deponent on his behalf, the CGS, Mr Raphael Eitan, who says in paragraph 23(d) on his affidavit: 'I am aware of the opinion of the second respondent who does not contest the strategic importance of the region under discussion but thinks that security needs can be effectuated by means other than establishing a settlement at the said place.'

This inconsistency between the Minister of Defence and the CGS on the very need for requisition has no parallel in all the case law of Israel; and it is also difficult to cite an example from other countries where a judge is required to choose between the opinions of two experts, one, the Minister responsible and the other, the head of the executive establishment.

* * *

As is widely known, courts can be asked to decide questions requiring special expertise, which is usually not in the judges' field. The opinions of reputable experts, submitted to us, can contradict each other completely. This may occur, for example, in trials raising medical issues or in cases of breach of patent touching on chemistry, physics, or other natural science. In matters of security, where the petitioner relies upon the opinion of a security expert and the respondent on that of another person who is both an expert and the one responsible for the security of the State, special weight is naturally given to the opinion of the latter.

* * *

At such an impasse, without reason to find the deponent on behalf of the respondents preferable to the opinions of other experts, we must ask ourselves: who bears the burden of proof? Must the petitioners convince us that the land was not requisitioned for the needs of the Army and security or should we perhaps require the respondents, the security authorities, to convince us that the requisition was needed for this purpose? I think that the burden rests upon the respondents. The confirmation by the Commander that the requisition was required for military needs does not automatically accord the presumption and certainly not the force of decisive evidence that this is definitely the case. Furthermore, we must bear in mind that the sincere subjective belief of the Commander as to the necessity of the requisition is not sufficient to exclude the question from judicial review. It is not the sincerity of his judgment but its accuracy that must convince us (see the well-known debate on *Liversidge* v. *Anderson* [7] and the article by R. F. V. Heuston in 86 *LQR* 33. See also *Ridge* v. *Baldwin* [8] and the *Kardosh* cases [6]). The law I cited at the opening of my remarks makes legal requisition conditional upon the existence of military necessity; obviously, then, the court will not sanction serious prejudice to a person's property unless it is satisfied that security needs are involved. Nor did the State Attorney argue that he is free of the obligation of persuasion and he went to great lengths to present to us all of the material. As I have said, where we have only evidence on the part of the respondents or the respondents' experts differ from the petitioners' experts, when harbouring concerns about the issue I might possibly give the respondents 'the benefit of the doubt'. Here, however, as I said, we have been told that the Defence Minister himself is not convinced of the necessity of this requisition. True, the post of Minister is political and he himself need not necessarily be an expert in the affairs of his Ministry. But today we have the conflicting opinion of a Minister of Defence who—as former Chief of Staff and Commander of the Air Force—is himself a distinguished expert on security matters, a fact which the State Attorney did not put into question. If such a Minister is not convinced, how can it be asked of us, the judges, that we should be convinced? If he sees no military necessity for establishing a settlement precisely at this place, who am I to differ from him?

This is the principal reason that leads me to distinguish this case from all the preceding cases and to arrive at a conclusion differing from that reached in those cases. There are two further, albeit less important, additions to be made to this conclusion. One is that in the *Rafiah Salient* case [4] and in *Beit-El* [3], I proceeded on the assumption that the Israeli settlements established on lands requisitioned from their Arab owners are essential for the security forces in their daily struggle against terrorists. 'One does not have to be a military and security expert', I said in *Beit-El*, 'to realize that terrorist elements operate more easily in an area inhabited only by a population that is indifferent or is sympathetic towards the enemy than in an area where there are also persons likely to guard against them and to report any suspicious movement to the authorities. Among the latter, terrorists will find no hide-out, assistance or supplies.'

The CGS, Lieut. Gen. Raphael Eitan, explained to us that at Elon Moreh the main security value in establishing a settlement on this site lies in its integration into the regional defence system in the event of 'total' war. I have perused again the affidavit submitted to us by Maj. Gen. Yisrael Tal in the matter of *Rafiah Salient* [4] and found that it only refers to terrorist operations in times of quiet. That was also my impression of Maj. Gen. Orli's opinion in *Beit-El* [3]. On looking at this affidavit again, however, I found that he also spoke about the needs of regional defence. These considerations were reflected in the judgment of my colleague, Landau J. In any event two requisitioned areas were there involved, one on the specific route of potential terrorists and the other bordering an important military camp (Beit-El). In this situation there could not have been any serious doubt regarding the enormous strategic value of these two sites. They and only they could fulfil a defence role, with no alternative available. At Elon Moreh, however, I cannot say that there doubtless exists a defence necessity.

The third manner in which the present case differs from the preceding cases stems from the affidavit of the settlers. It will be recalled that in the *Beit-El* affair [3], the settlers were joined as respondents to the petition and were not allowed to make any submissions; we assumed that their presence on the site was wholly dedicated to security needs and the defence of the homeland. In the words of my learned colleague, the Deputy President, '[s]ince the IDF is for the most part a reservists' army, the inhabitants of a civilian settlement are under military command even individually.' At that time I said, 'the settlers are subject to army control, either formally or by the force of circumstances. They are there by virtue and with the permission of the Army. I therefore still adhere to the view I held in the *Rafiah* case [4] that, as long as a state of belligerency exists, Jewish settlement in occupied territory serves actual security purposes.'

In the case at bar, we have heard the representatives of the settlers and it seems to me that we may not ignore the substance of their argument. . . . The settlers, it is very true, do not deny the security consideration, but in their opinion it is entirely secondary and incidental. As they state in their affidavit: '[a]ccordingly, with all due deference to the security point and although its correctness is not doubted by us, it is immaterial.'

These are trenchant remarks and it goes without saying that the settlers deserve praise for their candour in not masking their true motives. But I am left with a nagging question: these settlers one and all protest that they have come to settle in Elon Moreh not out of security considerations, and therefore their contribution to security—for all its benefit—is only incidental. Can it then be said of these settlers, as I expressed it in *Beit-El*, that they are at the location due to the permission of the Army? Although 'a person may be benefited in his absence', can a right or permission which the beneficiary positively rejects as loathsome be forced upon him? Let one thing be clear: without disassociating myself from the observations of my learned colleague, Landau J, I myself have no need to dispute with the settlers their religious or ideological debate. But it is our duty to inquire whether it is purely considerations of security which prompted the requisition of the land for the purpose of settling people at this location. It appears to me, then, that it is important to know what the attitude of the settlers is; if they did not come principally for security purposes, it is difficult for me to accept that this in fact is the purpose of their settlement.

* * *

Furthermore, in the case at bar, the State Attorney invited us to confirm with the authorities that the Geneva Convention is not contravened by the transfer of land to settlers for settlement needs. In his submission, land transfer does not contradict the humanitarian provisions of the Convention which are accepted by the State of Israel. It will be recalled that what is involved here is Article 49(b) of the Geneva Convention which prohibits an occupying power from deporting or transferring sections of its civilian population to the occupied territory. It is a mistake to think (as I read recently in a newspaper) that the Geneva Convention does not apply to Judea and Samaria. It applies, even though, as I said above, it is not 'justifiable' in this Court. Nor would I say that the 'humanitarian' provisions of the Convention are intended solely to protect the life, health, freedom, or honour of a person and not property. Who like us knows the value of possession? But the question whether voluntary settlement falls under the prohibition of 'transferring sections of the population' within the meaning of Article 49(b) of the Geneva Convention is not an easy one and, as far as we know, no answer has yet been found in international jurisprudence. Therefore now as well, I prefer not to answer this question, especially in view of the conclusion I have reached in this case; under both internal law and customary international law (Hague Convention, Article 52), a decision is not called for. Refraining from doing so, however, is not to be interpreted as agreement with the attitude of one or other of the parties.

For these reasons, in addition to those elucidated by my learned colleague, the Deputy President, I am of the opinion that the Order should be made absolute.

**Bechor J:**

* * *

The Deputy President also dealt with the question arising from the contradiction between requisitioning land for military needs, which is a temporary requisition, and establishing civilian settlements permanently. It is common knowledge that settlements have always constituted an inseparable part of the regional defence system. In the more general framework of the whole defence system of the Yishuv [the Jewish community], their role is also noted in *Beit-El* [3] and in *Matityahu* [2]. A distinction must, however, be drawn: the integration of civilian settlements into regional defence began many years before Israel achieved statehood, and continued within the State's territory after the statehood was attained. During these years the basis was always that the civilian settlements are permanent. This was not incorrect even from a legal point of view, since the post-statehood settlements were established in areas within the boundaries of the State where the law of the State applied. In the pre-State period as well, the intent was always to establish permanent settlements on land owned by the settling bodies. In the case at bar we are dealing with temporary requisition, and hence the contradiction between Elon Moreh and the creation of permanent settlements. This question has come sharply into focus for the first time in this petition, perhaps mainly as a result of the joinder of respondents 5 and 6 and the clear position they have adopted.

As I have said I concur with the judgment of Landau DP.

Order *nisi* made absolute.
Judgment given 22 October 1979.

# 31

# *Jamayat Askan Ala'almun Althaunia Alnahduda Almasaulia etc.* v. *Commander of IDF Forces in the Judea and Samaria Region and another*

[H.C. 393/82]
[37(4) PD 785 (1983)]

*Barak J, Y. Cohen J, and Avnor J*

Israeli cases referred to:

[1] HC 256/72—*Jerusalem District Electric Co.* v. *Minister of Defence*; 27(1) PD 124.
[2] HC 69,493/81—*Abu Aita* v. *Military Commander of the Judea and Samaria Region*; 37(2) PD 197.
[3] HC 619/78—*'Al Tliya' Weekly* v. *Minister of Defence*; 33(3) PD 505.
[4] HC 351/80—*Jerusalem District Electric Co.* v. *Minister of Industry and Energy* ; 35(2) PD 673.
[5] HC 390/79—*Dwaikat* v. *Government of Israel* (*the 'Elon Moreh' case*); 34(1) PD 1.
[6] HC 202/81—*Taviv* v. *Minister of Defence*; 36(2) PD 622.
[7] HC 97/79—*Abu Awad* v. *Military Commander of the Judea and Samaria Region*; 33(3) PD 309.
[8] HC 302/72—*Hilou* v. *Government of Israel*; 27(2) PD 169.
[9] HC 802/79—*Samara* v. *Military Commander of the Judea and Samaria Region*; 34(4) PD 1.
[10] HC 606,610/78—*Matoa* v. *Minister of Defence*; 33(2) PD 113.
[11] HC 258/79—*Amira* v. *Minister of Defence*; 34(1) PD 90.
[12] HC 629/82—*Mustafa* v. *Military Commander of the Judea and Samaria Region*; 37(1) PD 158.

# JUDGMENT

**Barak J:**

1. The petitioner is a co-operative society. Its purpose is the construction of a housing project for teachers who are members of the society who reside in Judea and Samaria. To that end, the society purchased land in Judea and Samaria and the members of the society applied for building permits. The applications were granted but subsequently cancelled by the respondents who requisitioned the land to construct two highways that would link towns in Judea with other towns in the area, including Israel . . .

2–4. * * *

## *The Position of the Respondents*

5–6. * * *

## *The Position of the Petitioner*

7–8. * * *

## *The Dispute*

9. * * *

## *The Normative Framework*

10–11. * * *

12. The Hague Regulations centre around two central axes: one securing the legitimate security interests of the occupant in an area subject to belligerent occupation; the other securing the needs of the civilian population in an area subject to belligerent occupation (*Jerusalem District Electric Co.* v. *Minister of Defence* [1]; *Abu Aita* v. *Military Commander* [2]). The Hague Regulations establish a certain balance between these two axes, emphasizing the military need in certain matter and emphasizing the needs of the civilian population in other matters:

> The law of war generally establishes a delicate balance between two magnetic poles: military need, on the one hand, and humanitarian considerations, on the other hand (Y. Dinstein, 'Legislative Authority in the Occupied Territories' (1972) 2 *Iyunei Mishpat* 505, 509).

In each of these two matters, both the 'military' need and the 'civilian' need, the principal point of departure is that the Military Commander does not inherit the rights and status of the defeated government. He is not the sovereign in the occupied territory (L. Oppenheim, 'The Legal Relations

Between the Occupying Power and the Inhabitants' (1917) 33 *LQR* 363). The powers of the defeated government are suspended and, under the rules of public international law, the Military Commander is vested with 'the supreme authority of government and administration in the region' (*'Al Tliya' Weekly* v. *Minister of Defence* [3]). From a legal point of view, these powers are temporary in nature, since the belligerent occupation is temporary in nature (see L. Oppenheim, *International Law* (7th edn. by H. Lauterpacht, London, 1952), ii, 436; see, too, H. Lauterpacht, *The Law of War on Land being Part III of the Manual of Military Law* (London, 1958), 143). This temporariness can be long-lived (see *Jerusalem District Electric Company* v. *Minister of Industry and Energy* [4]). International law does not set a time limit on its duration, and it lasts as long as the military government governs effectively in the region (see *Abu Aita* [2]).

13. We have seen that the considerations of the Military Commander are to secure security interests in the Region, on the one hand, and to secure the interests of the civilian population in the Region, on the other. In both cases the focus is on the Region. The Military Commander may not consider the national, economic, and social interests of his own State, as long as they do not affect his security interest in the Region or the interest of the local population. Even the military needs are local ones and not national security needs in the broad sense (*Dwaikat* v. *Government of Israel* (*'Elon Moreh'*) [5]). A region that is held in belligerent occupation is not an area open to economic or other exploitation. Thus, for example, a military government may not tax the residents of an area held in belligerent occupation for revenue designated for the treasury of the State on behalf of which it acts (see *Abu Aita* [2], at 271). Therefore the military government may not plan and implement a road system in a region held in belligerent occupation if the purpose of that planning and implementation is solely to constitute a 'service route' for its own State. The planning and implementation of a road system in occupied territory may be done for reasons pertaining to the benefit of the local population. Such planning and implementation cannot be done solely to serve the needs of the occupying State. Therefore, if the petitioner is right in that the purpose of the planning is not the needs of the Region (military or civilian) but only the needs of Israel, then its legal position is correct, that such purpose is an extraneous consideration for the Military Commander. It appears that the respondents themselves do not take issue with the said legal proposition, but disagree with the petitioner's position on the facts. It follows that this is the 'geometric place' in the legal analysis in which we must address the factual disagreement between the parties as to the purpose of the scheme.

14. We have no reason not to accept the respondents' position in the factual controversy that has been revealed between the parties. The planning considerations that underlie the scheme have been presented to us, and we

have no reason to doubt their veracity. The petitioner did not raise any fact to unsettle the respondents' position and, apart from a general argument, did not bring any evidence or proof that could cast doubt upon the respondents' affirmation. The picture that emerges from studying the material presented to us is of professional planning that takes into account the conditions and needs of the Region, and not only the conditions and needs of Israel.

15. * * *

16. In light of our conclusion—as to which we entertain no doubt or reservation—that the considerations of Israel and its civilian needs did not lie at the core of the road scheme and its implementation, the question remaining is the legal controversy between the parties concerning the power and authority of a military government to plan and implement a 'civilian' enterprise in the Region—without any military implication—that has long-term permanent implications, even beyond the time limits of the military government itself.

## *Securing the Population's Needs*

17. Different provisions of the Hague Regulations preserve various specific rights of the civilian population in an area under belligerent occupation. These rules are partial in character, and they contain a solution to a limited number of special problems. Together with these provisions, the Hague Regulations include a general 'meta' provision which establishes a general framework for review of actions taken by the occupying government. This provision is found in Article 43 of the Hague Regulations. In its French version this provision is as follows:

> *L'autorité du pouvoir légal ayant passé de fait entre les mains de l'occupant, celui-ci prendra toutes les mesures qui dépendent de lui en vue de rétablir et d'assurer, autant qu'il est possible, l'ordre et la vie publique en respectant, sauf empêchement absolu, les lois en vigeur dans le pays.*

The translation of this provision created certain difficulties (see E. H. Schwenk, 'Legislative Power of the Military Occupant Under Article 43, Hague Regulations', 54 *Yale LJ* 393 (1945)).

The Hebrew version of Article 43, as adopted in this Court in *Taviv* v. *Minister of Defence* [6] provides as follows:

> After the authority of legal government has passed in effect to the occupant, it must take all the measures within its capacity so as to restore and secure as far as possible the public order and life, while respecting the laws in effect in the country except where an absolute impediment thereto exists.

The opening part of this article refers to the authority of the Military Government to restore and secure 'the public order and life': this matter includes both the security needs of the Military Government itself and the needs of the civilian population subject to its rule (see Y. Dinstein, *The Laws of War* (Schocken, 1982–3), 216). The concluding part of this Article deals with a particular instance—that has a degree of special symbolism—in which a military government wishes to change the laws in effect in the region. The rule is that the laws that exist in the region must be respected and must not be changed except where legislative change is necessary for the purpose of carrying out the powers of the military government (whether in the civilian or military sphere), and inasmuch as is required for that purpose (see *Abu Aita* [2], at 310; Dinstein, in his aforementioned article in 2 *Iyunei Mishpat* at 509). In the present matter we are not dealing with a change in the existing legislation but with acts of planning, expropriation, and prohibition of construction within the framework of the existing legislation. It follows that the centre of gravity of our deliberation is found in the opening of Article 43 and not in its conclusion (*Jerusalem District Electric Co.* [4], at 688; *Abu Awad* v. *Military Commander of the Judea and Samaria Region* [7], at 314).

18. The opening of Article 43 of the Hague Regulations grants the Military Government authority and imposes upon it a duty to restore and secure the public order and life. This authority is twofold: first, restoring public order and life where they were disrupted in the past; secondly, securing the continued existence of public order and life. The Article does not limit itself to a special aspect of public order and life. It extends to public order and life in all of their aspects. Therefore, this authority also applies—in addition to military and security matters—to multifarious 'civilian' circumstances, such as economic, social, educational, hygienic, medical, traffic, and similar matters that are connected with life in a modern society.

* * *

19. The key question that underlies the legal controversy between the parties is related to the scope of the authority of the Military Government to secure public order and life. Does the Military Government have the same powers as an ordinary government, or does its military nature limit its authority, and if so in which circumstances? This question is not novel. Feilchenfeld was referring to it when he noted: 'Nations, tribunals and authors are by no means in agreement on the more practical question of how far authority of a belligerent occupant falls' (E. H. Feilchenfeld, *The International Economic Law of Belligerent Occupation* (Washington, 1942), 87).

Naturally, Article 43 determines a general formula but does not provide any details of specific solutions to concrete problems (see J. Stone, *Legal Controls of International Conflict* (New York, 1954), 728). We must therefore imbue the Article's general provision with concrete substance, taking into account the principled legal parameters that define the boundaries of the Military Government's authority.

20. It seems to me that the scope of the Military Government's authority—together with the military and security considerations—is limited by two main parameters: the one concerns the duty of the Military Government to act as a proper administration that cares for the local population in all areas of life; the other concerns the limitations of the Military Government, as a temporary government which is not sovereign but rather rules by virtue of the law of war. The first parameter tends to broaden the authority and duties of the Military Government to a degree of analogy with an ordinary government. The second parameter tends to reduce the authority and duties of the Military Government while creating a substantial difference between the Military Government's scope of authority and that of an ordinary government. It appears that the proper scope of the Military Government's authority is a product of the combination of the two parameters. The first parameter determines the optimal limit of the authority, whereas the second parameter determines its proper limits.

21. The first parameter which determines the scope of the Military Government's authority is concerned with a proper government that cares for the local population. To clarify the meaning of this parameter, it is necessary to examine the concept of the duties and powers of an ordinary and proper government. In this matter it should be noted that the Hague Regulations were formulated within the social reality that existed in the second half of the nineteenth century. This was a reality of laissez-faire in which the ordinary government did not tend to interfere in the social and economic life, on the one hand, and in which maximal protection was given to private property, on the other hand.

* * *

As a result, the Hague Regulations are characterized by a static approach, and not a dynamic approach, to all aspects of the Military Government. Private property is protected, but the economic and social interests of the region subject to military government are not dealt with in an appropriate manner.

* * *

This Court acts according to the Hague Regulations, so long as they have not been altered by new customs or an international agreement effective in Israel. However, within the framework of the Regulations themselves there is room to relate to the powers and functions of a proper government, according to the custom and practice of contemporary cultured nations, not according to social views that were evident over 100 years ago. Therefore, the concrete content of Article 43 of the Hague

Regulation with respect to securing the public order and life will not be established in accordance with the public order and life of the end of the nineteenth century but in accordance with the public order and life of a modern and cultured State at the end of the twentieth century.

22. In determining the scope of the Military Government's powers according to the formula concerning 'the public order and life' one should take into account the distinction between a short-term and a long-term military government. This distinction is a recurring theme in the legal literature on the laws of belligerent occupation. The Hague Regulations themselves were developed and formulated in the context of short-term military occupation. It appears that the military reality at that time had no previous experience, in principle, of long-term military occupations.

* * *

This distinction between short and long-term military government has significant effect on the content to be given to 'the public order and life'. As stated by Shamgar J in *Abu Aita* [2], at 313:

> The needs of any area, whether under military rule or otherwise, naturally change with the passage of time and the accompanying economic developments. As explained above, the drafters of the Regulations did not suffice with defining a duty that consists essentially in restoring the *status quo ante*. The duration of the military rule's existence could effect the nature of the needs, and as time goes by the need for co-ordination and reformation might become dominant. . . . The element of time is a factor that affects the span of authorities whether one considers military or area needs, or in balancing the two.

It is only natural that military and security needs predominate in a short-term military occupation. Conversely, the needs of the local population gain weight in a long-term military occupation (see Dinstein, *The Laws of War*, *op. cit.*, at 217). Therefore, legislative measures (such as new taxation or a new rate of taxation for an existing tax) that might be improper for a short-term military government could be proper for a long-term military government.

* * *

The fact that the Hague Regulations were formulated with a short-term military occupation in mind has the consequence that many questions arising in the day-to-day life of a long-term military occupation do not have appropriate answers in the Regulations. Here too we are unable to amend the Hague Regulations. We must apply them since they constitute part of our system of law. However, this distinction between military governments according to their time frame can be taken into account when considering proper policy in cases in which there is room for policymaking within the Regulations themselves. Article 43 is a classic example in this respect. Public order and life necessitate consideration of the time elements, and the fact that the Regulations as a whole were formulated with an eye to a short-term military government does not prevent the development of rules regarding the scope of authority of a long-term military government within the broad and flexible framework of Article 43 of the Hague Regulations.

* * *

23. The second parameter that influences the scope of the Military Government's authority is connected to the character of military rule, which by definition does not derive its vitality from the choice inhabitants of the region, which is not sovereign in its own right, and which draws its power from the laws of war. This rule is temporary in its essence, even if this temporariness is long-lasting. Therefore it is to be concluded from the very essence of the military rule that certain powers which are given to an ordinary ruler are not given to the military ruler.

* * *

It must be concluded that a military government is not permitted to introduce into an area subject to military occupation substantive changes of a permanent nature in the political, administrative, and legal institutions, except in extraordinary cases, for instance, where the existing institutions are opposed in their substance to fundamental notions of justice and morality.

24. * * *

25. As we have seen, it follows from the express language of Article 43 that the Military Government's authority extends not only to restoring but also to securing public order and life. Indeed, restoring and securing are not the same (*Abu Aita* [2], at 309). In addition to the authority to restore public order and life that have been disturbed, there exists the authority to secure public order and life, even where they have not been disturbed previously, or where they have already been restored.

26. The life of a population, like the life of an individual, is not static but is in perpetual development, growth and change. A military government cannot ignore this. It may not freeze life. . . .

The Military Government's authority therefore extends to taking measures necessary for growth, change, and progress. The conclusion is that a military government may develop industry, trade, agriculture, education, health and welfare services, and similar matters of proper administration that are necessary for securing the changing needs of a population in an area subject to belligerent occupation. This approach gives effect to the first of the two mentioned parameters. It expresses concern for the local population as befits a proper administration. Nevertheless, this approach does not ignore the second parameter, since it neither changes the temporary and special nature of the military government nor blurs the distinction between a military and ordinary government.

27. Sometimes growth and development cannot be secured within the framework of a long-term military government without fundamental investments that will bear fruit in the future. Such investments may lead to permanent changes in the region that will persist even after termination of the military government. May a military government plan and implement such actions? The first parameter, concerning proper government, certainly justifies the granting of authority to the military government to plan and implement such fundamental investments. Is there anything in the second parameter, concerning the temporariness of the military government, that negates such actions? . . .

Fundamental investments which might lead to permanent change that persists after termination of the military government are permitted if they are reasonably required for the needs of the local population. . . .

It appears to me, therefore, that long-term fundamental investments which could lead to permanent changes that might persist even after termination of the Military Government, are allowed if they are required for the benefit of the local population, provided that they do not bring about a substantial change in the fundamental institutions of the Region. This approach attains a suitable balance between, on one hand, the needs of a proper government that cares for the local population and secures its interests, not only in the short but also in the long term without freezing its development but rather considering the 'dynamics of life' (in the words of Shamgar J in *Abu Aita* [2], at 709) and on the other hand, the natural limitation of a military government that is temporary and derives its powers from the law of war.

28. The fundamental investments that are planned for the benefit of the local population might at times require planning and collaboration with factors outside the region. These factors could be a neighbouring State or the state of military government itself. Is there anything in the character of the military government to prevent it from planning under such circumstances? Certainly the interests of the local population could require such collaboration. It is only natural for a proper government to collaborate with others so as to realize its own purposes. Is there anything in the temporariness of the military government that would qualify this approach? The answer appears to be in the negative. Contact with factors outside the region—and certainly such contact with the State of the military government—is not an act of sovereignty that lies outside the authority of a military government (see *Abu Aita* [2], at 311).

29. We have seen that the military commander's authority is formed through a delicate balancing between the needs of a proper government and the limitations of a temporary government. This balancing does not create a point of equilibrium, but rather a surface or space within which there are several points of equilibrium. The military government may choose among them. It is not obliged to choose a specific option but may choose that option which it considers appropriate, provided that its considerations are proper according to the law of war and the rules of administrative law. Indeed a military government can be passive or it can be active. It can be satisfied with securing the essential minimum or wish to secure more than that. Sometimes a military government is prepared to make fundamental investments which will bring about permanent change, and sometimes it does not aim high. In the duration of a given military government there might be changes in the fundamental approach itself. This approach is influenced by various factors including the military government's physical capacity, the manpower at its disposal, military and civilian, and its monetary resources. This finds expression in Article 43 itself, according to which the military government must take 'all the measures within its capacity' so as to secure 'as far as possible' the public order and life:

> The degree to which it is possible to fulfil the duties is measured in view of the entire situation, that is, not only according to and in view of the area's needs but also in view of the legitimate military needs of the military administration . . . which is responsible for the belligerent occupation . . . while seeking a proper balance between the two (Shamgar J in *Abu Aita* [2], at 310).

Indeed, the most that can be indicated within the broad language of Article 43 is that there certainly exists a minimum standard with regard to securing the public order and life of the local population below which the military government functioning as a proper government may not sink, and that there certainly exists a maximal standard with regard to securing the public order and life of the local population above which the military government functioning as a temporary government may not rise, and that between these two there exists a field of authority within which there is permission to choose between various options. Each military government will choose the point of equilibrium that it considers appropriate according to its character and features, on the one hand, and its appreciation of the regional layout, on the other.

## *Legal Measures*

30. Which measures may a military government take so as to implement an action that lies within its authority? The apparent answer is that,

subject to specific provisions of the Hague Regulations and in accordance with the general provision of Article 43, the military government is given all the auxiliary powers that are reasonably required for implementing the authority. Thus, for example, it is commonly accepted that a military government may introduce or cancel a licensing system, issue or annul individual licences, grant or deny rights, appoint and remove officials, establish banks, and perform other actions that are required for implementing its powers (see G. von Glahn, *The Occupation of Enemy Territory* (Minneapolis, 1957), 202).

31. May a military government make use of local law so as to expropriate private property? The Hague Regulations determine comprehensive provisions with regard to the expropriation or requisition of property for military purposes. They do not contain any provision as to expropriation or taking possession for the benefit of the local population under local law. Should it be concluded from the silence of the Hague Regulations in this respect that this may not be done? Should it not be said that application of the local law is negated by the provision of Article 46 of the Hague Regulations that private property may not be confiscated? The answer to that is in the negative. The accepted approach is that the Regulations' provisions as to expropriation or requisition for military purposes do not exclude expropriation or requisition for 'civilian' purposes in accord with the local law. On the contrary: the accepted approach, which is derived from Article 46, is that a military government may expropriate or take possession of private property in accordance with the local law, provided that this is done in accordance with the conditions of that law and for the needs of the local population. As for the provision of Article 46, it was intended to apply in the absence of a local law that allows for expropriation and payment of compensation. . . .

To summarize: the local law allowing expropriation or requisition for public needs remains in effect in the period of belligerent occupation so long as it is not lawfully abrogated or amended. Under the law of war the power of expropriation is vested in the military government, which may exercise it provided three cumulative conditions are met: first, the person exercising the power must act in accordance with the requirements prescribed in the local law; secondly, the power must be exercised for the benefit of the local population as required by Article 43 of the Hague Regulations; thirdly, the person vested with the power must exercise it in accordance with the fundamental rules of Israeli administrative law, e.g. granting a right to be heard before expropriating or requisitioning (see Shamgar, *op.cit.*, at 48).

## *Judicial Review*

32. It appears that one can no longer question the ruling that the Supreme Court sitting as a High Court of Justice is authorized to exercise judicial review over actions of the Military Government in Judea, Samaria, and the Gaza strip. Indeed this issue was originally left unresolved (see *Hilou* v. *Government of Israel* [8], at 169; *Dwaikat* [5]). Over the years the status of the Military Government has been clarified and there is currently no doubt that this Court has the right of review under section 7 of the Courts Law 1957. The reason for this is that the Military Commander and his subordinates are public officials who exercise a public function by virtue of law (*Samara* v. *Military Commander* [9]; *Abu Aita* [2], at 230; E. Nathan, 'The Power of Supervision of the High Court of Justice over Military Government', in *Military Government in the Territories Administered by Israel 1967–1980, op.cit.*, at 109).

33. The judicial review jurisdiction of this Court extends both to examining the existence of a formal source for the Military Government's power (in either local law or security legislation) and to the manner of exercising such power. The latter examination is made in light of the rules of both customary international law and Israeli administrative law. In this respect one can say that every Israeli soldier carries in his kitbag the rules of customary public international law concerning the law of war and the fundamental rules of Israeli administrative law.

34. As to the scope of review, the decisions of this Court contain *dicta* according to which the areas of court intervention are very narrow (see *Hilou* [8], at 177, 179, 184; *Matoa* v. *Minister of Defence* [10], at 126; *Amira* v. *Minister of Defence* [11]). The meaning of these *dicta* is not that the grounds of review are restricted but that in matters of security the Court will not substitute the security considerations presented to the Court for those of the Military Commander. This approach is not specific to the Military Government but is a general one. In all areas of administrative law the Court does not superimpose itself as a public official but rather examines whether a reasonable and fair public official could have made such a decision. Indeed this Court has added that it is prepared to presume the integrity of the Military Commander's reasoning and that persuasive evidence is required to overcome that presumption. This special 'presumption' is surely limited to special military considerations. It has no application as regards the Military Government's 'civilian' power to secure the public order and life, and certainly not when dealing with a long-term military government. As we have seen, in a military government of this kind, the 'civilian' aspect predominates and there is no reason why this Court should not apply the same 'presumptions' to the Military Commander as to any other public official exercising lawful authority. The Military

Government concentrates a large amount of power and for the sake of the rule of law it is proper to exercise judicial review according to the ordinary tests. It appears that this is the course taken by the Court in the past (*Jerusalem District Electric Co.* v. *Minister of Energy* [4]; *Mustafa* v. *Military Commander* [12]) and there is no reason to depart from it in the future.

## From the General to the Particular

35. Bearing in mind these general principles concerning the authority of the Military Government we can now try to resolve the dispute between the parties. This dispute has two facets: one concerns the authority to plan a road system of national scope and size, the other concerns the authority to expropriate part of the petitioner's lands and to prohibit construction on the remaining part.

36. As we have seen, a military government must act as any proper administration in caring for the public life of the local population. To that end it is granted governmental powers. It must be taken into account that we are dealing with a long-term military government and significant changes occurring in the population. In these circumstances, a military government is authorized to make fundamental investments and long-term plans for the benefit of the local population. For that purpose it may also collaborate with its own State. In light of this, it is clear that there is nothing untoward in preparing a national road scheme: the transportation needs of the local population have increased; the condition of the roads cannot be frozen. The Military Government was therefore authorized to prepare a road scheme that would take into account present and future developments. It is true that the roads will certainly remain after termination of the military rule but that is immaterial. This planning does not in any way blur the distinction between a military and an ordinary government, and the fact that the planning was done in collaboration with Israel does not in itself disqualify the scheme provided it was made for the sake of the local population. Indeed, one can assume that the solution adopted in the road scheme is not the only one and that there are other possible solutions. That is not sufficient to justify our intervention. We are neither a supreme planning council nor engineers. Our judicial examination is critical and the question is whether a reasonable supreme planning council might have planned a scheme such as this. The answer to that is in the affirmative and there is nothing in the petitioner's affidavit or arguments to refute that. It is true that a different military government might have refrained from preparing a broad and comprehensive scheme. It is possible that such an approach could also have been one within the sphere of options open to a military government, but since the Military Government

chose to prepare a comprehensive scheme we find no legal fault in such choice as we are satisfied that it benefits the local population. As aforesaid, we have been convinced of that.

37. With the approval of the scheme, the petitioner's property rights are infringed. Part of its lands will be expropriated and construction is prohibited on the remainder. The petitioner will be paid compensation for its injury. All this is done in accord with the local law and within the scope of the local authority. As we have seen, the rules of public international law grant authority to a military government to affect property rights in accordance with and within the scope of the local law, if done for the benefit of the local population and if compensation is paid to affected persons. We sympathise with the petitioner but there is no reason to prefer it to others whose property would have been affected had another route been chosen.

## *Conclusion*

38. We have therefore reached the conclusion that the respondents acted lawfully and within their authority, and that for this reason the petition must be dismissed. That being the case, there is no need to discuss the other argument made by counsel for respondents, whereby the petitioner is estopped from applying in the present petition as it had exhausted its grounds of relief in the previous proceedings between the parties. We can leave that issue for further consideration.

The result is that we dismiss the petition. The interim order prohibiting changes in the surface is cancelled. The petitioner will bear the respondents' costs to the total amount of 50,000 shekels including attorney fees.

**Y. Cohen J**: I concur.

**Avnor J**: I concur.

Judgment given on 28 December 1983

# 32

# *Asser Al Aziz Abd Al Azis Abd Al Afu and others*
# v.
# *Commander of IDF Forces in the Judea and Samaria Region*

[H.C. 785/87]
[42(2) PD 4 (1988)]

*Shamgar P, Ben-Porat DP, S. Levin J, Bach J, and Goldberg J*

Israeli cases referred to:

[1] HC 606, 610/78—*Matoa* v. *Minister of Defence*; 33(2) PD 113, 121.
[2] HC 97/79—*Abu Awad* v. *Commander of IDF Forces*; 33(3) PD 309.
[3] HC 698/80—*Kawasma* v. *Minister of Defence*; 35(1) PD 617.
[4] HC 629/82—*Mustafa* v. *Commander of IDF Forces in the Judea and Samaria Region*; 37(1) PD 158, 161.
[5] HC 513, 514/85—*Nazal* v. *Commander of IDF Forces in the Judea and Samaria Region*; 39(3) PD 645.
[6] CA 31/63—*Feldberg* v. *Director of Value Added Tax*; 17 PD 1231.
[7] Cr.A 94/65—*Tourjeman* v. *Attorney General*; 19(3) PD 57.
[8] CA 165/82—*Kibbutz Hazor* v. *Rehovot Assessor*; 39(2) PD 70.
[9] Cr.A 174/54—*Shtempfer* v. *Legal Advisor to the Police*; 10 PD 5.
[10] Cr.A 336/61—*Eichmann* v. *Attorney General*; 16 PD 2033.
[11] CA 25, 145, 148/55—*Custodian for Absentee Property* v. *Samrah*; 10 PD 1825.
[12] Cr.A 131/67—*Kamiar* v. *State of Israel*; 22(2) PD 85.
[13] HC 69, 493/81—*Abu Aita* v. *Commander of IDF Forces in the Judea and Samaria Region*; 37(2) PD 197.
[14] HC 393/82—*Almasalia* v. *Commander of IDF Forces in the Judea and Samaria Region*; 37(4) PD 785.
[15] HC 390/79—*Dwaikat* v. *Government of Israel* (*The 'Elon Moreh' Case*); 34 PD 1.
[16] HC 27/88—*Hindi* v. *Commander of IDF Forces in the Judea and Samaria Region*; 42(2) PD 4.

[17] HC 845/87—*Rafiah* v. *Commander of IDF Forces in the Judea and Samaria Region*; 42(2) PD 4.
[18] HC 102, 150, 593, 690/82, 271/83—*Tzemel and others* v. *Minister of Defence*; 37(3) PD 365.
[19] HC 574/82—*Al Nawaar* v. *Minister of Defence*; 39(3) PD 449.
[20] CA 303/75—*State of Israel* v. *Raphael*; 29(2) PD 601.
[21] HC 609/82—*Pentomap Overseas (1981) Ltd* v. *Government Investment Centre*; 38(1) PD 757.
[22] CA 586, 626/82—*Insurance Corporation of Ireland Ltd* v. *State of Israel*; 41(2) PD 309.

English cases referred to:
[23] *R.* v. *Governor of Brixton Prison, ex parte Soblen* [1963] 2 QB 243 (CA).
[24] *Porter* v. *Freudenberg* [1915] 1 KB 857 (CA).

American cases referred to:
[25] *Ex parte Quirin*, 317 US 1 (1942).

## JUDGMENT

[*The military commanders of the various occupied territories acting pursuant to the Defence (Emergency) Regulations ordered the deportation of the petitioners from the territories, on the ground that they were involved in hostile activities against the State of Israel, thus endangering the security of the State and the public peace.*]

**Shamgar P:**

1–2. * * *

3. (a) The petitioners raised, as a central reason for their petitions, the argument that Article 49 of the Geneva Convention Relative to the Protection of Civilian Persons in Time of War, 1949 (hereinafter 'the Fourth Geneva Convention') forbids the deportation of any of the petitioners from Judea, Samaria, or the Gaza Strip, as the case may be. According to the argument, an absolute prohibition exists, with regard to a resident of one of the territories occupied by the IDF, against the application of Article 112 of the Defence (Emergency) Regulations 1945 or of any other legal provision (if such exists) whose subject is deportation. This is due to the provisions of the abovementioned international convention which, according to the contention, should be seen as a rule of public international law, binding upon the State of Israel and the Military Government bodies acting on its behalf and granting those injured the right of access to this Court.

The legal premise underlying this argument has been raised time and again before this Court and has been discussed either directly or partially and indirectly in a number of cases—see principally: *Matoa* v. *Minister of Defence* [1]; *Abu Awad* v. *Commander of the Judea and Samaria Region* [2]; *Kawasma* v. *Minister of Defence* [3]; *Mustafa* v. *Commander of IDF Forces* [4]; *Nazal* v. *Commander of IDF Forces* [5]. In order to complete the legal picture, see also Professor Y. Dinstein's article, 'The Rafiah Salient Judgment' (1973) 3 *Iyunei Mishpat* 934. . . .

(b) * * *

The opinions expressed therein are acceptable to me on the issue before us and I see no reason to add to what has already been said by this Court. As may be recalled, the statements of Landau P in *Kawasma* [3] complement those of Sussman J in *Abu Awad* [2], so far as they concern certain legal aspects of the provisions of the 1952 Jordanian constitution, whereas the decision in *Nazal* [5] touches on additional alternate objections, which were raised regarding the abovementioned legal question.

Since there have been no developments of any possible bearing on the assessment of the legal situation as expressed in various ways in the abovementioned judgments, I would see no need to go back and deal with the varied reasons for the interpretation of Article 49 above, which have already been presented in the previously cited decisions to which I subscribe. Nonetheless, I have read the remarks of my esteemed colleague, Bach J, and as he does not tend to follow the legal paths that were paved in *Abu Awad* [2] and *Kawasma* [3], and, as I disagree with his approach on this issue, I will present the gist of my view on this subject.

Afterwards, I will also deal with the new argument raised by the petitioners' learned counsel regarding the assimilation into our law of some of the rules of conventional international law.

(c) My comments will relate to the following areas:

(1) The accepted approach to interpretation under internal Israeli law;
(2) Principles of interpretation applicable to international conventions;
(3) Interpretation of the abovementioned Article 49.

(d) *The accepted interpretation in our law*—We accept that the interpretive rules applied in a given legal system are peculiar to that system and are not necessarily identical with those applied in another legal system.

* * *

The method of interpretation which our courts have applied for quite some time is that which attributes to the wording of the law the meaning which realizes its purpose; this is the interpretative method based on the legislative purpose which has recently received a thorough and penetrating examination in Barak J's book, *Judicial Discretion* (Papyrus, 1987).

The formation of rules of interpretation is not effected in a vacuum; rather it is adapted, as stated, to the system of law in which and from which these rules stem. The application of the said rules, in any concrete case in which the court is asked to give content to an enactment warranting interpretation, is carried out, as is accepted here, by applying judicial discretion. Applying judicial discretion is necessary, mainly, where clarification of the working of an enactment open to interpretation is required in the context of a decision regarding the weight to be given the words of the text, in determining the definition and scope of the legislative purpose. . . .

In other words, language does not govern the purpose; rather it serves it. The law is an instrument for realizing legal policy. Therefore, interpretation needs to aim toward emancipating the wording from its semantic bonds—if these bonds distance the wording from the legislative purpose which the words are intended to realize. Thus, for example, the legislative purpose may be reflected in the description of the legal situation which existed on the eve of the legislation being introduced (*Kibbutz Hazor* v. *Rehovot Assessor* [8], at 74).

* * *

In a nutshell, what has been said until now may be summarized thus: we have referred to the guidelines used in establishing the relation between the literal meaning of the written word and the correct legal interpretation, as far as this applies to our legal system. Interpretation in this sector seeks, as was said, to pave the way to a revelation of the legislative purpose. Setting the purpose in this form is directed to the sources which one may turn to in order to ascertain the purpose. It is customary in this matter to examine more than the text and, *inter alia*, also the legislative history; the legal and substantive context, and the meanings stemming from the structure of the legislation.

(e) *Interpretation in public international law*—Now the second question arises, i.e. what are the rules of interpretation relevant to our matter that are used in public international law?

Israel has not yet ratified the Vienna Convention of 23 May 1969 on the Law of Treaties, which came into force in 1980 for those who joined it (hereinafter, 'the Vienna Convention'). As an aside, what is said in Article 4 of the above Convention regarding non-retroactivity, in any case fundamentally limits the provisions relating to the question before us. Nonetheless, there is value, even if only for the sake of comparison, in an examination of the provisions of the Convention regarding interpretation.

On the issue of interpretation, Articles 31 and 32 of the said Convention state:

31. *General rule of interpretation*

1. A treaty shall be interpreted in good faith in accordance with the ordinary meaning to be given to the terms of the treaty in their context and in the light of its object and purpose.

2. The context for the purpose of the interpretation of a treaty shall comprise, in addition to the text, including its preamble and annexes;

(a) any agreement relating to the treaty which was made between all the parties in connexion with the conclusion of the treaty;

(b) any instrument which was made by one or more parties in connexion with the conclusion of the treaty and accepted by the other parties as an instrument related to the treaty.

32. *Supplementary means of interpretation*

Recourse may be had to supplementary means of interpretation including the preparatory work of the treaty and the circumstances of its conclusion, in order to confirm the meaning resulting from the application of Article 31, or to determine the meaning when the interpretation according to Article 31:

(a) leaves the meaning ambiguous or obscure; or

(b) leads to a result which is manifestly absurd or unreasonable.

It seems that from the first part of Article 31(1) one could conclude that the Convention sought to support that school of interpretation which emphasizes the text, as opposed to the alternative school of interpretation, no less accepted, which focuses on the intentions of the draftsmen of the Convention (see I. Brownlie, *Principles of Public International Law* (3rd edn., OUP, Oxford, 1979), 624). Yet, the second part of Article 31(1) and Article 32 form the bridge to the other theories of interpretation, also familiar to us from the earlier examination of our municipal law. That is, the provisions of the Convention leave ample space to enable examination of the purpose which led to its making. It is even possible to reflect upon the preparatory work describing the background to the making of the Convention, as material which can complement the plain understanding of the text, its purpose, and scope of application.

The accepted view is, as was stated, that one of the contributions of the Vienna Convention in this context was expressed in creation of a closeness and link between the two alternative theories of interpretation. In any event, an examination of the legislative purpose—which is one of the applicable methods of interpretation, unrelated to treaties—is among the recognized principles of interpretation. . . .

(f) The treatment of the questions of interpretation in our internal law and in public international law may be summarized by mentioning the conclusion, that not for naught has the subject before us been examined in *Abu Awad* [2] in the light also of its legislative purpose. This approach was necessitated by the method of interpretation customary in our legal system and by the doctrines of interpretation customary in public international law. As was already mentioned, the two systems do not maintain the exclusiveness of the literal method of interpretation, nor even a preference for it. Moreover, when for the purpose of the issue before us we adopt the interpretive approach as expressed in the specific area of law here discussed, namely public international law, we should recall Professor Yasseen's interpretive guidelines and the remarks of Starke mentioned above. From these sources emerge, *inter alia*, a stand rejecting the constriction of State authority and rejecting formalism, or an approach which ignores the special qualities of the field of law that we are discussing.

We shall now proceed to the application of the rules of interpretation to the issue before us.

(g) *Article 49 of the Fourth Geneva Convention*—What is the dispute regarding the interpretation of the above-mentioned Article 49? The relevant portions of the Article state:

> Individual or mass forcible transfers, as well as deportations of protected persons from occupied territory to the territory of the Occupying Power or to that of any other country, occupied or not, are prohibited, regardless of their motive.
>
> Nevertheless, the Occupying Power may undertake total or partial evacuation of a given area if the security of the population or imperative military reasons so demand. . . .
>
> The Occupying Power shall not deport or transfer parts of its own civilian population into the territory it occupies.

In *Abu Awad* [2], Sussman P comments (at 316–17) regarding the argument that the application of Regulation 112 of the Defence (Emergency) Regulations is contrary to Article 49 of the Fourth Geneva Convention:

> Neither have I found any substance in the argument that the exercise of the abovementioned Regulation 112 contradicts Article 49 of the Fourth Geneva Convention of August 1949 Relative to the Protection of Civilian Persons in Time of War. It is intended, as Dr. Pictet in his commentary on the Convention (p. 10) writes, to protect civilians from arbitrary action by the occupying army, and its purpose is to prevent acts such as the atrocities perpetrated by the Germans in World War II, during which millions of civilians were deported from their homes for various reasons, generally to Germany to serve the enemy in forced labour, along with Jews and others who were deported to concentration camps for torture and extermination.
>
> It is clear that the abovementioned Convention does not detract from the obligation of the Occupying Power to preserve public order in the occupied territory, an obligation imposed by Article 43 of the 1907 Hague Convention, nor does it detract from its right to employ the necessary means to ensure its own security (see Pictet, *Humanitarian Law and the Protection of War Victims*, at 115.) . . .
>
> It has nothing whatsoever in common with the deportations for forced labour, torture and extermination that were carried out by the Hitler regime. If the author was also referring to deportation of individuals in order to preserve the security of the occupied territory, then that is the opinion of an individual author, stated in vague terms with no substantiation whatsoever.

After a detailed analysis of the petitioners' arguments, Landau P decided in *Kawasma* [3] to accept the more far-reaching argument of the State regarding the applicability to our legal system of Article 49, which falls within the realm of conventional law, and therefore saw no need for additional comments on the content of the Article.

At the time no basis was given for the argument that Article 49 expresses a customary rule of international law; and given the material presented to us, the armed conflicts that have occurred since 1949 (India–Pakistan, Cyprus, and others) have not brought about legal decisions that would shed a different light on the issue. In any case if there are any, they were not brought to our attention by the parties. . . .

The background which the draftsmen of the Convention had in mind is clearly reflected in the deliberations of the Geneva Conference. The relevance of the background is twofold: it describes the flaw which the Convention seeks to rectify (H. Lauterpacht, 'Restrictive Interpretation and the Principle of Effectiveness in the Interpretation of Treaties' (1949) 26 *Brit. YB Int'l L* 48, 53, and compare *Feldberg* v. *Director of Value Added Tax* [6]); and the purpose that the draftsmen had in mind (O'Connell, *supra*, at 271; *Tourjeman* v. *Attorney General* [7], cited above, and the remarks of Learned Hand J as there quoted, at 80). It even sheds light on the legal situation for which they strove (*Kibbutz Hazor* [8]). This is also the reason that compelled Landau P in *Nazal* [5], to turn to the question whether the prohibition against deportation is within the realm of law rooted in custom or a conventional innovation.

(h) *What were the considerations guiding the draftsmen of the Convention*? An examination of *Actes de la Conférence Diplomatique de Genève de 1949* (Berne), ii, 648, 649, 743, 744, 810, 811, shows unequivocally that in using the term 'deportations', the participants in the deliberations referred to deportations such as those carried out during the Second World War. Thus it is stated for example at 810:

> *Bien qu'on se soit prononcé à l'unanimité pour condamner les déportations comme celles qui eurent lieu pendant la dernière guerre, la phrase qui se trouve au debut de l'article 45* [In the draft the current Article 49 bore the number 45–MS] *a suscité quelques difficultés, car il était peu aisé de concilier les idées exprimées dans des termes divers, en français, en anglais et en russe. Finalement, le Comité a décidé d'adopter un texte qui interdit les transferts individuels ou collectifs obligatoires ainsi que les déportations de personnes protégées, d'un territoire occupé dans un autre pays, mais qui autorise les transferts volontaires* (emphasis added by Shamgar P).

[Even though we have unanimously declared ourselves ready to condemn the deportations *such as those carried out during the Second World War*, the phrase found at the beginning of Article 45 created certain difficulties, since it was not easy to reconcile the ideas expressed in the various forms, in French, English and in Russian. Finally, the committee decided to adopt a text which forbids forced individual or collective transfer as well as the deportation of protected individuals, from an occupied territory to another country but which authorizes voluntary transfers (emphasis added by Shamgar P).[1]]

The Convention draftsmen referred to deportations such as those that took place during the last War and in the framework of the deliberations sought a text that would reflect the ideas that were expressed in different ways and in different languages.

Pictet agreed with this analysis. In his article, 'Convention de Genève—Protection de Civil', (1950) 76 *Recueil des Cours* 1, 96, Pictet pointed to the accomplishments of the Convention in contrast to the situation that prevailed before it, cited the futile attempts of the International Committee of the Red Cross in 1921 to prohibit the execution of hostages and deportations, and described the suffering of the civilian population during the Second World War:

*Des centaines de milliers d'entre eux servirent exposés aux déportations aux prises d'otage, à l'internement dans les camp de concentration, au pires sevices et à la mort* (Hundreds of thousands of them were exposed to deportations, to the taking of hostages, to internment in concentration camps, to the most severe brutality and to death).

Article 49, which prohibited deportations, was connected therefore with such provisions. As Pictet describes at 109–10: '[*q*]*uand on songe aux millions de personnes transférées de force au cours du dernier conflit et à leurs souffrances physiques et morales on ne peut que saluer avec reconnaissance un texte mettant fin a ces pratiques inhumaines. . . .*'

In his words: when one thinks about the millions of people who were forcibly transferred from place to place during the last conflict (i.e. the Second World War), and about their suffering, both physical and moral, one cannot but thankfully bless the text (of the Convention) which put an end to these inhuman practices.

Here, then, deportations, concentration camps, and the taking of hostages were linked together and the word 'deportations' was used in the context described above.

Incidentally, parallel to this, Article 34 of the Convention prohibits the taking of hostages, something which Pictet calls 'an innovation in international law' (*'constitue une innovation dans le droit international'*).

One is not speaking in this regard, even by inference, about the removal from the territory of a terrorist, infiltrator, or enemy agent, but rather about the protection of the entire civilian population as such from deportation, since the civilian population has more and more frequently become

[1] The original judgment provided no translation of the French. The editors' translation is unofficial.

a direct victim of war, despite its civilian character and despite its lack of involvement in active fighting.

M. H. Coursier ('Droit Humanitaire: Protection des Personnes Civiles en Temps' (1960) 99 *Recueil des Cours* 397, 399) cited the mass attacks against civilians in the context of the situation preceding the development of humanitarian law, when, unless expressly prohibited, everything was permitted. He mentions in this context the words of Grotius, according to which: '[*l*]*e massacre des femmes et des enfants est compris dans le droit de la guerre* (The massacre of women and children was permissible under the laws of war at the time).'

He saw the Convention as a necessity stemming from the numerical increase in civilian victims. In the First World War half a million civilians were killed as opposed to nine million soldiers. In the Second World War a kind of numerical parity was created as 24 million civilians and 26 million soldiers were killed. Coursier mentions the deportations in the context of forced labour, but makes no reference to the broad interpretations which would also apply the deportation prohibition to terrorists or enemy agents, whose deportation is necessary to protect the civilian population, for which the military authority is responsible.

That is also the case in B. M. Jankovici's book, *Public International Law* (New York, 1984), 375, 376. In discussing the prohibition against deportation, he refers to the millions of people who were tortured and killed in the concentration camps.

Also F. F. Spangenberg in *Die Zwangsarbeit der Bevölkerung Kriegsbesetzter Gebiete und das Völkerrecht* (Kiel, 1961) (Forced Labour of the Population in an Occupied Territory and The Law of Nations) describes the forced transfers and deportations in the war in connection with Article 49 and points out that *Die* 'Deportation' *als solche ist somit erstmalig absolut verboten* (translation: 'The "Deportation" is herewith first of all absolutely forbidden'). The reference is to the manner and form of deportation in the Second World War, about which he writes in his book. This is also the meaning of the text found in Schlochauer, *Wörterbuch des Völkerrechts* (De Gruyter (1962), iii, 560; see the entry entitled '*Vertreibung*' (Deportation)).

R. I. Miller, in *The Law of War* (Lexington) 88, creates a similar link between the various tribulations that mankind underwent in the Second World War, which he details, and the prohibition in Article 49:

In World War II at least 5 million persons were deported from occupied territories to Germany as part of the Nazi program of slave labor, persecution and death. Although HR–1907 does not prohibit deportation *per se*, its articles with respect to the safety and order of the inhabitants and requisitioning of supplies and services lead to the conclusion that forcible deportation is beyond the legitimate activities of an occupying power. The International Military Tribunal at Nuremberg and the Military Tribunals under Control Council Order No. 10, pursuant to their charters that defined 'deportation to slave labour or for any other purpose' to be war crimes, held the Nazi deportations to be unlawful. . . . Nevertheless, forcible deportation alone was held in the Krupp Trial to be a violation of customary law, as well as deportation for an illegal purpose (for example, forced labour in the territory of the occupying power) and deportation that disregards recognized standards of decency and humanity.

*Accordingly*, GC–949 provides that 'individual or mass forcible transfers' and deportations of protected persons from occupied territory to the territory of the occupying power, or any other country, are prohibited regardless of motive. The total or partial evacuation of a given area is permitted if the security of the population or imperative military reasons demand (emphasis pointing to the causal link is added by the author).

On the developing trend in the laws of war to protect the civilian population as such and to try to distinguish effectively between it and the fighters, see also Prof. F. Kalshoven, *The Law of Warfare* (Leiden, 1973), 28.

W. O'Brien, *The Conduct of Just and Limited War* (New York, 1981) presents the subject in a similar context, that is, in connection with the harm caused to a civilian population by transferring it from its location and in connection with the exception regarding evacuation of civilians on security grounds or for imperative military reasons:

The last specific prohibition of the positive international law *jus in bello* to be considered is that against forced displacement of civilians. With respect to international conflict, Article 49 of the 1949 Geneva Civilians Convention flatly prohibits massed forcible transfers or deportations of protected persons to the territory of the occupying power or to any other country, 'regardless of their motive'. Article 49 then provides that 'the Occupying Power may undertake total or partial evacuation of a given area if the security of the population or imperative military reasons so demand'. Conditions for such a transfer are to be limited to what is unavoidable.

It was also pointed out that the 1949 Geneva Convention was in this respect an improvement on and an extension of the agreement on the protection of civilians signed in Berne on 25 April 1918 between Germany and France, which also included provisions on deportation and forced labour (see Coursier, *supra*, at 397).

I would add that joining the subject of 'evacuation', as it appears in the second paragraph of Article 49, to the subject of 'deportations', where the matter of 'evacuation' is given as an exception to the 'deportation' prohibition and both are linked by the conjunction 'nevertheless', also affects the interpretation of the first paragraph of Article 49. In other words, tying the *evacuation* of a civilian population or portions thereof, which is permissible under certain circumstances, with *deportation* of the population, which is prohibited, teaches us also about the substance of the subject in the first paragraph. That is, *inter alia*, an example of an interpretation 'based on the context', to which the Vienna Convention refers.

The placing side by side of the subjects of the mass evacuation of a civilian population as such and the prohibition against deportation is also discussed in the works of P. la Pradelle, *La Conférence Diplomatique et les Nouvelles Conventions de Genève du 12 Aôut 1949* (Paris, 1951), 66–7, 185, and E. Castern, *The Present Law of War and Neutrality* (Helsinki, 1984). See also J. A. C. Gutteridge, 'The Geneva Conventions of 1949' (1949) 26 *Brit. YB Int'l L* 294, 323, n. 3.

The conclusion from everything said above is that the purpose which the draftsmen of the Convention had in mind was the protection of the civilian population, which had become a principal victim of modern-day wars, and the adoption of rules which would ensure that civilians would not serve as a target for arbitrary acts and inhuman exploitation. What concerned the draftsmen of the Convention were the mass deportations for purposes of extermination, mass population transfers for political or ethnic reasons or for forced labour. This concern is the 'legislative purpose' and this is the material context.

It is reasonable to conclude that the reference to mass and individual deportations in the text of the Article was inserted in reaction also to the Nazi methods of operation used in the Second World War, in which mass transfers were conducted, sometimes on the basis of common ethnic identity, or by rounding up people in ghettos, in streets, or houses, at times on the basis of individual summons through lists of names. Summons by name was done for the purpose of sending a person to death, to internment in a concentration camp, or for recruitment for slave labour in the factories of the occupier or in agriculture. Moreover, it seems that the summons to slave labour was always on an individual basis.

(i) The gist of the petitioners' argument is that the first paragraph of Article 49 prohibits any transfer of a person from the territory against his will.

The implications of this thesis are that Article 49 refers not only to deportations, evacuations, and transfers of civilian populations, as they were commonly defined in the period of the last war, but also to the removal of any person from the territory under any circumstances, whether after a legitimate judicial proceeding (e.g. an extradition request) or after proving that the residence was unlawful and without permission (see, for instance, *R.* v. *Governor of Brixton Prison, ex parte Soblen* [23], which uses the term deportation, and also Starke, *supra*, at 386) or for any other legal reason, based upon the internal law of the occupied territory.

According to the said argument, from the commencement of military rule over the territory there is a total freeze on the removal of persons, and whosoever is found in a territory under military rule cannot be removed for any reason whatsoever, as long as the military rule continues. In this matter there would be no difference between one dwelling lawfully or unlawfully in the territory, since Article 49 extends its protection to anyone termed a 'protected person', and this expression embraces, according to Article 4 of the Convention, all persons found in the territory, whether or not they are citizens or permanent residents thereof and even if they are there illegally as infiltrators (including armed infiltrators), as also follows from Pictet's remarks (*The Geneva Convention of 12 August 1949, Commentary*, ed. by J. S. Pictet (Geneva, 1958), iv 47).

The petitioners' submission rests essentially on one portion of the first paragraph of the Article, i.e. on the words 'transfers . . . deportations . . . regardless of their motive'. That is, according to this thesis, the reason or legal basis for the deportation is no longer relevant. Although the petitioners would agree that the background to the wording of Article 49 is that described above, the Article must now be interpreted according to them in its *literal and simple* meaning, thus including any forced removal from the territory.

(j) I do not accept the thesis described for a number of reasons: it is appropriate to present the implications of this argument in all its aspects. In this respect we should again detail what is liable to happen, according to the said argument, and what is the proper application of Article 49 in the personal sense and in the material sense.

*Ratione personae* is appropriate in reference to the term 'protected person', while *ratione materiae* relates to the following two basic matters: 'deportation' and 'regardless of their motive'.

From the personal aspect, Article 49 refers—as was already mentioned and as is universally accepted—to all those falling under the category of protected persons. This term is defined in Article 4 of the Convention, which in the relevant passage states:

> Persons protected by the Convention are those who, at a given moment *and in any manner whatsoever*, find themselves, in case of a conflict or occupation, in the hands of a Party to the conflict or Occupying Power of *which they are not* nationals (emphasis added by Shamgar P).

The definition employs a negative test, i.e. for our purposes, anyone who is not an Israeli national and is found in a territory occupied by our forces is *ipso facto* a protected person. This includes an infiltrator, spy, and anyone who entered the territory in any illegal manner. This interpretation is presented by Pictet in his *Commentary*, *supra*, at 47, who in reference to this matter states:

> The Article refers both to people who were in the territory before the outbreak of war (or the beginning of the occupation) and to those who go or are taken there as a result of circumstances: travellers, tourists, people who have been shipwrecked and even, it may be, *spies or saboteurs* (emphasis added).

The acceptance of the argument that the prohibition in Article 49 applies, whatever the motive for its personal application, means that if someone arrives in the territory for a visit of a limited period, or as a result of being shipwrecked on the Gaza coast, or even *as an infiltrator for the purpose of spying or sabotage* (and even if he is not a resident or national of the territory, for that is not a requirement of Article 4), it is prohibited to deport him so long as the territory is under military rule. In other words, the literal, simple, and all-inclusive definition of Article 49, when read together with Article 4, leads to the conclusion that the legality of a person's presence in the territory is not relevant, for his physical presence in the territory is sufficient to provide him with absolute immunity from deportation. According to this view, it is prohibited to deport an armed infiltrator who has served his sentence.

In order to demonstrate the implications of the petitioners' thesis, let us presume a set of theoretical circumstances: in *Ex parte Quirin* [25], the US Supreme Court heard the appeals of six Germans, former residents of the United States, who landed on the American coast during the Second World War in order to carry out acts of sabotage and spying. They were all sentenced to death in 1942.

The event took place in the territory of the United States; but had a similar incident occurred in an occupied territory (e.g. one of the islands held by the United States following the Second World War as occupied territory) after 1949, and it was decided not to execute the terrorists but to deport them back, whether in the framework of an exchange or in some other way, this would constitute, as it were, a serious violation of the Fourth Convention (Article 147). It is superfluous to add that the return of a deportee to his country of origin is not always done in accordance with his wishes, and the post-Second World War examples of this abound. There is no need to go as far as the United States in order to bring examples of infiltration for sabotage purposes, and that example was intended only to illustrate the point. In any event, from the thesis offered by the petitioners, it would follow that an infiltrator for sabotage purposes could not be deported before or after serving his sentence. The same would be true, according to this approach, of a person who came for a visit over the open bridges, yet stayed beyond the expiration of his permit. The literal and simple interpretation leads to an illogical conclusion.

(k) From here we shall proceed to the essence of the concept 'deportation' used in the Article. It is my opinion that, in accordance with the applicable rules of interpretation, one should not view the content of Article 49 as anything but a reference to such arbitrary deportations of groups of nationals as were carried out during the Second World War for purposes of subjugation, extermination, and for similarly cruel reasons.

If, on the other hand, one accepts the proposed interpretation of the petitioners, according to which deportation means any physical removal from the territory, then the above would apply, for instance, to deportation for the purposes of extradition of the protected person, for this too requires removing a person from the territory. Laws, judicial decisions, and legal literature use, in the context of extradition, the term deportation to refer to the stage of carrying out the 'extradition' or the 'rendition'. A murderer who escaped to the occupied territory would have a safe haven, which would preclude his transfer to the authorized jurisdiction. As we have already shown, in light of what is said in Article 4 of the Convention, no relevance is attached to the nationality or domicile of a protected person, and the mere presence in an occupied territory of one who is not a national of the occupying State is enough to qualify him as a protected person. (The subject of the applicability of conventions in territory under military rule is discussed, *inter alia*, in T. Meron's illustrative article, 'Applicability of Multilateral Conventions to Occupied Territories' in *Military Government in the Territories Administered by Israel 1967–1980* (ed. M. Shamgar (Jerusalem, 1982), 217, 218 no 8). The idea that a broad definition of Article 49 could prevent extradition is discussed in *New Rules for Victims of Armed Conflicts* by M. Bothe, K. J. Partsch, W. A. Solf (Hague, 1982), 693, in an examination of the Geneva Protocols of 1977.)

(l) Regarding the issue before us, the petitioners have directed our attention to the remarks of Pictet in *Commentary*, *supra*, at 368, who adopts the literal interpretation, according to which all deportations are prohibited no matter what the reason. One should see this interpretive view, which would apply Article 49 to as broad a group of circumstances as possible, in its context and within its limits. The desire for a literal and simple meaning, which may find expression in scholarly opinions in professional literature, does not bind the courts. Not only are there other contradictory viewpoints (see in this matter the remarks of Stone, which were quoted in Landau P's judgment in *Kawasma* [3]), but, more essentially, the court deals with the law as it exists and clarifies the meaning of a law or of a treaty, as the case may be, by adopting accepted rules of interpretation (see in this respect Lauterpacht, *supra*, at 80).

Were we to adopt the rules of interpretation used in our law, we could not accept the thesis proposed by the petitioners. The court would consider the flaw which the Convention was intended to correct (*Feldberg* [6]); would examine the material context and the structure of Article 49, which in its other provisions refers clearly and openly to evacuations and transfers of population (*Tourjeman* [7]); would attempt to lift the veil from the legislative purpose in order to adopt it as a standard of interpretation (*Kibbutz Hazor* [8]); and would be wary of and refrain from the adoption of a literal interpretation which is, so to speak, simple, but in law and in fact so simplistic that it leads the language of the law or the Convention, as appropriate, to a range of applicability that confounds reason (Barak, in his book *Judicial Discretion*, at 349), e.g. the absolute prohibition against the deportation of an infiltrator or spy, since deportations are prohibited, as it were, 'regardless of their motive'.

Essentially, even reference to the rules of interpretation of international conventions does not help the petitioner's argument. For even the Vienna Convention does not submit to the literal interpretation, but rather sees the words of the convention 'in their context and in the light of its object and purpose' (Article 31(1) of the Vienna Convention). The Convention permits us to examine the preparatory work and shies away from an interpretation whose outcome is 'manifestly absurd or unreasonable', and this description would apply at once to a prohibition against the deportation of an infiltrator (Lauterpacht, *Brit. YB Int'l L*, *supra*, at 89).

Here it is appropriate to add that one may not adopt a broad interpretation conditionally, that is, an interpretation which invokes the broad application selectively on the basis of the results and chooses between an outcome which is acceptable to the claimant and one which is not. Whoever accepts the literal and simple interpretation, according to which the term deportation includes any removal from the territory, and who sees the words 'regardless of their motive' as a catch-all, forgoes thereby the possibility of selection, as this would lead to a contradiction; one who adopts an interpretation that precludes discretion based on differentiating the motives cannot then at his convenience accept only part of the prohibition and reject the rest.

Thus, one cannot remove the sting by saying that the language of Article 49 prohibits deportation, under Regulation 112 of the Defence (Emergency) Regulations, and which also based on the implementation of a valid municipal law, but allows, on the other hand, the deportation of infiltrators, spies, and various enemy agents, or the extradition of criminals.

(m) Arising out of this answer to the petitioners' contention is the opposite question, namely, what then is the alternate interpretation of the words 'regardless of their motive'?

If we interpret the term 'deportation' as referring to the mass and arbitrary deportations whose descriptions are familiar to us, then the words referring to the motive do not change the essence; the reference to some possible motive simply serves to preclude the raising of arguments and excuses linking the mass deportations to, as it were, legitimate motives. In other words, whatever the motive, the basic essence of the prohibited act (deportation), to which the words of Article 49 are directed, does not change. The opposite is true: there is ground for the claim that the reference to 'some motive' is also among the lessons of the Second World War.

The words 'regardless of their motive' were intended to encompass all deportations of populations and mass evacuations for the purposes of labour, medical experiments, or extermination, which were founded during the war on a variety of arguments and motives, including some which were but trickery and deceit (such as relocation, necessary work, evacuation for security purposes, etc. . . .). Furthermore, the draftsmen of the Convention took into account the existing right of the military government to utilize manpower during wartime (see Regulation 52 of the 1907 Hague Regulations which deals with compulsory services, and Article 51 of the Fourth Geneva Convention which even today permits the subjection of protected persons to forced labour), but sought to clarify that mass deportation, as it had been carried out, is prohibited even when the motive is seemingly legitimate, except in the event of evacuation in accordance with the qualifications set out in the second paragraph of Article 49.

* * *

To summarize, this Court was competent to choose the interpretation resting upon the principles explained above over the literal interpretation urged by the petitioners. This Court has done so in *Abu Awad* [2], and I see no grounds for altering that conclusion, as its approach is acceptable to me. I also see no reasonable cause to deviate from the conclusion that served this Court in *Kawasma* [3], and which treated the matter as conventional law.

* * *

4. (a) This Court has indicated in its judgments that the abovementioned Article 49 is within the realm of conventional international law. In consequence of this determination, the petitioners have now raised a new thesis which holds that this Court's approach, which also forms the basis for the decisions in *Abu Awad* [2] and *Kawasma* [3], is founded in error. This approach holds that the rules of conventional international law (as opposed to customary international law) do not automatically become part of Israeli law unless they first undergo a legal adoption process by way of primary legislation.

This argument of the petitioners does not directly relate to the interpretation of Article 49; but it does seek to attack that part of the reasoning in our previous decisions in which this Court indicated that it saw no reason to delve into the question of the substantive interpretation of the abovementioned Article 49, since the Article reflects only conventional international law, and as such has not been assimilated into our country's law.

(b) The petitioners submit that not only does customary international law automatically become part of the municipal law (barring any contrary legislation), but that there are also parts of conventional international law which are automatically incorporated, without the need for adoption by way of legislation as a substantive part of Israeli municipal law. These are those parts of conventional international law which are within the realm of 'law-making treaties'. In this argument the petitioners based themselves on the statements of Lord McNair in two of his works (A. D. McNair, *The Law of Treaties* (Oxford, 1961), 89; A. D. McNair and A. D. Watts, *The Legal Effects of War* (4th edn., Cambridge, 1966), 371); on a judgment of the Court of Appeal in the matter of *Porter* v. *Freudenberg* [24]; on statements in B. Rubin's article, 'The Incorporation of International Treaties into the Country's Law by the Courts' (1983–4) 13 *Mishpatim* 210 and on Professor A. Rubenstein's article, 'The Changing Status of the Territories . . .' (1985–6) 11 *Iyunei Mishpat* 439, 446 (see English version in (1988) 8 *Tel-Aviv University Studies in Law* 59). They have also referred to portions of two articles which they believe lend support to the abovementioned thesis: Professor H. Lauterpacht, 'Is International Law A Part of the Law of England?' (1939) 25 *Transactions of the Grotius Society* 51; Professor F. A. Mann, 'The Enforcement of Treaties By English Courts' (1958–9) 44 *Transactions of the Grotius Society* 29.

5. (a) My conclusions, in answer to these arguments, have a threefold thrust:

(1) The suggested thesis does not accord with the accepted legal approach in Israel.
(2) One discerns no reasonable ground for changing or deviating from the existing legal situation, which in light of the existing constitutional structure, is also the desired legal situation.
(3) The legal situation in England, to which the petitioners sought to refer us (whether, in the petitioners' words, as a binding prototype or for purposes of comparison and persuasion), is not unequivocal, and does not necessarily coincide—certainly not in everyone's opinion—with the view that the petitioners suggested we adopt. There is much literature pointing to lack of clarity on this subject. Even in the above two articles (those of Professor Lauterpacht and Professor Mann), the scholars' dispute on the subject is presented.

Let us examine the subject in the above order.

(b) *The legal situation in Israel*—Israeli law on the relationship between international law and internal law—that is in order to decide whether a given provision of public international law has become part of Israeli law—distinguishes between conventional law and customary law (Prof. Y. Dinstein, *International Law and The State* (Schocken and Tel-Aviv University, 1971), 143). Professor Dinstein refers in this matter mainly to *Shtempfer* v. *Legal Advisor* [9]; *Eichmann* v. *Attorney General* [10];

*Custodian for Absentee Property* v. *Samrah* [11]; and *Kamiar* v. *State of Israel* [12].

The view that reflects the accepted opinion in this Court's decisions on the subject was also presented in *Abu Aita* [13], at 233 ff.; in the remarks of Barak J in *Almasalia* v. *Commander of IDF Forces* [14], 793, and in the remarks of Witkon J in *The Elon Moreh Case* [15], 29. See also M. Shamgar, 'Legal Concepts and Problems of the Israeli Military Government—The Initial Stage', in *Military Government in the Territories Administered By Israel 1967–1980*, *supra*, at 13, 47, 64, 69 and the abovementioned article of Professor Dinstein, at 937 (the last paragraph).

According to the consistent judgments of this Court, customary international law is part of the law of the land, subject to any contradictory provision in Israeli legislation.

c. * * *

The adoption of international treaties—in order to incorporate them as part of internal law and in order to render them enforceable through the national tribunals—is conditional upon a prior act of the legislator. As we shall see, international treaties may constitute a statement of the valid customary law—but then their content will be binding by virtue of the said customary status of the rule stated therein and not by virtue of its inclusion in the treaty. We shall return to this subject later in the discussion.

Based on what was said in *Samrah* [11], Professor Dinstein remarks in his book, *op. cit.*, at 147: '[t]he rules of conventional international law are not automatically incorporated into Israeli law, rather there is a need for special and explicit complementary legislation in order for them to become part of Israeli law.' In *Kamiar* [12] Cohn J reiterates (at 97) that '[n]o international treaty has legislative force so long as such status has not been granted in an explicit Law of the Knesset.'

(d) From the remarks of Cohn J one might surmise that there are rules of *conventional* international law which are expressed in law-making treaties and which *automatically* become part of municipal law without the requirement of any prior legislation. Such a conclusion is founded in error. We accept the relevant classification between declarative and constitutive treaties, and one must be exact and distinguish between them. To hold that an international conference's or the United Nations General Assembly's approval of the wording of a proposed treaty and invitation to States to join it is proof of the treaty's declarative nature is less than accurate. . . .

To summarize, according to the law applicable in Israel, an international treaty does not become part of Israeli law unless:

(1) its provisions are adopted by way of legislation and to the extent that they are so adopted; or
(2) the provisions of the treaty are but a repetition or declaration of

existing customary international law, namely, the codification of existing custom.

* * *

(e) When applying our remarks above to the issue before us, we must remember that Article 49 has been categorized in our judgments as conventional law which does not express customary international law.

* * *

6. (a) I have read the interesting articles, cited above, of Rubin and of Professor Rubinstein at 446, to which we were referred by the petitioners, but I have not been convinced that we should deviate from the existing and accepted law, as expressed in the rulings of this Court, on the methods of incorporating various rules of public international law into our legal system. Moreover, the existing law adequately reflects not only the prevailing, but also the desired, situation in terms of the power of the State to shape its law through its own independent legal tools. Adoption of the viewpoint suggested in the petitioners' arguments, according to which there is no need for Knesset legislation to assimilate into our law a rule of conventional public international law which finds expression in an international treaty joined by Israel, and which is not in the nature of codification of an existing customary rule, would, in fact, grant the Government legislative power, since according to our constitutional structure, the Government concludes and ratifies international treaties without any approval from the Knesset. In light of such outcome of the suggested thesis, a twofold doubt arises whether the described interpretive innovation is indeed desirable from the viewpoint of sound administration and the rule of law.

* * *

(b) To summarize this point: the system suggested by the petitioners would grant the Executive the power to infuse binding legal provisions into our legal system, without recourse to the legislator. . . .

(c) Another reason for the objection to the automatic adoption of a treaty which does not reflect customary international law lies in the substantive and basic difference between international law and municipal law, a matter which more than once has eluded the scrutiny of jurists interpreting rules of international law. Moreover, dependence on the automatic application of law-making treaties would subordinate Israeli law to provisions which had not been adapted to the conditions of the country, its interests, and its residents. In this context one must consider the fact that among the treaties presented in the professional literature by those jurists adhering to this thesis, and brought as leading examples of law-making treaties having immediate application, are treaties adopted by the United Nations and the International Labour Organization. While wanting to refrain from generalizations, the idea that the majority in these international bodies could automatically impose upon us provisions of binding law, which would be in force unless expressly annulled by the Knesset, is not attractive.

Also the attainment of clarity in determining the substance and limits of the law will necessarily be obstructed if we adopt the suggested approach. It is generally agreed that an *a priori* classification of the treaties is necessary in order to distinguish between those which apply automatically and those which require enabling legislation. Rules of differentiation and distinction are not defined clearly and simply. If we return, for example, to the remarks of Professor Lauterpacht, he determines that the said division is 'not clearly defined' (*ibid.* 75), and that is one of the reasons that the subject is marked by vagueness, dissention, and a lack of new and clear distinctions. In any event, the inclusion of an uncertain and unclearly defined element in our legal system does not seem desirable.

7. * * *

8. Often raised, peripherally to the discussion of the legal problems regarding the applicability of conventions, is the matter of the status of a *customary rule* of public international law in our internal law. The question of the nature and identification of a customary rule was discussed in detail in *Abu Aita* [13] at 238–42, and I therefore will not reiterate it here. However, it is worth taking note and repeating certain words of caution, which were included in the abovementioned judgment:

In his above cited work, *The Law of Armed Conflict* (vol. 2, at 3) Prof. G. Schwarzenberger gives two necessary warning signs that must be taken into account by anyone inquiring into the existence of a binding rule under the laws of war: one points to the tendency of creating the impression of greater certainty of the existence of binding legal rules that can be attained in the area of the laws of war in which belligerents seek to retain for themselves, as is natural—although it may not seem so to others—maximum freedom of action. The second warning concerns the obstacle set up by the unwarranted praise heaped on a given usage with which it is sought to dress up a particular interest with a universal rule that is inappropriate. The viewpoints of parties or sectors of States, parties interested in the upholding of a rule, do not reflect the existing law, but rather only a description of the legal situation they desire.

The practical conclusion that is to be reached at this stage is that a careful, detailed, and *all-inclusive* examination is required, giving proper weight to various opinions on a specific subject, to determine whether we are referring to a view acceptable to the overwhelming majority, or to only one of various possible viewpoints.

9. In *Hindi* v. *Commander of IDF Forces* [16], the petitioner again raised the argument that Regulation 112 of the Defence (Emergency) Regulations is not in force in Judea and Samaria.

This legal argument too has already been discussed and rejected in *Nazal* [5] and earlier in the abovementioned *Abu Awad* [2]. As stated, I see no reason to add to what has already been said in the matter.

10. Learned counsel for the petitioner in *Rafiah* v. *Commander of the IDF Forces* [17] raised, toward the close of the hearing, a new contention, which was not mentioned in the petition and in the arguments voiced before us in the course of the hearing. In his opinion, the Military Commander no longer has any authority to direct the deportation of the petitioner under Regulation 112 of the abovementioned Regulations, since with the signing of the Peace Treaty with Egypt, the Military Government terminated and the respondent no longer possesses the legal authority to issue such an order. Petitioner's counsel did not take the trouble, I regret, to base his contention on a reasoned legal argument. Thus, he did not explain which provisions of the Peace Treaty would lead us to the the above conclusion, or what rules of law sustain them.

I find the abovementioned contention unacceptable and the reason is both short and simple. *The Treaty of Peace between Israel and the Arab Republic of Egypt* was accompanied by an additional agreement between the States that concluded it, namely *a framework for peace in the Middle East agreed at Camp David.* According to this agreement, it was determined, *inter alia*, that further developments would ensue in the deployment of the Military Government at a certain stage, which need not be spelled out here, in the implementation of the said agreement. What emerges from this agreement is that, as long as the said stage has not arrived, the Military Government continues to function. There is no indication that the powers which signed the Peace Treaty had decided upon the abolition of the Military Government either at that time or at a subsequent stage prior to this time.

This Court has already ruled that as long as the military force exercises control over the territory, the laws of war will apply to it (*Tzemel and Others* v. *Minister of Defence* [18], at 373):

> The application of the provisions of the laws of war regarding the powers and obligations of a military force that has taken effective control of an area lying beyond the jurisdiction of its country's applicable law, can also be the result of belligerent action which provides the military force with control over a State against which *it is not* waging a war.

The court further stated at 374:

> even where the territory is seized from a country with which a state of belligerency exists (an armistice agreement does not terminate a state of belligerency) at the

time the military forces enter and seize effective control. If an agreement was subsequently signed, such as an agreement terminating the state of belligerency, the transfer of the territory, the powers, or both, to the previous authority, is disposed of in accordance with the terms of the said agreement. However, as long as the military force exercises control in the territory, the powers granted it and the limitations imposed upon it by virtue of the laws of war, remain in effect. This, of course, is entirely subject to the arrangement agreed upon by the duly authorized political bodies. See also *Al Nawaar* [19].

For our purposes it similarly emerges that, irrespective of the fact that a peace treaty has been signed, so long as the Military Government has not left the Gaza Strip and the relevant parties have not agreed otherwise, the respondent continues to hold the territory by force of belligerent occupation and is subject to the laws of customary international law that apply in war-time.

* * *

17. In summary, we have not found any abuse of authority, deviation from authority, lack of good faith, arbitrariness, unlawful discrimination, or similar shortcoming or irregularities that would invalidate the respondent's acts. In light of all of the facts presented to us, there is no room to doubt the veracity of the respondents' submissions and their reliability, and one cannot negate the legal and substantive basis for their decisions.

Accordingly, I would dismiss the petitions and set aside the orders issued pursuant to them.

**S. Levin J**: I concur.

**Goldberg J**: I concur.

**Ben-Porat DP**:

I concur in the instructive opinion of my esteemed colleague, Shamgar P. I would only add that in his judgment he mentioned and reviewed that interpretive approach which holds that one should interpret a treaty in a liberal and broad fashion, paying due attention to the intention of the treaty's draftsmen and to the purpose underlying its conclusion. For this purpose, a passage was quoted from Starke, *op cit.* at 511: '[t]reaties should be interpreted *in the light of existing international law* (emphasis added).'

A similar rule of interpretation is accepted by us in relation to legislative enactments, namely: two laws that deal *in pari materia* with the same subject and have the same purpose should be interpreted in a uniform manner, so as to create a suitable interpretive harmony between their provisions (see *State of Israel* v. *Raphael* [20], at 605; *Pentomap Overseas*

(*1981*) *Ltd* [21], at 766). I believe that one can apply this also to the present issue: Regulation 43 of the Hague Regulations, which is found in the section on 'Military Authority Over the Territory of a Hostile State', reads as follows:

> The authority of the legitimate power having in fact passed into the hands of the occupant, the latter shall take all the measures in his power to restore, and ensure, as far as possible, public order and safety, while respecting, unless absolutely prevented, the laws in force in the country.

The provisions of Article 49 of the Fourth Geneva Convention should be read (*inter alia*) in the light of the directive in Regulation 43 of the abovementioned Hague Regulations, so that the strict prohibition against the deportation of civilians, according to a simple reading of the text, should be qualified by the duty imposed under Regulation 43.

Let me clarify my position. One can deport individual residents of those territories to locations outside them, so long as their continued residence may harm public security and order in the occupied territories, and on condition that in the given circumstances no option other than deportation exists in order to protect the population of the territories. I would further add that one should read Article 49 of the Fourth Geneva Convention in the light of what is stated in Regulation 43 of the Hague Regulations, since the Hague Regulations bind Israel as part of *customary* international law, whereas the Geneva Convention has only *conventional* force. It is, therefore, understandable that greater weight should be accorded to the duty of ensuring security and public order in the occupied territories as set forth in Regulation 43.

**Bach J**:

1. I concur in the final conclusion reached by my esteemed colleague, the President, in these petitions; however, on one point of principle I must dissent from his opinion.

This point is the proper interpretation of Article 49 of the Fourth Geneva Convention (hereinafter 'The Convention'). Counsel for the petitioners requested that we re-examine this question and consider again an argument advanced on a number of occasions in the past—that the deportation of persons permanently residing in the territories occupied by the IDF, outside the boundaries of those territories, and into the territory of another State, is indeed in contravention of the provisions of Article 49 of the Convention.

2. In a reasoned decision given by Sussman P in *Abu Awad* [2], it was established explicitly that the deportation of a person from the territories of Judea, Samaria, and the Gaza Strip to one of the neighboring Arab States out of concern for State security is within the purview of the

Military Commander's authority under Regulation 112 of the Defence (Emergency) Regulations and outside the framework of actions to which Article 49 of the Convention applies.

In subsequent petitions, when this point was again raised on behalf of the petitioners, the Court was content to refer to the judgment in the abovementioned *Abu Awad* [2], expressing its concurrence in the ruling given in that case (e.g. see the judgment in *Nazal* [5], at 650–9) which is extensively quoted in the opinion of my esteemed colleague, the President. However, there have been instances when the court decided to reserve judgment on this point. Thus in *Kawasma* [3], Landau P reviewed the various arguments on this question and decided not to adopt a position regarding them when he stated (at 627):

> and I will refrain from deciding upon the legality of the deportation orders under Article 49(1) of the Geneva Convention, which for the time being must be regarded as a provision of conventional international law alone, upon which an individual cannot found his petition in court adjudicating according to the positive law of the forum country.

(I will return to this last argument below.) My opinion, therefore, does not contradict the conclusions of Landau P in *Kawasma* [3] and I am constrained to dissent only from the opinion expressed on this point in *Abu Awad* [2]. It should be recalled that in that same judgment in *Kawasma* [3], a minority opinion was delivered by Cohn J, who held that it was proper to make the order *nisi* absolute, and regard the deportation order as void.

3. Before I clarify my stand on this matter, and in order to make it easier to follow my arguments later, it would be useful to cite now the text of the relevant part of the aforesaid Article 49 as well as the reasoning of Sussman P in *Abu Awad* [2], which the petitioners requested us to reject.

The first two passages of Article 49 provide:

> Individual or mass forcible transfers, as well as deportations of protected persons from occupied territory to the territory of the occupying power or to that of any other country, occupied or not, are prohibited, regardless of their motive.
>
> Nevertheless, the occupying power may undertake total or partial evacuation of a given territory if the security of the population or imperative military reasons so demand. Such evacuations may not involve the displacement of protected persons outside the bounds of the occupied territory except when for material reasons it is impossible to avoid such displacement. Persons thus evacuated shall be transferred back to their homes as soon as hostilities in the area in question have ceased.

'Protected persons', in the sense of the Convention (according to the definition in Article 4 of the Convention), are 'those who at a given moment and in any manner whatsoever, find themselves, in case of a conflict or occupation, in the hands of a Party to the conflict or an Occupying Power of which they are not nationals.'

* * *

4. Professor Kretzmer, representing the Association for Civil Rights in Israel, submitted a comprehensive and exhaustive argument on this point on behalf of the petitioners, without ignoring the inherent difficulty of moving the court to deviate from precedents established by it in the past and affirmed in subsequent hearings. He stresses, however, that we are dealing with a conspicuous error in interpretation which it is incumbent upon us to correct, and that in contradistinction to previous compositions of the court, when dealing with this matter in the past, we are sitting now in an enlarged bench of five judges, and this fact as well can facilitate our adopting a decision to deviate from the aforesaid rule.

5. After examining the question in all its aspects, I am inclined to accept the position of the petitioners on this matter, and my reasons are these.

(a) The language of Article 49 is unequivocal and clear. The juxtaposition of the words *individual or mass forcible transfers as well as deportations* with the phrase *regardless of their motive* [emphasis added by the author of the judgment] admits, in my opinion, no room to doubt that the Article applies not only to mass deportations but to the deportation of individuals as well, and that the prohibition was intended to be total, sweeping and unconditional—'regardless of their motive'.

(b) I accept the approach which also found expression in the judgment of Sussman P in *Abu Awad* [2], namely that the Convention was framed in the wake of the Hitler rule in Germany, and in the face of the crimes perpetrated against the civilian population by the Nazis during the Second World War. Likewise, I would subscribe to the opinion that one may consider the historical facts accompanying the making of a convention and its purpose, in seeking the proper interpretation of its provisions. Also the Vienna Convention, upon which Professor Kretzmer relied in this context, is compatible with this possibility, since it provides in Article 31 '[a] treaty shall be interpreted in good faith in accordance with the ordinary meaning to be given to the terms of the treaty in their context and in the light of its object and purpose.'

On this issue I do not dissent at all from the opinion of the esteemed President and most of the authorities cited by him are acceptable to me as well. However, I find no contradiction between this 'historical approach' and a broad interpretation of the Article in question.

The crimes committed by the German army in occupied territories emphasized the need for a convention that would protect the civilian population and served as 'trigger' for its framing. But this fact does not in any way refute the thesis that when framing that convention the draftsmen decided to formulate it in broad forms, in a manner that would, *inter alia*, totally prevent the deportation of residents from those territories either to the occupying State or to another country.

The language of the Article, seen in its own context and in light of the treaty in its entirety, does not admit, in my opinion, the construction that it is intended to prevent only acts such as those committed by the Nazis for racial, ethnic, or nationalistic reasons.

We must not deviate, by way of interpretation, from the clear and simple meaning of the words of an enactment when the language of the provision is unequivocal and when the literal meaning does not contradict the legislative purpose or lead to an illogical and absurd result.

(c) The second portion of Article 49 supports the above interpretation. Here the Convention allows the evacuation of a population *within the territory*, i.e. from one place to another in the occupied area, if necessary for the security of the population or imperative from military purposes. It teaches us that the draftsmen of the Convention were aware of the need to safeguard security interests, and for this purpose even allowed the evacuation of populations within the occupied territories. The fact that this qualification was not included in the first portion, i.e. the deportation of residents beyond the borders for security reasons was not permitted, is significant.

(d) Other provisions of the Convention also illustrate an awareness by the draftsmen of the security needs of the occupying State, and indirectly support the stated broad interpretation of Article 49. Thus Article 78 opens: '[i]f the Occupying Power considers it necessary, for imperative reasons of security, to take safety measures concerning protected persons, it may, at the most, subject them to assigned residence or to internment.'

I accept Professor Kretzmer's contention that Articles 78 and 49 should be read together, to infer from them as follows: where a person poses a security risk, one may at most restrict his freedom of movement within the territory and detain him, but one cannot deport him to another country. This idea is also expressed by Pictet in his *Commentary*, *supra*, at 368. In discussing Article 78 of the Convention, he states:

> It will suffice to mention here that as we are dealing with occupied territory, the protected persons concerned will benefit by the provisions of Article 49 and cannot be deported; they can therefore only be interned, or placed in assigned residence, within the frontiers of the occupied country itself.

A similar conclusion emerges from an examination of Articles 35 and 48 of the Convention. The first part of Article 35, which deals with the fate of aliens in the territory of a party to the conflict, reads: '[a]ll protected persons who may desire to leave the territory at the outset of, or during a conflict, shall be entitled to do so, unless their departure is contrary to the national interests of the State.'

Article 48 of the Convention has a like provision concerning protected persons in the occupied territory, as follows: '[p]rotected persons who are not nationals of the Power whose territory is occupied, may avail themselves of the right to leave the territory subject to the provisions of Article 35.'

Again one sees an alertness to the need for permitting measures to protect the interests of the occupying State. To further such an interest, one can prevent the departure of persons from the occupied territories. The absence of a similar provision permitting deportation of a person from the territory for similar purposes is conspicuous, especially considering that Articles 48 and 49 are contiguous to each other.

Article 5 of the Convention, which deals specifically with spies and saboteurs, leads to the same conclusion. Its second paragraph reads:

> Where in occupied territory an individual protected person is detained as a spy or saboteur, or as a person under definite suspicion of activity hostile to the security of the Occupying Power, such a person shall, in those cases where absolute military security so requires, be regarded as having forfeited rights of communication under the present Convention.

The rights of communication accorded to protected persons under the Convention include the right to communicate with their families (see Article 25 of the Convention), the right to communicate with the Red Cross and other organizations (see Article 30 of the Convention), and the right to maintain free contact with an attorney (Article 72 of the Convention).

We see that under the Convention, the rights of spies and saboteurs can be denied in various ways, if the matter is deemed necessary for security reasons. Yet despite the alertness of the Convention's draftsmen to the security needs of the occupying power, there is no provision qualifying the sweeping prohibition in Article 49, and there is no allusion to the right to deport such persons to another State.

The abovementioned Articles of the Geneva Convention supplement the provisions of Regulation 43 of the Hague Regulations, which requires the occupying power to ensure public order and public welfare in the occupied territories, in the sense that they indicate the measures which may be adopted in order to fulfil this obligation. In any event, nothing in Regulation 43 of the Hague Regulations is incompatible with the simple and broad interpretation suggested for Article 49.

(e) A clear direction is discernible in the Convention. The freedom of movement of a 'protected person' can be limited, and he can even be arrested without trial, if it is necessary in order to protect security or another vital interest of the occupying State; this is in addition to the possibility of placing him on trial, punishing him, and even condemning him to death. But the 'protected person' cannot be deported; for the moment deportation to another country is carried out, the occupying State has no further control over him, and he therefore ceases to be a 'protected person'.

(f) Most scholars subscribe to the opinion that the above broad interpretation of Article 49 of the Convention is indeed the required interpretation. Thus at 279 of the abovementioned *Commentary* on the Convention, Pictet says the following regarding the first part of Article 49: '[t]he prohibition is absolute and allows of no exceptions, apart from these stipulated in paragraph 2.'

This opinion has been expressed in Israel on a number of occasions and in a consistent fashion by the learned scholar, Professor Dinstein. In his article 'Settlements and Deportations in the Occupied Territories' ( (1979–80) 7 *Iyunei Mishpat* 188), Professor Dinstein levels piercing criticism at the judgment in the above cited *Abu Awad* [2] and, relying on the text of Article 49 of the Convention, he writes, *inter alia*, as follows (at 193):

> No one would dispute that this paragraph was formulated on the basis of the bitter experiences of World War II. However, it is equally quite clear that the text of the paragraph is formulated as a total prohibition that admits no exception. A qualification that is based on military order and the security of the civilian population does appear in Article 49. However, these matters are not included in the first paragraph (which deals with deportation and exile outside the occupied territory), but rather in the second paragraph (which deals with a temporary evacuation that can and even must be performed within the occupied territory).

Likewise, the question of the authority to deport and evacuate in occupied territories is discussed in Professor Dinstein's book *The Laws of War* (Schocken and Tel-Aviv University, 1983). At 225 of the book, Professor Dinstein mentions the Articles of the Convention (such as Article 35), which permit restricting the freedom of the movement of residents of the occupied territories for the purposes of protecting certain interests of the occupying power, and he adds:

> The position is different when the departure—or more precisely, the removal—from the occupied territory is done by force. Article 49 of the Convention distinguishes between deportation and evacuation. Deportation is the forcible transfer of civilians—on an individual or collective basis—from the occupied territory to the territory of the occupying state or to another state (whether it is occupied or not). Deportation is prohibited unconditionally and without consideration of motives.

See also Professor Dinstein's 'The International Law of Belligerent Occupation and Human Rights' (1978) 8 *Isr. YB on HR* 104, 123.

This interpretation of Article 49 of the Convention has won nearly universal acceptance and I accept it as well.

6. My esteemed colleague, the President, attempts to demonstrate through a number of examples that the simple, literal interpretation of

Article 49 will lead to intolerable results. With all due respect, I do not believe that any of these aforesaid examples can lead to such a conclusion.

The learned President mentions the judgment of the US Supreme Court in *Ex parte Quirin* [25], which deals with German agents who infiltrated into the United States on an espionage mission, for which they were sentenced to death. It is clear that the case as such is not in point here, because it did not involve an occupied territory, only the territory of the United States itself, and the question of deportation did not arise there. The President is aware of this, nevertheless he expresses the following thought:

> The event took place inside the territory of the United States; but had a similar incident occurred in an occupied territory after 1949, and it was decided not to execute the terrorists but to deport them back, whether in the framework of an exchange or in some other way, this would constitute, as it were, a serious violation of the Fourth Convention.

It is difficult to see how such a hypothetical possibility can avail the arguments of my esteemed colleague. Let us in fact assume that those people spying against the United States were apprehended after 1949 in territory occupied by Americans. If we further assume that these people could expect a death sentence, then we may suppose that they would willingly have consented to be transferred to another country in order to save their lives. Nothing in the Convention prevents the willing transfer of protected persons to another country. Only forcible deportations are prohibited. But if we were to imagine that for one reason or another these German residents would not have agreed to leave the territory, then in truth the authorities of the United States could not deport them against their will to another country (if it were determined that they were 'protected persons'), without violating the Convention. If, for example, a spy with communist ideological sympathies were caught in the American occupation zone in Germany it would be permissible to arrest and punish him in every possible legal manner, but it would not be possible, according to the Geneva Convention, to deport him forcibly, not even to East Germany, the Soviet Union, or some other communist country. To the best of my knowledge, no such attempt was ever made. In any case, I do not find anything unreasonable or absurd in such an outcome.

My esteemed colleague, the President, also relies on the argument that, in light of the sweeping formulation of Article 4 of the Convention which includes a definition of the term 'protected persons' under the Convention, a literal interpretation of Article 49 would lead to the conclusion that one could not even deport terrorists who illegally infiltrate into the territory during the occupation; similarly that it would not be possible to extradite criminals from the territories to other States in accordance with extradition treaties.

The question regarding infiltrators could arise because of a certain difficulty in the interpretation of Article 4 of the Convention, which is not free of ambiguity. Thus when that same Article 4 states that '[p]ersons protected by the Convention are those who *find themselves* in case of a conflict or occupation in the hands of a Party to the conflict or occupation in the hands of a Party to the conflict or an Occupying Power' (emphasis added—G.B.) then there is perhaps room to argue that the reference is to people who, due to an armed conflict or belligerence between States, have fallen into a situation where against their will they *find themselves* in the hands of one of the parties to the conflict or in the hands of the occupying power; whereas people who subsequently penetrate into that territory with malicious intent are not included in that definition. If and when this problem arises in an actual case, there will be a need to resolve it through an appropriate interpretation of Article 4 of the Convention, but this does not suffice, in my opinion, to raise doubts concerning the interpretation of Article 49. In the matter before us, the aforesaid difficulty is in any case non-existent, since the petitioners are, by all opinions, permanent residents of the territories controlled by the IDF; and if the Convention under discussion applies to those territories, then the petitioners are undoubtedly included in the definition of 'protected persons'.

The same applies to the problem of extraditing criminals. The question of the feasibility of an extradition treaty between States, when it concerns people who are located in territories occupied by countries which are parties to the treaty, is thorny and complicated in itself; and whatever may be the answer to this question, one cannot draw inferences from this regarding the interpretation of Article 49. In any case, should it be established that it is indeed possible to extradite persons who are residents of occupied territories on the basis of the Extradition Law, 1954, and the treaties that were signed in accordance with it, then regarding the possibility of actually extraditing the persons concerned, I would arrive at the same ultimate conclusion as I do regarding the petitioners against whom the deportation orders were issued under Regulation 112 of the Defence (Emergency) Regulations, as will be detailed below.

7. Despite everything I have said above, I concur in the opinion of my esteemed colleague, the President, that these petitions should be dismissed. I do indeed see a need to dissent from the rule established in *Abu Awad* [2] regarding the interpretation of Article 49 of the Convention. On the other hand, I do not see any ground for deviating from the rule established and upheld in an appreciable number of judgments, that Article 49 of the Convention is solely a provision of conventional international law as distinguished from a provision of customary international law. Such a provision does not constitute binding law and cannot serve as a basis for petitions to the courts by individuals.

This opinion, which was clarified in *Matoa* [1] (at 120 and 127) by Witkon J and by Landau DP (as he then was) and upheld, as we have seen above, by, among others, Landau P in *Kawasma* [3], is deeply rooted in the judgments of this Court.

I would also mention the judgment of Barak J in *Almasalia* [14], in which (at 793) the declarative and hence binding nature of the Hague Regulations is explained. The judgment goes on to state:

> The same is not true of the Geneva Convention Relative to the Protection of Civilian Persons in Time of War, 1949, which even if applied to Israel's belligerent occupation in Judea and Samaria—this question is subject to bitter controversy and we will not express any position on it . . .—it is essentially a constitutive convention which does not adopt existing international customs but creates new norms, whose application in Israel requires a legislative act.

Only recently we re-examined the rule that a conventional international agreement has no binding force on the national level so long as it has not been adopted by the local legislator, and we upheld the existing rule on the subject [see *Insurance Corporation of Ireland Ltd* v. *State of Israel* [23], at 314].

I would agree in this regard with the judgment of Landau P in *Kawasma* [3], in which he expresses the opinion (at 646) that if the Convention is to be interpreted in such a manner as to prohibit the deportation of individuals in order to preserve security in occupied territory, then this provision does not constitute a part of customary international law but at most an addition to conventional international rules.

Landau P made reference in this context to the work of G. Von Glahn, *The Occupation of Enemy Territory* (Minneapolis, 1957), which states at 20: '[t]he 1949 Convention has resulted in most valuable additions to the *conventional* law of military occupation, such as treatment of civilians, *deportation*' (emphasis added).

On this point I agree with the reasoning of my esteemed colleague, the President, in his judgment on the present petitions.

8. I would further add that I see no grounds for our intervention in the decisions of the respondents in this matter for the sake of justice. Indeed my opinion is, as stated, that formally the deportation of the petitioners is included within the framework of acts to which Article 49 of the Convention applies. However, I also believe that the prevention of such acts of deportation was not the primary and dominant purpose of those who drafted the Convention.

I have not ignored the fact that representatives of the State have declared on a number of occasions before this Court that it is the intention of the Government to honour as policy the humanitarian provisions of the Convention.

Landau P expressed the opinion in *Kawasma* [3] (at 627–8), that:

> the decision of the State of Israel to honour in practice the humanitarian provisions of the Fourth Geneva Convention (see the article of M. Shamgar, 'The Observance of International Law in the Administered Territories' (1971) 1 *Isr. YB on HR* 262) is a political decision which does not pertain to the legal sphere with which this court is concerned.

I believe, however, with all due respect, that this determination is too sweeping. We have here a policy declaration that as a general rule obligates the Government, and cases may arise where in the framework of rules of administrative law we will instruct the Government to honour its obligations.

However, each case will be examined here in accordance with its circumstances, and in contrast to the interpretation of laws and conventions which at times require strict adherence to the meaning of words and terms, the Court enjoys a flexible and broad discretion when it examines a Government policy declaration in terms of its content and spirit.

It should not be overlooked that the Fourth Geneva Convention, with which we are dealing, includes a variety of provisions, the major portion of which are surely humanitarian in substance. But some are of public and administrative content and the Convention also contains provisions which can only partially be considered of a humanitarian nature. Article 49 of the Convention is indeed primarily of a humanitarian nature, but it seems that this aspect cannot predominate when it seeks, by virtue of its sweeping formulation, to prevent the deportation of individuals whose removal was decided upon because of their systematic incitement of other residents to acts of violence and because they constitute a grave danger to public welfare.

In Shamgar's article, 'The Observance of International Law in the Administered Territories' (1971) 1 *Isr. YB on HR*, it is stated (at 262–3): '[h]umanitarian law concerns itself essentially with human beings in distress and victims of war.'

This definition does not fit the deportation of members of terrorist organizations to one of the neighboring countries.

In any case, when we are dealing with people in respect of whom the elements of Regulations 108 and 112 in the Defence (Emergency) Regulations are satisfied, that is to say, where it has been demonstrated that their deportation is necessary for protecting public welfare and security in the Region, I would not suggest that we exercise our authority in the sphere of administrative law to order the respondents to refrain from carrying out the deportation of the petitioners, solely because the State has declared that in general it intends to honour the humanitarian provisions of the Convention.

It should be noted and further emphasized in this context that even counsel for the petitioners have not argued before us that the orders *nisi* should be made absolute because of the aforesaid declaration by the State, should their submission that the content of Article 49 of the Geneva Convention expresses customary international law be rejected.

There is, therefore, no room for our intervention, not even from the standpoint of the general considerations outlined above.

9. In light of what I have said, and as I also agree with those portions of the President's opinion which deal with the factual aspects of the petitions, I concur in the conclusion reached by my esteemed colleague in his judgment on the fate of these petitions.

*Judgment given on April 10, 1988.*

# Index